The Epistles of Paul The Apostle
to the

ROMANS

and to the

THESSALONIANS

CALVIN'S COMMENTARIES

CALVIN'S COMMENTARIES

The Epistles of Paul The Apostle

to the

ROMANS

and to the

THESSALONIANS

Translator
ROSS MACKENZIE

Editors
DAVID W. TORRANCE
THOMAS F. TORRANCE

Wm. B. Eerdmans Publishing Company
Grand Rapids, Michigan

REPRINTED . . . 1973

Reprinted, June 1980

ISBN 0-8028-2048-4

Published in Great Britain by Oliver and Boyd, Edinburgh

PHOTOLITHOPRINTED BY EERDMANS PRINTING COMPANY
GRAND RAPIDS, MICHIGAN, UNITED STATES OF AMERICA

INTRODUCTION

Chief Editions of John Calvin's Commentaries on the Epistles to the Romans and to the Thessalonians

1. *Latin.*

First edition, 1540, dedicated to Simon Grynaeus or Grynée of Basel, 18th October 1539. Strassburg, Vuendelinus Rihelius.

Another edition, 1551. Geneva, Ioannes Gerardus.

Another edition, 1556. Robertus Stephanus.

Also included in composite editions of the Commentaries on all Paul's Epistles: Geneva, Ioannes Crispinus, 1557; Thomas Curteus, 1565; Crispinus, 1572; Eustathius Vignon, 1580 and 1600.

Works, Volume 5, Part 3, Geneva, Ioannes Vignon and Iacobus Chouet, 1617.

Works, Amsterdam Edition, J. J. Schipper, Volume 7, 1667.

Commentaries of John Calvin on all the Epistles of Paul, Volume 1, Epistle to the Romans, etc., Volume 2, Epistles to the Thessalonians, etc., Gebauer, Halle, 1831 and 1832; Eichler, Berlin, 1834, 1864.

Corpus Reformatorum, Volume LXXVII, *Ioannis Calvini Opera quae supersunt Omnia*, Volume XLIX, Brunswick, 1892.

II. *French.*

Commentaire de M. Iean Calvin svr l'Epistre aux Romains, Geneva, Iean Girard, 1550.

In composite editions of the Commentaries on all Paul's Epistles, printed by Estienne Anastase, 1560; Conrad Badius, Geneva, 1561 and 1562, Paris, 1854-5; Sebastian Honoratus, Lyons, 1563; Soc. des livres rel., Toulouse, 1895; Société calviniste de France, Geneva, 1960 sqq.

III. *English.*

A Commentarie upon the Epistle of Saint Paul to the Romanes, written in Latin by M. Iohn Caluin, and newly translated into English by Christopher Rosdell, Preacher, London, 1577 and 1583.

Commentary on the Epistle to the Romans by J. C. To which is prefixed his life by T. Beza. Translated by Francis Gibson, A.B., Trinity College, Dublin. London, 1834. Philadelphia, 1836.

Calvin Translation Society. Translated by Henry Beveridge, Esq., Edinburgh, 1844. This translation was poorly done and was followed by another by the Rev. John Owen, Vicar of Thrussington, Edinburgh, 1849; new edition, Grand Rapids, Michigan, 1948.

JOHN CALVIN

to

SIMON GRYNAEUS,

a man worthy of all honour,
Greetings

I REMEMBER that three years ago we had a friendly discussion about the best way of interpreting scripture. The plan which you particularly favoured was also the one which at that time I preferred to any others. Both of us felt that lucid brevity constituted the particular virtue of an interpreter. Since it is almost his only task to unfold the mind of the writer whom he has undertaken to expound, he misses his mark, or at least strays outside his limits, by the extent to which he leads his readers away from the meaning of his author. Our desire, therefore, was that someone might be found, out of the number of those who have at the present day proposed to further the cause of theology in this kind of task, who would not only study to be comprehensible, but also try not to detain his readers too much with long and wordy commentaries. This view, I am aware, is not universally accepted, and those who do not accept it have their reasons for forming this opinion. I myself, however, am incapable of being moved by a love of abbreviation. But since the variation of thought which we find in the human mind makes certain things more pleasing to some than to others, let each of my readers here use his own judgment, provided no one wants to force all others to obey his own rules. Thus those of us who prefer brevity will not reject nor despise the efforts of those whose expositions of the sacred books are lengthier and more extensive, while they in turn will bear with us, even though they think that we are too short and compressed.

For my own part I could not prevent myself from trying to see what good my efforts in this regard might achieve for the Church of God. I am not at present confident that I have attained what at that time seemed best to us, nor did I expect that I could attain it when I began. But I have tried to modify my style, so that I might appear to have given my attention to that example. I leave it to you and those like you to estimate how far I have succeeded, since it is not my part to pass judgment. The fact that I have ventured to undertake the risk of interpreting this Epistle of Paul in particular will, I see, expose my design to widespread criticism. Since so many scholars of pre-eminent learning have previously devoted their efforts to explaining this Epistle, it seems unlikely that there is any room left for others to produce something better. I confess that although I promised myself some reward for my efforts, this thought at first held me back. I was afraid that I might incur the reputation of presumption, were I to turn my hand to this task after so many outstanding workmen. There are many ancient commentaries which deal with this Epistle, and many by more modern authors. They could indeed have had no more suitable object on which to bestow their labours, for if we understand this Epistle, we have a passage opened to us to the understanding of the whole of scripture.

I will say nothing of the ancient commentators, whose godliness, learning, sanctity and age have secured them such great authority that we should not despise anything which they have produced. With regard to those who are alive today, there is no point in mentioning them all by name. I will, however, express my views about those who have done the most significant work.

Philip Melanchthon has given us a great deal of light by reason of the outstanding character of both his learning, industry, and the skill in all kinds of knowledge in which he excels, in comparison with those who had published commentaries before him. His only object, however, seems to have been to discuss the points which were especially worth noting. He therefore dwells at length on these, and deliberately passes over many matters which can cause great trouble to those of average understanding. After Melanchthon came Bullinger, who has justly won great approval. Bullinger expounded doctrine with an ease of expression, and for this he has been widely commended. Finally there comes Bucer, who spoke the last word on the subject with the publication of his writings. In addition to his profound learning, abundant knowledge, keenness of intellect, wide reading, and many other varied excellences in which he is surpassed by hardly anyone at the present day, this scholar, as we know, is equalled by few and is superior to very many. It is to his especial credit that no one in our time has been more precise or diligent in interpreting scripture than he.

It would, I confess, be a mark of downright envy to want to compete with scholars such as these, and it never occurred to me to detract in the least from their praise. Let them retain both the favour and authority which, by the confession of all good men, they have earned. It will, however, I hope, be admitted that nothing has ever been so perfectly done by men that there is no room left for those who follow them to refine, adorn, or illustrate their work. I do not dare to say anything of myself, except that I thought that the present work would be of some profit, and that I have been led to undertake it for no other reason than the common good of the Church.

I further hoped that by using a different kind of writing I should not be exposed to the charge of envy. This was my particular fear. Melanchthon achieved what he intended by illustrating the principal points. While he was occupied in this primary task, he neglected many points which require attention. He did not, however, want to prevent others from examining them also. Bucer is too verbose to be read quickly by those who have other matters to deal with, and too profound to be easily understood by less intelligent and attentive readers. Whatever the subject with which he is dealing, so many subjects are suggested to him by his incredible and vigorous fertility of mind, that he does not know how to stop writing. Since, therefore, the former writer has not gone into every detail, while the latter has done so at greater length than can be read in a short time, I did not think that what I proposed to do had any appearance of rivalry. I was, however, in doubt for some time whether it would be advantageous to follow these and other scholars in gleaning certain passages in which I thought I might be able to assist humbler minds, or whether I should compose a continuous commentary in which I should have to repeat much that had previously been said by all these commentators, or at least by some of them. These writers, however, frequently vary from one another, and this fact creates much difficulty for simple-minded readers, who are hesitant as to which opinion they ought to accept. I thought, therefore, that I should not regret having undertaken this task if, by pointing to the best interpretation, I relieved them of the trouble of forming a judgment. Their own judgment, I believed, is somewhat erratic, but in particular I had decided to treat every point with such brevity that my readers would not lose much time in reading in the present work what is contained in other writings.

In short, I have striven to prevent any complaint that the present work is superfluous in many details. Of its usefulness I have nothing to say. Those who are favourably disposed, however, will perhaps admit, when they have read it, that they have got more out of my commentary than I may with any modesty dare to promise. Although I sometimes disagree with other writers, or at least differ from them in some respects, it is right that I should be excused in this regard. We ought to have such respect for the Word of God that any difference of interpretation on our part should alter it as little as possible. Its majesty is somehow diminished, especially if we do not interpret it with great discretion and moderation. If it be considered a sin to corrupt what has been dedicated to God, we assuredly cannot tolerate anyone who handles that most sacred of all things on earth with unclean or even ill-prepared hands.

It is, therefore, presumptuous and almost blasphemous to turn the meaning of scripture around without due care, as though it were some game that we were playing. And yet many scholars have done this at one time. We have continually found, however, that there is by no means universal agreement even among those who have not been found wanting in zeal for godliness, or piety and moderation in discussing the mysteries of God. God has never so blessed His servants that they each possessed full and perfect knowledge of every part of their subject. It is clear that His purpose in so limiting our knowledge was first that we should be kept humble, and also that we should continue to have dealings with our fellows. Even though it were otherwise highly desirable, we are not to look in the present life for lasting agreement among us on the exposition of passages of scripture. When, therefore, we depart from the views of our predecessors, we are not to be stimulated by any passion for innovation, impelled by any desire to slander others, aroused by any hatred, or prompted by any ambition. Necessity alone is to compel us, and we are to have no other object than that of doing good. We are to try to do the same also in expounding Scripture, but in the teachings of religion, in which God has particularly desired that the minds of His people should be in agreement, we are to take less liberty. My readers will have no difficulty in perceiving that I have studied both these points. But since it is not proper for me to make any judgment or pronouncement about myself, I willingly leave this verdict to you. If all men are right to defer for the most part to your judgment, I should defer to it in all the points in which you are more intimately known to me because of our close acquaintance. Such acquaintance usually lessens to some extent the esteem which we have for others, but in your case, as all scholars know well, it greatly increases it. Farewell.

STRASBURG, 18th October 1539

THE THEME OF THE
EPISTLE OF PAUL TO THE ROMANS

I AM in doubt whether it would be worth while to spend much time in speaking of the value of this Epistle. My uncertainty is due only to my fear that since my commendation of it falls far short of its grandeur my remarks may merely obscure the Epistle. It is due also to the fact that at the very beginning the Epistle introduces itself better and explains itself in a much better way than any words can describe. It will, therefore, be better for me to come now to the theme itself. This will prove to us beyond any doubt that among many other notable virtues the Epistle has one in particular which is never sufficiently appreciated. It is this—if we have gained a true understanding of this Epistle, we have an open door to all the most profound treasures of Scripture.

The whole of the Epistle is so methodical that even the beginning itself is artistically composed. The writer's art is evident in many points which we shall note as we proceed, but it is particularly displayed in the way in which the main argument is deduced. Having begun by proving his apostleship, Paul turns from this to commend the Gospel. But since this commendation is inevitably accompanied by a dispute concerning faith, he passes to this, taking the text as his guide. Thus he enters on the main subject of the whole Epistle, which is that we are justified by faith. In the discussion of this he is involved until the end of *chapter five*. The theme of these chapters, therefore, may be stated in this way: *Man's only righteousness is the mercy of God in Christ, when it is offered by the Gospel and received by faith.* But men are asleep in their sins, and flatter and deceive themselves by a false idea of righteousness which makes them think that they have no need of the righteousness of faith, unless they have already been cast down from all self-confidence. On the other hand, they are so intoxicated by the delights of their lustfulness, and so deeply sunk in their carefree ways, that they are not easily roused to seek after righteousness, unless they are smitten by fear of the divine judgment. Paul, therefore, does two things: he convinces them of their wickedness, and having done so rouses them from their sloth.

In the first place he condemns all mankind from the time of the creation of the world for their ingratitude, because they do not recognize the Artificer in the great excellence of His works. Indeed, when they are compelled to acknowledge Him, they do not honour His majesty with due respect, but in their vanity profane and dishonour it. He accuses all men of this ungodliness, which is the most detestable of all crimes. To prove more plainly that all men have departed from the Lord, Paul records the foul and terrifying deeds which men everywhere are liable to commit. This is a clear argument that they have fallen from God, for these evil deeds are evidences of the divine wrath, and are to be seen only in the ungodly. The Jews, however, and some of the Gentiles concealed their inward wickedness with a cloak of outward holiness, and were in no way, it seemed, to be condemned for these evil deeds, and therefore were assumed to be exempt from the common condemnation. It is for this reason that the apostle directs his remarks against that feigned sanctity. Since this mask of holiness could not be taken away from those self-styled saints, Paul summons them to the judgment of God, whose eyes do not fail to see even the hidden desires of men.

After this he makes a division in his discourse, and places the Jews and Gentiles separately before the judgment-seat of God. In the case of the Gentiles he deprives them of the excuse of ignorance which they pleaded. Their conscience, he says, was their law, and it more than sufficiently accused them. As far as the Jews are concerned, he strongly pleads with them to accept the very thing by which they defended themselves, viz. the holy scriptures. Since it was proved that they had transgressed the scriptures, they could not deny their wickedness, for the mouth of God had already passed sentence against them. At the same time Paul prevents the objection which they might have made, that the covenant of God, which was for them a mark of holiness, would have been violated if no distinction were made between them and others.

He shows here, first, that their possession of the covenant made them no better than others, since they have fallen from it in their unfaithfulness. Lest, however, he should detract from the constancy of the divine promise, he also grants that the covenant gave them some privilege, but this consisted in the mercy of God and not in their own merit. As far as their particular qualifications are concerned, therefore, they remain on a level with the Gentiles. He then proves from the authority of Scripture that Jews and Gentiles are all sinners. He also makes some reference here to the use of the law.

When he has clearly deprived mankind of trust in their own goodness and their glorying in righteousness, and has cast them down by the severity of the divine judgment, he now returns to his previous proposition that we are justified by faith. He explains what that faith means, and how we attain the righteousness of Christ by it.

He adds to this at the end of *chapter three* a remarkable conclusion, in order to repress the ferocity of human pride and prevent it from venturing to go against the grace of God. Lest the Jews should restrict this great favour of God to their own nation, he claims it also for the Gentiles.

In *chapter four* he argues from an example which he lays down as being clear, and therefore not liable to be disputed. Since Abraham is the father of the faithful, he ought to be regarded as a pattern and general type. Having proved, therefore, that Abraham was justified by faith, he teaches us that we ought to pursue the same course. By making a contrast between opposites Paul adds here that it follows that the righteousness of works disappears where we give place to the justification of faith. He confirms this by the testimony of David, who, since he makes the blessedness of man depend on the mercy of God, deprives man's works of the power to make him happy.

He then deals more fully with the subject on which he had briefly touched before—the Jews have no reason to exalt themselves above the Gentiles, since this blessedness is common to both. Scripture testifies that Abraham obtained righteousness when he was uncircumcised. Paul takes the opportunity of making some remarks in this passage on the use of circumcision. After this he adds that the promise of salvation depends on the goodness of God alone. If it is to depend on the law, it will not bring peace to men's consciences, where it ought to be firmly established, nor ever come to its fulfilment. In order, therefore, that our salvation may be sure and certain, we must consider the truth of God alone and not ourselves when we embrace it. In this we are to follow the example of Abraham who turned his attention from himself to the power of God. At the end of the chapter he compares two things which have similar points of comparison, in order to make a wider application of the example which he has quoted.

Chapter five touches on the fruit and effects of the righteousness of faith, but is almost wholly devoted to expanding what he has said, in order to make his point more clear. Paul argues *a maiori* to show how much we, who have been redeemed and reconciled to God, ought to expect from His love, which He poured forth to lost sinners in such abundance that He gave us His only begotten and only loved Son. He afterwards makes a comparison between sin and free righteousness, Christ and Adam, death and life, and law and grace. From this it is clear that however great our wrongs may be, they are swallowed up by the infinite goodness of God.

In *chapter six* he turns to discuss the sanctification which we obtain in Christ. As soon as the flesh has had a little taste of this grace, it is liable to gratify its vices and desires without disturbance, as though

7

grace were now ended. Against this Paul maintains here that we cannot receive righteousness in Christ without at the same time laying hold on sanctification. He takes his argument from baptism, by which we are admitted into fellowship with Christ. We are buried with Christ in baptism so that we may die to ourselves and be raised through His life to newness of life. It follows, therefore, that no one can put on the righteousness of Christ without regeneration. Paul uses this as the basis of exhortation to purity and holiness of life. Such purity and holiness must be displayed in those who have put aside the ungodly indulgence of the flesh, which seeks in Christ a greater freedom to sin, and who have been transferred from the kingdom of sin to the kingdom of righteousness. Paul also briefly mentions the abrogation of the law, in which the New Testament shines forth, for the Holy Spirit is promised in the New Testament, together with the remission of sins.

In *chapter seven* he enters into an impartial discussion concerning the use of the law. He had previously mentioned this while discussing another subject. We have been freed from the law, he says, because the law by itself could do nothing but condemn us. Lest, however, his argument should expose the law to reproach, he insists strongly that the law is free of all false accusation. It is our fault, Paul explains, that the law, which had been given for life, proved to be the means of death. At the same time he explains how the law increases sin. From this he passes to describe the struggle between the Spirit and the flesh experienced by the children of God as long as they are surrounded by the prison of our mortal body. Believers carry with them the remains of covetousness by which they are continually drawn from their obedience to the law.

Chapter eight contains many consolations to keep the consciences of believers from being terror-stricken or cast down when they have learned of the disobedience, or rather the imperfect obedience, of which he had previously accused them. To prevent the ungodly from flattering themselves on this score, he first states that this benefit belongs only to the regenerate in whom the Spirit of God lives and abounds. He therefore explains two truths. All those who have been grafted into Christ our Lord by His Spirit are beyond the danger or likelihood of condemnation, however burdened they may still be by their sins. In the second place, if those who remain in the flesh lack the sanctification of the Spirit, none of them has any share in this great blessing. After this Paul then explains how great is the assurance of our faith, since by His own testimony the Spirit of God drives away all our doubts and fears. He further shows by way of anticipating objections that our assurance of eternal life cannot be interrupted or disturbed by the present distresses to which we are subject in our mortal life. On the contrary, our salvation is promoted by such trials, and in comparison with the excellence of our salvation all our present ills will be reckoned as nothing. Paul confirms this by the example of Christ who, since He is the first-begotten and is the Head of the household of God, is thus the pattern to which we must all be conformed. Since, therefore, our salvation is secure, he concludes on a note of splendid praise in which he joyfully triumphs over the power and devices of Satan.

Most men were greatly distressed to see the Jews, who were the principal guardians and heirs of the covenant, reject Christ, for this proved to them either that the covenant was removed from the seed of Abraham, who disdained to fulfil it, or that this was not the promised Redeemer, since He had not made better provision for the people of Israel. Paul therefore begins to meet this objection at the beginning of *chapter nine*. He speaks first of His love towards his own people, that he might not give the appearance of speaking with malice. At the same time he makes a gracious reference to those distinctions by which the Jews excelled other nations, and passes gradually to his task of removing the offence which arose from their blindness. He divides the children of Abraham into two classes to show that not all those who were his physical descendants are to be regarded as his seed and share in the grace of the covenant. On the contrary, even strangers become his children if they are brought into the covenant by faith. There is an example of this truth in the case of Jacob and Esau. Paul, therefore, refers us back here to the election of God which we are to regard as the source of this whole matter. Since our election rests in the mercy of God alone, we seek its cause in human worthiness in vain. On the other hand, however, there is God's rejection. Although the justice of this rejection is beyond doubt, there is no higher cause for it than the will of God. Near the end of the chapter he shows that both the calling of the Gentiles and the rejection of the Jews have been witnessed to in the prophets.

In *chapter ten* he begins again by testifying to his love towards the Jews, and declares that their groundless trust in their works was the cause of their destruction. He prevents them from using the law as an excuse by saying that the law also leads us to the righteousness of faith. This righteousness, he adds, is offered without distinction to all nations by the kindness of God, but is accepted only by those whom the Lord has enlightened with special grace. Though more Gentiles than Jews had obtained this blessing,. he shows that this too was prophesied by Moses and Isaiah, the former of whom prophesied of the calling of the Gentiles and the latter the hardening of the Jews.

The question, however, remained whether the covenant of God had made some difference between the seed of Abraham and other nations.

In seeking to answer this, Paul first reminds us that the work of God is not to be confined to what the eye can see, for the elect often exceed our comprehension. Elijah was formerly mistaken when he thought that religion had perished in Israel, for there were seven thousand still alive. Paul also bids us not to be troubled by the vast number of unbelievers to whom we see the Gospel is repugnant. Finally, he asserts that the covenant remains even in the physical descendants of Abraham, but only in those whom the Lord has predestinated by His free election. He then turns to address the Gentiles, and warns them not to overleap restraint in vaunting their adoption. They are not to spurn the Jews as though they had been rejected, since they excel them only in the gracious acceptance of the Lord, which ought to give them more cause to be humble. God's covenant has not wholly departed from the seed of Abraham, for the Jews are at length to be provoked to jealousy by the faith of the Gentiles, so that God may gather all Israel to Himself.

The three chapters which follow are exhortatory, but are each different. *Chapter twelve* contains general rules for the Christian life. *Chapter thirteen* deals for the most part with the authority of magistrates. It is a likely assumption that there were some restless persons who thought that there could be no Christian liberty without the overthrow of the civil power. To avoid the appearance of laying any duties upon the Church than those of love, Paul shows that this obedience too is a part of love. After this he adds those precepts for the regulating of our life which he had not yet mentioned.

In the *next chapter* he gives an exhortation which was particularly necessary for that period. There were some whose obstinate superstition made them insist on the observance of the Mosaic rites, and they could not bear to neglect them without being most gravely offended. Those, on the other hand, who were confirmed in their rejection of these ceremonies deliberately showed their contempt for them in order to shatter this superstition. Both sides offended by their excesses. The superstitious despised the others as being contemptuous of the divine law, while the latter injudiciously mocked their simplicity. The apostle, therefore, commends to both a proper discretion, and bids the former refrain from contempt and abuse and the latter from taking too much offence. At the same time he prescribes the best way of exercising Christian liberty, which is to keep it within the limits of love and edification. He shows a proper regard for the weak by forbidding them to attempt anything against their conscience.

Chapter fifteen begins with a repetition of his general argument as a conclusion to his whole subject—the strong are to use their strength to confirm the weak. Since the Jews and Gentiles were continually arguing about the Mosaic ceremonies, he resolves all jealousy between them by removing the cause of their pride. He shows that the salvation of both rests on the mercy of God alone. It is on this that they are to rely, and lay aside all exalted thoughts of themselves, and it is by this that they are to be bound together in the hope of one and the same inheritance, and embrace each other wholeheartedly. Finally, since he wanted to digress in order to commend his apostleship which secured great authority for his doctrine, he took the opportunity of excusing and deprecating his presumption for having assumed the office of teacher among them with such confidence. He also gives them some grounds for hoping that he may come to them, although, as he had said at the beginning of the Epistle, he had hitherto sought and tried to do this in vain. He explains why he was at present prevented from coming—the churches of Macedonia and Achaia had entrusted to him the task of bringing to Jerusalem the alms which they had given to relieve the necessity of the believers who were in that city.

The last chapter is almost entirely taken up with greetings, though there are some admirable precepts here and there. It concludes with a notable prayer.

CHAPTER ONE

Paul, a servant of Jesus Christ, called to be an apostle, separated unto the gospel of God, which he promised afore by his prophets in the holy scriptures, concerning his Son, who was born of the seed of David according to the flesh, who was declared to be the Son of God with power, according to the spirit of holiness, by the resurrection of the dead; even Jesus Christ our Lord, through whom we received grace and apostleship, unto obedience of faith among all the nations, for his name's sake; among whom are ye also, called to be Jesus Christ's: to all that are in Rome, beloved of God, called to be saints: Grace to you and peace from God our Father and the Lord Jesus Christ. (1-7)

1. *Paul.* The question of the name Paul is not of such importance that we need spend much time in discussing it. Nothing can be added to the discussion which has not frequently been repeated by other interpreters. I should avoid making any reference to it at all but for the fact that it is possible to say something for those who may be interested without being unduly tedious, since my remarks on the subject will be brief.

The theory that the apostle assumed this name as a token of his successful conversion of the proconsul Sergius is disproved by Luke himself (Acts 13.7, 9), who makes it clear that Paul had this name earlier than that time. I think, too, that it is unlikely that this name had been given to Paul at the time of his own conversion. Augustine, I imagine, approved of this hypothesis simply because it provided him with the opportunity of some subtle argument in his discussion about the self-sufficient Saul who had become the inadequate servant of Christ. Origen, however, is more likely to be correct in his conclusion that Paul had two names. It may in fact have been the case that the family name of Saul had been given to him by his parents as an indication of his religion and race, while the surname Paul was added as an evidence of his right to Roman citizenship. This was an honour which had great importance in Paul's day, and which his parents would not want him to conceal, and yet they did not value it so greatly as to have him obscure the evidence of his Israelite origin. It was, however, the name Paul that he generally used in the Epistles, perhaps because it was a name which was better known and more common in the Churches to which he wrote, and was more acceptable in the Roman Empire, and less known among his own people. Paul, of course, had to avoid the

unnecessary suspicion and violent dislike which were occasioned by
the name of Jew at Rome and in the provinces, and also to avoid
arousing the passions of his fellow-countrymen, as well as take precautions for his own personal safety.

A servant of Jesus Christ. These are the titles by which Paul designates
himself in order to secure authority for his teaching. He does this in
two ways—*first*, by asserting his call to the apostleship, and, *second*, by
announcing to his readers that this vocation had something to do with
the Church at Rome. It was of great importance to Paul not only that
he should be regarded as an apostle by the call of God, but also that he
should be known as one who was destined for the Church at Rome.
He therefore states that he is a *servant* of Christ and called to the office
of apostle, in order to signify that his becoming an apostle was not a
casual intrusion. He then adds immediately after this that he was
separated, thus strengthening his insistence that he was not simply one
among many, but a particularly chosen apostle of the Lord. In this
sense too he is shifting his argument from the general to the particular,
since the apostleship is a particular kind of ministry. All who exercise
the office of teaching are regarded as belonging to the number of
Christ's servants, but apostles have a unique distinction which marks
them off from all others. Paul's separation, however (mentioned later),
expresses both the object and the use of his apostleship, for it was his
intention to make a brief reference to the purpose of his election to
that office. The title *servant of Christ*, therefore, which he applies to
himself, is a title which he shared with every other teacher. By
claiming the name of apostle, however, he gives himself a priority.
But since anyone who usurps the apostolic office has no claim to
authority, Paul reminds his readers that he has been appointed by God.

Thus the meaning of the passage is that Paul was no ordinary servant
of Christ, but an apostle, appointed by the call of God and not by any
presumptuous efforts of his own. There follows next a clearer explanation of his apostolic office, since it was his commission to preach the
gospel. I do not agree with those who refer this call which Paul is
describing to the eternal selection of God and interpret *separation* to
mean either his separation from his mother's womb (as mentioned in
Gal. 1.15), or his election (referred to by Luke) to preach to the
Gentiles. Paul's only boast is that the author of his call is God. There
was to be no suspicion that he was appropriating this honour from
personal presumption.

It should be noted here that not all are fit for the ministry of the
word. This requires a special call. Those who think that they are most
suitable should be careful not to assume the office without a call. We
shall discuss elsewhere the character of the call of apostles and bishops,

but the point to be noted is that the office of an apostle is the preaching of the Gospel. This very fact proves the absurdity of those dumb dogs whose mitre, crozier, and similar pretence are their only distinguishing marks, but whose boast is that they are the successors of the apostles.

The word *servant* means nothing more than minister, for it refers to an office. I mention this in order to get rid of the mistaken impression of those who indulge in needless speculation about the word, on the assumption that there is a contrast between the ministry of Moses and that of Christ.

2. *Which he promised afore.* A doctrine which is suspected of being of recent introduction loses a great deal of its authority, and so Paul establishes the credibility of the Gospel by its antiquity. It is almost as though he were saying that Christ had not come down to earth unexpectedly, or introduced a new kind of doctrine which had never been heard of before, for Christ with His Gospel had been *promised* and always expected from the beginning of the world. Since, however, antiquity frequently tends to be mythical, he introduces the prophets of God as his witnesses—and witnesses of supreme integrity—in order to remove any suspicion. In addition, he adds that their testimony was properly vouched, i.e. in the holy Scriptures.

We may gather from this passage what the Gospel is, for Paul teaches us that it had not been preached by the prophets, but only promised. If, therefore, the prophets promised the Gospel, it follows that the Gospel was revealed when our Lord was at last manifested in the flesh. Those who confuse the promises with the Gospel, therefore, are mistaken, since the Gospel is properly the appointed preaching of Christ made manifest, in whom the promises themselves are revealed.

3. *Concerning his Son.* In this important passage Paul teaches us that the whole Gospel is contained in Christ. To move even a step from Christ means to withdraw oneself from the Gospel. Since Christ is the living and express image of the Father, it need not surprise us that He alone is set in front of us as the One who is both the object and centre of our whole faith. The words, therefore, constitute a description of the Gospel, by which Paul summarizes its content. I have translated the words *Jesus Christ our Lord*, which follow, in the same case as *his Son*, since I feel that this suits the context better. The conclusion, therefore, must be that any due progress in the knowledge of Christ brings with it all that can be learned from the Gospel. On the other hand, to search for wisdom apart from Christ means not simply foolhardiness, but utter insanity.

Who was born. Divinity and humanity are the two requisites which we must look for in Christ if we are to find salvation in Him. His divinity contains power, righteousness, and life, which are communicated to us by His humanity. For this reason the apostle has expressly mentioned both in his summary of the Gospel, in stating that Christ was made manifest in the flesh, and that in the flesh He declared Himself to be the Son of God. So, too, John, after saying that *the Word became flesh*, adds that there was *the glory as of the only begotten from the Father* in His very flesh (John 1.14). The special note which Paul makes of the lineage and descent of Christ from His ancestor David is quite deliberate, for this particular phrase recalls us to the promise, and removes any doubt which we may have of His being the very One who was previously promised. The promise which had been made to David was so widely known that it seems to have been general among the Jews to call the Messiah the Son of David. The fact of Christ's descent from David contributes, therefore, to the confirmation of our faith. Paul adds *according to the flesh* to show that He possessed something better than the flesh—something which He had taken with Him from heaven, but had not received from David, i.e. the glory of the divine nature which he mentions immediately. In addition, Paul not only declares that Christ had real flesh by these expressions, but he also clearly distinguishes between Christ's human and divine nature, thus refuting the blasphemous nonsense of Servetus, who assigned to Christ flesh that was composed of three uncreated elements.

4. *Declared to be the Son of God*. Or, *determined (definitus)*. Paul is saying that the power of the resurrection represented the decree by which, as in Ps. 2.7, Christ was declared to be the Son of God: 'This day have I begotten thee.' 'Begetting' here refers to that which was made known. Certain interpreters find in this passage three separate proofs of the divinity of Christ—first, power (by this they mean miracles), second, the testimony of the Spirit, and third, the resurrection of the dead. I prefer, however, to join these three proofs and summarize them thus: Christ was declared to be the Son of God by the open exercise of a truly heavenly power, i.e. the power of the Spirit, when He rose from the dead. This power is laid hold of when it is sealed by the same Spirit in our hearts. The language of the apostle supports this interpretation. He says that Christ had been declared with *power*, because there was seen in Him the power which properly belongs to God and which proved beyond doubt that He was God. This was in fact made evident in His resurrection, just as Paul elsewhere, after declaring that the weakness of the flesh had been made manifest in Christ's death, extols the power of the Spirit in His resurrection (II Cor. 13.4). This glory, however, is not made known to us until the same Spirit imprints it on our hearts. The fact that Paul also includes the evidence which individual believers experience in their own hearts

with the stupendous power of the Spirit, which Christ manifested by rising from the dead, is clear from his express mention of sanctification. It is as though he were saying that the Spirit, as far as it sanctifies, confirms and ratifies that proof of its power which it once displayed. The Scriptures frequently ascribe titles to the Spirit of God, which serve to elucidate our present discussion. Thus the Spirit is called by our Lord *the Spirit of truth* (John 14.17), by reason of its effect as described in that passage. Furthermore, the divine power is said to have been displayed in the resurrection of Christ, because He rose by His own power, as He often testified: 'Destroy this temple, and in three days I will raise it up' (John 2.19), 'No one taketh it (*sc.* my life) away from me' (John 10.18). Christ gained victory out of death, to which He had yielded by reason of the weakness of His flesh, not by external aid, but by the heavenly operation of His own Spirit.

5. *Through whom we received grace and apostleship.* Having completed his definition of the Gospel, which he introduced in order to commend his office, Paul now returns to assert his own call, for it was a matter of great importance to him that this office should have the approval of those at Rome.

In distinguishing between grace and apostleship Paul is using a figure of speech, *hypallage*, to mean either apostleship freely bestowed, or the grace of apostleship. By this he implies that his appointment to this high office was wholly the work of divine favour, and not of his own merits. Although in the sight of the world his office held nothing but danger, toil, hatred, and disgrace, yet in the sight of God and His saints it has no common or ordinary merit, and is, therefore, deservedly to be reckoned a favour. The rendering *I received grace to be an apostle* may be preferable, and has the same meaning.

The expression *for His name's sake* is explained by Ambrose to mean that the apostle was appointed in the place of Christ to preach the Gospel, as he says in II Cor. 5.20, 'We are ambassadors on behalf of Christ.' The better interpretation, however, would appear to be that which takes *name* to mean knowledge, for the Gospel is preached in order that we should believe in the name of the Son of God (I John 3.23). Paul himself is said to have been a chosen vessel to bear the name of Christ amongst the Gentiles (Acts 9.15). *For his name's sake* therefore conveys the same sense as *that I may make known the character of Christ.*

Unto obedience. That is, we have received the commandment to bear the Gospel to all the Gentiles for their obedience by faith. By stating the purpose of his call Paul again reminds the Romans of his office, as though he were saying, 'It is my duty to discharge the responsibility entrusted to me, which is to preach the word. It is your responsibility to hear the Word, and wholly obey it, unless you want to make void the calling which the Lord has bestowed on me.'

We deduce from this that those who irreverently and contemptuously reject the preaching of the Gospel, the design of which is to bring us into obedience to God, are stubbornly resisting the power of God, and perverting the whole of His order. We are to note here also the nature of faith. It is referred to as *obedience*, because the Lord calls us by the Gospel, and we answer Him by faith as He calls us. So, on the other hand, the source of all our wilful disobedience of God is unbelief. I prefer the translation *into the obedience of faith* to *unto obedience*, since, except metaphorically, the latter is not strictly correct, although it is once used in Acts 6.7. Faith is properly that by which we obey the Gospel.

Among all the nations. It was not enough for Paul to have been appointed an apostle, unless his ministry had reference to the making of disciples. He therefore adds that his apostleship extends to all the Gentiles. He later refers to himself more distinctly as the apostle to the Romans when he says that they also are among the number of the nations to whom he was given to be a minister. The apostles also have in common the command to preach the Gospel throughout the whole world. They are not appointed to certain churches as pastors or bishops. Paul, in addition to his general responsibility for the apostolic function, was appointed by special authority as a minister to preach the Gospel among the nations. It is no objection to this statement that he was forbidden to pass through Bithynia and to preach the Word in Mysia (Acts 16.6-8). The purpose of this prohibition was not that his work should be limited to a certain area, but because it was necessary for him to go elsewhere for a time, since the harvest there had not yet fully ripened.

6. *Called to be Jesus Christ's.* Paul offers a reason more closely connected with those in the church at Rome, because the Lord had already given a sign by them, by which He declared that He was calling them to share the Gospel. It followed from this that if they wanted to have their own calling remain sure, they should not reject Paul's ministry, for Paul had been chosen by the same election of the Lord. I therefore take this clause *called to be Jesus Christ's* as an explanatory phrase, as though the particle *namely* were inserted. He means that they were partakers of Christ by His calling. Those who are to be heirs of eternal life are not only chosen by their Father in heaven to become His sons, but, having been chosen, are committed also to His care and trustworthiness as their Shepherd.

7. *To all.* By using this commendable order he shows what there is in us that is worthy of praise. (1) The Lord in His kindness has taken

us into His grace and love; (2) He has called us; (3) and He has called us to holiness. But this high honour is finally ours only if we do not neglect our calling.

There is here a very profound truth to which I shall briefly refer, and leave it to the consideration of individual readers. Our salvation does not, according to Paul, depend on our own power, but is entirely derived from the fountain of God's free and fatherly love towards us. The primary fact is this—God loves us. There is no other reason for His love than His own sheer goodness. On this, too, depends His calling, by which in His own time He seals His adoption in those whom He had freely chosen before. From this, however, we also deduce that there is no true association with the faithful for any who do not believe for certain that the Lord is favourable to them, even though they are undeserving and wretched sinners, and who aspire to holiness by the stimulation of His goodness, 'for God called us not for uncleanness, but in sanctification' (I Thess. 4.7). Since the Greek may be translated in the second person, I have seen no reason for changing it.

Grace to you and peace. It is a most desirable blessing to have God favourable to us. This is what 'grace' means. It is also a great blessing to have success and prosperity in all our affairs flow from Him. This is what 'peace' means. If God is angry, even though everything may seem to be favourable to us, our very blessing is changed into a curse. The only basis of our happiness, therefore, is the kindness of God. This allows us to enjoy true and undivided prosperity, while our very adversity itself promotes our salvation. Since Paul prays for peace from the Lord, we also understand from this that any blessing that comes to us is the fruit of God's benevolence. We must also note that at the same time he prays to the Lord Jesus Christ for these blessings. Our Lord deserves to be honoured in this way, for He is not only the administrator and disposer of His Father's bountiful goodness toward us, but He also works all things together with Him. It was, however, the special object of the apostle to show that all the blessings of God come to us through Christ.

There are some scholars who prefer to regard the word *peace* as signifying tranquillity of conscience. I do not deny that it sometimes has this meaning. But since it is certain that the apostle wished to give us here a summary of God's blessings, the former sense (which is suggested by Bucer) is much more appropriate. Paul wants to express the wish that believers should have the sum of happiness, and therefore goes, as he did before, to the very source itself, viz. the grace of God. This not only brings us eternal blessedness but is also the cause of all good things in this life.

First, I thank my God through Jesus Christ for you all, that your faith is proclaimed throughout the whole world. For God is my witness, whom I serve in my spirit in the gospel of his Son, how unceasingly I make mention of you, always in my prayers making request, if by any means now at length I may be prospered by the will of God to come unto you. For I long to see you, that I may impart unto you some spiritual gift, to the end ye may be established; that is, that I with you may be comforted in you, each of us by the other's faith, both yours and mine. (8-12)

8. *First, I thank my God.* The introduction in the present passage is one most suited to the case which Paul wants to put, since he takes the opportunity of preparing them for receiving his teaching by reasons connected with himself as well as with them. He argues from what he knows of them. He recalls the wide renown of their faith, and implies that since they are honoured with the open approbation of the churches, they cannot reject the Lord's apostle without disappointing the good name which they universally enjoyed. Such conduct would be discourteous, and in some measure a breach of trust. As this fame of theirs ought, therefore, with good reason to have induced the apostle who had formed a good opinion of their obedience to undertake the teaching and instruction of the Romans according to his office, so they were obliged in turn not to despise his authority. He disposes them to adopt a receptive attitude from a consideration of his own character, by testifying his sincere affection toward them. There is nothing more effective in securing confidence in a counsellor than the impression that he is sincerely anxious for us, and is studying our interest.

It is worth noting, first of all, that Paul commends their faith in such a way as to imply that it had been received from God. From this we learn that faith is a gift of God. If thanksgiving is the acknowledgment of a benefit, whoever thanks God for faith acknowledges that it is His gift. When we find that the apostle always begins his congratulations with thanksgiving, we may know that the lesson we are being given is that all our blessings are the gifts of God. We should also accustom ourselves to such forms of expression as may ever rouse us more keenly to acknowledge God as the bestower of all good things, and to stir up others at the same time to a similar attitude. If it is right to do this in little blessings, how much more ought we to do so in regard to faith, which is neither a commonplace nor an indiscriminate gift of God. Furthermore, we have here an illustration of how thanksgiving ought to be given *through Jesus Christ,* according to the command of the apostle in Heb. 13.15, which shows how it is in His name that we both seek and find mercy from the Father. Finally, Paul refers to God as *my God*. This is the special privilege of the faithful, on whom alone God bestows this honour. There is implied in this a mutual relationship, which is expressed in the promise, 'And ye shall be my people, and I will be your God' (Jer. 30.22), though I prefer to restrict the phrase to the character which Paul bore as a mark of God's approval of the obedience which he rendered to the Lord in preaching the Gospel. Thus Hezekiah calls God the God of Isaiah when he desires to declare that Isaiah was a true and faithful prophet (Isa. 37.4). Thus also God is called *par excellence* the God of Daniel, because Daniel had maintained the purity of His worship (Dan. 6.20).

That your faith is proclaimed throughout the whole world. The approbation of honourable men was to Paul equivalent to that of the whole world in estimating the faith of the Romans, for the testimony of unbelievers, who detested the faith, could not be sincere or credible. We should, therefore, understand that the faith of the Romans had been voiced in the whole world by all of the faithful who were able to form a proper opinion of it, and pass a right judgment on it. The fact that this small and despised handful of men was unknown to unbelievers even at Rome was of no importance, since their judgment had not the slightest weight with Paul.

9. *For God is my witness.* He shows his love by its effects. Had he not been greatly attached to them, he would not have commended them to the Lord with such concern. In particular he would not have so earnestly wanted to promote their salvation by his own efforts. His concern and desire, therefore, are unequivocal proofs of his affection for them, for these can never exist unless they have their source in love. Since, however, Paul knew that it was desirable to convince the Romans of his sincerity in order to establish confidence in his preaching, he added an oath—the unavoidable course whenever an assertion, which requires to be established beyond doubt, is called in question. If an oath is merely an appeal to God for the confirmation of what we are saying, we must grant the wisdom of the apostle's oath, which he took without thereby infringing the commandment of Christ.

It is evident from this that it was not Christ's design (as the Anabaptists superstitiously imagine) to abolish oaths entirely, but rather to restore the true observance of the Law. The Law, while allowing an oath, condemns only perjury and unnecessary pledge on oath. If, therefore, we would take an oath properly, we should imitate the serious and reverent attitude which is exhibited by the apostles. To understand this form of oath, however, we should understand that in appealing to God as a witness, we are summoning Him as the One who exacts a penalty if we swear deceitfully, as Paul states elsewhere in these words: 'I call God for a witness upon my soul' (II Cor. 1.23).

Whom I serve in my spirit. Since irreverent mockers of God are accustomed to appeal to His name as a mere pretext with as much assurance as presumption, Paul here commends his own devotion in order to secure for himself the confidence of the Romans. Those who are possessed of a fear of the Lord and a reverence for Him will shrink from taking a false oath. Paul also sets his spirit against an external appearance of religion. Since many make a pretence of being worshippers of God, and outwardly appear to be so, he bears witness that he worships God from the heart. It may also be that he was alluding to the ancient ceremonies in which alone the Jews thought that the worship of God consisted. He means, therefore, that, although he was not trained in these, he was nevertheless a sincere worshipper of God, as he states in Phil. 3.3: 'We are the circumcision, who worship by the Spirit of God, and glory in Christ Jesus, and have no confidence in the flesh.' He glories, therefore, that He served God with sincere devotion of heart, which is true religion and proper worship.

As I have already mentioned, it was also of importance to Paul that he should declare his devotion to God, in order that his oath might be more readily believed. Perjury is a mockery to the godless, while to the devout it is more to be dreaded than a thousand deaths. Where there is a real fear of God, there must also be a real respect for His name. It is the same, therefore, as if Paul were saying that he was well aware of the sacredness and reverence required in taking an oath, and that he was not calling God to witness flippantly, as the irreverent are in the habit of doing. His own example, therefore, teaches us that whenever we take an oath we ought to give such evidence of respect that the name of God, which we use in our talk, may retain its due weight. He then gives a proof from his own ministry that his worship of God did not spring from mere pretence. It was the most complete evidence of his devotion to the glory of God that he denied himself, and did not hesitate to face all the hardships of reproach, poverty, death, and hatred, in promoting the Kingdom of God.

Some interpret this clause to mean that Paul wanted to commend the worship which he had said he offered to God because it was agreeable to the command of the Gospel, in which a spiritual worship is enjoined upon us. The former interpretation is by far the better one, viz. that he was devoting his service to God in the preaching of the Gospel. In the meantime, however, he distinguishes himself from the hypocrites who had other motives than the worship of God, since most of them were driven by ambition, or something of the sort, and were far from discharging their ministry faithfully and from the heart. The conclusion is that Paul is sincere in his office of teaching, for the fact that he has spoken of his own devotion is appropriate to the particular case in hand. We deduce from this some useful teaching which ought to add no small encouragement to ministers of the Gospel when they hear that in preaching the Gospel they are rendering an acceptable and valuable service to God. Is there anything that should prevent them from doing so, when they know that their labours are so pleasing to God and approved by Him as to be considered an act of the highest worship? Paul further calls it *the gospel of his Son*. It is by this that Christ is made known, and He is appointed by the Father to glorify the Father in turn while He Himself is glorified.

How unceasingly I make mention of you. Paul continues to express the greater vehemence of his affection by his very constancy in praying for them. It was a great proof of his affection that he never prayed to the Lord without making mention of them. In order that the meaning of this passage may be clearer, I take the word πάντοτε, always, to mean 'in all my prayers', or, 'whenever I address God in my prayers, I make mention of you'. Paul is not speaking here of any invocation of God, but of those prayers to which the saints spontaneously devote themselves. The apostle might frequently have voiced some ejaculatory prayer or other without remembering the Romans, but whenever he prayed to God with deliberate premeditation, he remembered them as well as others. He speaks particularly, therefore, of *prayers*. It is to prayer that the saints deliberately devote themselves, even as we see that the Lord Himself sought a place of retirement for such a purpose. At the same time, however, Paul denotes the frequency, or rather the continuance, of his habit of prayer by saying that he devoted himself to prayer *unceasingly*.

10. *Always in my prayers making request.* It is unlikely that we shall study earnestly to promote the welfare of those whom we are not prepared to help by our own efforts also. Having stated, therefore, that he was anxious for their well-being, Paul now adds that he is proving his love to them in the sight of God by another way, viz. by requesting that he might be of use to them. The full sense of the passage will appear by supplying *also* and reading as follows: 'Making also request, if by any means I might have a prosperous journey by the will of God.' By this he shows that he not only was expecting success in his journey by the grace of God, but would also judge the success of his journey by the approval of the Lord.

11. *For I long to see you.* Even though he was absent, he could have confirmed their faith by his doctrine, but since advice always comes better from one who is present, Paul wanted to be with them. He explains the object of his advice, in order to demonstrate that he

wanted to undertake the trouble of a journey not for his own advantage, but for theirs. By *spiritual gift* he means the capabilities which he possessed either of preaching, exhortation, or prophecy, and which he knew he had acquired by the grace of God. He has here strikingly pointed out the lawful use of these gifts by the word *impart*, for different gifts are given to each individual, so that all may contribute generously to their common interests, and communicate to one another the gifts possessed individually (Rom. 12.3; I Cor. 12.11).

To the end ye may be established. Paul modifies his words about imparting, lest he should appear to regard them as those who had still to be instructed in the first elements of the Gospel, and who had not yet been properly initiated into Christ. He says, therefore, that he was most anxious to help them at the point where those who have made the greatest progress still require assistance, for we all need to be confirmed until we have attained to 'the measure of the stature of the fulness of Christ' (Eph. 4.13). Not being satisfied with this modest assertion, he modifies it by showing that he did not usurp the position of teacher without a desire also to learn from them, as though he said, 'I am anxious to confirm you according to the measure of the grace conferred on me, that your example may also add to the eagerness of my faith, and that we may both thus benefit one another.'

Note how modestly he expresses what he feels by not refusing to seek strengthening from inexperienced beginners. He means what he says, too, for there is none so void of gifts in the Church of Christ who cannot in some measure contribute to our spiritual progress. Ill will and pride, however, prevent our deriving such benefit from one another. Such is our superiority and such the intoxicating effect of our stupid boasting, that every one of us despises and disregards others, and considers that he possesses a sufficient abundance for himself. With Bucer I translate the Greek verb in the sense of *exhorting* rather than of comforting, since it suits the context better.

And I would not have you ignorant, brethren, that oftentimes I purposed to come unto you (and was hindered hitherto), that I might have some fruit in you also, even as in the rest of the Gentiles. I am debtor both to Greeks and to Barbarians, both to the wise and to the foolish. So, as much as in me is, I am ready to preach the gospel to you also that are in Rome. (13-15)

13. *And I would not have you ignorant, brethren.* Paul now confirms the declarations which he had given up to this point of his constant request to the Lord to be allowed to visit them at some time, since his professions might have appeared empty if he neglected to seize the opportunities when offered. He says that it had not been the effort but

the opportunity which had been wanting, as he had been prevented from his frequently projected purpose of visiting Rome.

We learn from this that the Lord frequently upsets the purposes of his saints in order to humble them, and by such humiliation to teach them to look to His providence, on which they are to depend. Strictly speaking, however, their plans are not frustrated, since they have no purposes apart from the will of the Lord. It is blasphemous affrontery to determine one's future plans without taking consideration of God, as though they were within our power to arrange. This is what James sharply reproves (4.13).

Paul says that he was *hindered*. We may take this to mean that the Lord employed him in more urgent business, which he could not have neglected without damage to the Church. Thus the things which hinder believers and unbelievers differ, for the latter feel that they are hindered only when they are unable to move from the unmitigable hand of the Lord, while believers are content to be prevented by some genuine reason, and do not allow themselves to attempt anything which is either beyond their duty or contrary to the edification of the Church.

That I might have some fruit in you also. Paul is no doubt referring to that fruit which the apostles were sent out by the Lord to gather: *I chose you, and appointed you, that ye should go and bear fruit, and that your fruit should abide* (John 15.16). He calls the fruit his own, although he had not gathered it for himself, but for the Lord. There is no truer characteristic of believers than that they should promote the glory of the Lord, with which their whole happiness is connected. He recollects that this had befallen him *in the rest of the Gentiles*, in order to inspire the Romans with the hope that his coming to them would not be unprofitable, since it had been of advantage to so many Gentiles.

14. *Both to Greeks and to Barbarians.* The epithets *wise* and *foolish* explain the meaning of *Greeks* and *Barbarians*. Erasmus translated by *learned* and *ignorant*, quite a good rendering, but I have preferred to retain Paul's very words. Paul, therefore, argues from his own office to show that his assurance that he was capable of teaching the Romans, however much they excelled in learning, prudence, and skill, should not be ascribed to his arrogance, since the Lord had been pleased to make him a debtor even to the wise. There are two points to be considered here. The first is that the Gospel is appointed and offered to the wise by the commandment of God in order that the Lord may subject all the wisdom of this world to Himself, and make every talent and every kind of science, and the sublimity of all the arts, give place to the simple nature of His teaching. The wise are reduced to the same level as the ignorant, and made so gently receptive as to tolerate

as their fellow-disciples under their Master, Christ, those whom they would not previously have condescended to take as their scholars. In the second place, the unlearned are by no means to be debarred from this school, nor are the learned to avoid it through groundless apprehension. If Paul was a debtor to them, and is to be thought of as having been a debtor of good faith, he no doubt discharged what he owed. They will, therefore, in this case find what they will be capable of enjoying. All teachers also have here a rule to follow, viz. to accommodate themselves in a modest, courteous way to the ignorant and unlearned. By doing so they will more patiently endure much stupidity of conduct and bear with innumerable instances of pride, which might otherwise overcome them. It is, however, their duty to remember that their obligations to the foolish mean that they are not to indulge their folly beyond moderation.

15. *So, as much as in me is, I am ready to preach the gospel to you also that are in Rome.* He concludes what he had thus far said of his own desire to go to Rome, and since it seemed to be a part of his duty to spread the Gospel among them in order to gather fruit for the Lord, he earnestly desired to fulfil the calling of God as far as the Lord would allow.

For I am not ashamed of the gospel: for it is the power of God unto salvation to every one that believeth; to the Jew first, and also to the Greek. For therein is revealed a righteousness of God by faith unto faith: as it is written, But the righteous shall live by faith. (16-17)

16. *I am not ashamed of the gospel of Christ.* Paul anticipates an objection by declaring in advance that he has no regard for the taunts of the ungodly. In so doing, however, he takes the opportunity of commending the merits of the Gospel, that it might not be spurned by the Romans. He hints indeed that it was contemptible in the eyes of the world, when he says that he is not ashamed of it himself. Thus he prepares them for bearing the reproach of the cross of Christ, that they might not undervalue the Gospel when they saw it exposed to the fears and taunts of the ungodly. On the other hand, however, he proves its supreme value to believers. If, in the first place, the power of God ought to be highly esteemed, that power shines forth in the Gospel. If goodness is worthy of being sought and loved by us, the Gospel is the instrument of that goodness; and it ought to be both honoured and esteemed, since respect is due to the power of God, and we ought to love it in proportion as our salvation is thus secured.

Note, however, how much Paul attributes to the ministry of the Word, when he declares that God exerts His power there for our salvation. He is not speaking here of any secret revelation, but of preaching by word of mouth. It follows from this that those who withdraw themselves from hearing the Word preached are wilfully rejecting the power of God and repelling His hand of deliverance far from them.

Because God does not work effectually in all men, but only when the Spirit shines in our hearts as the inward teacher, he adds *to every one that believeth*. The Gospel is indeed offered to all for their salvation, but its power is not universally manifest. The fact that the Gospel is the taste of death to the ungodly arises not so much from the nature of the Gospel itself, as from their own wickedness. By setting forth one way of salvation, it cuts off confidence in every other way. When men withdraw from this one salvation they find in the Gospel a sure evidence of their own ruin. When, therefore, the Gospel invites all to partake of salvation without any difference, it is rightly termed the doctrine of salvation. For Christ is there offered, whose proper office is to save that which had been lost, and those who refuse to be saved by Him shall find Him their Judge. In Scripture the word salvation is throughout set in opposition to death, and when it occurs, we must consider what is the subject under discussion. Since, therefore, the Gospel delivers from ruin and the curse of eternal death, the salvation which it secures is eternal life.

To the Jew first, and also to the Greek. Under the word *Greek* Paul here includes all the Gentiles as the comparison proves, for he intended the two classes to include all mankind. It is probable that he chose this nation in particular to designate other nations because, in the first place, they were the first after the Jews to have been admitted into participation in the Gospel covenant, and, secondly, because the Greeks had a better knowledge than the Jews on account of their geographical proximity and the widespread knowledge of their language. By a figure of speech he therefore unites the Gentiles with the Jews in the participation of the Gospel, without depriving the Jews of their eminence and rank, since they were first in the promise and call. Paul, therefore, maintains for the Jews their prerogative, but he immediately adds the Gentiles as being sharers with them of the Gospel, though in a lesser degree.

17. *For therein is revealed a righteousness of God by faith unto faith.* This is an explanation and confirmation of the preceding clause, which stated that the Gospel is 'the power of God unto salvation'. If we seek salvation, i.e. life with God, we must first seek righteousness, by which we may be reconciled to Him, and obtain that life which consists in His benevolence alone through His being favourable to us. In order that we may be loved by God we must first be righteous, for He hates unrighteousness. The meaning is, therefore, that we can obtain

salvation from no other source than the Gospel, since God has nowhere else revealed to us His righteousness, which alone delivers us from death. This righteousness, the basis of our salvation, is revealed in the Gospel: hence the Gospel is said to be *the power of God unto salvation*. In this way we argue from cause to effect.

Note further how rare and valuable a treasure God bestows on us in His Gospel, viz. the communication of His righteousness. By the *righteousness of God* I understand that which is approved at His tribunal, as on the other hand that which is reckoned and counted as righteousness in the opinion of men, even though it is a mere triviality, is generally referred to as the 'righteousness of men'. Paul, however, is without doubt alluding to the many prophecies in which the Spirit is throughout setting forth the righteousness of God in the future kingdom of Christ. Some commentators explain the meaning to be 'what is given to us by God'. I certainly grant that the words will bear this meaning, because God justifies us by His Gospel, and thus saves us. And yet the former sense seems to me more suitable, although I would not spend much time on the question. It is of more importance that some scholars think that this *righteousness* consists not only in the free remission of sins, but in part also in the grace of regeneration. I hold, however, that we are restored to life because God freely reconciles us to Himself, as we shall later show at greater length in the proper place.

In place of the expression *to every one that believeth* which he had used before he now says *by faith*. Righteousness is offered by the Gospel, and is received by faith. He adds *unto faith*, for in proportion to the advance of our faith and our progress in knowledge the *righteousness of God* increases in us, and its possession is in a degree confirmed. When we first taste the Gospel we do indeed see the countenance of God turned graciously toward us, but at a distance. The more our knowledge of true religion increases, we see the grace of God with greater clarity and more familiarity, as though He were coming nearer to us. The suggestion that there is here an implied comparison between the Old and New Testaments is subtle rather than well-founded, for Paul is not here comparing the fathers who lived under the Law with us, but marks the daily progress of every believer.

As it is written, But the righteous shall live by faith. He proves the righteousness of faith by the authority of the prophet Habakkuk, who, in predicting the destruction of the proud, adds at the same time that *the just shall live by his faith.* We live in the presence of God only by righteousness. It therefore follows that our righteousness depends on faith. The verb in the future tense designates the undivided perpetuity of the life of which he is speaking, as though he had said, 'It shall not continue for a moment, but shall endure for ever.' The ungodly are also inflated with the delusion of having life, but 'when they are saying, Peace and safety, then sudden destruction cometh upon them' (I Thess. 5.3). Theirs, therefore, is a shadow which endures only for a moment, while the faith of the righteous alone brings everlasting life. What is the source of that life but the faith which leads us to God, and makes our life depend on Him? Paul's reference to this passage from Habakkuk would have been irrelevant, unless the prophet meant that we stand firm only when we rest on God by faith. He ascribed the life of the ungodly to faith only in so far as they renounce the pride of the world and gather themselves together for the protection of God alone. Habakkuk does not, it is true, explicitly deal with this question, and hence he makes no mention of free righteousness, but it is sufficiently evident from the nature of faith that this passage is rightly applied to our present subject. From his argument we necessarily also infer the mutual relationship between faith and the Gospel, for since *the just* is said to *live by his faith*, he maintains that such a life is received by the Gospel.

We see now the main or cardinal point of the first part of this Epistle: we are justified by faith through the mercy of God alone. We do not so far have this in Paul's actual words, but it will be quite easily seen later from the context that the righteousness which is based on faith depends wholly on the mercy of God.

> For the wrath of God is revealed from heaven against all ungodliness
> and unrighteousness of men, who hold down the truth in unrighteousness;
> because that which may be known of God is manifest in them; for God
> manifested it unto them. For the invisible things of him since the creation
> of the world are clearly seen, being perceived through the things that are
> made, even his everlasting power and divinity; that they may be without
> excuse: because that, knowing God, they glorified him not as God,
> neither gave thanks; but became vain in their reasonings, and their
> senseless heart was darkened. Professing themselves to be wise, they
> became fools, and changed the glory of the incorruptible God for the
> likeness of an image of corruptible man, and of birds, and of fourfooted
> beasts, and creeping things. (18-23)

18. *For the wrath of God is revealed from heaven against all ungodliness and unrighteousness of men.* Paul now argues from a comparison of opposites in order to prove that righteousness is bestowed or conferred only by the Gospel, for he demonstrates that without it all are condemned. Salvation, therefore, will be found in the Gospel alone. The first proof of confirmation which he adduces is the fact that, although the structure of the world and the most splendid ordering of the elements ought to have induced man to glorify God, yet there are

none who discharge their duty. This is proof that all men are guilty of sacrilege, and of base and iniquitous ingratitude.

There are some who suggest that this is Paul's first proposition, so that he may begin his discourse with repentance, but I feel that it is here that Paul begins his controversial matter, and that the main theme has been stated in the preceding sentence. His object is to instruct us where salvation is to be sought. He has stated that we can obtain it only by the Gospel, but because the flesh will not willingly humble itself to the point of ascribing the praise of salvation to the grace of God alone, Paul shows that the whole world is guilty of eternal death. It follows from this that we must recover life by some other means, since in ourselves we are all lost. A careful examination of each word will greatly assist us to understand the meaning of the passage.

Some interpreters distinguish between ungodliness and unrighteousness, maintaining that ungodliness refers to the profanation of the worship of God, and unrighteousness to a want of justice to men. Since, however, the apostle refers this unrighteousness immediately to the neglect of true religion, we shall interpret both as having the same meaning. *All ungodliness of men* is to be taken by hypallage as meaning *the ungodliness of all men*, or the ungodliness of which all men stand convicted. One thing is designated by the two different expressions, viz. ingratitude to God, because we offend against God in two ways. Ἀσέβεια, ungodliness, implies a dishonouring of God, while ἀδικία, unrighteousness, means that man by transferring to himself what belongs to God, has unjustly deprived God of His due honour. The word *wrath*, referring to God in human terms as is usual in Scripture, means the vengeance of God, for when God punishes, He has, according to our way of thinking, the appearance of anger. The word, therefore, implies no emotion in God, but has reference only to the feelings of the sinner who is punished. Paul then says that the wrath of God is *revealed from heaven*, although the expression *from heaven* is taken by some as an adjective, as though he said *the wrath of the God of heaven*. In my opinion, however, it is more emphatic to say, 'Let a man look where he will, he will find no salvation, for *the wrath of God* is poured out on the whole world to the full extent of heaven.'

The truth of God means the true knowledge of God, and to *hold down* the truth is to suppress or obscure it: hence they are accused of theft. *In unrighteousness* is a Hebrew phrase and means unjustly (*injuste*), but we have tried to keep the meaning clear.

19. *Because that which may be known of God is manifest in them.* Paul thus designates what is right or expedient for us to know of God, and he means all that refers to the showing forth of the glory of the Lord, or, which is the same thing, whatever ought to induce and excite us

to glorify God. This means that we cannot fully comprehend God in His greatness, but that there are certain limits within which men ought to confine themselves, even as God accommodates to our limited capacity (*ad modulum nostrum attemperat*) every declaration which He makes of Himself. Only fools, therefore, seek to know the essence of God. The Spirit, the Teacher of perfect wisdom, not without reason recalls our attention to *that which may be known*, τὸ γνωστόν, and Paul will immediately explain how this may be known. The force of the passage is increased by the preposition *in* (*in ipsis* rather than the simple *ipsis*). Although in Hebrew phraseology, which the apostle frequently uses, the particle בְּ, *in*, is often redundant, he seems in this instance to have intended to indicate a manifestation of God's character which is too forceful to allow men to escape from it, since undoubtedly every one of us feels it engraved on his own heart. By saying *God manifested it* he means that man was formed to be a spectator of the created world, and that he was endowed with eyes for the purpose of his being led to God Himself, the Author of the world, by contemplating so magnificent an image.

20. *For the invisible things of him since the creation of the world are clearly seen.* God is invisible in Himself, but since His majesty shines forth in all His works and in all His creatures, men ought to have acknowledged Him in these, for they clearly demonstrate their Creator. For this reason the apostle, in his Epistle to the Hebrews, calls the world a mirror or representation (*specula seu spectacula*) of invisible things (Heb. 11.3). He does not recount in detail all the attributes which may be held to belong to God, but he tells us how to come to the knowledge of His eternal power and divinity. He who is the Author of all things must necessarily be without beginning and self-created. When we have made this discovery about God, His divinity now reveals itself, and this divinity can exist only when accompanied by all the attributes of God, since they are all included in that divinity.

That they may be without excuse. This clearly proves how much men gain from this demonstration of the existence of God, viz. an utter incapacity to bring any defence to prevent them from being justly accused before the judgment-seat of God. We must, therefore, make this distinction, that the manifestation of God by which He makes His glory known among His creatures is sufficiently clear as far as its own light is concerned. It is, however, inadequate on account of our blindness. But we are not so blind that we can plead ignorance without being convicted of perversity. We form a conception of divinity, and then we conclude that we are under the necessity of worshipping such a Being, whatever His character may be. Our judgment, however, fails here before it discovers the nature or character of God. Hence the apostle in Heb. 11.3 ascribes to faith the light by which a man can gain real knowledge from the work of creation. He does so with good reason, for we are prevented by our blindness from reaching our goal. And yet we see just enough to keep us from making excuse. Both of these truths are well demonstrated by Paul in Acts 14.17, when he says that the Lord in times past left the nations in their ignorance, yet He did not leave them without witness, ἀμάρτυροι, since He gave them rain and fruitful seasons from heaven. This knowledge of God, therefore, which avails only to prevent men from making excuses, differs greatly from the knowledge which brings salvation. This latter is mentioned by Christ, and Jeremiah teaches us to glory in it (John 17.3; Jer. 9.24).

21. *Because that, knowing God.* He clearly declares here that God has put into the minds of all men the knowledge of Himself. In other words, He has so demonstrated His existence by His works as to make men see what they do not seek to know of their own accord, viz. that there is a God. The world does not exist by chance, nor has it proceeded from itself. We must always, however, note the degree of knowledge which they have continued to hold, as we see from what follows.

They glorified him not as God. No conception of God can be formed without including His eternity, power, wisdom, goodness, truth, righteousness, and mercy. His eternity is evidenced by the fact that He holds all things in His hand and makes all things to consist in Himself. His wisdom is seen, because He has arranged all things in perfect order; His goodness, because there is no other cause for His creation of all things, nor can any other reason than His goodness itself induce Him to preserve them. His justice is evident in His governing of the world, because He punishes the guilty and defends the innocent; His mercy, because He bears the perversity of men with so much patience; and His truth, because He is unchangeable. Those, therefore, who have formed a conception of God ought to give Him the praise due to His eternity, wisdom, goodness, and justice. Since men have not recognized these attributes in God, but have conjured up an imaginary picture of Him as though He were an insubstantial phantom, they are justly said to have wickedly robbed Him of His glory. It is not without reason that Paul adds that *neither gave they thanks,* for there is no one who is not indebted to God's infinite kindnesses, and even on this account alone He has abundantly put us in His debt by condescending to reveal Himself to us. *But they became vain in their reasonings, and their senseless heart was darkened,* i.e. they forsook the truth of God and turned aside to the vanity of their own reason, which is completely undiscriminating and impermanent. Their *senseless heart* being thus *darkened* could understand nothing correctly, but in every way was borne headlong into error and falsehood. This was their unrighteousness, that the seed of true knowledge was immediately choked by their wickedness before it grew to maturity.

22. *Professing themselves to be wise, they became fools.* It is commonly inferred from this passage that Paul is here alluding to the philosophers who lay particular claim to a reputation for wisdom. The drift of his argument is held to show that when the superiority of the great is reduced to nothing, the ordinary people would have no grounds for supposing that they had anything which was worth commending. Interpreters who take this view do not seem to me to have been influenced by sufficiently conclusive reasoning, for it was not peculiar to philosophers to imagine that they were wise in the knowledge of God, but it was equally common to all nations and classes of men. All men have sought to form some conception of the majesty of God, and to make Him such a God as their reason could conceive Him to be. This presumptuous attitude to God is not, I maintain, learned in the philosophical schools, but is innate, and accompanies us, so to speak, from the womb. It is evident that this evil has flourished in all ages, so that men have allowed themselves every liberty in devising superstitious practices. The arrogance, therefore, which is here condemned is that, when men ought in humility to have given glory to God, they sought to be wise among themselves, and to reduce God to the level of their own low condition. Paul maintains this principle, that if a man is estranged from the worship of God, it is his own fault, as though he said, 'Because they have exalted themselves in pride, they have been made foolish by the righteous vengeance of God.' There is also an obvious reason which militates against the interpretation which I reject. The error of forming an image of God (*de affingenda Deo imagine*) did not originate with the philosophers, but was received from others, and also stamped by their own approval.

23. *And changed the glory of the incorruptible God.* Having imagined such a God as they could comprehend by their carnal sense, it was impossible for them to acknowledge the true God, but they invented a fictitious new God, or rather a phantom in His stead. What Paul says is that they *changed the glory of God.* In the same way as one might substitute one child for another, they departed from the true God. Nor are they excused on the pretext that they believe, nevertheless, that God dwells in heaven, and that they regard the wood not as God but as His image (*pro simulacro*), for it is an insult to God to form so gross an idea of His Majesty as to dare to make an image of Him. None of them can be exempted from the blasphemy of such presumption,

neither priests, politicians, nor philosophers. Even Plato, the most sound-minded of them, sought to trace some form in God (*formam in Deo*).

The utter senselessness to which we therefore draw attention here is that all men have desired to make themselves a figure of God. This is a sure proof that their ideas of God are gross and illogical. In the first place they have defiled the majesty of God by forming Him in the likeness of *corruptible man* (I prefer this rendering to that of *mortal man* which is adopted by Erasmus), since Paul opposes not only the mortality of man to the immortality of God, but His incorruptible glory to the very pitiable condition of man. Furthermore, not being content with so great an offence, they even descended to the vilest of beasts, making their stupidity appear yet more evident. The reader will see a description of these abominable practices in Lactantius, Eusebius, and Augustine in his *City of God*.

> *Wherefore God gave them up in the lusts of their hearts unto uncleanness, that their bodies should be dishonoured among themselves: for that they exchanged the truth of God for a lie, and worshipped and served the creature rather than the Creator, who is blessed for ever. Amen. For this cause God gave them up into vile passions: for their women changed the natural use into that which is against nature: and likewise also the men, leaving the natural use of the woman, burned in their lusts one toward another, men with men working unseemliness, and receiving in themselves that recompense of their error which was due. And even as they refused to have God in their knowledge, God gave them up unto a reprobate mind, to do those things which are not fitting; being filled with all unrighteousness, wickedness, covetousness, maliciousness; full of envy, murder, strife, deceit, malignity; whisperers, backbiters, hateful to God, insolent, haughty, boastful, inventors of evil things, disobedient to parents, without understanding, covenant-breakers, without natural affection, unmerciful: who, knowing the ordinance of God, that they which practise such things are worthy of death, not only do the same, but also consent with them that practise them. (24-32)*

24. *Wherefore God gave them up.* Ungodliness is a hidden evil, and therefore Paul uses a more obvious proof to show that they cannot escape without just condemnation, since this ungodliness was followed by effects which prove manifest evidence of the wrath of the Lord. If, however, the wrath of the Lord is always just, it follows that there had been something which rendered them liable to condemnation. Paul, therefore, now uses these signs to prove the apostasy and defection of men, for the Lord punishes those who have alienated themselves from His goodness by casting them headlong into destruction and ruin of

many kinds. By comparing the vices of which they were guilty with the ungodliness of which he accused them before, he shows that they were suffering punishment through the just judgment of God. Since nothing is dearer to us than our own honour, it is the height of blindness when we do not hesitate to bring disgrace upon ourselves. It is, therefore, the most suitable punishment for a dishonour done to the divine Majesty. This is the theme which Paul pursues to the end of the chapter, but he deals with it in various ways, for it required considerable enlargement.

In short, therefore, what Paul is saying is that man's ingratitude to God is inexcusable. Their own case proves for certain that the wrath of God is mercilessly venting itself against them. They would never, like beasts, have plunged into such disgusting acts of lust had they not incurred the detestation and hostility of God in His Majesty. Since, therefore, the most flagrant vice is everywhere practised, he concludes that undoubted proofs of divine vengeance are evident in the human race. Now if this vengeance of God never rages without reason or unjustly, but is always kept within the limits of what is right, Paul tells us that it is clear from this that destruction, no less certain than just, menaces the whole of humanity.

It is quite unnecessary at this point to enter into a long discussion of how God gives men up to wickedness. It is certain indeed that He not only permits men to fall into sin, by allowing them to do so, and by conniving at their fall, but that He also ordains it by His just judgment, so that they are forcibly led into such mad folly not only by their own evil yearnings but by the Devil as well. Paul, therefore, adopts the word *give up* in accordance with the constant usage of Scripture. Those who think that we are led into sin by the permission of God alone do too great violence to this word, for as Satan is the minister of the wrath of God and His 'executioner', he is armed against us not merely in appearance, but by the orders of the Judge. God, however, is not on this account cruel, nor are we innocent, since Paul clearly shows that we are delivered up into His power only if we deserve such punishment. This exception alone must be made, that the cause of sin, the roots of which always reside in the sinner himself, does not arise from God, for it is always true that *O Israel, thou hast destroyed thyself; but in me is thine help* (Hos. 13.9).

By connecting the evil desires of the human heart with *uncleanness* he indirectly gives us to understand the fruit which our heart will bring forth when it is once left to itself. The expression *among themselves* is emphatic, for it significantly expresses how deep and indelible are the marks of vile conduct which they have imprinted on their bodies.

25. *For that they exchanged the truth of God for a lie.* He repeats what

he has previously said, though in different words, in order to fix it deeper in our mind. When they exchange the truth of God for a lie, His glory is obliterated. It is right that those who have tried not only to deprive God of His honour, but also to blaspheme His name, should be covered with every kind of ignominy. *And worshipped and served the creature rather than the Creator.* I have given this translation in order to include two words in the one construction. Paul properly points out the sin of idolatry, for religious honour cannot be given to the creature without taking it away from God in an unworthy and sacrilegious manner. It is an empty excuse to pretend that the images are worshipped for God's sake, since God does not acknowledge such worship, nor regard it as acceptable. It is not the true God at all who is then worshipped, but a false God whom the flesh has devised for itself. The words which are added, *Who is blessed for ever. Amen,* I interpret as having been used for the purpose of exposing idolatry to greater reproach, the sense of the passage being thus, 'We ought to honour and adore God alone, and we are not permitted to take anything from Him, however small.'

26. *For this cause God gave them up unto vile passions.* Having introduced an intervening clause, he returns to his former remarks about the 'vengeance of the Lord', and adduces as his first proof of it the fearful crime of unnatural lust. This proves that men have not only abandoned themselves to bestial desires, but have become worse than beasts, since they have reversed the whole order of nature. He then enumerates a long catagloue of vices which existed in all ages, but at that time prevailed universally without any restraint at all.

It makes no difference that they were not all involved in such vicious corruption, for in reproving the general corruption of men it is proof enough if everyone without exception is forced to admit to some faults. We must, therefore, take it that Paul is here dealing with those monstrous deeds which had been common in all ages, and were at that time universally prevalent. It is astonishing how frequently this abominable act, which even brute beasts abhor, was then indulged in. Other vices, too, were commonly practised. He then recites a catalogue of vice, which comprehends the whole human race. Although all men are not thieves, murderers, or adulterers, yet there are none who are not to be found corrupted by some vice or another. Paul refers to those acts which are shameful even in popular estimation, and serve to dishonour God, as *vile passions.*

27. *That recompense of their error which was due.* Those whose hostility has prevented them from beholding the glory of God, by blinding their eyes to the light which He has offered them, deserve to be blinded, so that they may forget themselves, and not see what is to

their benefit. And those who were not ashamed to extinguish to the utmost of their power the glory of God which alone gives us light deserve to become blind at noonday.

28. *And even as they refused to have God in their knowledge, God gave them up unto a reprobate mind.* In these words we should note the reference which felicitously sums up the just relation between sin and punishment. Because *they refused to have God in their knowledge*, which alone directs our minds to true wisdom, the Lord gave them a perverted mind, which could not choose anything right. In saying that they *refused*, he means that they had not pursued the knowledge of God with the attention which they ought to have displayed, but, on the contrary, had deliberately turned their thoughts away from God. He means, therefore, that by a perverted choice, they had preferred their own vanities to God. Thus, the error by which they were deceived was self-chosen.

To do those things which are not fitting. As Paul had hitherto referred to only one execrable example, which was commonly practised by many, but not by all, he begins to enumerate here the vices from which none is to be found free. As we have said, though every vice may not appear in each individual, yet all men are conscious of some wrong conduct, so that everyone can be accused of obvious depravity for his own part. In the first place, by *not fitting* he means that their behaviour was contrary to every decision of reason and inconsistent with human responsibility. The evidence of a perverted mind which he offers is that men bound themselves without reflection to those crimes which common sense ought to have despised.

It is, however, wasted effort to relate these vices so as to connect them with one another, since this was not Paul's design. Rather he set them down as they occurred to him. We shall very briefly explain the meaning of each.

29. *Unrighteousness* means the violation of human justice, when each does not receive his due. I have translated πονηρίαν by *wickedness*, according to the opinion of Ammonius, who explains that πονηρόν, the wicked man, is the δραστικὸν κακοῦ, the doer of evil. The word therefore means acts of maliciousness or unrestrained licence, but maliciousness is the depravity and perversity of mind which strives to do harm to our neighbour. I have translated Paul's πορνείαν by *lust*, though I have no objection to the rendering *fornication*, for he means the inward desire as well as the outward act.[1] The meaning of the words *covetousness, envy*, and *murder*, is quite certain. The word *strife* includes quarrels, fighting, and sedition. We have rendered κακοήθεια by *malignity*, notorious and signal wickedness, when a man has become

[1] Calvin's version has *libidine* (A.V. fornication). The R.V. omits the word.

callous and hardened by custom and evil habit in the corruption of his ethical standards.

30. The word θεοστυγεῖς undoubtedly means *haters of God*,[1] for there is no reason to take it in its passive sense (*hated by God*), since Paul is here proving men's guilt by their obvious wickedness. By the *haters of God*, therefore, he means those who see that His justice stands in the way of their acts of wickedness. *Whisperers* and *backbiters* are to be distinguished in the following way: the *whisperers* destroy the friend-ships of good men by their secret accusations, inflame their minds to anger, speak against the innocent, and sow discord. *Backbiters*, with innate malignity, spare the reputation of none, and, as though driven by a passionate urge to speak evil of people, revile the deserving as well as the innocent. We have translated ὑβριστάς as *maleficos* (R.V. *insolent*), for Latin writers habitually speak of notable wrongs, such as acts of plunder, theft, burning, and sorcery, as *maleficia*. It was to these acts that Paul desired to refer here. I have rendered the word ὑπερήφανους which Paul uses as *haughty*, the meaning of the Greek. The word in origin suggests that the haughty are 'elevated', and look down with contempt on all who are beneath them, and cannot tolerate the sight of any equals. The *boastful* are those who are inflated with over-confident vanity, and the *covenant-breakers* are those who destroy the bonds of society by their wrongdoing, or those in whom there is no sincerity or constancy of faith, and who may be called truce-breakers.

31. Those who are *without natural affection* have laid aside the primary natural affections towards their own kind. Since Paul holds that want of mercy is a proof of the depravity of human nature, Augustine, in arguing against the Stoics, concludes that mercy is a Christian virtue.

32. *Who, knowing the ordinance of God, that they which practise such things are worthy of death.* Though this passage is explained in various ways, the following appears to me the truest interpretation—men had completely abandoned themselves to unrestrained licence in their sinning, and by erasing all distinction between good and evil, approved both in themselves and in others those things which they knew to be displeasing to God, and would be condemned by his righteous judg-ment. It is the height of evil when the sinner is so completely void of shame that he is not only pleased with his own vices, and will not tolerate their condemnation, but also encourages them in others by his consent and approval. This desperate wickedness is thus described in Scripture: They 'rejoice to do evil' (Prov. 2.14); 'Thou hast opened thy feet to every one that passed by, and multiplied thy whoredom' (Ezek. 16.25). A man who feels shame may still be healed; but when such a lack of shame has been acquired through the practice of sin,

[1] R.V. 'hateful to God'.

that vice, and not virtue, pleases us and has our approval, there is no more any hope of amendment. This, then, is the interpretation which I offer. Paul, it seems, meant to condemn here something more grievous and wicked than the mere perpetration of vice. I do not know what this may be, if we do not mean that which is the height of wickedness—when wretched men, casting away all shame, undertake the patronage of vice rather than the righteousness of God.

CHAPTER TWO

Wherefore thou art without excuse, O man, whosoever thou art that judgest: for wherein thou judgest another, thou condemnest thyself; for thou that judgest dost practise the same things. And we know that the judgment of God is according to truth against them that practise such things. (1-2)

1. *Wherefore thou art without excuse, O man.* This rebuke is directed at the hypocrites who draw attention by their displays of outward sanctity, and even imagine that they have been accepted by God, as though they had afforded Him full satisfaction. Paul, therefore, having shown the grosser vices as a proof that none are just before God, now attacks this class of sanctimonious persons, who could not have been included in his first catalogue. Now the inference is too plain and simple for anyone to wonder how the apostle derived his argument. He therefore makes them *without excuse*, because they themselves knew the judgment of God, and yet transgressed the law, as though he said, 'Although you do not consent to the vices of others, and, indeed, give the impression of being an avowed enemy and reprover of them, yet, because you are not free from them, if you really examine yourself, you cannot offer any defence of your conduct.'

For wherein thou judgest another, thou condemnest thyself. Besides the elegant play upon the two Greek verbs κρίνειν and κατακρίνειν (*to judge, to condemn*), we should note the exaggeration which Paul uses in condemning them. It is exactly as though he were saying: 'You are doubly deserving of condemnation, for you are guilty of the same vices which you condemn and reprove in others.' It is a well known saying that those who demand from others a rule of life lay claim to innocence, moderation, and every virtue, and that they are unworthy of any pardon if they commit the same wrongs which they have undertaken to amend in others.

For thou that judgest dost practise the same things. This is the literal translation, but the meaning is: 'Although you judge, yet you do the same.' He states that they were doing this because they were not in the right state of mind, for sin properly belongs to the mind. And so they condemn themselves in this respect, because while reproving a thief, adulterer, or slanderer, they did not simply pass judgment on persons, but on the vices which are inseparable from them.

2. *And we know that the judgment of God is according to truth against*

them. Paul's design is to shake the hypocrites out of their self-complacency, so that they may not think that they have really gained anything if they are applauded by the world, or acquit themselves from guilt. A very different judgment awaits them in heaven. He accuses them, moreover, of inward impurity. This, however, cannot be proved and convicted by human testimony, since it is hidden from human eyes, and so he appeals to the judgment of God, from which the darkness itself is not hidden, and which must necessarily be felt by sinners, whether they want it or not.

The *truth* of this judgment consists in two facts: first, God will punish sin without any respect of persons, whoever may be the one in whom He has detected it. Second, He does not regard external appearances, nor is He satisfied with any work, if it does not proceed from real sincerity of heart. It follows from this that the mask of a feigned piety will not prevent Him from punishing secret wickedness with His judgment. The phrase *according to truth* is a Hebraism, for *truth* in Hebrew often means the inward integrity of the heart, and is thus opposed not only to palpable falsehood, but also to the external appearance of good works. Hypocrites are aroused only when they are informed that God will take account not only of their spurious righteousness, but also of their secret feelings.

And reckonest thou this, O man, who judgest them that practise such things, and doest the same, that thou shalt escape the judgment of God? Or despisest thou the riches of his goodness and forbearance and long-suffering, not knowing that the goodness of God leadeth thee to repentance? but after thy hardness and impenitent heart treasurest up for thyself wrath in the day of wrath and revelation of the righteous judgment of God; who will render to every man according to his works: to them that by patience in well-doing seek for glory and honour and incorruption, eternal life: but unto them that are factious, and obey not the truth, but obey unrighteousness, shall be *wrath and indignation, tribulation and anguish, upon every soul of man that worketh evil, of the Jew first, and also of the Greek; but glory and honour and peace to every man that worketh good, to the Jew first, and also to the Greek.* (3-10)

3. *And reckonest thou this, O man.* It is a rule of rhetoric to refrain from vehement rebuke until the offence has been proved. Paul, therefore, may seem to some to have acted unwisely here in passing so severe a censure before he has completed his intended accusation. This, however, is not the case. His proof that they were guilty of sin was sufficiently conclusive, since he did not accuse them before men, but convicted them by the judgment of conscience. Paul clearly thought that he had proved what he intended, viz. that if they examined

themselves, and submitted to the scrutiny of the divine judgment, they would not be able to deny their iniquity. It was not urgently necessary for Paul to rebuke their feigned sanctity so severely and incisively, for men of this kind have staggering self-assurance, unless they are shaken from their empty confidence. Let us, therefore, remember that the best way to overcome hypocrisy is to rouse it from its drugging effects and draw it to the light of the divine judgment

That thou shalt escape the judgment of God? Paul's argument proceeds from the less to the greater. If our sins are to be subject to the judgment of men, much more should they be subject to the judgment of God, who is the only true judge of all. Men are led by a divine instinct to condemn evil deeds, it is true, but this is only a faint and obscure resemblance of the divine judgment. Those who think that they can escape the judgment of God, though they do not allow others to escape their own judgment, are extremely foolish. Paul repeats the word *man* for the purpose of comparing man to God.

4. *Or despisest thou the riches of his goodness?* There does not seem to me to be any dilemma here, as some scholars maintain, but rather the anticipation of a possible objection. Since hypocrites are generally inflated with prosperity, as though they had merited the mercy of God by their good deeds, and thus become more hardened in their contempt of Him, the apostle anticipates their arrogance. He proves by a contrary argument that they have no cause to imagine that God is propitious to them on account of their outward prosperity, since He has a very different design by which to do men good, viz. to convert sinners to Himself. Where, therefore, the fear of God does not prevail, confidence in prosperity is a contempt and mockery of His measureless goodness. It follows from this that those whom God has spared in this life will have a heavier punishment inflicted on them, because they have added their rejection of the fatherly invitation of God to their other wickedness. Although all the favours of God are so many proofs of His fatherly goodness, yet because He has often a different object in view, the ungodly are wrong to congratulate themselves on their prosperity, as though they were dear to Him, while He kindly and bountifully supports them.

Not knowing that the goodness of God leadeth thee to repentance? The Lord shows us by His kindness that He is the one to whom we ought to turn if we are anxious for our well-being, and at the same time He raises our confidence of expecting mercy. If we do not use the bountifulness of God for this end, we abuse it, although it is not always received in the same way. While the Lord treats His own servants favourably, and gives them earthly blessings, He makes His benevolence known to them by signs of this kind, and accustoms them at the same time to seek the sum of all good things in Himself alone. When He treats the transgressors of His law with the same indulgence, His object is to mollify their stubbornness by His own kindness; yet He does not declare that He is pleased with them, but rather calls them to repentance. If anyone objects that the Lord is pleading to deaf ears so long as He does not inwardly touch their hearts, our answer must be that in this instance it is our own wicked nature which is to be blamed. I prefer *leadeth* rather than *calleth*, for it is more significant. I do not, however, take this in the sense of driving, but of leading rather by the hand.

5. *But after thy hardness and impenitent heart treasurest up for thyself.* Impenitence follows when we have become hardened to the admonitions of the Lord, for those who have no anxiety for repentance openly provoke the Lord.

We may learn from this remarkable passage what I have already referred to, viz. that the ungodly not only heap up for themselves daily a more serious judgment from God as long as they live here, but that the gifts of God also, which they continually enjoy, will increase their condemnation, for they will be called to give an account of them all. They will then find that they will be justly accused of the ultimate wickedness of having been made worse by the goodness of God, which at least ought to have corrected them. Let us, therefore, take care not to lay up for ourselves this treasure of misfortune by an unlawful abuse of the blessings of God.

In the day of wrath. Literally, *into the day* (Greek, εἰς ἡμέραν, *for the day*). The ungodly now heap around themselves the wrath of God, the force of which will be poured on their heads on that day. They are heaping up for themselves hidden destruction, which will then be taken out of the treasures of God. The day of the last judgment is called *the day of wrath* when it is the ungodly to whom reference is being made, though it will be a day of redemption to believers. Thus all other visitations of the Lord are always described as fearful and terrifying to the ungodly, but pleasant and joyful to the godly. Hence whenever Scripture mentions the nearness of the Lord, it bids the godly exult with joy. When, however, it returns to the reprobate, it smites them with nothing but terror and fear. 'That day is a day of wrath,' says Zephaniah, 'a day of trouble and distress, a day of wasteness and desolation, a day of darkness and gloominess, a day of clouds and thick darkness' (Zeph. 1.15). There is a similar description in Joel 2.2, and Amos declares, 'Woe unto you that desire the day of the Lord! wherefore would ye have the day of the Lord? it is darkness, and not light' (Amos 5.18). By adding the word *revelation* Paul intimates what this *day of wrath* is to be, viz. that the Lord will then manifest His judgment. Although each day He gives indications of it, yet He suspends and holds back the clear and full manifestation of it until that day when the books will be opened, the sheep separated from the goats, and the wheat cleansed from the tares.

6. *Who will render to every man according to his works.* Paul has to deal with unseeing pretenders to sanctity, who think that the wickedness of their hearts is well concealed, provided only it is covered with some appearance of empty works. He has, therefore, pointed out the true righteousness of works which God will value, in case they should confidently assume that it was enough to please Him by bringing words and mere trifles. This sentence, however, is not as difficult as it is generally assumed. By punishing the wickedness of the reprobate with just vengeance, the Lord will repay them what they deserve; and again because He sanctifies those whom He has previously resolved to glorify, He will also crown their good works, but not on account of any merit. This cannot, however, be proved from the present verse, which, while it declares what reward good works are to have, does not state their value, or the price that is due to them. It is foolish to assume that a thing has merit because it is rewarded.

7. *To them that by patience in well-doing.* The Latin version has *perseverantia*, but the reading *patientia* signifies more than perseverance. Perseverance means that one is not wearied in a continuance of well-doing. But endurance is also required in the saints, by which they may hold fast in spite of their various trials. Satan does not allow them easy access to the Lord, but tries to impede them with innumerable obstacles, and to turn them aside from the right way. When Paul says that believers, by continuing in good works, *seek for glory and honour*, he does not mean that they have any other aspiration than God, or that they are striving to attain any greater or more worthy object, but they cannot seek Him without at the same time aiming to attain the blessedness of His kingdom. This is here described in the paraphrase given in these words. The meaning, therefore, is that the Lord will give eternal life to those who strive to attain immortality by studying to do good works.

8. *But unto them that are factious.* The passage is a little confused. In the first place the general sense of the passage is interrupted. The thread of the argument demanded that the second part of the comparison should correspond to the first, thus: 'The Lord will give eternal life to those who by perseverance in good works seek glory, honour, and incorruption, but to the contentious and disobedient, eternal death.' The conclusion should then be supplied, 'Glory, honour, and incorruption have been secured for the former, while wrath and affliction are laid up for the latter.' In the second place the words *wrath, indignation, tribulation,* and *anguish,* are applied to two different

clauses in the context. This, however, by no means confuses the meaning of the passage, and we must accept this in apostolic writings. It is from other writers that eloquence is to be learned: here spiritual wisdom is to be sought in an inadequate literary style which lacks polish and refinement.

The factiousness here mentioned means rebelliousness and obstinacy, for Paul is contending with hypocrites who laugh God to scorn by their gross and callous indulgence. By *truth* is meant simply the rule of the divine will, which is the only light of truth. It is the common characteristic of all unbelievers that they always choose to submit to iniquity rather than to take upon themselves the yoke of God, and whatever obedience they may pretend, they do not cease to clamour and struggle stubbornly against the Word of God. As those who are manifestly evil scoff at this truth, so hypocrites have no hesitation in setting up in opposition to it their artificial form of worship. The apostle further adds that such disobedient persons *obey unrighteousness*. Those who have refused to yield to the law of the Lord have no middle course which will keep them from falling into the bondage of sin. The just reward of hot-headed presumption is that those who are unwilling to render obedience to God are brought under the bondage of sin.

Wrath and indignation. The essential meaning of the word necessitates this translation. Θύμος in Greek means what in Latin is called *excandescentia*, indignation (v. Cicero, *Tusc.* IV), viz. a sudden blaze of anger. For the rest I follow Erasmus. Note, however, that of the four which are here mentioned, the last two are the effects of the former. Those who experience the anger and displeasure of God are immediately confounded.

Although Paul might have offered a brief description in a couple of words of the blessedness of true believers, and also the ruin of the reprobate, he enlarges on both subjects in order to strike men more effectively with fear of the wrath of God, and whet their desire for obtaining grace through Christ. We never fear the judgment of God as we ought, unless it is vividly portrayed before our eyes; nor are we really consumed with a desire for future life, unless aroused by many incentives.

9. *Of the Jew first, and also of the Greek.* Almost certainly *Jew* is contrasted here simply with Greek. Later on Paul refers to those whom he at present designates Greeks as Gentiles. The Jews, however, take precedence in this instance, for in preference to others they have both the promises and the warnings of the Law. It is as though Paul had said, 'This is the universal law of the divine judgment, which will begin with the Jews, and include the whole world.'

*For there is no respect of persons with God. For as many as have sinned
without law shall also perish without law: and as many as have sinned
under law shall be judged by law; for not the hearers of a law are just
before God, but the doers of a law shall be justified.* (11-13)

11. *For there is no respect of persons with God.* Up to this point Paul
has in general accused the whole of mankind of being guilty, but now
he begins to bring home his accusation to the Jews and to the Gentiles
separately. At the same time he informs them that no distinction
between them could prevent them from both being liable to eternal
death without distinction. The Gentiles pretended ignorance as their
defence, the Jews gloried in the honour of having the law. From the
one Paul removes their attempts at evasion, and from the other their
false and futile boasting.

The whole human race, therefore, is divided into two classes, for
God had separated the Jews from all the rest. The Gentiles, however,
all received the same treatment. He now teaches us that this distinction
is no reason why both should not be involved in the same guilt. The
word *person* is used in Scripture of all external realities which are
commonly held to possess some value or honour. When, therefore,
we read that God is no respecter of persons, we should understand that
what He regards is purity of heart or inward integrity, and not the
things which are usually valued by men, e.g. family, country, dignity,
wealth, etc., so that *respect of persons* is to be taken here as the choosing
or distinction between different nations. If the objection is raised that
there is, therefore, no free election of God, the answer must be that
there is a twofold acceptance of men before God: first, when in His
unmotivated goodness He calls us from nothing and elects us, since
there is nothing in our nature which is able to enjoy His approbation;
and second, when He has regenerated us, and bestows upon us also
His gifts, and shows favour to the image of His Son, which He re-
cognizes in us.

12. *For as many as have sinned without law.* In the previous part of
this section he attacks the Gentiles who, though they had no Moses
given to them to promulgate and ratify the law from the Lord, were
not, he maintains, prevented by this from bringing upon themselves
the just sentence of death by their sins. The knowledge of a written
law was not necessary for the just condemnation of a sinner. Let us,
therefore, consider the plea of those who through misplaced mercy
attempt, on the grounds of ignorance, to exempt from the judgment
of God the Gentiles who are deprived of the light of the Gospel.

And as many as have sinned under law. As the Gentiles, led astray by
the fallacies of their reason, plunge headlong into destruction, so the

Jews possess a law by which they are condemned, for long ago the sentence was pronounced, 'Cursed be he that confirmeth not the words of this law to do them' (Deut. 27.26). A worse condition, therefore, awaits Jewish sinners, since their condemnation is already pronounced in their own law.

13. *For not the hearers of a law are just.* Paul anticipates the objection which the Jews might have adduced. They gloried in their unique knowledge of the law, because they perceived that it was the rule of righteousness (Deut. 4.1). To refute this mistaken impression he asserts that the hearing or the knowledge of the law is not of such consequence as to afford righteousness, but that works must be brought forth in accordance with the saying, 'He that doeth them shall live in them' (Lev. 18.5).[1] The sense of this verse, therefore, is that if righteousness is sought by the law, the law must be fulfilled, for the righteousness of the law consists in the perfection of works. Those who misinterpret this passage for the purpose of building up justification by works deserve universal contempt. It is, therefore, improper and irrelevant to introduce here such lengthy discussions on justification to solve so futile an argument. The apostle urges here on the Jews only the judgment of the law which he had mentioned, which is that they cannot be justified by the law unless they fulfil it, and that if they transgress it, a curse is instantly pronounced upon them. We do not deny that absolute righteousness is prescribed in the law, but since all men are convicted of offence, we assert the necessity of seeking for another righteousness. Indeed, we can prove from this passage that no one is justified by works. If only those who fulfil the law are justified by the law, it follows that no one is justified, for no one can be found who can boast of having fulfilled the law.

For when Gentiles which have no law do by nature the things of the law, these, having no law, are a law unto themselves; in that they shew the work of the law written in their hearts, their conscience bearing witness therewith, and their thoughts one with another accusing or else excusing them; *in the day when God shall judge the secrets of men, according to my gospel, by Jesus Christ.* (14-16)

14. *For when Gentiles which have no law do by nature the things of the law.* He now repeats the proof of the first part of the sentence, for he is not satisfied with condemning us by mere assertion, and pronouncing the just judgment of God upon us, but endeavours to convince us of it by arguments, in order to arouse us to a greater desire and love for Christ. He shows that ignorance is offered in vain as an excuse by the Gentiles, since they declare by their own deeds that they

[1] See Rom. 10.5; Gal. 3.12.

do have some rule of righteousness. There is no nation so opposed to everything that is human that it does not keep within the confines of some laws. Since, therefore, all nations are disposed to make laws for themselves of their own accord, and without being instructed to do so, it is beyond all doubt that they have certain ideas of justice and rectitude, which the Greeks refer to as προλήψεις, and which are implanted by nature in the hearts of men. Therefore they have a law, without the law; for although they do not have the written law of Moses, they are by no means completely lacking in the knowledge of right and justice. They could not otherwise distinguish between vice and virtue, the former of which they restrain by punishing it, while commending the latter, and showing their approval of it, and honouring it with rewards. Paul contrasts nature with the written law, meaning that the Gentiles had the natural light of righteousness, which supplied the place of the law by which the Jews are taught, so that they were *a law unto themselves.*

15. *In that they shew the work of the law written in their hearts,* i.e. they prove that there is imprinted on their hearts a discrimination and judgment, by which they distinguish between justice and injustice, honesty and dishonesty. Paul does not mean that it is engraved on their will, so that they seek it and pursue it diligently, but that they are so mastered by the power of truth as not to be able to disapprove of it. They would not have instituted religious rites if they were not convinced that God ought to be worshipped, or been ashamed of adultery and theft if they did not regard them both as evil.

There is no basis for deducing the power of the will from the present passage, as if Paul had said that the keeping of the law is within our power, for he does not speak of our power to fulfil the law, but of our knowledge of it. The word *hearts* is not to be taken for the seat of the affections, but simply for the understanding, as in Deut. 29.4, 'The Lord hath not given you an heart to know,' and in Luke 24.25, 'O foolish men, and slow of heart to believe.'

We cannot conclude from this passage that there is in men a *full* knowledge of the law, but only that there are some seeds of justice implanted in their nature. This is evidenced by such facts as these, that all the Gentiles alike institute religious rites, make laws to punish adultery, theft, and murder, and commend good faith in commercial transactions and contracts. In this way they prove their knowledge that God is to be worshipped, that adultery, theft, and murder, are evils, and that honesty is to be esteemed. It is not to our purpose to inquire what sort of God they take Him to be, or how many gods they have devised. It is sufficient to know that they think that there is a God, and that honour and worship are due to Him. It is of no consequence whether they permit the coveting of another man's wife, possessions, or anything which was his, or whether they connive at anger and hatred, since it will not be right for them to covet what they know it is wrong to do.

Their conscience bearing witness therewith. The testimony of their own conscience, which is equivalent to a thousand witnesses, was the strongest pressure which he could bring to bear on them. Men are sustained and comforted by their consciousness of good actions, but inwardly harassed and tormented when conscious of having done evil —hence the pagan aphorism that a good conscience is the largest theatre, but a bad one the worst of executioners, and torments the godly with more ferocity than any furies can do. There is, therefore, a certain natural knowledge of the law, which states that one action is good and worthy of being followed, while another is to be shunned with horror.

Notice Paul's scholarly definition of conscience—there are, he says, some arguments which we adopt by which to defend a right course of action which we have taken, while on the other hand there are others which accuse and convict us of our evil deeds. Paul refers these arguments of accusation or defence to the day of the Lord, not because they will only then appear, for they are constantly operative in fulfilling their function in this life, but because they will then also take effect. The purpose of Paul's argument here is to prevent anyone from despising the arguments as being of no consequence or enduring significance. As before, he has put *in the day* rather than *until the day*.

16. *When God shall judge the secrets of men.* This extended description of God's judgment is most appropriate to the present passage. He informs those who wilfully conceal themselves in the hideaways of their moral insensibility that those innermost thoughts, which are at present entirely hidden in the depths of their hearts, will then be brought to the light. So in another passage Paul seeks to show the Corinthians how little human judgment is worth which stops short at outward appearances. He bids them wait until the Lord comes 'who will both bring to light the hidden things of darkness, and make manifest the counsels of the hearts' (I Cor. 4.5). In hearing this, let us recall the admonition that, if we desire the real approval of our Judge, we must strive for sincerity of heart.

He adds the expression *according to my gospel* to prove that he is offering a doctrine which corresponds to the inborn judgments of mankind, and he calls the Gospel *his* Gospel on account of his ministry. The true God alone has the authority to give the Gospel to men. The apostles had only the dispensation of it. We need not be surprised that the Gospel is in part said to be the messenger and proclamation of the future judgment. If the fulfilment and completion of its promises are deferred to the full revelation of the heavenly kingdom, it must necessarily be connected with the last judgment. Furthermore, Christ cannot be preached without proving to be resurrection for some, and destruction for others. Both of these, resurrection and destruction, have reference to the day of judgment. I apply the words *by Jesus Christ* to the day of judgment, although there are other explanations, the meaning being that the Lord will execute His judgment by Christ, who has been appointed by the Father to be the Judge of the living and the dead. This judgment by Christ is always reckoned by the apostles among the chief articles of the Gospel. If we adopt this interpretation, the sentence, which would otherwise be inadequate, will gain in depth.

But if thou bearest the name of a Jew, and restest upon the law, and gloriest in God, and knowest his will, and approvest the things that are excellent, being instructed out of the law, and art confident that thou thyself art a guide of the blind, a light of them that are in darkness, a corrector of the foolish, a teacher of babes, having in the law the form of knowledge and of the truth; thou therefore that teachest another, teachest thou not thyself? thou that preachest a man should not steal, dost thou steal? thou that sayest a man should not commit adultery, dost thou commit adultery? thou that abhorrest idols, dost thou rob temples? thou who gloriest in the law, through thy transgression of the law dishonourest thou God? For the name of God is blasphemed among the Gentiles because of you, even as it is written. (17-24)

17. *But if thou bearest the name of a Jew, and restest upon the law.* Some old manuscripts read εἰ δέ, and if this reading were generally accepted I should approve of reading it. But since the majority of manuscripts is opposed to this reading, and the meaning is otherwise appropriate, I retain the old reading, especially since there is only the small difference of one word which is involved.

Having now dealt with the Gentiles, Paul returns to the Jews, and in order to quell all their empty pride more forcibly, he grants them all those privileges which transported and filled them with pride. He then shows how insufficient these are for the attainment of true glory, and, indeed, how much they contribute to their dishonour. In the name *Jew* Paul includes all the privileges of the nation which they vainly pretended had been derived from the law and the prophets, and by this term he understands all Israelites, all of whom were then, without distinction, referred to as Jews.

It is uncertain at what time this name first originated, but it was undoubtedly first used after the Dispersion. Josephus, in his *Antiquities,* XI, considers that it was derived from Judas Maccabaeus, under whose

auspices the liberty and honour of the people, which had for some time
fallen into disrepute, and been almost buried, revived again. On the
assumption that this suggestion is unsatisfactory, although I consider
it probable, I will offer another conjecture of my own. I certainly think
it very likely that, after they had been deprived of their honours by so
many defeats, and scattered abroad, they were not able to retain any
definite tribal distinctions. The national census could not be made at
the appointed time, and there was no civil government in existence,
which was necessary to preserve an order of this kind. Their places of
habitation were scattered and dispersed, and the hardships by which
they had been worn out no doubt made them less attentive to their
genealogical records. If, however, this hypothesis is disallowed, it
cannot be denied that there was the likelihood of such a danger in such
a confused situation. Whether, therefore, they meant to provide for
the future, or to remedy the evil which they were already enduring,
they all, I imagine, assumed at the same time the name of the tribe in
which the purity of their religion had been preserved for the longest
time, and which excelled in the unique privilege of being the tribe
from which the Redeemer was expected to come. Their last refuge
in their extremities was to console themselves with the expectation of
the Messiah. It was at any rate by the name of Jews that they professed
themselves to be the heirs of the covenant which the Lord had made
with Abraham and his seed.

And restest upon the law, and gloriest in God. Paul does not mean that
they had rested in the study of the law, as though they had devoted
their attention to the keeping of it, but, on the contrary, blames them
for not observing the end for which the law had been given. They had
neglected to observe it, and were inflated with pride simply because
they were persuaded that the oracles of God belonged to them. In the
same way they *gloried in God*, but not as the Lord commanded us by
his prophet (Jer. 9.24), that we should humble ourselves, and seek our
glory in Him alone. Without any knowledge of the goodness of God
they made Him peculiarly their own, although they did not inwardly
possess Him, and assumed that they were His people, for the sake of
empty ostentation before their fellow men. This, then, was not the
glorying of the heart, but the boasting of the tongue.

18. *And knowest his will, and approvest the things that are excellent.* Paul
now concedes to the Jews their knowledge of the divine will, and their
approval of the things that were useful, which they had gained from
the teaching of the law. There are two kinds of approval—one, the
approval of choice, when we embrace the good of which we have
approved, and the other, the approval of judgment, by which we
distinguish good from evil, although we do not by any means pursue

it vigorously or studiously. The Jews were so learned in the law that they could pass judgment on the conduct of others, but were disinclined to regulate their own life accordingly. When Paul rebukes their hypocrisy, however, we may infer (provided our judgment proceeds from sincerity) that it is only when we listen to God that we rightly approve the things that are useful. His will, as it is revealed in the law, is here appointed as the guide and instructor of what is rightly to be approved.

19. *And art confident that thou thyself art a guide.* Paul grants them still more, as if they had not only sufficient for themselves, but also the means of enriching others. He grants, in fact, that they had such an abundance of learning as might also have contributed to others.

20. I take the words which follow, *having in the law the form of knowledge,* causatively, to mean 'because you have the form of knowledge'. They professed themselves to be the teachers of others, because they seemed to carry in their inmost being all the secrets of the law. The word *form* is not used to mean pattern, for Paul has used μόρφωσιν, and not τυπόν, but he intended, I think, to point out the pompous appearance of their teaching, which is commonly called 'show'. It certainly appears that they had none of the knowledge of which they boasted. Paul, however, by indirectly ridiculing their vicious abuse of the law, shows on the other hand that right knowledge must be sought from the law, in order that the truth may rest on a sure foundation.

21. *Thou, therefore, that teachest another, teachest thou not thyself?* The praise which he has given to the Jews up to this point was such as might justly have adorned them, provided marks of a truer character were not wanting. Since, however, it included average qualifications, which even the ungodly may possess and corrupt by abuse, it is by no means sufficient to constitute true glory. But Paul, not content with merely rebuking and upbraiding their arrogance in trusting in these alone, turns his words of praise to their reproach. The man who not only renders useless the gifts of God, which are otherwise of great value and quality, but also vitiates and corrupts them by his depravity, deserves the utmost reproach. He is a perverse counsellor who does not consult his own good, and is wise only for the benefit of others. Paul, therefore, shows that the praise which they appropriated to themselves proved to be to their own disgrace.

Thou that preachest a man should not steal, dost thou steal? He seems to have alluded to the passage in Ps. 50.16, in which God says to the wicked

'What hast thou to do to declare my statutes,
And that thou hast taken my covenant in thy mouth?

Seeing thou hatest instruction,
And castest my words behind thee.
When thou sawest a thief, thou consentedst with him,
And hast been partaker with adulterers.'

This rebuke applied to the Jews in the old days, who relied on the mere knowledge of the law, and lived no better than if they had no law. It may be turned against us in the present time, unless we take good care. Indeed, it may well be applied to many who boast of some extraordinary knowledge of the Gospel, and yet abandon themselves to every kind of profligacy, as though the Gospel were not the rule of life. Let us, therefore, to prevent such a careless attitude towards the Lord, bear in mind the kind of judgment that threatens such verbal juggling, which boasts of the word of God by sheer garrulity.

22. *Thou that abhorrest idols, dost thou rob temples?* Paul skilfully compares sacrilege to idolatry as being virtually the same. Sacrilege is simply a profanation of the divine majesty, a sin not unknown to heathen poets. For this reason Ovid (*Metamor.* III) accuses Lycurgus of sacrilege, for despising the rites of Bacchus, and in his *Fasti* he refers to the hands which violated the majesty of Venus as sacrilegious. Since, however, the Gentiles ascribed the majesty of their gods to idols, they called it sacrilege only if anyone plundered what was dedicated to their temples, in which, as they believed, the whole of religion was centred. So at the present time, where superstition prevails rather than the Word of God, the only kind of sacrilege which they acknowledge is the stealing of what belongs to churches, since their only god is in idols, and their only religion in pomp and splendour.

We are here warned, first, not to flatter ourselves and to despise others when we have performed only a part of the law, and, second, not to boast in having external idolatry removed while we do not strive in the meantime to expel and eradicate the impiety which lies deep within our hearts.

23. *Thou who gloriest in the law, through thy transgression of the law dishonourest thou God?* Every transgressor of the law dishonours God, since we are all born in order to worship Him in holiness and righteousness. Paul, however, justly charges the Jews in this respect with special guilt, for when they proclaimed God as their law-giver, without being over-anxious to regulate their lives according to His rule, they clearly proved that they paid little regard to the Majesty of God, which they so easily despised. In the same way at the present time, those who argue wildly about the doctrine of Christ, while trampling on it by their unrestrained and wanton way of life, dishonour Christ by transgressing His Gospel.

24. *For the name of God is blasphemed.* I think that this quotation is taken from Ezek. 36.20, rather than from Isa. 52.5, because there are none of the reproaches against the people in Isaiah, with which the whole chapter in Ezekiel is filled. Some scholars hold that this is an argument from the less to the greater, in this sense: 'The prophet justly upbraided the Jews of his time, because the glory and power of God were ridiculed among the Gentiles on account of their captivity, as though He had been unable to preserve the nation which He had taken under His protection. If He did that to them, then you, much more than they, are a disgrace and reproach to God, for you are blaspheming His religion, which men judge by your utterly corrupt morals.' I do not reject this interpretation, but prefer a simpler one: 'We see that all the reproaches flung at the people of Israel fall on the name of God, because the Jews, since they are reckoned and esteemed to be the people of God, carry the name of God engraved on their foreheads. They boast in the name of God, but they dishonour Him among men by their infamous conduct.' It is a monstrous thing that those who derive their glory from God should disgrace His holy name. At least He deserved to receive a different reward from them than that.

> *For circumcision indeed profiteth, if thou be a doer of the law: but if thou be a transgressor of the law, thy circumcision is become uncircumcision. If therefore the uncircumcision keep the ordinances of the law, shall not his uncircumcision be reckoned for circumcision? and shall not the uncircumcision which is by nature, if it fulfil the law, judge thee, who with the letter and circumcision art a transgressor of the law? For he is not a Jew, which is one outwardly; neither is that circumcision, which is outward in the flesh: but he is a Jew, which is one inwardly: and circumcision is that of the heart, in the spirit, not in the letter; whose praise is not of men, but of God.* (25-29)

25. *For circumcision indeed profiteth, if thou be a doer of the law.* Paul anticipates the objection which the Jews might have adduced in opposition to him in the defence of their own cause. If circumcision was a symbol of the covenant of the Lord, by which He had chosen Abraham and his seed as His peculiar people, they did not seem on this account to have made an empty boast. Since, however, they neglected what the sign signified, and looked only on the external appearance, he answers that they had no reason to lay claim to anything on account of a mere sign. The true character of circumcision was a spiritual promise, which required faith. The Jews neglected both the promise and the faith, and for this reason their confidence was vain. It is on this account that here, as in his Epistle to the Galatians, Paul omits to state the main use of circumcision, and applies what he says to their

glaring error. We should note this carefully, for if Paul were explaining the whole nature and purpose of circumcision, it would have been inconsistent not to have made mention of grace and the free promise. In both cases, however, he speaks according to the demands of his subject, and therefore he discusses only that part which was disputed.

The Jews thought that circumcision was of itself sufficient for the purpose of obtaining righteousness. Arguing, therefore, in their own terms, Paul gives this reply, that if this benefit is expected from circumcision, the condition is that the person who is circumcised must prove himself to be wholly and perfectly a worshipper of God. Circumcision, therefore, requires perfection. The same may also be said of our baptism. If anyone puts his trust in the water of baptism alone, and thinks that he is justified, as though he had obtained holiness from that ordinance itself, we must adduce in objection to this the end of baptism, which is that the Lord thereby calls us to holiness of life. The grace and promise, which baptism testifies and seals to us, would not in this case be mentioned, because we have to deal with those who are content with the empty shadow of baptism, and neither regard nor consider what is of real importance in it. We may note that when Paul is speaking to believers about signs apart from theological controversy, he connects them with the efficacy and fulfilment of the promises which belong to them. But when he is arguing with unreasoning interpreters, who are unacquainted with the nature of signs, he omits all mention of the true and proper character of signs, and directs all his arguments against their false interpretation.

Many scholars, seeing that Paul adduces circumcision rather than any other work of the law, suppose that he is depriving only ceremonies of righteousness. The facts, however, are quite different. Those who dare to set up their own merits against the righteousness of God always boast in external observances more than in real goodness. No one who is seriously touched or moved by the fear of God will ever dare to raise up his eyes to heaven, since the more he strives to attain true righteousness, the clearer he will discern how far he is from it. With regard to the Pharisees, who are content with making an external pretence of holiness, we need not wonder that they so easily delude themselves. Paul, therefore, having left the Jew nothing but this poor subterfuge of boasting of their justification by circumcision, now takes from them even this empty pretence as well.

26. *If therefore the uncircumcision keep the ordinances of the law.* The argument is very powerful. The means are always inferior to the end, and subordinate to it. Circumcision has reference to the law, and must therefore be inferior to it. It is accordingly of more importance to keep the law than circumcision, which was established for the sake of the

law. It follows from this that the uncircumcised, provided he keeps
the law, far excels the Jew with his barren and unprofitable circumcision, if he is a transgressor of the law. Although he is polluted by
nature, yet he shall be sanctified by keeping the law in such a way that
uncircumcision shall be imputed to him as circumcision. The word
uncircumcision is to be taken in its proper sense in the second clause, but
pejoratively in the first for the Gentiles, the thing for the persons.

It should be added furthermore that one ought not to be over-
anxious to understand who are the observers of the law of whom Paul
speaks here, since no such can be found. Paul's intention was simply
to propose the hypothesis that if any Gentile could be found who kept
the law, his righteousness would be of more value without circumcision than the circumcision of the Jews without righteousness. I do
not, therefore, refer the following words, *And shall not the uncircumcision which is by nature judge thee?*, to persons, but to the illustration
which it provides, as when it is said that the Queen of the south shall
come (Matt. 12.42), and the men of Nineveh shall stand up in the
judgment (Luke 11.32). The very words of Paul lead us to this view.
The Gentile, he says, who observes the law, shall judge you, who are a
transgressor, although he is uncircumcised and you have the literal
circumcision.

27. *Who with the letter and circumcision art a transgressor.* The meaning,
by hypallage, is *by literal circumcision.* Paul does not mean that the Jews
were violating the law because they had the literal circumcision, but
because they continued, although they had the external rite, to neglect
the spiritual worship of God, viz. piety, righteousness, judgment, and
truth, which are the chief heads of the law.

28. *For he is not a Jew, which is one outwardly.* The meaning is that a
true Jew is not to be judged either by his natural descent, the title of
his profession, or an external symbol, and that the circumcision which
constitutes a Jew does not consist in an external sign only, but that both
are internal. The observations which Paul adds concerning true
circumcision are taken from various passages of Scripture, and even
from its general teaching. The people everywhere are commanded to
circumcise their hearts, and this is what the Lord promises to do. The
cutting off of the foreskin did not mean the minor destruction of one
part, but the cutting off of the whole nature. Circumcision, therefore,
was the mortification of the whole flesh.

29. The words which Paul adds, *in the spirit, not in the letter*, are to
be understood thus: by *the letter* he means the outward rite without
godliness, and by *the spirit* he means the purport (*finem*) of this rite,
which is spiritual. Since the whole importance of signs and rites depend
on their purpose (*a fine pendeat*), if this purpose is removed, the letter

alone remains, which in itself is useless. Paul's reason for saying this is that where the voice of God sounds, all that He commands, if men do not receive it in sincerity of heart, will remain in the letter, i.e. in dead writing (*in frigida scriptura*). If, however, it penetrates into the heart, it is in some measure transformed into the spirit. There is an allusion here to the difference between the old covenant and the new, as Jeremiah notes, 31.33, in a passage where the Lord declares that He will ratify and establish His covenant, after He has put His law in their inward parts, and written it in their hearts. Paul also had the same point in mind in another context (II Cor. 3.6), where he compares the law with the Gospel, and calls the former the *letter*, which is not only dead, but even *killeth*, while the latter he adorns with the title of *spirit*. Those who have made *the letter* to be the genuine meaning, and *the spirit* the allegorical meaning, have completely misinterpreted the passage.

Whose praise is not of men. Because the eyes of men are fixed on mere appearances, he denies that we ought to be satisfied with what is commended by human opinion. This is often deceived by external splendour. We should, rather, be satisfied with the eyes of God, from which the deepest secrets of the heart are not hidden. Thus he recalls hypocrites, who deceive themselves with false opinions, to the tribunal of God.

CHAPTER THREE

What advantage then hath the Jew? or what is the profit of circumcision?
Much every way: first of all, that they were entrusted with the oracles of
God. (1-2)

1. *What advantage then hath the Jew?* Paul has admirably contended
that circumcision by itself brought no advantage to the Jews. Since,
however, he could not deny that there was some difference between
the Gentiles and the Jews which had that sign as its distinguishing mark
from the Lord, and since it was inconsistent to deny and invalidate a
distinction which God had appointed, it remained for him to remove
this objection also. It was quite clear that the boasting of the Jews from
this source was misplaced. There was still, however, the doubt concerning the purpose for which God had established circumcision. The
Lord would not have appointed it, unless He had intended some
benefit by it. He therefore asks, by way of meeting the objection, what
it was that made the Jew superior to the Gentile. He adds his reason
for asking this question by a farther question, *What is the profit of*
circumcision? For circumcision distinguished the Jews from other men,
just as Paul calls ceremonies a middle wall which separated men from
one another (Eph. 2.14).

2. *Much every way.* That is, very much. He here begins to give the
sacrament its proper place of honour. But he does not allow that the
Jews should boast on this account. When he says that they had been
marked with the sign of circumcision, by which they were counted the
children of God, he does not admit that they had attained this superiority through any merit or worthiness of their own, but through the
benefits of God. Regarded as men, therefore, they were, as Paul shows,
equal to others; but if we take into account the favours of God, in this
respect they were to be distinguished, as Paul informs us, from other
nations.

First of all, they that were entrusted with the oracles of God. Some
commentators hold that there is here a *non sequitur*, for Paul sets down
more than he afterwards expounds. The word *first* is not, apparently,
a note of number, but simply means *chiefly* or *especially*, and is to be
taken in this sense: 'The fact of their being entrusted with the oracles
of God alone ought to be sufficient to secure their dignity.' It is worth
noting that the advantage of circumcision does not consist in the mere
sign, but its value is derived from the Word. Paul is here asking what

benefit the sacrament conferred on the Jews, and he answers that God had deposited with them the treasures of heavenly wisdom. It follows from this that apart from the Word no excellence remains. By *oracles* he means the covenant which God at first revealed to Abraham and to his posterity, and afterwards sealed and interpreted by the law and the prophets.

The oracles were committed to the Jews to keep safe for as long as it pleased the Lord to continue His glory among them. They were then to publish them, at the time of His disposing, throughout the whole world. The Jews were, firstly, keepers of the oracles of God, and secondly stewards. If the Lord's favouring of a nation with the giving of His Word is to be regarded as such a great benefit, we can never sufficiently despise our ingratitude for receiving it with so much neglect or carelessness, not to say disdain.

For what if some were without faith? shall their want of faith make of none effect the faithfulness of God? God forbid: yea, let God be found true, but every man a liar; as it is written, That thou mightest be justified in thy words, And mightest prevail when thou comest into judgment. (3-4)

3. *For what if some were without faith?* As before, while regarding the Jews as exulting in a bare sign, Paul would allow them not even a spark of glory, so now, while considering the nature of a sign, he testifies that its merit is not destroyed even by their empty pride. Since therefore, he had apparently suggested above that whatever grace there might have been in the sign of circumcision, it had been wholly destroyed through the ingratitude of the Jews, by way of meeting the objection he now asks again what opinion we should form of it. There is here a kind of reticence, since Paul expresses less than he desires to be understood. It would have been true to say that a great part of the nation had renounced the covenant of God. But as this would have been a very offensive thing to say of the Jews, he mentioned only *some*, in order to lessen the hardness of his censure.

Shall their want of faith make of none effect the faithfulness of God? Καταργεῖν properly signifies *to render void and ineffectual*. This meaning is most suited to the present passage. Paul's inquiry is not so much whether the unbelief of men prevents the truth of God from remaining firm and constant in itself, but whether its effect and fulfilment among them may thereby be impeded. The meaning, therefore, is, 'Since most of the Jews are breakers of the covenant, is the covenant of God abrogated by their perfidy in such a way that it produces no fruit among them?' To this he answers that it is impossible that the truth of

God should lose its constancy through human wickedness. Therefore although the greater part of the Jews had broken the covenant of God and trampled upon it, yet it retained its efficacy and exerted its power, if not in all men universally, at least in that nation. The meaning of the sentence is that the grace of the Lord and His blessing unto eternal salvation prevails among them. This, however, can be so only when the promise is received by faith. In this way the mutual covenant is confirmed on both sides. He means, therefore, that there were always some in the Jewish nation who, continuing to believe in the promise, had not fallen from the privileges of the covenant.

4. *Yea, let God be found true, but every man a liar.* However others may interpret this verse, I regard it as an argument from the necessary consequence of its opposite. By this consequence Paul invalidates the objection which has gone before. If the two propositions, that God is true and that man is a liar, stand together, and indeed agree, it follows that the truth of God is not rendered void by the falsehood of men. If Paul had not contrasted these two principles at this point, his later attempt to refute the absurdity of how God may be just, if He commends His justice by our injustice, would have been to no purpose. The meaning, therefore, is quite clear—the faithfulness of God, so far from being overthrown by the perfidy and apostasy of men, becomes thereby more evident. *God*, he says, *is true*, not only because He is prepared to stand faithfully by His promises, but also because He fulfils in deed whatever He declares in Word; for He says, 'As my power, so also shall my work be.' Man, on the other hand, is *a liar*, not only because he often breaks his pledge, but because by nature he seeks after falsehood and shuns the truth.

The first proposition is the primary axiom of all Christian philosophy. The latter is taken from Ps. 116.11, where David confesses that there is no certainty from or in man.

This is a remarkable passage, and contains a much needed consolation. Such is the wickedness of men in rejecting or despising the Word of God, that he would often doubt its certainty, if he did not recall that the truth of God does not depend on the truth of man. But how does this agree with what Paul has just previously said, that in order to make the divine promise effectual, faith, which receives it, is required from men for its efficacy? Faith is opposed to falsehood. The question certainly seems to be difficult, but the answer is not—the Lord, in spite of the lies of men, which otherwise are hindrances to His truth, will still find a way for it where there is no way, that He may emerge victorious by correcting in His elect the inborn unbelief of our nature, and by subjecting to His obedience those who seemed to be invincible. It should be added that Paul is now arguing about the corruption of nature and not about the grace of God, which is the remedy for that corruption.

That thou mightest be justified in thy words. The meaning is, So far are our falsehood and lack of faith from destroying the truth of God, that they make it more clear and prominent. David testifies to this, saying that God, whatever He may determine to do to him, since he is a sinner, will always be a just and righteous Judge, and overcome all the slanders of the ungodly who would murmur against His righteousness. By the *words* of God David means the judgments which He pronounces upon us. It is too forced to understand by this, as is commonly done, the *promises* of God. The particle *that*, therefore, is not final, and does not refer to a far-fetched consequence, but suggests the conclusion, 'Against thee only have I sinned, therefore thou wilt punish me justly.' The objection immediately added, 'How shall the righteousness of God remain perfect if our iniquity enhances its glory?' proves that Paul has quoted this passage of David in its true and proper sense. As I have just observed, Paul has detained his readers by this difficulty to no effect and inopportunely if David did not mean that God in His wonderful providence made even the sins of men glorify His own righteousness. The second clause in Hebrew is, *And that thou mightest be pure in thy judgment.* This expression means simply that God in all His judgments is worthy of praise, however much the ungodly may clamour and with hatred endeavour to efface His glory by their complaints. Paul has followed the Greek version, which also suited his purpose here better. We know that, in quoting Scripture, the apostles often used freer language than the original, since they were content if what they quoted applied to their subject, and therefore they were not over-careful in their use of words.

The following, therefore, will be the application of the present passage: 'If any of the sins of men are required to set forth the glory of the Lord, and He is especially glorified by His truth, it follows that even human falsehood serves to confirm rather than to overturn His truth.' Although the word κρίνεσθαι may be taken actively as well as passively, yet the Greek translators undoubtedly took it in a passive sense, contrary to the meaning of the prophet.

But if our unrighteousness commendeth the righteousness of God, what shall we say? Is God unrighteous who visiteth with wrath? (I speak after the manner of men.) God forbid: for then how shall God judge the world? But if the truth of God through my lie abounded unto his glory, why am I also still judged as a sinner? and why not (as we be slanderously reported, and as some affirm that we say), Let us do evil, that good may come? whose condemnation is just. (5-8)

61

5. *But if our unrighteousness commendeth the righteousness of God.* It was necessary for the apostle to introduce this thought, although it is a digression from the main subject, lest he should seem to give the ill-disposed an opportunity of speaking evil, which he knew they would readily take. Since they were watching for every opportunity of slandering the Gospel, they had, in the testimony of David, the means available to frame their calumny. 'If God looks only for the glorification of men, why does He punish them when they offend, since by their offence they glorify Him? He has certainly no reason to be offended, if the cause of His displeasure is derived from the means of His glorification.' There is no doubt that this was a commonplace slander, as Paul will presently repeat. For this reason he could not pass it over without comment. But to prevent it being thought that he was here expressing his own opinion, he prefaces what he is saying by stating that he is assuming the character of the ungodly. In a single phrase he sharply attacks human reason, the property of which, he intimates, is always to speak against the wisdom of God. He does not say that he is speaking *as the ungodly*, but *after the manner of men*. This is, in fact, the case, since all the mysteries of God are paradoxes to the mortals who have such audacity that they do not hesitate to rise against them and insolently attack what they cannot understand. We are thereby reminded that if we desire to become capable of comprehending these mysteries, we must especially strive to become disentangled from our own reason, and devote and give ourselves entirely to the obedience of His word. The word *wrath*, used here for judgment, refers to punishment, as though he had said, 'Is God unjust, in punishing those sins which set forth His righteousness?'

6. *God forbid.* In checking this blasphemy he does not give a direct answer to the objection, but begins first by expressing his abhorrence of it, lest the Christian religion should appear to be accompanied by such great absurdities. This expression of abhorrence is much stronger than any simple denial which he might adopt, for he implies that this irreverent expression ought to be regarded with horror, and not listened to. He adds presently what we may term an indirect refutation, for he does not entirely remove the slander, but simply states in reply that their objection was absurd. Moreover, he draws an argument from the office of God Himself, in order to prove its impossibility—*God shall judge the world.* He cannot, therefore, be unjust.

This argument is not derived, as some state, from the mere power of God, but from His actual power, which shines in the whole course and order of His works. The meaning is that the office of God is to judge the world, i.e. to settle it by His righteousness, and reduce to the best order any disorder which may be in it. God, therefore, can

determine nothing unjustly. Paul seems to have alluded to the passage
in Moses (Gen. 18.25), in which it is stated that while Abraham prays
God not to deliver Sodom entirely to destruction, he says, 'That be
far from thee to do after this manner, to slay the righteous with the
wicked, that so the righteous should be as the wicked; that be far from
thee: shall not the Judge of all the earth do right?' A similar expression
is found in Job 34.17, 'Shall even one that hateth right govern?'
Although unjust judges are often found among men, this is either
because, contrary to law and right, they usurp their authority, or
because they are raised to that position of power without consideration,
or because their standards deteriorate. There is no such failure in God.
Since, therefore, He is by nature Judge, He must of necessity be just,
for He cannot deny Himself. Paul, therefore, reasons from the impossibility that God, whose property and essential nature it is to rule
the world in uprightness, should wrongfully be charged with unrighteousness. Although this teaching of Paul extends to the continued
government of God, I allow that it has particular reference to the last
judgment, when at last a real restoration of right order will take place.
If, however, the reader wants to have a direct refutation, by which to
check such blasphemies as these, the following sould be the sense: 'It
is not from the nature of unrighteousness that the righteousness of God
appears more clearly. Rather, God's goodness overcomes our wickedness in such a way as to give it a different direction.'

7. *But if the truth of God through my lie abounded unto his glory.* There
is no doubt that this objection is brought forward in the person of the
ungodly. It is an explanation of the former verse, and would have been
connected with it if the apostle had not been moved by the affront to
God, and broken off the sentence in the middle. The sense is that if
the truth of God is made more clear, and in some measure is established
by our falsity, and if thereby also more glory redounds to Him, it is
quite unjust that the one who has served the glory of God should be
punished as a sinner.

8. *And why not, Let us do evil.* The sentence is elliptical, and we are
to understand some completing phrase such as, *And why is it not rather
said (as we are slanderously reported)* that we are to do evil, that good may
come? The apostle, however, does not think that this wicked misrepresentation is worth answering, although it may be argued out of
court with very good reason. The pretext of the ungodly was simply
that if God is glorified by our iniquity, and if there is nothing more
seemly for a man to do in this life than to promote the glory of God,
then let us sin to advance His glory. The answer to this is simple—
evil of itself cannot produce anything but evil. And if the glory of
God is made more radiant by our sin, then this is not the work of man,

but the work of God, who, as a wonderful craftsman, knows how to overcome our wickedness and direct it to another end, so as to turn it, contrary to our intended design, to the promotion of His own glory. God has prescribed godliness, which consists in obedience to His word, as the way by which He would have us glorify Him, and the man who transgresses these bounds does not strive to honour God, but to dishonour Him. The fact that the outcome is different is to be ascribed to the providence of God rather than to human wickedness, which is prepared not only to injure but indeed even to overturn the Majesty of God.

(*As we be slanderously reported.*) Since Paul speaks with such reverence about the secret judgments of God, it is surprising that his enemies went to such lengths of maliciousness to slander him. There has never been reverence or seriousness among the servants of God great enough to restrain the filthy, virulent tongues of men. It is, therefore, no new thing that our doctrine, which we ourselves know to be the pure Gospel of Christ (and all the angels, as well as believers, bear witness), should be encumbered at this present time by so many accusations, and be rendered odious by our opponents. We can conceive of nothing more monstrous than that the charge, which we read of here, had been laid against Paul for the purpose of treating his preaching with contempt among the ignorant. Let us, therefore, bear the slanderous abuse by the ungodly of the truth which we preach, and let us not cease on this account to guard constantly the simple confession of it, since it has sufficient power to crush and disperse their falsehoods. But let us, after the example of the apostle, oppose as much as we are able their malicious devices, that the base and the abandoned may not speak evil of our Creator with impunity.

Whose condemnation is just. Some take this in an active sense, to mean that Paul agreed with them that their objection was absurd, in order that no one should think that the doctrine of the Gospel was connected with such paradoxes. I prefer the passive sense, however. It would have been inconsistent simply to express approval of such wickedness, which merited rather severe condemnation, and this, I think, is what Paul has done. Their perversity was to be condemned on two accounts: first, because this impiety had been able to gain their mental assent; and second, because in slandering the Gospel, they dared to draw their calumny from that source.

What then? are we in worse case than they? No, in no wise: for we before laid to the charge both of Jews and Greeks, that they are all under sin. (9)

9. *What then? are we in worse case than they?* Paul returns from the

digression to his subject. To prevent the Jews from stating that they were being deprived of their rights, he mentions in detail the distinctions of honour by which they exalted themselves over the Gentiles, and now at length replies to the question whether they surpassed the Gentiles in any respect. His answer seems to be slightly different from what he had said above, since he now deprives of all dignity those on whom he previously had bestowed so much. There is, however, no disagreement, for those privileges in which he had admitted their pre-eminence were external to themselves, and dependent on the goodness of God and not on their own merit. Paul inquires whether they had any worthiness in which they could glory in themselves. The two answers, therefore, which he gives agree with one another in such a way that one follows from the other. When he extolled their privileges, including them among the benefits of God alone, he showed that they had nothing of their own. The answer which he now gives could have been inferred at once from this, for if their chief excellence lies in the fact that the oracles of God are deposited with them, and if they possess this pre-eminence by no merit of their own, then they have no cause for boasting in the sight of God. But note the sanctified skill of the apostle in addressing the Jews in the third person when he ascribed pre-eminence to them. While stripping them of every privilege, he numbers himself among them to avoid giving offence.

For we before laid to the charge both of Jews and Greeks. The Greek verb αἰτιᾶσθαι, which Paul here uses, is properly a forensic term, and I have therefore preferred to render it *We have brought a charge.* A plaintiff is said to establish a charge in an action which he is prepared to substantiate by other testimonies and proofs. The apostle has summoned all mankind to the tribunal of God, in order to include all under the one condemnation. It is pointless to object that the apostle here not merely brings a charge, but more especially proves it. No charge is true unless it is based on firm and valid proofs, as Cicero says when he distinguishes in a certain passage between an accusation and a reproach. To be *under sin* means that we are justly condemned before God as sinners, or that we are held under the curse which is due to sin. As righteousness brings with it absolution, so also sin is followed by condemnation.

As it is written, There is none righteous, no, not one: There is none that understandeth, There is none that seeketh after God; They have all turned aside, they are together become unprofitable; There is none that doeth good, no, not so much as one: Their throat is an open sepulchre; With their tongues they have used deceit: The poison of asps is under their lips: Whose mouth is full of cursing and bitterness: Their feet are

*swift to shed blood; Destruction and misery are in their ways; And the
way of peace have they not known: There is no fear of God before
their eyes.* (10-18)

10. *As it is written.* Paul's reasoning has hitherto been designed to
convince men of their iniquity. He now begins to argue from authority
which for Christians is the strongest kind of proof, provided the
authority derives from God alone. Let teachers of the Church learn
from this the character of their office. If Paul here asserts no doctrine but
what he confirms by the sure testimony of Scripture, much less ought
those who have no other commission but to preach the Gospel, which
they have received through Paul and others, to attempt that course.

There is none righteous. Giving the sense rather than the actual
expressions, the apostle seems to have stated the general position first
before coming to particulars. He defines the substance of what the
prophet declares to be in man, viz. *that there is none righteous,* and
afterwards enumerates in detail the fruits of this righteousness.

11. The first effect is that *there is none that understandeth.* This ignorance is soon proved by their failure to *seek after God.* The man in whom
there is no knowledge of God, whatever other learning he may
otherwise possess, is empty, and even the very sciences and the arts,
which are good in themselves, are emptied of significance when they
lack this basis.

12. He adds: *There is none that doeth good,* which means that they
had put off all sense of humanity. As our best bond of mutual connexion resides in the knowledge of God (since, as He is the common
Father of all, He reconciles us perfectly, and apart from Him there is
nothing but disunion), so inhumanity generally follows our ignorance
of God, when each, treating others with contempt, loves himself and
seeks his own interest.

13. He adds further: *Their throat is an open sepulchre,* i.e. a gulf to
swallow men up. This is more than if he had said that they were
man-eaters, ἀνθρωποφάγους, since it is the height of enormity that a
man's throat should be big enough to swallow and devour men entirely. The expressions *their tongues* are full of *deceit,* and *the poison of
asps is under their lips* mean the same thing.

14. In addition he says that their *mouth is full of cursing and bitterness.*
This vice is the opposite of the former. The meaning is that they
breathe forth wickedness from every part. If they speak pleasantly,
they deceive, and blend poison with their flatteries. But if they express
what is in their hearts, it is *cursing* and *bitterness* which come forth.

15. The expression which Paul adds from Isaiah, *Destruction and
misery are in their ways,* is a most striking one, for it is a description of

ferocity of immeasurable barbarity, which produces solitude and waste by destroying everything wherever it goes. Pliny gives this same description of Domitian.

17. There follows the phrase, *The way of peace have they not known.* They are so habituated to rapine, acts of violence and wrong, savagery and cruelty, that they do not know how to act in a kind or friendly way.

18. In his conclusion he again repeats, in different words, what we stated at the beginning, viz. that all wickedness flows from a disregard of God. When we have forsaken the fear of God, which is the essential part of wisdom, there is no right or purity left. In short, since the fear of God is the bridle by which our wickedness is held in check, its removal frees us to indulge in every kind of licentious conduct.

Lest anyone should regard these quotations as having been forced from their original meaning, let us consider each of them in their contexts. David, in Ps. 14.3, says that there was such perversity in men that God, when looking on them all in succession, could not find even one righteous man. It therefore follows that this infection had spread into the whole human race, since nothing is hidden from the sight of God. At the end of the Psalm, it is true, he speaks of the redemption of Israel, but we shall soon show in what manner, and to what extent, the saints are delivered from this condition. In other Psalms he complains of the wickedness of his enemies, foreshadowing in himself and his descendants a type of the kingdom of Christ. In his adversaries, therefore, are represented all those who, being estranged from Christ, are not led by His Spirit. Isaiah expressly mentions Israel, and his accusation therefore applies still more to the Gentiles. There is no doubt that human nature is described in these words, in order that we may see what man is when left to himself, since Scripture testifies that all who are not regenerated by the grace of God are in this state. The condition of the saints would be in no way better unless this depravity were amended in them. That they may still, however, remember that they are not different from others by nature, they find in what remains of their carnal nature, from which they can never escape, the seeds of those evils which would continually produce their effect in them, if they were not prevented by being mortified. For this they are indebted to the mercy of God and not to their own nature, We may add that although all the vices here enumerated do not appear in every individual, this does not prevent their being justly and truly ascribed to human nature, as we have already noted above, chapter 1.26.

Now we know that what things soever the law saith, it speaketh to them that are under the law; that every mouth may be stopped, and all the world may be brought under the judgment of God: because by the works

of the law shall no flesh be justified in his sight: for through the law
cometh *the knowledge of sin.* (19-20)

19. *Now we know.* Leaving the Gentiles, he expressly addresses those
words to the Jews, whom it was a much greater task to subdue, because,
being no less destitute of true righteousness than the Gentiles, they
took God's covenant as their covering, as though the fact of their
having been separated from the rest of the world by the election of
God were sufficient holiness for them. Paul in fact mentions the means
of escape which he well knew the Jews had available. Whatever
unfavourable expressions the law had used of mankind, the Jews
usually applied them to the Gentiles, as though *they* were exempt from
the common condition of men. No doubt they would have been so,
had they not fallen from their own position. To prevent them, therefore, from being impeded by any false conceit of their own worthiness,
and from confining to the Gentiles alone what applied to them in
common with others, Paul here anticipates the objection, and shows
from the design of Scripture that they were not only one with the
majority of men, but that they had peculiarly come under that condemnation. We see the apostle's diligence in refuting these objections,
for to whom but the Jews had the law been given? And was it not
designed to be a means of instructing them? What it states of others is
therefore incidental, or πάρεργον, as the saying goes. The law applies
its teaching mainly to its own disciples.

It speaketh to them that are under the law. He says that the law was
destined for the Jews. It follows from this that it properly referred to
them. Under the word *law* Paul also includes the prophets, and so the
whole of the Old Testament.

That every mouth be stopped. That is, that every evasion and every
occasion for excuse may be cut off. The metaphor is taken from
courts of law, where the defendant, if he has anything to plead as a
lawful defence, requests leave to speak, in order to clear himself of
the accusations laid to his charge. But if his conscience oppresses him,
he is silent, and without saying a word awaits his condemnation, since
he has already been condemned by his own silence. The expression in
Job 40.4, *I lay mine hand upon my mouth*, has the same meaning, for Job
says that although he had some kind of excuse, yet he would cease to
justify himself, and submit to the sentence pronounced by God. The
following clause contains the explanation, for his mouth is stopped,
and he is so bound by the judgment against him as to have no means
of escape. In other passages to be silent before the face of the Lord is
to tremble at His Majesty, and to stand as it were voiceless with
astonishment at His radiance.

20. *Because by the works of the law shall no flesh be justified.* Even among learned scholars there is some doubt about what is meant by *the works of the law.* While some extend them to include the observance of the whole law, others restrict them to ceremonies alone. The addition of the word *law* induced Chrysostom, Origen, and Jerome to accept the latter opinion, for they thought that this addition had a peculiar connotation, to prevent the passage from being understood of all works. This difficulty, however, has a very easy solution. Works are just before God to the extent that we seek to render worship and obedience to Him by them. In order, therefore, to remove more explicitly the power of justification from all works, Paul has used the term of those works which have the greatest ability to justify, if any such exist. For the law has the promises, without which there would be no value in our works before God. We see, therefore, the reasons for Paul's express mention of *the works of the law,* for it is by the law that our works are evaluated. Even the schoolmen were quite aware of this, for they had a well-worn cliché that works are meritorious not by any intrinsic worthiness, but by the covenant of God. They are mistaken, since they do not see that our works are always corrupted by vices which deprive them of any merit. The principle, however, is still true that the reward for works depends on the free promise of the law. Paul, therefore, rightly and wisely does not argue about mere works, but makes a distinct and explicit reference to the keeping of the law, which was properly the subject of his discussion.

The arguments adduced by other learned scholars in support of this opinion are weaker than they should have been. They hold that the mention of circumcision is offered as an example which refers only to ceremonies. We have, however, already explained why Paul mentioned circumcision, for only hypocrites are inflated with confidence in their works, and we know that they boast only in external appearances. Circumcision also, in their view, was a sort of initiation into the righteousness of the law, and therefore seemed to them at the same time a work of the highest honour, and, indeed, the basis of the righteousness of works. They oppose circumcision on the grounds of what Paul says in the Epistle to the Galatians, where, in dealing with the same subject, he refers only to ceremonies. Their argument, however, is not sufficiently strong to achieve what they want. Paul was arguing with those who inspired the people with false confidence in ceremonies, and to remove this confidence he does not confine himself to ceremonies, nor does he specifically discuss their value, but he includes the whole law, as we see in the passages which are all derived from that source. The dispute which was maintained at Jerusalem by the disciples was of the same character.

We contend, however, not without reason, that Paul is here speaking of the whole law. We are abundantly supported by the thread of reasoning which he has followed up to this point, and continues to follow. There are many other passages which do not allow us to think otherwise. It is, therefore, a memorable truth of the first importance that no one can obtain righteousness by keeping the law. Paul has given his reason for this, and he will presently repeat it—all men without exception are guilty of transgression and condemned of unrighteousness by the law. These two propositions—to be justified by works, and to be guilty of transgression—are opposed to one another, as we shall see more fully when we proceed. The word *flesh*, if not particularly specified, signifies men, though it seems to convey a somewhat more general sense, just as it is more expressive to say, *All mortals*, than to say, *All men*, as we find in Gallius.

For through the law cometh *the knowledge of sin*. Paul argues from the opposite—we do not get righteousness from the law, because it convinces us of sin and condemnation—since life and death do not issue from the same fountain. His argument from the opposite effect of the law, that it cannot confer righteousness on us, holds good only if we maintain that it is an inseparable and unvarying circumstance of the law to show man his sin and cut off his hope of salvation. By itself, since it teaches us what righteousness is, the law is indeed the way to salvation; but our depravity and corruption prevent it from being of any advantage to us in this respect. It is also necessary in the second place to add this, that any man who has been found to be a sinner is deprived of righteousness. It is frivolous to invent, as the sophists do, a half-righteousness, so that works in part may justify. Man's corruption prevents any achievement in this regard.

But now apart from the law a righteousness of God hath been manifested, being witnessed by the law and the prophets; even the righteousness of God through faith in Jesus Christ unto all them that believe; for there is no distinction. (21-22)

21. *But now apart from the law.* It is not certain why he calls the righteousness which we obtain by faith *the righteousness of God*, whether it is because it alone stands in the presence of God, or because the Lord in His mercy confers it upon us. As both interpretations will suit, we do not argue for one or the other. This righteousness, therefore, which God communicates to man, and which alone he accepts and acknowledges as righteousness, has been revealed, he says, *apart from the law*, i.e. without the aid of the law. The law is understood to mean works, for it is not proper to refer it to teaching, which he soon cites as a witness to the free righteousness of faith. I shall presently show that

it is pointless and lacking in flexibility to restrict *the law* to ceremonies. We know, therefore, that the merits of works are excluded. We also see that Paul does not confuse works with the mercy of God, but removes and eradicates all confidence in works and establishes mercy alone.

I am well aware that Augustine gives a different explanation. He considers that the righteousness of God is the grace of regeneration and this grace is free, he states, because God renews us, unworthy as we are, by His Spirit. He excludes from this the works of the law, i.e. those works by which men endeavour to deserve well of God by themselves, without self-renewal. I am also perfectly well aware that some modern theorists proudly adduce this doctrine as though it had been revealed to them at this very time. But it is evident from the context that the apostle includes all works without exception, even those which the Lord produces in His own people. Abraham was regenerated and led by the Spirit of God at the time when Paul denies that he had been justified by works. He therefore excludes from man's justification not only works which are morally good, as they are commonly termed, and which are performed by the natural instinct, but also all those which even believers can possess. Again, if it is a definition of the righteousness of faith to say, *Blessed are they whose iniquities are forgiven* (Ps. 32.1), there is no dispute about different kinds of works, but the merit of works is abolished, and the remission of sins alone is established as the cause of righteousness.

The two propositions, that man is justified by faith through the grace of Christ, and yet that he is justified by the works which proceed from spiritual regeneration, are held to be in the fullest agreement, because God freely renews us, and we also receive His gift by faith. But Paul suggests a very different principle, viz. than men's consciences will never be at peace until they rest on the mercy of God alone. In another passage, having taught us that God was in Christ in order to justify men, he expresses the mode of His justification—by *not reckoning unto them their trespasses.* In the same way, in his Epistle to the Galatians he sets the law in opposition to faith with regard to the effect of justification, because the law promises life to those who do what it commands (Gal. 2.16), and requires not only the outward performance of works, but also a sincere love of God. It follows, therefore, that no merit of works is admitted in the righteousness of faith. It appears evident, therefore, that it is a frivolous objection to say that we are justified in Christ, because we are renewed by the Spirit in so far as we are members of Christ, that we are justified by faith, because we are united by faith to the body of Christ, and that we are freely justified, because God finds nothing in us but sin.

We are, therefore, *in Christ*, because we are out of ourselves; and therefore *in faith*, because we rest on the mercy of God alone, and on His free promises; and therefore *freely*, because God reconciles us to Himself by burying our sins. Nor can this be confined to the commencement of justification, as those interpreters fondly suppose, for the definition, *Blessed are they whose iniquities are forgiven*, was effected in David after a lengthy period of training in the service of God. And Abraham, though a rare example of holiness, thirty years after his call had no works in which to glory before God, and therefore his belief in the promise was imputed to him for righteousness. When Paul teaches us that God justifies men by not imputing their sins, he quotes a passage which is daily repeated in the Church. That peace of conscience, which is disturbed on the score of works, is not a one-day phenomenon, but ought to continue through our whole life. It follows from this that until our death we are justified only as we look to Christ alone in whom God has adopted us, and now regards us as accepted. Those, too, who falsely accuse us of asserting that according to Scripture we are justified by faith alone, since the exclusive particle *alone* is nowhere to be found in Scripture are refuted by this same argument. But if justification does not depend either on the law, or on ourselves, why should it not be ascribed to mercy alone? And if it is of mercy alone, then it is of faith alone.

The particle *now* may simply be taken adversatively, without temporal reference, as we often use *now* for *but*. If, however, a temporal reference is preferred (and I willingly admit it, to avoid any suspicion of evasion), it is not the abrogation of ceremonies alone which is to be understood, for the intention of the apostle was simply to illustrate by comparison the grace by which we surpass the fathers. The meaning will therefore be that the righteousness of faith had been revealed by the preaching of the Gospel after the appearance of Christ in the flesh. It does not, however, follow from this that it had been hidden before the coming of Christ, for a double manifestation is to be thought of here—the first in the Old Testament, which consisted of the word and sacraments, the other in the New, which, in addition to the ceremonies and promises, contains their fulfilment in Christ. To this is added also a fuller clarity by the Gospel.

Being witnessed by the law and the prophets. Paul adds this, that the Gospel should not seem to be contrary to the law in conferring free righteousness. As, therefore, he has denied that the righteousness of faith needs the assistance of the law, so now he asserts that it is confirmed by its testimony. And if the law bears testimony to free righteousness, it is evident that it was not given to teach men how to obtain righteousness for themselves by works. Those, therefore, who wrest the law for this purpose, pervert it. But, if proof of this truth is desired, one should examine in order the main heads of the Mosaic teaching, and it will be found that in the beginning man, having been cast from the kingdom of God, had no other means of restoration than that contained in the evangelical promises concerning the blessed seed, by whom, it was foretold, the serpent's head was to be bruised, and in whom a blessing had been promised to the nations. We shall find in the commandments proof of our iniquity, and from the sacrifices and oblations we shall learn that satisfaction and purification are found in Christ alone. If we come to the prophets, we shall find the clearest promises of free mercy. On this, see my *Institutes*.

22. *Even the righteousness of God.* Paul briefly shows what this justification is like, viz. that it is to be found in Christ and apprehended by faith. By reintroducing the name of God, however, he appears to make Him the author, and not merely the approver, of the righteousness of which he speaks, as though he said that it flows from Him alone, or that its origin is in heaven, but that it is disclosed to us in Christ.

The order, therefore, to be followed in discussing the subject in hand is as follows: First, the cause of our justification is to be referred not to the judgment of men but to the tribunal of God, before whom only perfect and absolute obedience to the law is reckoned as righteousness, as is clear from the promises and warnings of the law. If there is no one who has attained to such precise holiness, it follows that all men are destitute of righteousness in themselves. Second, it is necessary that Christ should come to our aid, for He who alone is just can render us just by transferring to us His own righteousness. We see now how the righteousness of faith is the righteousness of Christ. When, therefore, we are justified, the efficient cause is the mercy of God, Christ is the substance (*materia*) of our justification, and the Word, with faith, the instrument. Faith is therefore said to justify, because it is the instrument by which we receive Christ, in whom righteousness is communicated to us. When we are made partakers of Christ, we are not only ourselves righteous, but our works also are counted righteous in the sight of God, because any imperfections in them are obliterated by the blood of Christ. The promises, which were conditional, are fulfilled to us also by the same grace, since God rewards our works as perfect, inasmuch as their defects are covered by free pardon.

Unto all them that believe (Calvin: *Unto all and upon all them that believe*). For the sake of amplification he repeats the same truth in different expressions, in order to express more fully what we have already heard, viz. that faith alone is here required, that believers are not distinguished by external marks, and that it is therefore of no importance whether they are Gentiles or Jews.

*For all have sinned, and fall short of the glory of God; being justified
freely by his grace through the redemption that is in Christ Jesus: whom
God set forth to be a propitiation, through faith, by his blood, to shew
his righteousness, because of the passing over of the sins done aforetime,
in the forbearance of God; for the shewing, I say, of his righteousness at
this present season: that he might himself be just, and the justifier of him
that hath faith in Jesus. (23-26)*

For there is no distinction. Paul urges on all without distinction the
necessity of seeking righteousness in Christ, as though he said, 'There
is no other way of obtaining righteousness. There is not one method
for justifying some, and a different one for others, but all alike must be
justified by faith, because all are sinners, and have therefore no cause
for glorifying before God.' He takes it for granted that everyone is
conscious of sin when he comes to the tribunal of God, and is dis-
comfited and lost beneath a sense of his own shame, so that no sinner
can bear the presence of God, as we see in the example of Adam. Paul
attacks again with an argument from the opposite side, and for this
reason we should notice his following points. Since all men are sinners,
Paul infers that they are deficient or completely lacking in the praise
of righteousness. There is, therefore, according to his teaching no
righteousness except that which is perfect and absolute. If there were
such a thing as half righteousness, it would not be necessary to deprive
a man entirely of all glory because he was a sinner. The fiction of what
is called partial righteousness is hereby sufficiently refuted. If it were
true that we are partially justified by works, and partially by the grace
of God, this argument of Paul, that all are deprived of the glory of God
because they are sinners, would have no force. It is, therefore, certain
that there is no righteousness where there is sin, until Christ abolishes
the curse. This is precisely what Paul is saying in Gal. 3.10, that all
who are under the law are exposed to the curse, and that we are
delivered from it through the kindness of Christ. *The glory of God*
means the glory which is in the presence of God, as in John 12.43,
where it is said that they loved the glory of men more than the glory
of God. Thus Paul summons us from the applause of a human court
to the tribunal of heaven.

24. *Being justified freely by his grace.* The participle is here used for
the verb according to the Greek usage. The meaning is that since there
is nothing left for men in themselves but to perish, having been smitten
by the just judgment of God, they are therefore freely justified by His
mercy, for Christ comes to the aid of their wretchedness, and communicates Himself to believers, so that they find in Him alone all those
things of which they are in want. There is, perhaps, no passage in the

whole of Scripture which more strikingly illustrates the efficacy of this righteousness, for it shows that the mercy of God is the efficient cause, Christ with His blood the material cause, faith conceived by the Word the formal or instrumental cause, and the glory of both the divine justice and goodness the final cause.

With regard to the efficient cause, Paul says that we are *justified freely*, and justified, what is more, by His grace. Thus he has twice used the expression that all is of God and nothing from ourselves. It would have been sufficient to oppose grace to merit, but to prevent our entertaining the idea of a truncated righteousness, he has more clearly asserted his meaning by repetition, and has claimed for the mercy of God alone the whole effect of our righteousness which the sophists divide into parts and mutilate, lest they should be constrained to admit their own poverty.

Through the redemption that is in Christ Jesus. This is the material cause—the fact that Christ by His obedience satisfied the judgment of the Father, and by undertaking our cause freed us from the tyranny of death by which we were held captive. Our guilt is taken away by the expiatory sacrifice which He offered. Here again the fiction of those who make righteousness a quality receives its best refutation. If we are accounted righteous before God because we are redeemed at a price, we certainly borrow from some other source what we do not have. Paul soon explains more clearly the value and object of this redemption, viz. that it reconciles us to God, for he calls Christ a propitiation or (and I prefer to use an allusion to an older figure) a mercy-seat. What he means is that we are righteous only in so far as Christ reconciles the Father to us. But we must now examine what he says.

25. *Whom God set forth to be a propitiation.* The Greek verb προτιθέναι sometimes means *to determine beforehand*, and sometimes *to set forth*. If we take the former meaning, Paul is referring to the free mercy of God in having appointed Christ as our Mediator to reconcile the Father to us by the sacrifice of His death. It is no ordinary commendation of the grace of God that of His own accord He sought out a way by which to remove our curse. Certainly the present passage seems to agree with that in John 3.16: 'God so loved the world, that he gave his only begotten Son.' Should we, however, adopt the other meaning, the sense will be the same, that in His own time God *set* Him *forth*, whom He had appointed Mediator. There is, I think, an allusion in the word ἱλαστήριον, as I have said, to the ancient mercy-seat, for he informs us that in Christ there was exhibited in reality that which was given figuratively to the Jews. Since, however, the other view cannot be disproved, if the reader prefers to accept the more simple sense, I shall leave the question open. Paul's particular meaning here is made

quite clear from what he says, viz. that God, apart from Christ, is always angry with us, and that we are reconciled to Him when we are accepted by His righteousness. God does not hate in us His own workmanship, that is, the fact that He has created us as living beings, but He hates our uncleanness, which has extinguished the light of His image. When the washing of Christ has removed this, He loves and embraces us as His own pure workmanship.

A propitiation, through faith, by his blood. I prefer this literal retention of Paul's language, since I think that his intention was to use a single idea to declare that God is reconciled to us as soon as we put our trust in the blood of Christ, because by faith we come to the possession of this benefit. By mentioning *blood* alone he did not mean to exclude other parts of redemption, but rather to include the whole of it in a single word, and he mentioned the blood, in which we are washed. Thus, the whole of our expiation is denoted by taking a part for the whole. Having just stated that God has been reconciled in Christ, he now adds that this reconciliation is brought to pass by faith, at the same time stating what should be the chief object of our faith in looking to Christ.

Because of the passing over of the sins done aforetime. The causal pre-position is equivalent in meaning to *for the sake of remission,* or, *to this end, that he might blot out sins.* This definition or explanation confirms again what I have already frequently hinted at, viz. that men are justified not because they are such in reality, but by imputation. Only he uses various forms of expression for the purpose of making it more clear that there is no merit of ours in this righteousness. If we obtain it by the remission of sins, we conclude that it is beyond ourselves; and further, if remission itself is an act of the liberality of God alone, every merit falls to the ground.

The question, however, may be asked why Paul restricts pardon to sins that are past. Although this passage is explained in various ways, I think it is probable that Paul was thinking of legal expiations, which were indeed evidences of satisfaction to come, but which could by no means placate God. There is a similar passage in Heb. 9.15, in which it is stated that the redemption of the transgressions which remained under the old covenant was brought by Christ. We are not, however, to understand that only the transgressions of former times were expiated by the death of Christ. This is a completely nonsensical idea which some extremists have drawn from a distorted view of this passage. Paul teaches simply that until the death of Christ there had been no price for placating God, and that this was not performed or accomplished by legal types—hence the truth has been suspended until the fulness of time came. We may say further that those things which involve us daily in guilt must be regarded in the same light, for there is only one propitiation for all.

To avoid that inconsistency, some scholars have maintained that former sins are forgiven, lest it should appear that licence was being given to sin in the future. It is true certainly that no pardon is offered except for sins committed, not because the advantage of redemption fails, or is lost, if we fall afterwards—as Novatus and his sect imagined —but because it is the dispensation of the Gospel to set before the intending sinner the judgment and wrath of God, and before the sinner His mercy. The explanation already offered is, however, the true sense.

The additional phrase, that this remission was through *the forbearance of God*, means simply *gentleness*. This has restrained the judgment of God, and prevented it from being inflamed for our destruction, until He received us at last into His favour. There appears to be here rather an implied anticipation, and to prevent the objection that this grace had appeared only at a late stage, Paul instructs us that it was an evidence of forbearance.

26. *For the shewing,* I say, *of his righteousness.* The repetition of this clause is emphatic and deliberately intended by Paul, since it was very necessary. There is no greater difficulty than to persuade a man to deprive himself of all honour and to ascribe it to God, although Paul intentionally mentions this new demonstration of God's justice to make the Jews open their eyes to it.

At this present season. He rightly applies what had been at all times to the period when Christ was revealed, for God openly manifested in His Son what had formerly been known in obscurity and in shadow. Thus the coming of Christ was a time of God's good pleasure, and the day of salvation. God gave some proof of His righteousness in all ages, but when the Sun of righteousness arose, it appeared in far greater brightness. We should, therefore, notice the comparison between the Old and New Testaments, for the righteousness of God was clearly revealed only when Christ appeared.

That he might himself be just. This is a definition of that righteousness which he said had been revealed when Christ was given, and which, as he has taught us in the first chapter, is made known in the Gospel. He affirms that it consists of two parts. The first is that God is just, not indeed as one among many, but as one who contains in Himself alone all the fulness of righteousness. He receives the full and complete praise which is His due only as He alone obtains the name and honour of being just, while the whole human race is condemned of unrighteousness. The other part refers to the communication of righteousness, for God does not by any means shut His riches within Himself, but pours them forth upon mankind. The righteousness of God, therefore, shines in us in so far as He justifies us by faith in Christ, for Christ was given in vain for our righteousness, if there were no enjoyment of Him by faith. It follows from this that in themselves all men are unrighteous and lost, until a remedy from heaven was offered to them.

Where then is the glorying? It is excluded. By what manner of law? of works? Nay: but by a law of faith. We reckon therefore that a man is justified by faith apart from the works of the law. (27-28)

27. *Where then is the glorying?* Having deprived men of all confidence in works with sufficiently conclusive reasons, the apostle now reproaches them with their vanity. His exclamation here was necessary, for it would have been insufficient for him in this case to offer his teaching, if the Holy Spirit did not thunder against our pride with greater vehemence, in order to lay it low. Boasting, he says, is excluded beyond all doubt, since we can produce nothing of our own which merits the approbation or commendation of God. If, however, merit is a matter of boasting, whether it is termed 'congruous merit' or 'condign merit',[1] by which a man may conciliate God to himself, we see that both of these are here destroyed. Paul is not concerned with the diminution or moderation of merit, but does not leave a single particle remaining. Besides, if faith removes glorying in works in such a way that it cannot be purely preached without wholly depriving men of all praise by ascribing everything to the mercy of God, it follows that no works are of avail in the attainment of righteousness.

Of works? In what sense does the apostle deny here that our merits are excluded by the law, since he has before proved our condemnation by the law? If the law delivers us all over to death, what glory shall we get out of it? Does it not rather deprive us of all glorying, and cover us with shame? He showed then that our sin is laid open by the judgment of the law, because we have all ceased to observe it. He means here that if righteousness consisted in the law of works, our boasting would not be excluded; but since it is by faith alone, there is nothing that we can claim for ourselves, for faith receives all from God, and brings nothing except a humble confession of want.

This contrast between faith and works should be carefully noticed, for works are mentioned here universally without any addition. He

---

[1] This is a reference to the mediaeval scholastic distinction between *meritum de congruo* and *meritum de condigno*. *Meritum de congruo* refers to the meriting of 'first-grace' which God, in accordance with His promise, confers as a fitting reward for good works; *meritum de condigno* refers to meriting of 'eternal life' which God, in accordance with His promise, confers upon those who already in a state of grace perform good works through the assistance of supernatural grace.

is therefore speaking not of ceremonial observances alone, nor specifically of any external works, but includes all the merits of works which can possibly be imagined.

The word *law* is here improperly applied to faith, but this does not obscure the meaning of the apostle in the least. He means that when we come to the rule of faith, all glorying in works is destroyed. It is as if he were saying that the righteousness of works is indeed commended in the law, but that of faith has its own law, which leaves no righteousness in any kind of works.

28. *We reckon therefore that a man is justified by faith.* Paul states his main proposition as being now incontrovertible, and adds an explanation, for when works are expressly excluded, much light is thrown on justification by faith. For this reason our opponents spend their greatest efforts in their attempts to involve faith in the merits of works. They allow indeed that man is justified by faith, but not by faith alone. In fact, they bestow on love the power of justification, though in what they say they ascribe it to faith. But Paul affirms in this passage that justification is free in such a way as to make it quite evident that no merit of works can at all be associated with it. I have already explained why he refers to them as the works of the law, and I have proved at the same time that it is quite absurd to restrict them to ceremonial observances. It is also an erroneous misrepresentation to mean by the works of the law the works of the letter which are done without the Spirit of Christ. Contrariwise, the word *law* which he adds means the same as though he called them meritorious, since what is referred to is the reward promised in the law.

When James says that man is not justified by faith alone but also by works, this is in no way opposed to the preceding view. The best way of reconciling the two views is to consider the nature of the argument used by James. The question is not how men may attain righteousness for themselves in the presence of God, but how they may prove to others that they are justified. James is refuting the hypocrites who make the empty boast that they have faith. It is, therefore, grossly illogical not to admit that the word *justify* is taken by James in a different sense from Paul, since they are dealing with different subjects. The word *faith* is also no doubt capable of various meanings, and this ambiguity must be taken into account for a correct judgment to be formed on the question. James, as we may learn from the context, meant no more than that man is not rendered or proved righteous by a feigned or dead faith, unless he proves his righteousness by his works. On this subject, see my *Institutes*.

Or is God the God of Jews only? is he not the God of Gentiles also?

Yea, of Gentiles also: if so be that God is one, and he shall justify the
circumcision by faith, and the uncircumcision through faith. (29-30)

29. *Or is God the God of Jews only?* The second proposition is that
this righteousness does not belong to the Jews more than to the
Gentiles. It was of great importance that this point should be urged,
in order that a free passage might be made for the kingdom of Christ
through the whole world. He does not, therefore, ask simply or
precisely whether God was the Creator of the Gentiles—this was
admitted without dispute—but whether He would declare Himself as
their Saviour also. After He had made the whole human race equal,
and had reduced them to the same condition, any distinction between
them was from God and not from themselves, who were on a common
level. But if it is true that God desires to make all the peoples of the
earth partakers of His mercy, then salvation (and righteousness, which
is necessary for salvation), are extended to all. By the name *God*,
therefore, is conveyed the mutual relationship which is often mentioned
in Scripture: 'And ye shall be my people, and I will be your God' (Jer.
30.22). The fact that for a certain time God chose for Himself a peculiar
people did not invalidate the principle of creation, that all men were
formed after the image of God, and were being educated in the world
to the hope of a blessed eternity.

30. *And he shall justify the circumcision by faith.* When he says that
some are justified *by* faith, and others *through* faith, he seems to have
indulged in a variety of expressions in pointing out the same truth, in
order to touch in passing on the foolishness of the Jews, who imagined
that there was a distinction between themselves and the Gentiles. On
the subject of justification, however, there was not the slightest difference. If men are made partakers of this grace by faith alone, and if
faith is the same in them both, it is absurd to make a distinction where
there is so great a similarity. I am, therefore, of the opinion that the
words are ironical, as though he were saying: 'If anyone wants to make
a difference between Gentile and Jew, let it be this—the Jew obtains
righteousness *by* faith, and the Gentile *through* faith.' It may be, however, that the following distinction is preferred, that the Jews are
justified by faith, because they are born as the heirs of grace, while the
right of adoption is transmitted to them from the fathers, but that the
Gentiles are justified through faith, because the covenant comes to
them from outside.

Do we then make the law of none effect through faith? God forbid: nay,
we establish the law. (31)

31. *Do we then make the law of none effect?* When the law is opposed

to faith, the flesh immediately suspects that there is some incompatibility between the two, as if they were opposed to each other. This misunderstanding is prevalent particularly among those whose minds are coloured by a false view of the law, and who, disregarding the promises, seek in the law only the righteousness of works. On this account the Jews severely attacked not only Paul, but also our Lord Himself, as if all His preaching aimed at the abrogation of the law—hence the protest which He made: 'I came not to destroy (the law), but to fulfil' (Matt. 5.17).

This suspicion extended to the moral as well as the ceremonial law; for since the Gospel puts an end to the Mosaic ceremonies, its intention is held to be the destruction of the ministry of Moses. And further, since the Gospel obliterates all righteousness of works, it is believed to be opposed to all those testimonies of the law in which the Lord affirms that He has prescribed there the way of righteousness and salvation. I therefore take this defence of Paul to refer not only to ceremonies, nor to what are called moral precepts, but to the whole law in general.

The moral law is truly confirmed and established through faith in Christ, since it was given to teach man of his iniquity, and to lead him to Christ, without whom the law is not fulfilled. In vain the law proclaims what is right, yet it accomplishes nothing but the increase of inordinate desires, in order finally to bring upon man greater condemnation. When, however, we come to Christ, we first find in Him the exact righteousness of the law, and this also becomes ours by imputation. In the second place we find in Him sanctification, by which our hearts are formed to keep the law. True, we keep it imperfectly, yet at least we are aiming at it. The argument is the same in the case of ceremonies. These cease and vanish away when Christ comes, but they are truly confirmed by Him. In themselves they are vain and shadowy images, and will be found to possess reality only in reference to a better end. Their highest confirmation, therefore, lies in the fact that they have attained their truth in Christ. Let us, therefore, also remember to preach the Gospel in such a way that we establish the law by our manner of teaching, but let the only support of our preaching be that of faith in Christ.

CHAPTER FOUR

What then shall we say that Abraham, our forefather according to the flesh, hath found? For, if Abraham was justified by works, he hath whereof to glory; but not toward God. For what saith the scripture? And Abraham believed God, and it was reckoned unto him for righteousness. (1-3)

1. *What then shall we say?* Paul confirms his argument by an example, and his proof is sufficiently conclusive, since both in content and in person the points of correspondence are all alike. Abraham was the father of the faithful. We should all be conformed to him. But there is also only one way, and not more than one, by which all may attain righteousness. In many other matters one example would not be sufficient to make a general rule. Since, however, in the person of Abraham there was exhibited a mirror or pattern of righteousness, which belongs in common to the whole Church, Paul rightly applies what has been written of him alone to the whole body of the Church. At the same time also he restrains the Jews, who had no more plausible basis for glorying than the boast that they were the sons of Abraham, for they would never have dared to ascribe to themselves more sanctity than they ascribed to the holy patriarch. Now that it is agreed that he has been freely justified, his posterity, who claim a righteousness of their own by the law, ought to have been overcome by shame and hold their peace.

According to the flesh. Between this clause and the word *father* there is inserted in Paul's text the verb εὑρηκέναι, thus: 'What shall we say that Abraham our forefather *has found* according to the flesh?' On this account some interpreters hold that the question is: 'What has Abraham *obtained* according to the flesh?' If this exposition is satisfactory, the words *according to the flesh* will mean *naturally* or *from himself.* It is, however, probable that they are to be connected with the word *forefather* as an epithet. Since we are usually more influenced by familiar examples, the dignity of their race, in which the Jews took much pride, is again expressly mentioned. Some regard this as having been added by way of contempt. The children of Adam are elsewhere called carnal in this sense, because they are not spiritual or legitimate. But I think that the expression was used because it belonged peculiarly to the Jews, for it was a greater honour to be the children of Abraham by nature and carnal descent than by mere adoption, provided there was also faith. He therefore concedes to the Jews a closer bond of union, but only in order more deeply to impress upon them not to depart from the example of their father.

2. *For if Abraham was justified by works.* The argument is incomplete and ought to be put in this form: 'If Abraham was justified by works, he can boast in his own merit, but he has no reason for boasting before God. Therefore he is not justified by works.' Thus the clause *but not toward God* is the minor proposition of the syllogism, and to this should be added the conclusion which I have stated, though it is not expressed by Paul. He calls it 'glorying' when we pretend to have anything of our own which in the judgment of God deserves a reward. Which of us will claim for himself the least particle of merit, when it is not granted to Abraham?

3. *For what saith the scripture?* This is the proof of his minor proposition or assumption, in which he denied that Abraham had any ground for glorying. If Abraham is justified because he embraces the goodness of God, by faith, it follows that he has no cause for glorying, since he brings nothing of his own except the acknowledgment of his own misery which seeks for mercy. Paul is assuming that the righteousness of faith is the place of help and refuge for the sinner who is destitute of works. If there were any righteousness by the law or by works, it would reside in men themselves. But men get the faith which they lack from elsewhere. It is for this reason rightly termed the imputed righteousness of faith.

The passage quoted is taken from Gen. 15.6, in which the word *believe* should not be restricted to any particular expression, but refers to the whole covenant of salvation and the grace of adoption which Abraham is said to have apprehended by faith. There is mentioned there, it is true, the promise of a future seed, but it was grounded on free adoption. It ought, however, to be noted that salvation is not promised without the grace of God, nor the grace of God without salvation; and again, that we are not called to the grace of God or to the hope of salvation without having righteousness offered to us at the same time.

If we take this position, it is clear that those who think that Paul wrested the Mosaic statement from its context, do not understand the principles of theology. Since there is a particular promise stated in the passage, they understand that Abraham acted rightly and honourably in believing it, and was so far approved by God. But their interpretation here is mistaken, first, because they have not perceived that *believing* extends to the whole context, and ought not therefore to be restricted to one clause. The principal mistake, however, is in their failure to begin with what is asserted of the grace of God. God bestowed His grace to make Abraham more certain both of His adoption and His fatherly favour, in which is included eternal salvation by Christ. For this reason Abraham, in believing, embraces nothing but the grace offered to him, lest it should be of no effect. If this is imputed to him for righteousness, it follows that the only ground of his right-eousness was his trust in the goodness of God, and his daring to hope for all things from Him. Moses does not relate what men thought of Abraham, but the character which he had before the tribunal of God. Abraham, therefore, seized the kindness of God which was offered to him in the promise, and by which he perceived that righteousness was being communicated to him. In order to determine the meaning of righteousness, it is necessary to understand this relation between promise and faith, for there is the same relationship between God and us as juridically exists between giver and recipient. We attain right-eousness only because it is brought to us by the promise of the Gospel, and thus we discern that we possess it by faith.

I have already explained, and I intend to explain more fully when I come, if the Lord will allow me, to deal with his Epistle, how we are to reconcile this passage with James, who appears to contradict it. Let us simply note that those to whom righteousness is imputed are justified, since Paul uses these two expressions as synonyms. We conclude from this that the question is not what men are in themselves, but how God regards them, not because purity of conscience and integrity of life are distinguished from the free favour of God, but because, when the reason for God's love to us and His acknowledg-ment of us as just is questioned, it is necessary that Christ should be seen to be the one who clothes us with His own righteousness.

Now to him that worketh, the reward is not reckoned as of grace, but as of debt. But to him that worketh not, but believeth on him that justifieth the ungodly, his faith is reckoned for righteousness. (4-5)

4. *Now to him that worketh.* By 'him that worketh' Paul does not mean the man who is given to good works, a pursuit which ought to be zealously followed by all the children of God, but the one who merits something by his own achievements. Similarly, by 'him that worketh not' he means the one who is due nothing by the merit of his works. He does not want believers to be indolent, but merely forbids their being mercenary-minded by demanding something from God as their due.

We have already stated that the discussion here is not how we are to regulate our life, but rather concerns the reason for our salvation. Paul argues from opposites that God does not repay righteousness to us as a debt, but bestows it as a gift. I agree with Bucer, who proves that the form of Paul's argument is not derived from a single expression, but from the whole sentence, thus: 'If there is any man who merits anything by his work, that which is merited is not freely imputed to him, but rendered to him as his due.' Faith is reckoned as righteousness not because it brings any merit from us, but because it lays hold of the goodness of God. Therefore righteousness is not our due, but is freely bestowed. Since Christ justifies us by faith of His own good will, Paul always sees in this our self-emptying, for what do we believe, except that Christ is our expiation to reconcile us to God? The same truth is given in different words in Gal. 3.11, where it is said, 'that no man is justified by the law in the sight of God, is evident: for, The righteous shall live by faith; and the law is not of faith; but, He that doeth them shall live in them.' Since the law promises a reward to works, Paul concludes from this that the righteousness of faith, which is free, does not agree with the righteousness of works. It will be different if faith justifies on the basis of works. We ought carefully to observe these comparisons, which entirely remove all merit.

5. *But believeth on him that justifieth the ungodly.* This is a highly emphatic circumlocution. In it Paul expresses the substance and nature both of faith and righteousness. He clearly shows that faith brings us righteousness, not because it is a meritorious virtue, but because it obtains for us the grace of God. Paul not only states that God is the giver of righteousness, but also condemns us of unrighteousness, in order that the bounty of God may help our necessity. In short, only those who feel in themselves that they are ungodly will attain to the righteousness of faith. This circumlocution is to be related to the subject of the passage, viz. that faith adorns us with the righteousness of another, which it begs from God. Here again God is said to justify us while He freely forgives sinners and favours with His love those with whom He might justifiably be angry, i.e. while His mercy abolishes our unrighteousness.

Even as David also pronounceth blessing upon the man, unto whom God reckoneth righteousness apart from works, saying, Blessed are they whose iniquities are forgiven, And whose sins are covered, Blessed is the man to whom the Lord will not reckon sin. (6-8)

6. *Even as David also pronounceth blessing.* We see from this that those who limit the works of the law to ceremonies are merely cavilling, since what he previously referred to as the works of the law he now simply, and without any addition, calls works. If it is agreed that the simple and unrestricted language which we find in this passage is to be understood as applying without distinction to every work, it must hold good throughout the whole argument. There is nothing

more inconsistent than to remove the power of justification from ceremonies alone, since Paul excludes all works without distinction. To this is added the negative clause that God justifies men by *not* imputing their sin. By these words we also learn that righteousness for Paul is nothing other than the remission of sins, and finally, that this remission is also unmerited, because it is imputed without works, as the very word remission indicates. Debt is not remitted when the creditor is paid, but when the creditor of his own accord cancels the debt through his pure generosity. Let us therefore have done with those who teach us to buy the forgiveness of our sins by making satisfaction. Paul borrows his argument from this type of remission in order to prove that the gift of righteousness is free. How can they agree with Paul? They say that we must satisfy the justice of God by our works, in order to obtain the pardon of our sins. Paul here rather argues, that the righteousness of faith is free and independent of works, since it depends on the remission of sins. His argument would certainly be false if any works were required in the remission of sins.

The ridiculous assertions of the schoolmen about half-remission are equally refuted by the same words of David. They absurdly maintain that although the fault is forgiven, the punishment is retained by God. But the Psalmist declares not only that our sins are covered, i.e. removed from the sight of God, but he also adds that they are not imputed. How can it be consistent for God to demand the punishment of those sins which He does not impute? We are therefore left with the glorious statement that he who is cleansed before God by the free remission of sins is justified by faith. We may also deduce from this the unending continuance of free righteousness throughout our whole life. When David, wearied by the long continued torment of his conscience, gives voice to this declaration, he is assuredly speaking from his own experience. And yet he had worshipped God now for many years. Having made great progress, therefore, he at length experienced the misery of all who are summoned to the tribunal of God, and he declares that there is no other way of obtaining happiness than for the Lord to receive us into His favour by not imputing our sins. Thus, too, is refuted the fallacy of those who absurdly imagine that the righteousness of faith is merely an initial act, and that afterwards believers retain by their works the possession of that righteousness which they had first attained without any merits of their own.

It in no way detracts from Paul's argument that works, and other blessings also, are sometimes stated to be imputed for righteousness. In Ps. 106.30 it is written that it was imputed to Phinehas, the priest of the Lord, for righteousness, because he avenged the reproach of Israel by exacting punishment on an adulterer and a harlot. We are told, it is true, that a man has performed a righteous deed, but we know that one act does not justify a person. What is required is obedience, perfect and complete in all its parts, according to the promise, 'He who shall do these things shall live in them' (Lev. 18.5). How then is this vengeance which he inflicted imputed to him for righteousness? It was necessary that he should first have been justified by the grace of God, for those who are already clothed with the righteousness of Christ have God favourably disposed not only to them, but also to their works. The spots and blemishes of these works are covered by the purity of Christ, lest they should come into judgment, and being unpolluted by any defilements, are thereby considered righteous. It is quite clear that apart from such forbearances no human work at all can please God. But if the righteousness of faith is the only reason why our works are counted just, how absurd is the argument that righteousness is not by faith alone, because it is attributed to works. My answer to this is the incontrovertible argument that all works would be condemned of unrighteousness, if justification were not by faith alone.

The same is true of happiness. It is those who fear the Lord, walk in His ways (Ps. 128.1), and meditate on His law day and night (Ps. 1.2) who are pronounced blessed. Since, however, no one does this as perfectly as he should in order to satisfy fully the commandment of God, all blessings of this kind are useless until we are made blessed by being purified and cleansed by the remission of sins. It is thus that we become capable of enjoying the blessedness which the Lord promises to His servants on account of their diligent attention to the law and good works. The righteousness of works, therefore, is the effect of the righteousness of faith, and the blessedness which arises from works is the effect of the blessedness which consists in the remission of sins. If the cause ought not and cannot be destroyed by its own effect, the intentions of those who strive to destroy the righteousness of faith by works are quite wrong.

Someone may ask, 'Why may we not use these quotations to prove that man is justified and made blessed by works? For the words of Scripture declare that man is justified and made blessed by works as much as by faith and the mercy of God.' We should consider here the order of causes as well as the dispensation of the grace of God. No declaration about either the righteousness of works or the blessedness which comes from doing them has any effect unless it has been preceded by this true righteousness of faith alone, and unless this righteousness alone fulfils all its functions. It is this, therefore, that must be built up and established, in order that the former may grow and come forth from it as fruit from the tree.

Is this blessing then pronounced upon the circumcision, or upon the uncircumcision also? for we say, To Abraham his faith was reckoned for righteousness. How then was it reckoned? when he was in circumcision, or in uncircumcision? Not in circumcision, but in uncircumcision.
(9-10)

Because Paul mentions only *circumcision* and *uncircumcision*, many interpreters unwisely conclude that the only question at issue is the attainment of righteousness by the ceremonies of the law. But we should consider the class of men with whom Paul is arguing, for we know that while hypocrites generally boast of meritorious works, yet they mask their conduct in their outward appearances. The Jews also had a particular reason of their own for their estrangement from a true and genuine righteousness by a gross abuse of the law. Paul said that only those whom God reconciles to Himself by free pardon are blessed. It follows from this that all those whose works come into judgment are cursed. The principle is now stated that men are justified not by their own worthiness, but by the mercy of God. But even this is not yet enough, unless remission of sins precedes all works. Of these the first was circumcision, which initiated the Jewish people into obedience to God. He therefore proceeds to demonstrate this too.

Let us always remember that circumcision is here considered as the 'initial' work of the righteousness of the law. The Jews did not boast in it as the symbol of the grace of God, but in their 'meritorious observance of the law, and regarded themselves as better than others on the grounds of possessing greater excellence before God. We see now that the dispute is not about a single rite, but that every work of the law is included in this class, i.e. every work which ought to receive reward. Circumcision is particularly mentioned, because it was the basis of the righteousness of the law.

Paul argues from the opposite side that if the righteousness of Abraham is the remission of sins (and he assumes this), and if he attained this before circumcision, it therefore follows that remission of sins is not given for previous merits. We see that the argument is taken from the order of cause and effect, for cause always precedes effect, and Abraham possessed righteousness before he had circumcision.

And he received the sign of circumcision, a seal of the righteousness of the faith which he had while he was in uncircumcision: that he might be the father of all them that believe, though they be in uncircumcision, that righteousness might be reckoned unto them; and the father of circumcision to them who not only are of the circumcision, but who also walk in the steps of that faith of our father Abraham which he had in uncircumcision. (11-12)

11. *And he received the sign.* By way of anticipating an objection Paul shows that, although it did not justify, circumcision had not been unprofitable and superfluous, seeing that it had another very excellent use, viz. the office of sealing and as it were ratifying the righteousness of faith. In the meantime he suggests from the very purpose of circumcision that it was not the cause of righteousness, although it tends to confirm the righteousness of faith already obtained in uncircumcision, and therefore in no way detracts or takes away from that righteousness.

This is a notable passage in regard to the general benefits of the sacraments. These, as Paul testifies, are seals by which the promises of God are in a manner imprinted on our hearts, and the certainty of grace confirmed. Although by themselves they are unprofitable, yet God has designed them to be the instruments of His grace, and by the secret grace of His Spirit promotes the benefit of the elect by their means. Although to the reprobate they are lifeless and useless symbols, yet they always retain their power and character. Even if our unbelief should deprive us of their effect, yet it does not undermine or extinguish the truth of God. The principle therefore remains, that sacred symbols are testimonies by which God seals His grace on our hearts.

It should be stated in particular that a twofold grace has been represented by the sign of circumcision. God had promised Abraham a seed that was blessed. From this seed salvation was to be looked for for the whole world. On this depended the promise, 'I will be a God unto thee' (Gen. 17.7). Free reconciliation to God was therefore included in that sign, and the analogy corresponded to it sufficiently for believers to look forward to the promised seed. God for His part demanded integrity and holiness of life, and showed by the symbol how this might be attained, viz. by the circumcision of everything in man that is born of the flesh, because his whole nature is corrupted. He therefore instructed Abraham by the outward sign to circumcise spiritually the corruption of his flesh. Moses has also alluded to this in Deut. 10.16. In order to show that this was not the work of man, but of God, he commanded the circumcision of tender infants who, by reason of their age, could not as yet have performed that command. Moses has expressly mentioned spiritual circumcision as a work of the divine power, as we see in Deut. 30.6 where he says, 'The Lord will circumcise thine heart.' The prophets afterwards explained this same idea much more clearly.

In conclusion, as now in baptism there are two parts, so formerly in circumcision there were the two parts which testified both to newness of life and to the forgiveness of sins. Although in the case of Abraham righteousness preceded circumcision, this is not always so in the sacraments, as we see from Isaac and his posterity. God, however, desired to provide such an illustration once at the beginning, so that salvation might not be limited to outward signs.

That he might be the father of all them that believe. Note how the circumcision of Abraham confirms our faith in free righteousness. Circumcision is the sealing of the righteousness of faith, in order that righteousness may be imputed to us also who believe. Thus with remarkable skill Paul turns against his opponents the objections which they might have offered. If the very truth and significance of circumcision are to be found in uncircumcision, there is no ground for the Jews to vaunt themselves so greatly above the Gentiles.

There is, however, this possible doubt: Should we also follow the example of Abraham and confirm the same righteousness by the sign of circumcision? If we should, then why has the apostle omitted to mention this? It is surely because he thought that his remarks settled the question. When it has been admitted that circumcision avails only to seal the grace of God, it follows that it is of no benefit to us today, for we have a divinely instituted sign in its place. Since, therefore, there is now no necessity for circumcision where baptism exists, Paul was not inclined to enter into a profitless dispute about something which was already settled, viz. why the righteousness of faith should not be sealed to the Gentiles in the same way as it was to Abraham. To believe *in uncircumcision* means that the Gentiles do not introduce the seal of circumcision, being content with their own condition. The proposition διά is thus put for ἐν.

12. *To them who not only are of the circumcision.* The word *are* is here to be taken for *are reckoned*, for Paul is alluding to the physical descendants of Abraham who have only outward circumcision, and glory confidently in it. They neglect, however, the other chief point, viz. to imitate the faith of Abraham, which alone secured his salvation. It appears from this how careful Paul is to distinguish faith from the sacrament, not only so that no one may be satisfied with the one but not the other, as though it were sufficient for one's justification, but also to prove that faith alone may fulfil every requirement. While he allows that circumcised Jews are justified, he expressly excepts circumcision, provided they follow the example of Abraham in pure faith. What does faith *in uncircumcision* mean, if not to show that it alone is sufficient without any other aid? We must therefore avoid confusing the two causes of justification by separating the two.

The scholastic dogma by which the sacraments of the Old and New Testaments are distinguished is refuted by the same argument. The schoolmen deny the power of justification to the former, assigning it to the latter. If, however, Paul is correct in his argument when he

proves that circumcision does not justify because Abraham was justified
by faith, the same argument also holds good for us. We deny, therefore, that men are justified by baptism, since they are justified by the
same faith as that of Abraham.

*For not through the law was the promise to Abraham or to his seed, that
he should be heir of the world, but through the righteousness of faith.* (13)

13. *For not through the law was the promise.* Paul now repeats more
distinctly the contrast between the law and faith which he had touched
on before. We should note this carefully; for if faith borrows nothing
from the law in order to justify, we understand from this that it relates
to the mercy of God alone. The fond fancy of those who would have
this refer to ceremonial observances, is easily disproved, for if works in
any way contributed towards justification, he would not have said
through the (written) law, but rather *through the law of nature*. Paul does
not oppose spiritual holiness of life to ceremonies, but faith and its
righteousness. The upshot, therefore, is that the inheritance had been
promised to Abraham, not because he had merited it by observing the
law, but because he had obtained righteousness by faith. Men's
consciences, it is certain (as Paul will presently add), enjoy true peace
only when they feel that they are being freely given what is not their
legal right.

It follows from this also that the benefit, the cause of which applies
equally to both, belongs to the Gentiles as much as to the Jews; for if
the salvation of men is based on the goodness of God alone, those who
exclude the Gentiles from it are restricting and impeding its course as
much as it is possible for them to do.

That he should be heir of the world. Since he is now dealing with
eternal salvation, the apostle seems to have led his readers to the world
somewhat inopportunely, but he includes in the word *world* generally
the restoration which was hoped for from Christ. While the restoration of the life of believers was in fact the principal object, it was,
however, necessary that the fallen state of the whole world should be
repaired. In Heb. 1.2 the apostle calls Christ the heir of all the blessings
of God, because the adoption which we have procured by His grace
has restored to us the possession of the inheritance from which we fell
in Adam. But since under the type of the land of Canaan not only was
the hope of a heavenly life displayed to Abraham, but also the full and
perfect blessing of God, the apostle rightly teaches us that the dominion
of the world was promised to him. The godly have a taste of this in
the present life, for however often they may be oppressed by difficulty
and want, yet because they partake with a peaceable conscience of those
things which God created for their use, and enjoy earthly blessings

G   91

from a favourable and willing Father as pledges and foretastes of eternal life, their poverty does not prevent them from acknowledging earth, sea, and heaven as their right.

Although the ungodly devour the riches of the world, they can call nothing their own, but rather snatch what they have by stealth, for they usurp it under the curse of God. It is a great comfort to the godly in their poverty that, although they live sparingly, yet they are stealing nothing of what belongs to others, but are receiving their lawful allowance from the hand of their heavenly Father until they see the full possession of their inheritance, when all creatures will serve their glory. Both heaven and earth shall be renewed for this purpose, that they may according to their measure contribute towards making the kingdom of God more glorious.

For if they which are of the law be heirs, faith is made void, and the promise is made of none effect: for the law worketh wrath; but where there is no law, neither is there transgression. (14-15)

14. *For if they which are of the law be heirs.* Paul argues from the untenable or absurd position that the grace which Abraham obtained from God had not been promised to him by legal agreement, or with regard to works. He does so because if it had been laid down as a condition that God regarded as worthy of adoption only those who deserve it, or who perform the law, no one would dare to have any confidence that adoption applied to him. Who is conscious of such perfection as to determine that the inheritance is due to him by the righteousness of the law? His faith would therefore be nullified, for the impossible condition would not only keep men's minds in suspense and anxiety, but also smite them with fear and trembling. Thus the effect of the promises would vanish, because they are of no avail except when received by faith. If our adversaries would give their whole attention to this one reason, the controversy between us might easily be settled.

The apostle assumes it as beyond doubt that the promises of God are ineffectual if we do not receive them with full assurance of mind. But what would happen if the salvation of men were based on the observance of the law? Men's consciences would have no certainty, but would be troubled with unceasing disquiet, and at length succumb to despair. The promise itself, the fulfilment of which would depend on an impossibility, would vanish without producing any fruit. Away then with those who teach pitiable folk to procure salvation for themselves by works, since Paul expressly declares that the promise is abolished if it depends on works. We should particularly recognize that when we rely on works faith is reduced to nothing. We also learn from this what faith is, and the character which the righteousness of works ought to exhibit, if men are to be able to trust in it with confidence.

The apostle tells us that faith perishes if our soul does not rest securely in the goodness of God. Faith is therefore not the mere acknowledgment of God or of His truth, nor is it even the simple persuasion that there is a God, and that His Word is truth, but is the sure knowledge of divine mercy which is conceived from the Gospel, and brings peace of conscience in the presence of God and repose. The sum of the matter is, therefore, that if salvation depends on the observance of the law, the mind will not be able to have any confidence in it, and indeed all the promises offered to us by God will prove of no effect. We are thus in a lost and deplorable condition if we are sent back to works to find out the cause or the certainty of salvation.

15. *For the law worketh wrath.* This is a confirmation of the last verse, and is taken from the opposite effect of the law. Since the law produces nothing but vengeance, it cannot bring grace. The law would, it is true, point out the way of life to men of virtue and integrity, but since it orders the sinful and corrupt to do their duty without supplying them with the power to do it, it brings them in their guilt to the judgment seat of God. Such is the corruption of our nature that the more we are taught what right and justice are, the more openly is our iniquity, and particularly our obstinacy, detected, and thus the judgment of God falls more heavily.

By *wrath* we should understand the judgment of God, the meaning it frequently has. Those who maintain that the wrath of the sinner is inflamed by the law, because he hates and blasphemes the Lawgiver whom he sees opposed to his lusts, are ingenious in what they say, but their argument is not sufficiently relevant to the present passage. The common use of the expression, and also the reason which Paul immediately adds, make it clear that Paul meant quite simply that it is condemnation alone which the law brings upon us all.

But where there is no law, neither is there transgression. This is the second proof by which he confirms his statement. It would have been difficult otherwise to see how the wrath of God is kindled against us by the law if the reason had not been made more apparent. The reason is that when we have perceived the knowledge of the righteousness of God by the law, the less excuse we have the more we grievously sin against Him. Those who despise the known will of God deservedly suffer a heavier punishment than those who offend through ignorance. The apostle, however, does not speak of the simple transgression of righteousness from which no man is exempted, but rather, by *transgression* means that a man, having been taught what pleases and displeases God, knowingly and wilfully transgresses the boundaries prescribed by the word of God. In a single phrase, *transgression* here is not a simple offence, but means a wilful obstinacy in violating righteousness. The particle οὗ, *where*, which I take as an adverb, is rendered by some commentators as *cujus*, *of which*, but the former reading is the more appropriate and more generally accepted. Whichever reading we may follow, the meaning remains the same, viz. that he who is uninstructed by the written law is not guilty of so great a transgression as the man who obstinately breaks and transgresses the law of God.

> *For this cause it is of faith, that it may be according to grace; to the end that the promise may be sure to all the seed; not to that only which is of the law, but to that also which is of the faith of Abraham, who is the father of us all (as it is written, A father of many nations have I made thee) before him who he believed, even God, who quickeneth the dead, and calleth the things that are not, as though they were. (16-17)*

16. *For this cause it is of faith.* The completion of the argument may be summed up thus: If we become heirs of salvation by works, then faith in our adoption will disappear, and the promise of it will be abrogated. But it is necessary that both faith and promise should be certain. Our adoption, therefore, comes to us by faith, so that it may be secured, by being based on the goodness of God alone. The apostle, we see, estimates faith by its unshakable certainty, and considers hesitancy and doubt as unbelief, which abolishes faith and abrogates the promise. This, however, is the doubt which the schoolmen call moral conjecture, and which they substitute for faith.

That it may be according to grace. The apostle first shows here that nothing but pure grace is put before faith. The object of faith is pure grace. If grace took merit into account, Paul's assertion that whatever it obtains for us is unmerited would be wrong. I will repeat this again in different words—If grace is everything that we obtain by faith, then all consideration for works is finished. The following passage removes all ambiguity more clearly by showing that the promise is finally secured only when it rests on grace. This expression of Paul confirms the state of uncertainty in which men are placed as long as they depend on works, because they deprive themselves of the fruit of the promises. From this also we may easily deduce that grace does not mean, as some imagine, the gift of regeneration, but unmerited favour, for as regeneration is never perfect, it would never suffice to appease their consciences, nor of itself ratify the promise.

Not to that only which is of the law. Although this expression applies elsewhere to the fanatical zealots of the law who bind themselves to its yoke and glory in the confidence which they have in it, here it means simply the Jewish nation, to whom the law of the Lord had been delivered. Paul informs us in another passage that all who remain bound to the dominion of the law are subject to a curse, and therefore their exclusion from participation in grace is certain. He is not, therefore, referring to the servants of the law who, having adhered to the righteousness of works, renounce Christ, but to the Jews who had been brought up in the law and became followers of Christ. The sentence will become clearer if we word it thus: 'Not to those only who are of the law, but to all who imitate the faith of Abraham, even though they did not have the law before.'

Who is the father of us all. The relative has the force of a causative particle. Paul desires to show that the Gentiles were partakers of this grace, since they have been taken into his seed by the same prophecy which conferred the inheritance on Abraham and his seed. Abraham is stated to have been appointed the father, not of one nation, but of many. By this the future extension of grace, at that time confined within the limits of Israel alone, was prefigured, for they could not have been counted as the offspring of Abraham unless the promised blessing were extended to them. The past tense of the verb, by the common usage of Scripture, denotes the certainty of the divine counsel. Although there was not the least evidence at that time for such a thing, yet, since the Lord had so decreed, Abraham is rightly said to have been appointed the father of many nations. Let us put in parenthesis the statement of Moses, so that this sentence may be read without a break: 'Who is the father of us all before him whom he believed, even God.' It was necessary also to explain the form of that relationship, that the Jews might not glory excessively in their physical descent. He therefore says that Abraham is 'the father of us all before God', meaning, 'our spiritual father', for he has this privilege not by his physical relationship to us, but by the promise of God.

17. *Before him whom he believed, even God, who quickeneth the dead.* The purpose of this circumlocution, in which the very substance of the faith of Abraham is expressed, is to provide a transition to the Gentiles from his example. Abraham was to attain to the promise which he heard from the mouth of the Lord in a wonderful way, since there was no sign of the promise. He was promised a seed as though he were in virility and full vigour. He was, however, past procreation, and therefore it was necessary for him to raise his thoughts to the power of God which gives life to the dead. There is, therefore, no absurdity if the Gentiles, who are otherwise barren and dead, are brought into the fellowship. Those who deny that they are capable of grace do wrong to Abraham, whose faith was sustained by the thought that it makes no difference whether those who are called to life by the Lord

are dead or not, for His power can easily raise the dead, even by speaking to them. We have here, moreover, the type and pattern of our general calling, by which our beginning is set before our eyes (not that which relates to our first birth, but which relates to the hope of the future life), namely, that when we are called of God we arise out of nothing. Whatever character we may seem to possess, we have not as much as a spark of any goodness which can render us fit for the kingdom of God. The only way by which we shall hear the call of God is that we must completely die to ourselves. The condition of our divine calling is that the dead are raised by the Lord, and that those who are nothing begin by His power to be something. The word *calling* should not be restricted to preaching, but is to be taken in the usual sense of Scripture of raising from the dead, and is meant to express more strongly the power of God who raises up by a single nod those whom He wills.

Who in hope believed against hope, to the end that he might become a father of many nations, according to that which had been spoken, So shall thy seed be. (18)

18. *Who in hope believed against hope.* If we adopt this reading the sense will be that when there was no good reason—and, indeed, when all reason was against him—yet he continued to believe. There is nothing more inimical to faith than to bind understanding to sight, so that we seek the substance of our hope from what we see. We may also read 'above hope', perhaps more appropriately, as if he were saying that by his faith he had far surpassed any conception that he could have formed. If our faith does not ascend on heavenly wings so as to look down from afar on all the feelings of the flesh, it will always stick fast in the mud of the world. Paul uses the word hope twice in the same sentence, in the first case to mean the argument for hope which can be derived from nature and carnal reason, in the second to refer to faith given by God. The meaning is that when he had no grounds for hope, Abraham still relied in hope on the promise of God, and considered that the fact that the Lord had promised was a sufficient ground for hope, however incredible the fact might be in itself.

According to that which had been spoken. I have chosen this translation in order to refer it to the time of Abraham. Paul means that when very many temptations were driving him to despair at possible failure, Abraham turned his mind to the promise which had been given to him, 'Thy seed shall equal the stars of heaven and the sands of the sea.' Paul deliberately cited only part of the quotation, in order to stimulate us to read the Scriptures. In all their quotations from Scripture the apostles take scrupulous care to arouse us to a more careful perusal of them.

And without being weakened in faith he considered his own body now as good as dead (he being about a hundred years old), and the deadness of Sarah's womb: yea, looking unto the promise of God, he wavered not through unbelief, but waxed strong through faith, giving glory to God, and being fully assured that, what he had promised, he was able also to perform. Wherefore also it was reckoned unto him for righteousness.

(19-22)

19. *And without being weakened in faith.* Alternatively, by omitting one of the negatives,[1] we may render the passage thus: 'Nor did he, though weak in faith, consider his own body.' But this does not affect the sense. He now shows more closely the circumstances which might have hindered, and indeed wholly prevented, Abraham from receiving the promise. Issue was promised to him from Sarah at a time when he was by nature incapable of reproducing and Sarah of conceiving. All that he could see in or around himself was opposed to the fulfilment of the promise. He therefore ceased to think about what he could see, and, as it were, forgot himself in order to make room for the truth of God. We are not, however, to imagine that he had no regard whatever for his own body, now incapable of reproduction, since Scripture affirms on the contrary that he reasoned with himself thus:

'Shall a child be born unto him that is an hundred years old? and shall Sarah, that is ninety years old, bear?' But because he laid aside such considerations, and resigned his whole judgment to the Lord, the apostle says that he 'considered not his own body'. It was a mark of greater constancy to withdraw his attention from the obvious fact which thrust itself upon him than if he had never contemplated any such thing.

Both this passage and Gen. 17 and 18 quite clearly prove that the body of Abraham had become incapable of reproduction on account of his age before He received the Lord's blessing. We cannot, therefore, admit the opinion of Augustine, who states somewhere that the impediment was in Sarah alone. The absurdity of the objection which induced him to have recourse to this solution ought not to influence us. Augustine holds that it is ridiculous to call Abraham incapable of reproduction in his hundredth year, since he had many children born to him some time afterwards. God, however, more fully demonstrated His power by that very act. When Abraham, who before had been like a dry, withered tree, was revived by the heavenly blessing, he not only had the power to beget Isaac, but having been restored to the age

---

[1] Calvin's version reads: 'Considered *not* his own body.'

of virility, was afterwards able to produce other offspring. It may be objected that it is not contrary to the ordering of nature that a man should beget children at that age. Although I admit that such a thing is not a prodigy, yet it is little short of miraculous. Consider too the number of toils, sorrows, wanderings, and distresses, which had wearied that saint through all his life. We shall have to admit that he had been as much worn out and exhausted by his toils as by his age. Finally, his body is not called barren without qualification, but comparatively. It was unlikely that one who in the flower and vigour of his life had been incapable of reproduction should only now begin when his powers had decayed.

The expression *without being weakened in faith* should be understood to mean that he had not wavered or fluctuated, as we tend to do in a time of uncertainty. Faith has a double weakness—one which succumbs to the temptations of adversity, and makes us fall from the power of God; the other which arises from imperfection, yet does not extinguish faith itself. However much the mind is enlightened, much ignorance still remains, and however much the heart is established, much doubt still clings to it. The faithful, therefore, are continually at conflict with ignorance and doubt, those vices of the flesh. In this conflict their faith is often severely shaken and distressed, but it finally emerges victorious, so that in weakness itself they may be said to have the greatest strength.

20. *Looking unto the promise of God, he wavered not through unbelief.* I have good grounds for my translation, although I do not follow the Vulgate or Erasmus. The apostle seems to have intended to say that Abraham had not weighed the evidence in the balance of unbelief to see whether the Lord could fulfil His promise. A proper inquiry into any subject means that we examine it dispassionately, and refuse to admit anything which seems credible without thorough investigation. Like the Virgin Mary, when she inquired of the angel how his message would come to pass, and other similar instances in Scripture, Abraham asked how this could happen, but it was the question of a person struck with wonderment. When, therefore, a message is brought to the saints concerning the works of God, the greatness of which exceeds their comprehension, they break out into expressions of wonder, but from wonder they soon pass on to a contemplation of the power of God. The ungodly, however, mock at their inquiries, and reject them as mythical. This, as we see, was the case with the Jews when they asked Christ how He could give His flesh to be eaten. It was for this reason that Abraham was not reproved when he laughed and inquired how a child could be born to a man a hundred years old and to a woman of ninety, for in his wonderment he nevertheless yielded to the power of the Word of God. On the other hand, similar laughter and inquiry

on the part of Sarah was rebuked, because she accused the promises of God of being unreal.

If these observations are applied to our present subject, it will be evident that the justification of Abraham and that of the Gentiles had exactly the same source. The Jews, therefore, insult their own father if they oppose the calling of the Gentiles as absurd. Let us also remember that we are all in the same condition as Abraham. Our circumstances are all in opposition to the promises of God. He promises us immortality: yet we are surrounded by mortality and corruption. He declares that He accounts us just: yet we are covered with sins. He testifies that He is propitious and benevolent towards us: yet outward signs threaten His wrath. What then are we to do? We must close our eyes, disregard ourselves and all things connected with us, so that nothing may hinder or prevent us from believing that God is true.

But waxed strong through faith. This is opposed to the previous clause where Paul had said that he was not weak in faith, implying that he had overcome unbelief by the constancy and firmness of his faith. The only one who will emerge victorious from this struggle will be the man who gets his defence and strength from the Word of God. When Paul adds *giving glory to God*, we must note that no greater honour can be given to God than by sealing His truth by our faith. On the other hand, no greater insult can be shown to Him than by rejecting the grace which He offers us, or by detracting from the authority of His Word. For this reason the main thing in the worship of God is to embrace His promises with obedience. True religion begins with faith.

21. *Being fully assured that, what he had promised, he was able also to perform.* Since all men acknowledge the power of God, Paul seems to say nothing out of the ordinary about Abraham's faith; but experience shows that one of the most difficult attainments is to ascribe to the power of God the honour of which it is worthy. There is no obstacle, however small and insignificant, which does not lead the flesh to suppose that the hand of God is restrained from accomplishing His work. The result is that in the slightest possible trials the promises of God slide away from us. As I have said, it is an undisputed fact that no one denies the omnipotence of God, but as soon as any obstacle is raised to impede the course of His promise, we degrade His power. We ought, therefore, to make the following verdict in making a comparison, in order that the power of God may receive its rightful honour from us—the power of God is as necessary to overcome the obstacles of the world as the strong rays of the sun are to disperse the clouds. We tend always to make the excuse that our frequent doubts about His promises do not detract from His power, because the supposition that God promises more in His Word than He can perform

(which would be wrong, and plainly a blasphemy against God) is by no means the cause of our hesitation, but is the defect which we feel in ourselves. We do not sufficiently exalt the power of God, if we do not consider it greater than our weakness. Faith, therefore, ought not to look to our weakness, misery, and defects, but should fix its whole attention on the power of God alone. If it depended on our righteousness or dignity, it would never reach the consideration of God's power. The proof of unbelief, which he mentioned before, is our measuring of the power of the Lord by our own standard. Faith does not suppose that God can do all things while in the meantime remaining unmoved, but rather locates His power in His continual activity, and applies it in particular to what is effected by His Word. The hand of God, therefore, is always ready to accomplish what He has spoken.

It seems strange to me that Erasmus preferred to regard the relative as masculine. Although the sense is not altered by the different gender, I prefer to come more close to the Greek words used by Paul. The verb, I know, is passive, but a slight change would have lessened the harshness.

22. *Wherefore also it was reckoned unto him for righteousness.* It becomes more clear now why and how his faith brought righteousness to Abraham: it was because he depended on the Word of God, and did not reject the grace which God had promised. This relation between faith and the Word is to be carefully maintained and committed to memory, for faith can bring us no more than it has received from the Word. The man, therefore, who comes to the decision that God is true, having in his mind only a general and confused knowledge of God, will not immediately be righteous, unless He rests secure on the promise of His grace.

Now it was not written for his sake alone, that it was reckoned unto him; but for our sake also, unto whom it shall be reckoned, who believe on him that raiseth Jesus our Lord from the dead, who was delivered up for our trespasses, and was raised for our justification. (23-25)

23. *Now it was not written for his sake alone.* Since, as we have reminded readers above, the proof afforded by an example is not always conclusive, to prevent his statement from being called in question, Paul expressly affirms that in the person of Abraham there had been exhibited an example of a common righteousness which applies equally to all.

We are reminded in this passage of the duty of seeking profit from scriptural examples. The pagan writers have truly said that history is the teacher of life, but there is no one who makes sound progress in it as it is handed down to us by them. Scripture alone lays claim to an office of this kind. In the first place it prescribes general rules by which we may test all other history, so as to make it serve our advantage. In the second place, it clearly distinguishes what actions we ought to follow, and what to avoid. But as far as doctrine is concerned, which is its especial province, it is alone in showing us the providence of God, His righteousness and goodness towards His people, and His judgments against the wicked.

Paul maintains, therefore, that the record of Abraham's life was not written for his own sake alone. It does not refer to the individual calling of one particular person, but is a description of the way to obtain righteousness, which is one and unchanging among all believers. It is this which is exhibited in the father of all the faithful, who ought to command universal regard.

If, therefore, we would make a right and proper use of the sacred histories, we must remember that we ought to use them in such a way as to draw from them the fruit of sound doctrine. They instruct us how to form our life, how to strengthen our faith, and how we are to arouse the fear of the Lord. The example of the saints will be of assistance in the ordering of our lives, if we learn from them sobriety, chastity, love, patience, moderation, contempt of the world, and other virtues. The help of God, which was always available to them, will contribute to the confirmation of our faith, and His protection, and the fatherly care which He exercised over them, will afford us consolation in time of adversity. The judgments of God, and His punishments inflicted on the wicked, will also be of assistance to us, provided they inspire in us the fear which fills our hearts with reverence and devotion.

By stating that it was not *for his sake alone*, he seems to suggest that it was partly written for his sake. For this reason some interpreters understand that what Abraham obtained by faith was recorded to his praise, because the Lord wishes His servants to be had in everlasting remembrance, as Solomon says, 'The memory of the just is blessed' (Prov. 10.7). May we not, however, take the words *not for his sake alone* more simply to mean that it was not on Abraham's account only —as though it were some singular privilege which could not be suitably introduced as an example, but was related to our instruction, since we must be justified in the same way? This would certainly be a more fitting sense.

24. *Who believe on him that raised Jesus our Lord.* I have reminded readers above of the value of these circumlocutions inserted by Paul. He introduces them according to the general context of the passages in order to give us different views of the substance of our faith. The resurrection of Christ is the most important part of this, for it is the

ground of our hope in the life to come. Had he simply said that we believe in God, it would not have been so easy for us to gather how this could serve to obtain righteousness. But when Christ comes forth and offers us a sure pledge of life in His own resurrection, we see clearly from what source the imputation of our righteousness flows.

25. *Who was delivered up for our trespasses.* He pursues and illustrates at greater length the doctrine to which I have just referred. It is of great importance to us not only to have our minds directed to Christ, but also to have a clear picture of how He has attained our salvation. Although Scripture, where it deals with our salvation, dwells on the death of Christ alone, yet on this occasion the apostle goes farther, and as he proposed to give a more explicit account of the cause of our salvation, he enumerates its two parts. He says, firstly, that our sins were expiated by the death of Christ, and, secondly, that our righteousness was obtained by His resurrection. The sum is that when we possess the benefit of Christ's death and resurrection, righteousness is fulfilled in all its parts. There is no doubt that by separating the death of Christ from His resurrection, Paul is accommodating his language to our ignorance, because otherwise it is true that our righteousness has been procured by the obedience of Christ which He displayed in His death, as the apostle will teach us in the following chapter. Since Christ, however, has made known to us how much He had achieved by His death by rising from the dead, this distinction will also teach us that our salvation was begun by the sacrifice by which our sins were expiated, and finally completed by His resurrection. The beginning of righteousness is our reconciliation to God, and its completion is the reign of life when death has been destroyed. Paul, therefore, means that satisfaction for our sins had been accomplished on the cross, for the destruction of our sins by Christ was necessary in order that Christ might restore us to the Father's favour. This could be accomplished only by His suffering in our place the punishment which we were unable to endure. 'The chastisement of our peace', says Isaiah, 'was upon Him' (Isa. 53.5). Paul says that He was *delivered*, rather than that He died, because expiation depends on the eternal goodwill of God, who chose this way of reconciliation.

And was raised for our justification. It would not have been sufficient for Christ to expose Himself to the wrath and judgment of God, and undergo the curse due to our sins, unless He also emerged as victor over the curse, and having been received into the glory of heaven, reconciled God to us by His intercession. The power of justification, therefore, which overcame death is ascribed to His resurrection, not because the sacrifice of the cross, by which we are reconciled to God, has in no way contributed towards our justification, but because the perfection of this grace is revealed more clearly in His new life. I cannot agree with those who refer this second clause to newness of life, for the apostle has not begun to deal with this. It is certain, too, that both clauses have the same point of reference. If, therefore, justification signifies newness of life, then His death for our sins would have meant that He acquired grace for us to mortify the flesh—a sense which no one admits. As, therefore, Paul said that Christ died for our sins, because He delivered us from the calamity of death by suffering death as a punishment for our sins, so now He is said to have been raised for our justification, because He fully restored life to us by His resurrection. He was first struck by the hand of God, so that in the person of a sinner (*in persona peccatoris*) He might sustain the misery of sin, and afterwards was exalted into the kingdom of life, so that He might freely give His people righteousness and life. Paul, therefore, is still speaking of imputed justification. The passage which follows immediately in the next chapter will confirm this.

CHAPTER FIVE

Being therefore justified by faith, let us have peace with God through our Lord Jesus Christ; through whom also we have had our access by faith into this grace wherein we stand; and let us rejoice in hope of the glory of God. (1-2)

1. *Being therefore justified by faith.* The apostle begins to illustrate by their effects his assertions up to this point concerning the righteousness of faith. The whole of this chapter, therefore, consists in amplifying what he has stated. These amplifications, however, not only explain, but also confirm his argument. He had previously maintained that if righteousness is sought by works, faith is abolished, for wretched souls, who have no constancy in themselves, will be troubled by constant unrest. Paul, however, now teaches us that our souls are quietened and pacified when we have obtained justification by faith—we *have peace with God.* This is the particular fruit of the righteousness of faith, and any desire to seek for security of conscience by works (which we see among the irreligious and the ignorant) will be unsuccessful, for the heart is either lulled asleep by disregard or forgetfulness of the judgment of God, or else it is full of fear and trembling until it rests in Christ, who alone is our peace.

Peace, therefore, means serenity of conscience, which originates from the awareness of having God reconciled to oneself. This serenity is possessed neither by the Pharisee, who is inflated by a false confidence in his works, nor by the senseless sinner, who, since he is intoxicated with the pleasure of his vices, feels no lack of peace. Though neither of these seems to be in open conflict with God, unlike the man who is struck with a sense of sin, yet because they do not truly approach the judgment seat of God, they have no experience at all of harmony with him. A dulled conscience implies a departure from God. Peace with God is opposed to the drunken security of the flesh, because the rousing of oneself to give an account of one's way of life is of first importance. No one will stand without fear before God, unless he relies on free reconciliation, for as long as God is judge, all men must be filled with fear and confusion. The strongest proof of this is that our opponents do nothing but idly bandy words when they lay claim to righteousness by works. Paul's conclusion is based on the principle that wretched souls are always uneasy, unless they rest in the grace of Christ.

2. *Through whom also we have had our access by faith into this grace.*

Our reconciliation with God is dependent upon Christ. He alone is the beloved Son, and we are all by nature the children of wrath. But this grace is communicated to us by the Gospel, because it is the ministry of reconciliation. By the benefit of this reconciliation we are brought into the kingdom of God. Paul, therefore, has rightly set before our eyes the sure pledge in Christ of the grace of God, in order to draw us more effectively from confidence in our works. He teaches us by the word *access* that salvation begins with Christ, and thus excludes the preparations by which foolish men imagine that they can anticipate the mercy of God. It is as if he said, 'Christ meets the undeserving, and stretches forth His hand for their deliverance.' He adds immediately afterwards that it is through the continuance of the same grace that our salvation remains firm and secure. By this he means that our perseverance is not founded on our own power or industry, but on Christ. When, however, he says at the same time that we *stand*, he indicates how deeply rooted the Gospel ought to be in the hearts of the godly, so that they may be strengthened by its truth, and stand firm against all the devices of the flesh and the Devil. By this word *stand* he means that faith is not the fleeting persuasion of a day, but is so fixed and deeply submerged in our minds as to continue throughout our life. The man, therefore, whose faith gives him a place among the faithful is not driven to believe by a sudden impulse, but remains in the place divinely appointed for him with such constancy and steadfastness that he never ceases to cleave to Christ.

And let us rejoice in hope of the glory of God. The reason not only for the emergence of the hope of the life to come, but also for our daring to rejoice in it, is that we rest on the sure foundations of the grace of God. Paul's meaning is that, although believers are now pilgrims on earth, yet by their confidence they surmount the heavens, so that they cherish their future inheritance in their bosoms with tranquillity. This passage demolishes the two most troublesome doctrines of the sophists, first, that in which they bid Christians be satisfied with moral conjecture in discerning the grace of God towards them, and second, that in which they teach that we are all in a state of uncertainty concerning our final perseverance. But if there is no certain knowledge for the present, and no constant and unhesitant persuasion for the future, who dare glory? The hope of the glory of God has shone upon us by the Gospel, which testifies that we shall be partakers of the divine nature, for when we shall see God face to face, we shall be like him (II Pet. 1.4; I John 3.2).

And not only so, but let us also rejoice in our tribulations: knowing that tribulation worketh patience; and patience, probation; and probation, hope: and hope putteth not to shame; because the love of God hath been shed abroad in our hearts through the Holy Ghost which was given unto us. (3-5)

3. *And not only so, but let us rejoice.* Paul anticipates any possible sneer that Christians, for all their glorying, are still strangely harassed and distressed in this life, which is a far from blessed condition. He declares that their calamities, so far from impeding their happiness, even promote their glorying. To prove this point he argues from the effects. He employs an admirable climax, in which he finally concludes that all the afflictions which we suffer contribute to our salvation and final good.

His assertion that the saints glory in their tribulations is not to be understood to mean that they did not dread or flee from adversity, or were not sore distressed by its bitterness when it occurred (for no patience would result from their difficulties if they had no feeling of bitterness). They are, however, rightly said to glory, because in their grief and sorrow they are greatly consoled by the thought that all their sufferings are dispensed to their good by the hand of a most indulgent Father. Believers have always sufficient grounds for glorying when their salvation is promoted.

We learn, therefore, from this, what is the purpose of our tribulations, if we would show ourselves to be the sons of God. These should accustom us to patience, and if they do not, our depravity renders the work of the Lord void and ineffectual. His proof that adversity is no obstacle to the glorifying of believers is demonstrated by the fact that they experience the help of God, which nourishes and confirms their hope, by patiently enduring their adversity. It is certain, therefore, that those who do not learn patience do not make good progress. It is no objection to this that Scripture records complaints of the saints which are filled with despair. On occasion the Lord so besets and crushes His people for a time as scarcely to allow them to breathe or recollect their source of consolation; but in a moment He restores to life those whom he had almost submerged in the darkness of death. Thus Paul's affirmation is always fulfilled in them: 'We are pressed on every side, yet not straitened; perplexed, yet not unto despair; pursued, yet not forsaken; smitten down, yet not destroyed' (II Cor. 4.8-9).

Tribulation worketh patience. This is not the natural effect of tribulation, which, as we see, provokes a great part of mankind to murmur against God, and even to curse Him. But when an inner submissiveness, which is infused by the Spirit of God, and the consolation, which is conveyed by the same Spirit, have taken the place of our obstinacy, then the tribulations, which in the stubborn can produce only indignation and discontent, become the means of begetting patience. 4. *And patience, probation.* In a similar climax James seems to follow a different order, for he says that *experience worketh patience.* We shall, however, reconcile the two if we understand that the meaning of the words is different. Paul means by the word *probation* the experience which believers have of the sure protection of God, when, relying on His aid, they overcome all difficulties. Standing firm and patiently enduring, they experience the strength of the power of the Lord which He has promised will always be present among His people. James uses the same word to mean tribulation itself, according to the common usage of Scripture, because by tribulations God proves and tries His servants—hence tribulations are also often called temptations.

According to the present passage, therefore, we make the proper progress in patience when we regard it as having been established for us by the power of God, and thus for the future entertain the hope that we shall never be without the grace of God, which has always succoured us in our necessity. Paul, therefore, adds that hope arises from experience, for we are ungrateful for the benefits which we have received if we do not confirm our hope for the future by calling them to our remembrance.

5. *And hope putteth not to shame.* That is, it regards our salvation as most certain. This clearly shows that affliction is used by the Lord to try us, so that our salvation may thereby be gradually advanced. Those troubles, therefore, which in their own way are the supports of our happiness, cannot distress us. Thus Paul's assertion is proved, that the godly have grounds for glorying in the midst of their afflictions.

Because the love of God hath been shed abroad in our hearts. I do not refer this to the last phrase only, but to the whole of the two preceding verses. We are stimulated to patience by tribulation, and patience is a proof to us of divine help. This further encourages us to hope, for however we may be beset and seem to be worn out, we do not cease to feel the divine kindness towards us. This is the richest consolation, and much more abundant than when all is well with us. Since what appears to be happiness is misery itself when God is hostile to us and displeased with us, so when He is favourably disposed towards us, our very calamities will undoubtedly issue in prosperity and joy. All things must serve the will of the Creator, who, according to His fatherly favour towards us (as Paul again repeats in chapter 8), over-rules all the trials of the cross for our salvation. This knowledge of the divine love towards us is instilled into our hearts by the Spirit of God, for the good things which God has prepared for those who worship Him are hidden from the ears, eyes and minds of men, and the Spirit alone can reveal them. The participle *shed abroad* is very emphatic, and means that the revelation of divine love towards us is so plentiful that it fills our hearts. Being thus shed abroad through every part of us, it not only mitigates our sorrow in adversity, but like a sweet seasoning gives a loveliness to our tribulations.

He says further that the Spirit is *given*, i.e. bestowed on us by the unmotivated goodness of God, and not conferred in return for our merits, as Augustine has noted well. He is, however, mistaken in his interpretation of the love of God. His explanation is that we endure adversity with constancy, and are thus confirmed in our hope, because having been regenerated by the Spirit, we love God. This is a devout sentiment, but not what Paul means. Love is not to be taken here in an active, but in a passive sense. It is certain, too, that what Paul is teaching us is that the true source of all love is the conviction which believers have of the love which God bears them. This is no light persuasion only with which they are tinged, but their minds are thoroughly permeated with it.

For while we were yet weak, in due season Christ died for the ungodly. For scarcely for a righteous man will one die: for peradventure for the good man some one would even dare to die. But God commendeth his own love toward us, in that, while we were yet sinners, Christ died for us. Much more then, being now justified by his blood, shall we be saved from the wrath of God through him. (6-9)

6. *Christ died for the ungodly.* In my translation I have not ventured to allow myself the liberty of rendering this, 'in the time in which we were weak', though I preferred this sense. The present argument proceeds from the greater to the less, and Paul will afterwards pursue it at greater length. Although he has not woven the thread of his discourse too distinctly, the irregularity of its structure will not affect the meaning. 'If Christ', he says, 'had mercy on the ungodly, if He reconciled His enemies to the Father, and accomplished this by virtue of His death, He will now much more easily save them when they are justified, and keep in His grace those whom He has restored to grace, especially since the efficacy of His life is now added to His death.' Some interpreters hold that the time of weakness means the period when Christ first began to be manifested to the world, and they consider that those who were *yet weak* were those who were like children under the tuition of the law. The expression, however, I maintain, relates to every Christian believer, and the time referred to is the period which precedes the reconciliation of each to God. We are all born the children of wrath, and are kept under that curse until we become partakers of Christ. By those who are *weak* he means those who have nothing in themselves but sin, for immediately afterwards he calls them

ungodly. There is nothing unusual in taking weakness in this sense, since in I Cor. 12.22 he calls the less honourable parts of the body *feeble*, and in II Cor. 10.10 he calls his own bodily presence *weak*, because it has no dignity. This meaning will frequently recur a little further on. When, therefore, we were *weak*, i.e. when we were completely unworthy and unfit to be regarded by God, at that very time Christ died for the ungodly. Faith is the beginning of godliness, from which all those for whom Christ died were estranged. This is also true of the fathers of old, who obtained righteousness before the death of Christ, for they derived this benefit from His death which was still to come.

7. *For scarcely for a righteous man will one die.* Reason compels me to expound the particle γάρ in an affirmative or declarative sense, rather than causally, the meaning being, 'It is a very rare occurrence indeed among men that any should die for a righteous man, although this may occasionally happen. But even if we admit that this may happen, none will be found willing to die for the ungodly, as Christ did.' The passage thus employs a comparison to amplify what Christ has done for us, since there does not exist among mankind such an example of kindness as Christ has showed to us.

8. *But God commendeth his own love toward us.* The verb συνίστησι has more than one meaning. The more suitable here is that of confirming. It is not the apostle's object to arouse us to give thanks, but to establish the confidence and security of our souls. God, therefore, *confirms*, i.e. declares His love toward us to be most certain and true, because He did not spare Christ His Son for the sake of the ungodly. Herein is His love manifested, that without being influenced by any love of ours, He first loved us of His own good pleasure, as John tells us (John 3.16). The word *sinners* (as in many other passages) means those who are wholly corrupt and given to sin—see John 9.31, 'God heareth not sinners', i.e. the wicked and the guilty. The woman who was a 'sinner' means the woman who lived a shameful life (Luke 8.37). This appears more clearly from the contrast which immediately follows —*being now justified by his blood*. Since he contrasts these two things, and refers to those who are delivered from the guilt of sin as *justified*, it necessarily follows that *sinners* means those who are condemned for their evil deeds.

The sum of the whole is that if Christ has attained righteousness for sinners by His death, He will now much more protect them from destruction when they are justified. In the last clause he applies the comparison between less and greater to his own doctrine. It would not have been enough for Christ to have once procured salvation for us, were He not to maintain it safe and secure to the end. This is what the apostle now asserts, declaring that we have no need to fear that

Christ will terminate the bestowal of His grace upon us before we have come to our appointed end. Such is our condition since He has reconciled us to the Father, that He purposes to extend His grace to us more effectively, and to increase it day by day.

For if, while we were enemies, we were reconciled to God through the death of his son, much more, being reconciled, shall we be saved by his life. (10)

10. This is an explanation of the previous verse, amplified by making a comparison between Christ's life and His death. We were enemies, he says, when Christ presented Himself to the Father as a means of propitiation. We are now made friends by His reconciliation, and if this was accomplished by His death, His life will have much greater power and efficacy. We have, therefore, ample proof to strengthen our minds with confidence in our salvation. We have been reconciled to God by the death of Christ, Paul holds, because His was an expiatory sacrifice by which the world was reconciled to God, as I have shown in chapter 4.

The apostle, however, seems here to be contradicting himself. If the death of Christ was a pledge of the divine love towards us, it follows that we were even then acceptable to Him. But now he says that we were *enemies*. My answer to this is that because God hates sin, we are also hated by Him in so far as we are sinners. But in so far as He receives us into the body of Christ by His secret counsel, He ceases to hate us. Our return to grace, however, is unknown to us, until we attain it by faith. With regard to ourselves, therefore, we are always enemies, until the death of Christ is interposed to propitiate God. This double aspect ought to be noted. In no other way do we recognise the free mercy of God than if we are persuaded of His refusal to spare His only-begotten Son, because He loved us when there was discord between us and God. Again, we do not sufficiently understand the benefit conferred on us by the death of Christ, unless this is the beginning of our reconciliation to God, so that we are convinced that it is by the expiation that has been made that God, who before was justly hostile to us, is now propitious to us. Thus, since our reception into favour is ascribed to the death of Christ, the meaning is that the guilt, for which we were otherwise punishable, has been taken away.

And not only so, but we also rejoice in God through our Lord Jesus Christ, through whom we have now received the reconciliation. (11)

11. *And not only so.* He now rises to the highest degree of glorying for while we glory that God is ours, every blessing which can be conceived or desired is obtained and flows from this source. God is not only the highest of all our blessings, but also contains in Himself

the sum and all the parts of these blessings, and He is made ours through Christ. By the benefit, therefore, of our faith we have attained the position of lacking nothing that is necessary for our happiness. Paul's repeated advocacy of reconciliation is not without effect. First, we are to learn to fix our eyes on the death of Christ, whenever our salvation is concerned. Second, we are to know that we are to place our confidence in nothing else but the expiation of our sins.

Therefore, as through one man sin entered into the world, and death through sin; and so death passed unto all men, for that all sinned:— for until the law sin was in the world: but sin is not imputed when there is no law. Nevertheless death reigned from Adam until Moses, even over them that had not sinned after the likeness of Adam's transgression, who is a figure of him that was to come. (12-14)

12. *Therefore, as through one man sin entered into the world.* He now begins to enlarge on the same doctrine by a comparison of opposites. If the purpose of Christ's coming was to redeem us from the calamity into which Adam had fallen, and taken all his posterity headlong with him, a clearer realization of what we possess in Christ can come only when we have been shown what we have lost in Adam. The comparison, however, is not similar in all respects. Paul, therefore, makes a correction, which we shall notice at the proper place. We shall also point out any difference which may occur. The incompleteness of the sentence renders it somewhat obscure, since the second clause of the comparison, which balances the first, is not expressed. We shall, however, endeavour to make both plain when we come to the passage concerned.

Sin entered into the world. Note the order which he follows here. He says that sin had preceded, and that death followed from sin. There are some interpreters who maintain that such was our ruin as a result of the sin of Adam, that we perished through no fault of our own, but merely because he had as it were sinned for us. Paul, however, expressly affirms that sin has spread to all who suffer the punishment of sin. He presses the point more closely when he shortly afterwards assigns a reason why all Adam's posterity are subject to the dominion of death. It is because we have all sinned. To *sin,* as the word is used here, is to be corrupt and vitiated. The natural depravity which we bring from our mother's womb, although it does not produce its fruits immediately, is still sin before God, and deserves His punishment. This is what is called original sin. As Adam at his first creation had received for his posterity as well as for himself the gifts of divine grace (*divinae gratiae dotes*), so by falling from the Lord, in himself he corrupted, vitiated, depraved, and ruined our nature—

having lost the image of God (*abdicatus a Dei similitudine*), the only
seed which he could have produced was that which bore resemblance
to himself (*sui simile*). We have, therefore, all sinned, because we are
all imbued with natural corruption, and for this reason are wicked and
perverse. The attempt at one time by the Pelagians to elude Paul's
words by saying that sin descended by imitation from Adam to the
whole human race was a frivolous deceit, because in this case Christ
would be only an example and not the cause of righteousness. Further,
the inference is also plain that Paul is not dealing here with actual sin,
for if every person was responsible for his own guilt, why did Paul
compare Adam with Christ?. It follows, therefore, that the allusion
here is to our innate and hereditary depravity.

For until the law sin was in the world. The parenthesis here anticipates
an objection. Since there does not appear to be transgression without
the law, there might have been some doubt whether sin existed before
the law. Its existence after the law was incontrovertible. The only
question was of the time preceding the law. Paul, therefore, gives the
answer that although God had not by that time passed judgment by a
written law, the human race would still have been under a curse, even
from the womb. Those, therefore, who led a wicked and reprobate
life before the law was promulgated were by no means absolved from
the condemnation of sin, for there was always a God to whom worship
was due, and some rule of righteousness in existence. This interpretation is so plain and clear that it provides a sufficient refutation of any
contrary explanation.

But sin is not imputed when there is no law. We are asleep in our sins
if the law does not reprove us, and even although we are quite aware
of our evil actions, yet we suppress as much as we can the knowledge
of evil which forces itself upon us, or at least we obliterate it by quickly
forgetting it. While the law convicts and reproves us, it arouses us to
return to a consideration of the judgment of God. The apostle, therefore, notes the perversity of men, when not aroused by the law, in
having laid aside to a great degree the distinction between good and
evil, and indulged their lusts without care or disturbance, as if there
were no judgment of God. The punishment of Cain, the deluge which
destroyed the whole world, the downfall of Sodom, and the punishment inflicted on Pharaoh and Abimelech on account of Abraham, and
finally, the plagues brought upon the Egyptians, testify that God has
laid men's iniquities to their charge. The many complaints and
expostulations with which men accuse one another of iniquity, and on
the other hand the apologies by which they carefully exculpate their
conduct, prove also that they have accused one another of wrong.
There are many examples to prove that all men have been conscious

both of good and evil. For the most part, however, they connived at their own evil deeds, so as to impute no sin to themselves, unless forced to do so. When, therefore, Paul asserts that sin is not imputed without the law, he is speaking comparatively, because when men are not goaded to action by the law, they sink into indolence.

Paul has wisely introduced this sentence, in order that the Jews might learn more clearly from it the gravity of their offence in being openly condemned by the law. If those whom God has never cited as guilty before His tribunal were not immune from punishment, what will become of the Jews, to whom the law, like a herald, proclaims their guilt—indeed threatens judgment? We may offer another reason too why Paul expressly states that sin has reigned before the law without having been imputed. He does so in order that we may know that the cause of death does not proceed from the law, but is only demonstrated by it. He declares, therefore, that all men were miserably lost immediately after the fall of Adam, although their destruction was finally revealed by the law. It will suit the context better to translate the adversative δέ by 'although'. The meaning will be that although men may indulge themselves, they cannot escape the judgment of God even while the law does not convict them.

14. *Death reigned from Adam until Moses.* Paul explains more clearly that the heedless and abandoned life which men led from Adam to the time when the law was promulgated was of no avail to them. The distinction between good and evil had been dismissed, and therefore without the warning of the law the recollection of sin was buried, because sin still prevailed to condemn them. Death, therefore, reigned also then, because the judgment of God could not be destroyed by men's blindness and hardness of heart.

Even over them that had not sinned. This passage is generally understood of little children, who, without being guilty of any actual transgression, die through original sin. I prefer, however, to interpret it generally as referring to all those who sinned without the law. This verse is to be connected with the preceding words, in which it was stated that those who had no law did not impute sin to one another. They did not, therefore, sin *after the likeness of Adam's transgression,* because they did not have the will of God made known to them by a sure revelation as he had. The Lord had forbidden Adam to touch the fruit of the tree of the knowledge of good and evil. To them, however, the only command which He had given was the testimony of conscience. The apostle, therefore, wanted to imply that this difference between Adam and his posterity could not exempt them from condemnation. Infants are also in the meantime included in the universal catalogue.

Who is a figure of him that was to come. This sentence is put in place of a second clause. Only one part of the comparison is expressed; the other is omitted by anacoluthon, the meaning therefore being, 'As by one man sin entered into the whole world, and death by sin, so by one man righteousness returned, and life by righteousness.' Paul's assertion that Adam was a type of Christ need not surprise us, for some resemblance is always apparent, even in complete opposites. Since, therefore, we are all lost through Adam's sin, and restored through the righteousness of Christ, Adam is not improperly called a type of Christ. We should note, however, that Adam is not called the type of sin, nor Christ the type of righteousness, as if they preceded us only by their example. The two are rather contrasted, and we should note this, in order to avoid falling into the misunderstanding, and indeed the fatal error, of Origen, who theorizes on the corruption of mankind in non-Christian philosophical terms, and not merely weakens but almost entirely destroys the grace of Christ. Erasmus is even less to be forgiven, since he goes to such lengths in excusing so gross a misunderstanding.

> *But not as the trespass, so also is the free gift. For if by the trespass of the one the many died, much more did the grace of God, and the gift by the grace of the one man, Jesus Christ, abound unto the many.* (15)

15. *But not as the trespass.* There now follow the corrections of the comparison which he has introduced above. The apostle, however, does not so minutely discuss the points of difference between Christ and Adam, as oppose the errors into which his readers might otherwise easily fall. We shall add what he omits to say in his explanation. Although he frequently mentions the difference between Adam and Christ, all his repeated statements lack a balancing clause, or at least are elliptical. These, it is true, are faults in his language, but in no way do they detract from the majesty of that heavenly wisdom which is delivered to us by the apostle. On the contrary, the singular providence of God has passed on to us these profound mysteries in the garb of a poor style, so that our faith might not depend on the power of human eloquence, but on the efficacy of the Spirit alone.

He does not as yet expressly state the reason for the correction which he makes, but simply informs us that the grace acquired by Christ belongs to a greater number than the condemnation contracted by the first man. I do not know whether all my readers will agree with those who think that Paul is here merely debating a point. We may quite appropriately infer that if the fall of Adam had the effect of producing the ruin of many, the grace of God is much more efficacious in benefiting many, since it is granted that Christ is much more powerful to save than Adam was to destroy. But since the argument of those who do not want to accept the passage in this sense cannot be disproved, I leave it to my readers to choose whichever of the two interpretations they prefer. The passage which follows cannot be reckoned as a logical inference, nevertheless it follows the same argument. It is probable, therefore, that Paul is simply connecting or modifying by the exception which he makes the statements which he had made concerning the resemblance between Christ and Adam.

We should note, however, that Paul does not here contrast the larger number with the many, for he is not speaking of the great number of mankind, but he argues that since the sin of Adam has destroyed many, the righteousness of Christ will be no less effective for the salvation of many.

In saying that *by the trespass of the one the many died*, he means that corruption has descended from him to us. It is not his fault that we perish, as though we ourselves were not to be blamed; but Paul ascribes our ruin to Adam, because his sin is the cause of our sin. By our sin I mean that which is natural and innate in us.

The grace of God, and the gift by the grace. Grace is properly opposed to offence, and the gift which proceeds from grace to death. Grace, therefore, means the pure goodness of God, or His unmerited love, of which He has given us a proof in Christ, in order to relieve our misery. The *gift* is the fruit of this mercy which has come to us, viz. the reconciliation by which we have obtained life and salvation. It is also righteousness, newness of life, and every other similar blessing. This clearly reveals the absurd definition of grace given by the schoolmen, who would have it merely a quality infused into the hearts of men. Grace, properly speaking, is in God, and it is the effect of grace which is in us. Paul says that it was by *the one*, because the Father has made Him the fountain out of whose fulness all may draw. He thus teaches us that not even a drop of life can be found beyond Christ, nor is there any other remedy for our poverty and want than that which He conveys to us from His own abundance.

And not as through one that sinned, so is the gift: for the judgment came of one unto condemnation, but the free gift came of many trespasses unto justification. (16)

16. This is the particular reason for his correction of the comparison between Adam and Christ—guilt prevailed from one offence to our universal condemnation, but grace, or rather the free gift, is efficacious to justify us from our many offences. This is an explanation of the preceding sentence, because He had not yet expressed how or in what respect Christ surpasses Adam. If we admit this distinction between

Christ and Adam, it will be seen that those who have taught that what
we recover in Christ is merely freedom from original sin, or the corruption contracted from Adam, have held blasphemous views. Note,
too, that the numerous offences, from which he affirms that we are
cleansed by the benefits of Christ, are to be understood not only of
the transgressions which each one of us has committed before baptism,
but also of the sins by which the saints daily contract new guilt, and
which would deservedly subject them to condemnation, did this grace
not afford them constant relief.

In contrasting *gift* with *judgment*, Paul means by the latter strict
justice, and by the former free pardon, for condemnation comes from
strict justice, but absolution from pardon. To put it in a different way,
if God deals with us according to justice, we are all lost. But He
justifies us freely in Christ.

For if, by the trespass of the one, death reigned through the one; much
more shall they that receive the abundance of grace and of the gift of
righteousness reign in life through the one, even Jesus Christ. (17)

17. *For if, by the trespass of the one.* Paul again corrects in general the
comparison which he had made, and dwells still further on it. It was
not at all his purpose to follow out every particular subject, but to
determine the main points. He had stated before that the power of
grace had been more abundant than the power of sin, and on this basis
he consoles and confirms believers, and, at the same time, stimulates
and encourages them to ponder over the kindliness of God. His
intention in this earnest repetition is that men may worthily proclaim
the grace of God, and be led from self-confidence to trust in Christ,
so that when we have obtained His grace, we may enjoy full assurance.
This ultimately is the source of our gratitude. The meaning of the
whole passage is that since Christ surpasses Adam, the sin of Adam is
overcome by the righteousness of Christ. The curse of Adam is over-
turned by the grace of Christ, and the life which Christ bestows
swallows up the death which came from Adam. The parts of this
comparison, however, do not correspond. Paul ought to have said
that the blessing of life reigns and flourishes more and more through
the abundance of grace, instead of which he says that believers 'shall
reign'. The sense is the same, however, for the kingdom of believers
is in life, and the kingdom of life is in believers.

Worth noticing here also are the two differences between Christ and
Adam which the apostle omitted, not because he thought they were
of no importance, but because it had no connexion with his present
argument to enumerate them.

The first difference is that we are condemned by Adam's sin not by imputation alone, as though we were being punished for another's sin; but we suffer his punishment because we too are guilty, since God holds our nature, which has been corrupted in Adam, guilty of iniquity. But the righteousness of Christ restores us by a different means to salvation. We are not accounted righteous because we have righteousness within us, but because we possess Christ Himself with all His blessings, given to us by the Father's bounty. The gift of righteousness, therefore, does not signify a quality with which God endows us, for this is a misinterpretation, but is the free imputation of righteousness. The apostle is expounding his interpretation of the word *grace*.

The second difference is that Christ's benefit does not come to all men in the manner in which Adam involved his whole race in condemnation. The reason for this is quite obvious. Since the curse, which we derive from Adam, is conveyed to us by nature, we need not be surprised that it includes the whole of mankind. In order, however, that we may participate in the grace of Christ, we must be ingrafted into Him by faith. The mere fact of being a man, therefore, is enough to entail participation in the wretched inheritance of sin, for it dwells in human flesh and blood. It is necessary, however, to be a believer in order to enjoy the righteousness of Christ, for we attain to fellowship (*consortium*) with Him by faith. Fellowship with Christ is communicated to infants in a peculiar way. They have the right of adoption in the covenant, by which they come into communion with Christ (*in Christi communionem*). I am referring to the children of the godly, to whom the promise of grace is directed. The others are by no means exempted from the common lot.

So then as through one trespass the judgment came *unto all men to condemnation; even so through one act of righteousness* the free gift came *unto all men to justification of life.* (18)

18. *So then as through one trespass.* The sentence is defective, but will be completed by reading the words *condemnation* and *justification* in the nominative case. We must do this to complete the sense. The verse is also the general conclusion of the preceding comparison, for Paul omits to mention the correction which he had inserted, and now completes the comparison. 'As by the offence of one man we were made sinners, so the righteousness of Christ is efficacious to justify us.' He does not, however, say that Christ's righteousness, δικαιοσύνη, is thus efficacious, but His justification, δικαίωμα. Christ, Paul reminds us, was not privately righteous on His own account, but the righteousness with which He was endowed was more extensive, in order that He might enrich believers with the gift conferred upon Himself. Paul makes grace common to all men, not because it in fact extends to all,

but because it is offered to all. Although Christ suffered for the sins of
the world, and is offered by the goodness of God without distinction
to all men, yet not all receive Him.

The two words which he has just used, *judgment* and *grace*, might
also be repeated in this form—'As by the judgment of God the sin of
one man issued in the condemnation of many, so grace will be efficacious for the justification of many.' In my judgment *justification of life*
means absolution, which restores life to us, or is 'life-giving'. Our
hope of salvation is God's being propitious towards us, and we cannot
be accepted by Him unless we are righteous. Life has therefore its
origin in justification.

For as through the one man's disobedience the many were made sinners,
even so through the obedience of the one shall the many be made righteous.
(19)

19. This is not a tautology, but a necessary explanation of the previous verse. Paul shows that the offence of the one man is such as to
render us guilty ourselves. He had previously said that we are condemned, but to prevent anyone from laying claim to innocence, he
desired also to add that everyone is condemned, because he is a sinner.
When he afterwards states that we are made righteous by the obedience
of Christ, we deduce from this that Christ, in satisfying the Father,
has procured righteousness for us. It follows from this that righteousness exists in Christ as a property, but that that which belongs properly
to Christ is imputed to us. At the same time he explains the character
of the righteousness of Christ by referring to it as *obedience*. Let us note
here what we are required to bring into the presence of God, if we wish
to be justified by works, viz. obedience to the law, and not a partial
obedience, but absolute obedience in every respect. If a righteous man
has fallen, none of his former righteousness is remembered. We are
also to learn from this the falsity of the self-conceived schemes which
men thrust upon God for the purpose of satisfying His justice. Only
when we follow what God has commanded us do we truly worship
Him, and render obedience to His Word. Let us, therefore, have
nothing to do with those who confidently lay claim to the righteousness of works, which can exist only when there is full and complete
observance of the law. This, it is certain, nowhere exists. We similarly
deduce that those who boast before God of works of their own invention, which He regards as being no better than dung, are out of
their minds, for obedience is better than sacrifice.

And the law came in beside, that the trespass might abound; but where
sin abounded, grace did abound more exceedingly: that, as sin reigned

in death, even so might grace reign through righteousness unto eternal life through Jesus Christ our Lord. (20-21)

20. *And the law came in beside.* What he states here is dependent on his previous observation that sin existed before the law was published. When this point had been established, the question which immediately followed was, 'For what purpose was the law given?' It was necessary, therefore, to solve this difficulty also. But since he had no opportunity on that occasion of a longer digression, he deferred consideration of it to the present passage. He now shows in passing that the law entered in order that sin might abound. He is not here describing the whole use and office of the law, but is dealing only with the one part which served his present purpose. In order to set forth the grace of God, he tells us that it was necessary that men's destruction should be more clearly revealed to them. Men were indeed shipwrecked before the law was given, but since they seemed to be surviving, even in their destruction, they were submerged into the deep, in order that their deliverance might appear more remarkable when, contrary to human expectation, they emerge from the floods which overwhelm them. It was not unreasonable that the law should in part be given for the very reason that it might again condemn men who had once already been condemned. We are quite justified in using any means to bring men, and indeed to force them when they have been proved guilty, to have a sense of their own wickedness.

That the trespass might abound. The general method of interpreting this passage since the time of Augustine is well known. When lust is checked by the restraints of the law, it is all the more stimulated. It is a natural tendency in man to strive for that which is forbidden. The increase here referred to I take simply to be that of knowledge and obstinacy, for sin is placed before men's eyes by the law, so that they may constantly be compelled to see that condemnation is laid up in store for them. Thus sin, which men would otherwise cast behind them, takes possession of their conscience. Now that the law has been given, and the will of God, which is wantonly tramped under foot, is made known, those who before simply transgressed the bounds of justice come to despise the divine authority. It follows from this that sin is increased by the law, because the authority of the Lawgiver is then despised and His majesty degraded.

Grace did abound more exceedingly. Grace came to the help of mankind after sin had overwhelmed them and held them in its power. Paul teaches us that the extent of grace is more strikingly revealed because it is poured out in so copious a flood while sin abounds as not only to overcome the flood of sin, but even to swallow it up. From this we may learn that our condemnation is not set before us in the law for the purpose of making us continue in it, but to acquaint us intimately with our misery, and lead us to Christ, who is sent to be a physician to the sick, a deliverer to the captives, a comforter to the afflicted, and a defender to the oppressed (Isa. 61.1).

21. *That, as sin reigned in death, even so might grace reign through righteousness.* As sin is said to be the sting of death, because death has no power over men except on account of sin, so sin executes its power by death. It is therefore said to exercise its dominion by death. In the last clause the order of the words is confused, but not unintentionally. If Paul had said 'in order that righteousness may reign by Christ', his contrast would have been straightforward. He was not, however, content to compare opposites, and adds the word *grace*, so that he might more deeply imprint on our memory the truth that the whole of our righteousness does not proceed from our own merit, but from the divine kindness. He had previously said that death itself had reigned. He now ascribes the idea of reigning to sin. But the end or effect of sin is death. He states that it *reigned*, in the past tense, not because it has ceased to reign in those who are born only of flesh, but he distinguishes between Adam and Christ in such a way as to assign to each his proper time. As soon, therefore, as grace of Christ begins to prevail in individuals, the reign of sin and death ceases.

CHAPTER SIX

What shall we say then? Shall we continue in sin, that grace may abound? God forbid. We who died to sin, how shall we any longer live therein? (1-2)

1. *What shall we say then?* Throughout this chapter the apostle maintains that those who imagine that Christ bestows free justification upon us without imparting newness of life shamefully rend Christ asunder. He goes further, however, and proposes the objection that if men continued in sin this would seem to provide an opportunity for grace to be displayed. We know how inclined the flesh is to use any excuse for self-indulgence. Satan, too, so readily devises all kinds of slander by which to discredit the doctrine of grace. We ought not to be astonished if, when the flesh has heard of justification by faith, it strikes so often against different obstacles, since every truth that is preached of Christ is quite paradoxical to human judgment. We must, however, continue in our course. Christ is not to be suppressed because to many He is a stone of offence and a rock of stumbling. As He will prove to be the destruction of the ungodly, He will likewise be resurrection for the godly. We must, however, always meet unreasonable questions, lest Christian doctrine should appear to involve any absurdity.

The apostle now pursues the objection which is most commonly laid against the preaching of divine grace. This is that if it is true that the grace of God will assist us more liberally and abundantly in proportion as we are overwhelmed with a greater burden of sin, nothing is better for us than to provoke the wrath of God by being submerged in the depths of sin, and by frequent perpetration of new offences, for only then shall we experience more abounding grace, which is the greatest benefit we can desire. We shall see later how we are to refute this misconception.

2. *God forbid.* Some interpreters hold that the apostle's only desire was to reprove indignantly such an unreasoning and foolish attitude. Other passages, however, prove how frequently he made this answer even in the course of a lengthy argument. Here too he will shortly disprove with a great deal of care the slander against his doctrine of grace. In the first place, however, he rejects it by an indignant negative, in order to warn his readers that there is no greater contradiction than to nourish our vices by the grace of Christ, which is the means of restoring our righteousness.

We who have died to sin. He now argues from the opposite side. He who sins, lives to sin. We are dead to sin by the grace of Christ. Therefore it is false to maintain that that which abolishes sin gives it strength. The truth is rather that believers are never reconciled to God without the gift of regeneration. Indeed, we are justified for this very purpose, that we may afterwards worship God in purity of life. Christ washes us by His blood, and renders God propitious to us by His expiation, by making us partakers of His Spirit, who renews us to a holy life. It would, therefore, be a most absurd inversion of the work of God if sin were to acquire strength by means of the grace which is offered to us in Christ. Medicine does not foster the disease which it destroys. We ought further to bear in mind the point to which I have already referred, that Paul is not here dealing with the state in which God finds us when He calls us into fellowship with His Son, but the state in which we ought to be when He has shown mercy to us, and freely adopted us. By using an adverb to denote future time, Paul shows the kind of change which ought to follow justification.

Or are ye ignorant that all we who were baptized into Christ Jesus were baptized into his death? We were buried therefore with him through baptism into death: that like as Christ was raised from the dead through the glory of the Father, so we also might walk in newness of life. (3-4)

3. *Or are ye ignorant?* Paul proves his previous assertion that Christ destroys sin in His people from the effect of baptism, by which we are initiated into faith in Him. It is beyond question that we put on Christ in baptism, and that we are baptized on this principle that we may be one with Him. Paul now assumes a second principle. We truly grow up into the body of Christ (*in Christi corpus vere coalescere*) only when His death produces its fruit in us. Indeed, he teaches us that this fellowship of His death is the focal centre of baptism. It is not a washing alone, but also the mortification and putting to death of the old man, which is there set forth. It is evident from this that the efficacy of Christ's death appears from the moment when we are received into His grace. The efficacy of this fellowship of the death of Christ is described forthwith.

4. *We were buried therefore with him.* He now begins to show what is meant by our baptism into the death of Christ, though he does not yet give a full explanation. Baptism means that being dead to ourselves, we may become new creatures. Paul rightly passes from the fellowship of Christ's death to the sharing of His life. Because these two are inseparably connected, our old man is destroyed by the death of Christ, so that His resurrection may restore our righteousness, and make us new creatures. And since Christ has been given to us for life,

why should we die with Him, if not to rise again to a better life? Christ, therefore, puts to death what is mortal in us in order that He may truly restore us to life.

Let us notice, moreover, that the apostle does not simply exhort us here to imitate Christ, as though he had said that the death of Christ is an example which it is appropriate for all Christians to follow. Without doubt he has something higher in mind. What he does is to propound a doctrine which he will later use as a basis for exhortation. His doctrine, as we may clearly see, is that the death of Christ is efficacious to destroy and overthrow the depravity of our flesh, and His resurrection to renew a better nature within us. It also states that by baptism we are admitted into participation in this grace. Having laid this fundamental proposition, Paul may very properly exhort Christians to strive to live in a manner that corresponds to their calling. It is irrelevant to argue that this power is not apparent in all the baptized, for Paul, because he is speaking to believers, connects the reality and the effect with the outward sign (*substantiam et effectum externo signo coniungit*) in his usual manner. We know that whatever the Lord offers by the visible symbol is confirmed and ratified by their faith. In short, he teaches us what the truth of baptism is, when rightly received. Thus he testifies that all the Galatians who had been baptized into Christ had put on Christ (Gal. 3.27). We must always use these terms while the institution of the Lord and the faith of believers correspond, for we never have naked and empty symbols (*nuda et inania symbola*), except when our ingratitude and wickedness hinder the working of the divine beneficence.

Through the glory of the Father. That is, by the splendid power by which He declared Himself truly glorious, and displayed the magnificence of His glory. Thus in Scripture the power of God, which was operative in the resurrection of Christ, is often set forth in elevated terms, and with good reason. It is of great importance that we should extol, by explicit mention of the incomparable power of God, not only our faith in the last resurrection, which far surpasses the perception of the flesh, but also the other benefits which we receive from the resurrection of Christ.

> *For if we have become united with him by the likeness of his death, we shall also by the likeness of his resurrection; knowing this, that our old man was crucified with him, that the body of sin might be done away, that so we should no longer be in bondage to sin. (5-6)*

5. *For if we have become united.* Paul confirms the argument which he had previously given by using plainer expressions. The comparison which he introduces removes all ambiguity, since our ingrafting

signifies not only our conformity to the example of Christ, but also the secret union (*arcanam coniunctionem*) by which we grow together with Him, in such a way that He revives us by His Spirit, and transfers His power to us. Therefore, as the graft has the same life or death as the tree into which it is ingrafted, so it is reasonable that we should be as much partakers of the life as of the death of Christ. If we are ingrafted into the likeness (*in similitudinem*) of Christ's death, and His death is inseparable from His resurrection, our death will therefore be followed by our resurrection. But the words can be interpreted in two ways—either that we are ingrafted into Christ into the likeness of His death, or that we are simply ingrafted into His likeness. The first reading would require that the Greek dative ὁμοιώματι should refer to the means of our ingrafting. I do not deny that this has a deeper sense, but since the other meaning is more appropriate to the simplicity of the expression, I have preferred to use it. It makes little difference, however, since both amount to the same thing. Chrysostom holds that by the expression 'likeness of death' Paul means 'death', as elsewhere by 'being made in the likeness of men' (Phil. 2.7) he means 'being made man'. It seems to me, however, that there is greater significance than this in the expression. Besides referring to *resurrection*, it seems to imply that we do not die a natural death like Christ, but that there is this similarity between our death and His—as Christ died in the flesh which He had assumed from us, so we die in ourselves, that we may live in Him. Our death, therefore, is not the same as Christ's but is similar to it, for we are to notice the analogy (*analogia*) between the death of this present life and our spiritual renewal.

Become united (*insiticii facti*). This word has great emphasis, and clearly shows that the apostle is not exhorting us, but rather teaching us about the benefit which we derive from Christ. He does not require from us any duty which our care or diligence can achieve, but speaks of the ingrafting which is accomplished by the hand of God. There is no reason for studiously applying the metaphor or comparison in every particular, for the disparity between the grafting of trees and our spiritual ingrafting will at once be evident. In the grafting of trees the graft draws its nourishment from the root, but retains its own natural quality in the fruit which is eaten. In spiritual ingrafting, however, we not only derive the strength and sap of the life which flows from Christ, but we also pass from our own nature into His. The apostle desired to point quite simply to the efficacy of the death of Christ, which manifested itself in putting to death our flesh, and also the efficacy of His resurrection in renewing within us the better nature of the Spirit.

6. *Knowing this, that our old man was crucified with him.* The 'old' man

is called old as the 'Old' Testament is called old in reference to the New. He begins to be old when his regeneration is begun, and his old nature is gradually put to death. Paul is referring to our whole nature which we bring from the womb, and which is so incapable of receiving the kingdom of God that it must die in the same proportion as we are renewed into true life. This 'old man', he says, is fastened to the cross of Christ, for by its power he is slain. Paul referred explicitly to the cross in order to show more distinctly that the only source of our mortification is our participation in the death of Christ. I do not agree with those interpreters who explain that Paul used the word *crucified* rather than *dead*, because our old man is still alive, and in some measure flourishing. The interpretation is quite correct, but hardly relevant to the present passage. The *body of sin*, which he mentions a little later, does not mean flesh and bones, but the whole mass of sin, for man, when left to his own nature, is a mass of sin. The expression *that so we should no longer be in bondage to sin* points to the purpose of its destruction. It follows that as long as we are children of Adam and no more than men, we are so completely held in bondage to sin that we can do nothing but sin. But when we are ingrafted into Christ, we are delivered from this miserable constraint, not because we at once cease to sin altogether, but in order that we may finally become victorious in the conflict.

For he that hath died is justified from sin. But if we died with Christ, we believe that we shall also live with him; knowing that Christ being raised from the dead dieth no more; death no more hath dominion over him. For the death that he died, he died unto sin once: but the life that he liveth, he liveth unto God. Even so reckon ye also yourselves to be dead unto sin, but alive unto God in Christ Jesus. (7-11)

7. *For he that hath died is justified.* The argument is derived from the inherent nature or effect of death. If death destroys all the actions of life, we who have died to sin ought to cease from those actions which it exercised during the continuance of its life. *Justified* means freed or reclaimed from bondage. Just as the prisoner who is absolved by the sentence of the judge is freed from the bond of his accusation, so death, by releasing us from this life, sets us free from all its responsibilities.

Furthermore, although such an example is nowhere to be found among men, there is no reason for regarding this statement as an empty speculation, or for despairing because we do not find ourselves among the number of those who have wholly crucified the flesh. This work of God is not completed on the day when it is begun in us, but gradually increases, and by daily advancement is brought by degrees to its completion. We may summarize Paul's teaching in the following way:

'If you are a Christian, you must show in yourself a sign of your communion in the death of Christ (*communionis cum morte Christi*), and the fruit of this is that your flesh will be crucified together with all its desires. Do not assume, however, that this communion is not a real one if you find traces of the flesh still existing in you. But you are continually to study to increase your communion in the death of Christ, until you arrive at the goal.' It is well with the believer if his flesh is continually mortified, and it is no small attainment when the Holy Spirit has taken control of the realm which has been wrested from the flesh. There is another fellowship (*communicatio*) in the death of Christ of which the apostle often speaks, as in II Cor. 4, viz. the bearing of the cross, which is followed by our participation (*consortium*) in eternal life.

8. *But if we died with Christ, we believe that we shall also live with him.* His sole purpose in repeating this statement is to add the declaration which afterwards follows, that *Christ being raised from the dead dieth no more.* He wishes to teach us by this the duty laid on Christians of pursuing this new way of life as long as they live. If they ought to represent in themselves the image of Christ, both by mortifying the flesh and by the life of the Spirit, the mortifying of the flesh must be done once and for ever, while the life of the Spirit must never cease. This is not, as we have already stated, because our flesh is mortified in us in a single moment, but because we must not shrink from putting it to death. If we return to our own filthiness, we deny Christ, for we can have communion with Him only by newness of life, even as He Himself lives an incorruptible life.

9. *Death no more hath dominion over him.* Paul seems to imply that death had once enjoyed dominion over Christ. And indeed when He gave Himself up to death for us, in some measure He surrendered and subjected Himself to its power, on this condition, however, that it was not possible that He should be held bound by its pains, or yield to it, or be overcome by it. By submitting, therefore, to its dominion for a moment, He destroyed it for ever. To speak, however, in more simple terms, the *dominion* of death refers to the voluntary condition of Christ's death, which was terminated by His resurrection. The meaning is that Christ, who now gives life to believers by His Spirit, or breathes His own life into them by His secret power from heaven, was freed from the dominion of death when He arose from the dead, in order to deliver all His people from the same dominion.

10. *He died unto sin once.* Paul had stated that after the example of Christ we have for ever been freed from the yoke of death. He now applies this statement to his declaration that we are no longer subject to the tyranny of sin. He proves this from the final cause of Christ's death, for Christ died in order that He might destroy sin. We must

also note the reference to Christ in this form of expression. He is not stated to have died to sin for the purpose of ceasing to commit sin—as we must say in our own case—but because He died on account of sin, so that, by constituting Himself a ransom (ἀντίλυτρον), He might annihilate its power and authority. The apostle says that Christ died *once* (Heb. 10.14), not only because He has sanctified believers for ever by the eternal redemption which He procured by His one oblation and the cleansing of sin accomplished by His blood, but also for the purpose of establishing a common likeness between ourselves and the Redeemer (*ut in nobis quoque mutua similitudo respondeat*). Although spiritual death makes continual headway within us, yet we are properly said to die once, when Christ reconciles us by His blood to the Father, and regenerates us also at the same time by the power of His Spirit.

But the life that he liveth, he liveth unto God. It is the same sense whether we read *with God* or *in God*. Paul is showing that Christ is living in the immortal and incorruptible kingdom of God a life now subject to no mortality. A type of this immortal life should appear in the regeneration of the godly. We must keep in mind here the word *likeness.* Paul does not say that we shall live in heaven, as Christ does, but he makes the new life, which we live on earth after our regeneration, match (*conformem*) His life in heaven. His statement that we are *to die unto sin* after the example of Christ does not mean that our death may be said to be the same as His, for we die to sin when sin dies in us. In Christ's case it was different, for it was by dying that He destroyed sin. Paul had previously stated that we believe that we shall share the life of Christ. The word *believe* clearly shows that He is speaking of the grace of Christ. Had he only been warning us of our duty, he would have spoken as follows: 'Since we are dead with Christ, we ought likewise to live with Him.' The word *believe* denotes that Paul is here dealing with the doctrine of faith, which is founded on the promises, as if he had said, 'Believers should have the assurance that their mortification in the flesh through the benefit of Christ is such that the same Christ will maintain their newness of life to the end.' The future tense of the verb *to live* does not refer to the last resurrection, but simply denotes the continuing course of our new life in Christ, as long as we are pilgrims on the earth.

11. *Even so reckon ye also yourselves to be dead unto sin.* Paul now adds the definition of his analogy (*analogiae definitio*), to which I have referred. He applies to us his two statements concerning Christ dying once to sin and living for ever to God, and instructs us how we may now die while we live, viz. by renouncing sin. He does not, however, omit the other part of the analogy, i.e. how we are to live when we

have once embraced the grace of Christ by faith. Although the mortification of our flesh is only beginning in us, yet the life of sin is destroyed by this very means, so that our spiritual newness, which is divine, may afterwards continue for ever. If Christ did not put sin finally to death in us, His grace would be lacking in stability and permanence.

The meaning, therefore, of the passage is this: 'This is the view you are to take of your case—as Christ died once to destroy sin, so you have died once in order that in future you may cease from sin. Indeed, you must make daily progress in the mortification of your flesh which has been begun in you, until sin is wholly destroyed. As Christ was raised to an incorruptible life, so you are regenerated by the grace of God, in order that you may lead the whole of your life in holiness and righteousness, since the power of the Holy Spirit, by which you have been renewed, is eternal, and will flourish for ever.' I prefer, however, to retain Paul's words *in Christ Jesus,* rather than to render with Erasmus *by Christ Jesus,* because this conveys more clearly the ingrafting by which we are made one with Christ.

Let not sin therefore reign in your mortal body, that ye should obey the lusts thereof: neither present your members unto sin as instruments of unrighteousness; but present yourselves unto God, as alive from the dead, and your members as instruments of righteousness unto God.

(12-13)

12. *Let not sin therefore reign.* He now begins his exhortation, which is a natural consequence of the doctrine which he had delivered concerning our fellowship with Christ. Though sin resides in us, it is ridiculous that it should have the power to exercise dominion over us, for the power of sanctification ought to be superior to it, so that our life may testify that we are truly members of Christ.

The word *body,* as I have already maintained, is not to be taken in the sense of flesh, skin, and bones, but for the whole body of man's existence. We may quite certainly infer this from the present passage, for the other clause, which he will shortly add concerning the parts of the body, extends also to the soul. Paul thus refers disparagingly to earthly man, for the corruption of our nature prevents our aspiring to anything worthy of our origin. Thus also in Gen. 6.3, God, while He complains that man, like the brute animals, has become flesh, leaves him nothing but an earthly nature. The affirmation of Christ that what is born of the flesh is flesh (John 3.6) conveys the same idea. The objection that there is a difference in the case of the soul is easily answered by the assertion that in our present degenerate state our souls are fixed to the earth, and so enslaved to our bodies that they have fallen from their proper excellence. In a word the nature of man is termed corporeal, because he has been deprived of heavenly grace (*privatus coelesti gratia*), and is only a kind of deceptive shadow or image (*fallax tantum umbra vel imago*). There is the additional fact that this body is contemptuously referred to by Paul as *mortal*, for the purpose of teaching us that the whole of human nature is liable to death and destruction. He now gives the name of sin to that original depravity which dwells in our hearts, and which impels us to sin, and from which properly all our evil deeds and wickedness flow. Paul sets lust between sin and ourselves, so that sin, as it were, lords it over us, while our inordinate desires are sin's edicts and commands.

13. *Neither present your members unto sin.* When sin has once acquired dominion in our mind, all our faculties are immediately applied to its service. Paul, therefore, here describes the reign of sin by its consequences, in order to point out more clearly what course we must follow if we would cast off its yoke. In referring to our members as *instruments*, Paul is using a military metaphor, as if he were saying that as a soldier has his arms always in readiness, in order that he may use them whenever he is ordered by his general, but never uses them unless commanded to do so, so Christians ought to regard all their members as the weapons of spiritual warfare. If, therefore, they prevent the proper use of any of their members, they are serving sin. But they have sworn an oath of service to God and Christ, and by this they are bound. They are, therefore, under obligation to refrain from all dealings with the camps of sin. Let those whose members are all in readiness to commit every kind of abomination, as though they were the prostitutes of Satan, consider here by what right they lay claim to the name of Christian.

Against this, Paul now bids us give ourselves wholly to God, so that we may restrain our hearts and minds from straying where the lusts of the flesh may draw us. We are to look to the will of God alone, eager to receive His commands, and prepared to obey His orders. Our members, too, are to be dedicated and consecrated to His will, so that all our powers of soul and body may aspire to His glory alone. The reason for this is that, since our former life has been destroyed, the Lord has not in vain created us for another, to which our actions ought to correspond.

For sin shall not have dominion over you: for ye are not under the law, but under grace. What then? shall we sin, because we are not under law, but under grace? God forbid. Know ye not, that to whom ye present yourselves as servants unto obedience, his servants ye are whom ye obey; whether of sin unto death, or of obedience unto righteousness?

But thanks be to God, that, whereas ye were servants of sin, ye became obedient from the heart to that form of teaching whereunto ye were delivered; and being made free from sin, ye became servants of righteousness. (14-18)

14. *For sin shall not have dominion over you.* It is not necessary to spend long in repeating and refuting interpretations which have little or no appearance of truth. There is, however, one interpretation which can be maintained with greater probability than the rest. *Under the law* is taken to mean *being subject to the letter of the law,* which does not renew the mind, while *under grace,* on the other hand, implies freedom from corrupt desires by the Spirit of grace. I am not, however, altogether in favour of this interpretation, for if we adopt this sense, what is the object of the question which follows—'Shall we sin, because we are not under law?' The apostle would never have put such a question if he had not understood that we are freed from the rigour of the law, so that God no longer deals with us according to the high demands of justice. It is, therefore, beyond question that he intended here to indicate some deliverance from the bondage of the very law of the Lord. I will briefly explain my view without entering into controversy.

In the first place, we have here, I think, an encouragement for the comfort of believers, lest they should fail in their attempts to attain to holiness through a sense of their own weakness. He had exhorted them to apply all their powers in obedience to righteousness, but since they carry about the remains of the flesh, they cannot do other than walk with uncertainty. Lest, therefore, they should lose spirit from realizing their own weakness and become despondent, he takes the opportunity of giving them new heart from the comforting thought that their works are not now exacted according to the strict rule of the law, but that God forgives their impurity and accepts them with kindness and indulgence. The yoke of the law cannot be borne without breaking and crushing those who carry it. It remains, therefore, for believers to flee to Christ and implore His help as the defender of their liberty; for such is His character. Christ submitted Himself to the bondage of the law, although He was not otherwise a debtor to its demands, in order that, in the words of the apostle, He might redeem those who were under the law (Gal. 4.5).

Not to be *under law,* therefore, means that it is a dead letter which condemns us, because we have not the power to perform it. It also means that we are no longer subject to the law in so far as it requires of us perfect righteousness, and pronounces death on all who have transgressed any part of it. Likewise, by the word *grace* we understand both parts of redemption, i.e. the forgiveness of sins, by which God imputes righteousness to us, and the sanctification of the Spirit, by whom He forms us anew to good works. The adversative particle, in my opinion, is causal, as is often the case, and means, 'Because we are under grace, we are not, therefore, under the law.' The meaning will now be quite clear. The apostle is desirous of comforting us and preventing us from growing wearied in striving to do what is right, because we still feel many imperfections in ourselves. However much the stings of sin may torment us, they cannot subdue us, for we are enabled to conquer them by the Spirit of God. Since we are under grace, too, we are freed from the strict demand of the law. We are to understand here, moreover, that the apostle takes it for granted that all those who are without the grace of God are bound by the yoke of the law, and held under its condemnation. So, on the other hand, we may argue that as long as men are under the law, they are subject to the dominion of sin.

15. *What then? shall we sin?* Because the wisdom of the flesh is always exclaiming against the mysteries of God, Paul had to add this statement in order to counter a possible objection. Since the law is the rule of good living, and has been given to govern men, we hold that if it is broken all discipline at once falls to the ground, the restraints are shattered, and ultimately no difference or distinction between good and evil is left. But our misconception here consists in our supposing that the righteousness which God approves in His law is abolished when the law is abrogated. This abrogation, however, does not at all apply to the precepts which teach us the right way to live, for Christ confirms and sanctions these, and does not abrogate them. The proper solution to the objection is that the only part of the law which is removed is the curse, to which all men who are beyond the grace of Christ are subject. Although Paul does not expressly state this, he hints at it.

16. *God forbid. Know ye not.* This is not the bare denial it has been supposed to be, as if Paul preferred to express his abhorrence of such a question rather than to disprove it, since he proceeds immediately to refute the objection from the nature of the contrast which he is making, almost in the following sense: 'There is such a great difference between the yoke of Christ and that of sin, that no one can bear them simultaneously. If we sin, we give ourselves up to the service of sin. Believers, on the other hand, have been redeemed from the tyranny of sin in order to serve Christ. It is, therefore, impossible for them to remain bound to sin.' It will be better to examine more closely the order taken by Paul in pursuing his argument.

Whom ye obey. The relative *whom* may here be taken, as it often is, in a causal sense. Thus one might say, 'There is no kind of wickedness which the parricide, *who* has not shrunk from committing the worst of all crimes, an act from which even wild beasts would shrink, will not do.' Paul draws his argument partly from the effects and partly from the nature of the correlatives. In the first place, their obedience is an indication to Paul that they are *servants*, since obedience proves that power to command belongs to the one who thus forces others into subjection to himself. The argument here is taken from the effect of slavery. A second truth follows from this: if we are slaves, then sin has dominion over us.

Or of obedience unto righteousness. The phraseology is not strictly correct. If Paul had wanted to balance the parts of the sentence, he should have said, *or of righteousness unto life*. Since, however, the change in the words does not alter the sense of the passage, he preferred to express the nature of righteousness by the word *obedience*. This, however, by metonymy, denotes the commandments of God themselves. His use of the word without any addition indicates that it is God alone who has authority over the consciences of men. Although God's name is not mentioned, obedience is nevertheless referred to God, since it cannot be a divided obedience.

17. *But thanks be to God.* Paul applies his comparison to the case before him. Although the only truth of which his readers needed to be reminded was that they were no longer the servants of sin, he adds a thanksgiving. He does so for the purpose, first, of teaching them that their deliverance from sin was not attributable to their own merit, but to the singular mercy of God. At the same time, however, their very thanksgiving should teach them how great God's goodness is. This, therefore, should arouse them more vigorously to a hatred of sin. Paul's giving of thanks is on account of their deliverance from sin, which followed when they ceased to be what they were before, and has no reference to the period in which they were the servants of sin. This implied comparison between their former and their present state is emphatic. The apostle attacks those who slander the grace of Christ, showing that when grace ceases to abound, the whole human race is held captive under the dominion of sin, but that the kingdom of sin comes to an end as soon as grace puts forth its power.

We may deduce from this that we are not freed from the bondage of the law in order to sin, since the law does not lose its dominion until the grace of God claims us for Him, in order to renew righteousness in us. It is impossible, therefore, for us to be subject to sin when the grace of God reigns within us. As we have stated above, the spirit of regeneration is included in this word *grace*.

Ye became obedient from the heart. Paul compares here also the hidden power of the Spirit with the external letter of the law, as though he said, 'Christ forms our hearts inwardly in a better way than the compulsion of the law, with its threats and terrors.' This destroys the calumny of those who hold that if Christ frees us from the subjection of the law, He brings us liberty to sin. Christ, however, does not deliver His followers to unbridled lasciviousness, so that they may prance about without restraint, like horses let loose in the fields, but conducts them to a lawful manner of life. Erasmus, following the Vulgate, has chosen to translate this as *form*, but I feel compelled to retain the word *type*, the word which Paul uses. The word *pattern* may, perhaps, be preferred, for I think that Paul is referring to the express image of the righteousness which Christ engraves on our hearts. This corresponds to the prescribed rule of the law, according to which all our actions are to be formed, so that they may not turn aside to the right or to the left.

18. *And being made free from sin.* The meaning is that it is absurd for anyone to continue in bondage after he has gained his freedom. He ought to maintain the state of freedom which he has received. It is not fitting, therefore, for believers to be brought again under the dominion of sin, from which they have been set at liberty by Christ. The argument here is derived from the efficient cause, and the argument which follows is derived from the final cause: 'You have been liberated from the bondage of sin, in order that you may pass into the kingdom of righteousness. It is fitting, therefore, that you should wholly forget sin, and turn your whole heart to righteousness, into the service of which you have been brought.'

It is to be noted that no one can serve righteousness, unless he has first been liberated by the power and kindness of God from the tyranny of sin, as Christ Himself testifies, 'If the Son shall make you free, ye shall be free indeed' (John 8.36). If the beginning of goodness depends on the act of deliverance which the grace of God alone effects, how shall we prepare ourselves to receive that grace by the power of our free will?

I speak after the manner of men because of the infirmity of your flesh: for as ye presented your members as servants to uncleanness and to iniquity unto iniquity, even so now present your members as servants to righteousness unto sanctification. (19)

19. *I speak after the manner of men.* He states that he is speaking after the manner of men as far as form, but not substance, is concerned. Thus, too, Christ in John 3.12 says that He was telling of earthly things, while speaking of heavenly mysteries. He did not do so, however, with such sublimity as the dignity of His theme required, because He accommodated Himself to the capacity of an ignorant and simple people. The apostle speaks thus by way of preface, the better to prove

the gross and evil character of the slander which imagines that the liberty obtained by Christ gives licence to sin. At the same time also He admonishes believers that there is no greater absurdity, and, indeed, no greater dishonour or shame than that the spiritual grace of Christ should have less influence over them than earthly freedom. 'By comparing sin and righteousness', he is saying, 'I could show how much greater should be the enthusiasm which you display in being drawn into the service of righteousness than you showed in your obedience to sin. But I omit such a comparison, so as to make allowance for your weakness. In order, however, that I may treat you with the greatest indulgence, I may surely make this just demand of you—at least you should not practise righteousness in a colder or more careless way than you have served sin.' Paul avoids here having to state his full meaning, as when one desires more to be understood than the words express. He exhorts them, however, even though his words do not appear to require so much, to obey righteousness with the greater care, since it is more worthy of being served than sin.

As ye presented your members. That is, the readiness with which all your faculties before obeyed sin clearly proved in how pitiful a condition the depravity of your flesh held you in enslavement and bondage. Be now, therefore, no less eager and ready in performing the commandments of God, and do not let your activity in doing good be less now than once it was in sinning. Paul does not, as in I Thess. 4.7, observe the same order in the antithesis in contrasting uncleanness with holiness, yet his meaning is quite clear.

In the first place there are, he maintains, two kinds of sin—uncleanness and iniquity. Of these, the former is contrasted with chastity and holiness, while the latter refers to injuries inflicted on our neighbour. He also repeats the word *iniquity* twice, in a different sense. In the first instance it means plunder, frauds, perjury, and wrongs of every kind, in the second, universal corruption of life. It is as if he had said, 'You have prostituted your members in committing works of wickedness, so as to make the kingdom of iniquity prevail in you.' By *righteousness* I understand the law and the rule of righteous living, the purpose of which is sanctification, so that believers may consecrate themselves in purity to the service of God.

For when ye were servants of sin, ye were free in regard of righteousness. What fruit then had ye at that time in the things whereof ye are now ashamed? for the end of those things is death. But now being made free from sin, and become servants to God, ye have your fruit unto sanctification, and the end eternal life. For the wages of sin is death; but the free gift of God is eternal life in Christ Jesus our Lord. (20-23)

20. *For when ye were servants of sin.* Paul repeats the distinction between the yoke of sin and of righteousness which he had mentioned before. Sin and righteousness are so opposed to one another that anyone who devotes himself to the one must leave the other. Paul compares the two so that, in examining them separately, we may see more clearly what is to be expected from each. A comparison throws more light on our consideration of the nature of any subject which we may be discussing. Paul, therefore, balances sin and righteousness against one another. Having made this distinction, he then shows what we may expect to follow from each.

Let us remember, therefore, that the apostle is still arguing from opposites. 'While you were the servants of sin, you were cut off from righteousness. Now, however, the situation is reversed, and it is your duty to serve righteousness, because you have been delivered from the yoke of sin.' By *free in regard of righteousness* he means those who are not forced by the restraints of obedience to serve righteousness. The liberty of the flesh, on the other hand, frees us from obedience to God, only to put us in bondage to the devil. It is, therefore, a despicable and accursed liberty, which triumphs in our destruction with unrestrained, or rather frenzied, violence.

21. *What fruit then had ye?* Paul could express his meaning with greater force only by appealing to their consciences, and by confessing the shame which they felt as it were in their own person. As soon as the godly begin to be enlightened by the Spirit of Christ and the preaching of the Gospel, they freely acknowledge that the whole of their past life, which they lived without Christ, is worthy of condemnation. So far from trying to excuse it, they are in fact ashamed of themselves. Indeed, they go farther, and continually bear their disgrace in mind, so that the shame of it may make them more truly and willingly humble before God.

The words, *whereof ye are now ashamed,* are important. How blind is the self-love which afflicts us when we are so wrapped in the darkness of our sins that we do not consider the extent of the uncleanness which is in us! The light of the Lord alone can open our eyes to behold the foulness which lies concealed in our flesh. Only those, therefore, who have learned well to be earnestly dissatisfied with themselves, and to be confounded with shame at their wretchedness, are imbued with the principles of Christian philosophy. Paul finally shows even more plainly from what follows how much believers ought to be ashamed when they understand that they had been close to destruction, and on the very edge of death. Indeed, they would already have entered the gates of death, had they not been drawn back by the mercy of God.

22. *Ye have your fruit unto sanctification.* Paul has before said that sin

has two consequences. So too, he now states, has righteousness. Sin, in this life, brings the torments of an evil conscience, and after this life eternal death. From righteousness we gather the fruit which it bears in this life, viz. sanctification. For the future, we hope for eternal life. This, unless we are immeasurably stupid, ought to create in our minds a hatred and horror of sin, and a love of and a desire for righteousness. Some render τέλος as 'tribute', but I do not think that this is Paul's meaning. Although it is true that death is the punishment which we bear on account of sin, the word 'tribute' will not suit the other clause to which Paul has applied it, for he does not go on to say that life is the tribute of righteousness.

23. *For the wages of sin is death.* Some interpreters hold that in comparing death to the rations allotted to soldiers, Paul is referring bitingly to the unpleasant nature of the wages which are paid to sinners, for the Greek word is sometimes taken in the sense of military rations. He seems, however, rather to be making an oblique reference to the blind appetites of those who are lured to their destruction by the enticements of sin, like fish by the hook. It will, however, be more simple to render the word 'wages', for death, surely, is a sufficiently ample reward for the wicked. This verse is a conclusion to the previous one, and, as it were, an epilogue to it. Paul does not, however, repeat the same idea in different words in vain, for he intended to make sin more detestable by doubling its terror.

But the free gift of God is eternal life. It is wrong to render this statement, *eternal life is the gift of God*, as though righteousness were the subject, and the gift of God the predicate. This sense does not preserve the contrast. Sin, as Paul has already taught us, produces only death. He now adds that this gift of God, viz. our justification and sanctification, brings us the blessedness of eternal life. We may, however, express it in this way: 'As the cause of death is sin, so righteousness, which is Christ's gift to us, restores eternal life to us.'

In the meantime, however, we may deduce from this with utter certainty that our salvation is wholly of the grace and pure kindness of God. Paul could have stated alternatively that the wages of righteousness is eternal life, thus balancing the two clauses, but he saw that it is through the gift of God that we obtain life, and not by our own merits. This gift, too, is not a single, unaccompanied gift, for since we are clothed with the righteousness of the Son, we are reconciled to God, and renewed by the power of the Spirit to holiness. He has added, therefore, *in Christ Jesus*, to call us away from any conceit about our own dignity.

CHAPTER SEVEN

Or are ye ignorant, brethren (for I speak to men that know the law), how that the law hath dominion over a man for so long time as he liveth? For the woman that hath a husband is bound by law to the husband while he liveth; but if the husband die, she is discharged from the law of the husband. So then if, while the husband liveth, she be joined to another man, she shall be called an adulteress: but if the husband die, she is free from the law, so that she is no adulteress, though she be joined to another man. Wherefore, my brethren, ye also were made dead to the law through the body of Christ; that ye should be joined to another, even to him who was raised from the dead, that we might bring forth fruit unto God. (1-4)

Although Paul had given an adequate, if brief, explanation concerning the abrogation of the law, the question was a difficult one, and might have given rise to many others. He now considers, therefore, at greater length in what way the law is abrogated with regard to us. He then shows how greatly we may benefit from this, for while the law holds us in bondage apart from Christ, it can only condemn us. To prevent anyone, therefore, from accusing the law on this account, he takes up and refutes the objections of the flesh in this notable passage, in which he well expresses the use of the law.

1. *Or are ye ignorant, brethren?* Paul's general proposition is that the law was given to men in order to govern this present life. It has no longer any place after death. To this he will afterwards add the hypothesis that we are dead to the law in the body of Christ. Some interpreters understand that the dominion of the law continues to bind us for as long as its use is in force. This view, however, is rather obscure, and does not harmonize so well with the proposition which comes immediately next. I prefer, therefore, to follow those who regard the statement as referring to the life of man, and not to the existence of the law. Paul's question is more emphatic in affirming the certainty of his subject. It shows that it was not new or unknown to any of them, but was acknowledged equally by all.

(*For I speak to men that know the law.*) This parenthesis has the same reference as his proposition. He knew that they were not so inexperienced in the law as to have any doubts on the subject in question. Although the proposition and the parenthesis might both be understood of all laws, it is better to take them as referring to the law of God, which is the subject now under discussion.

It is childish to suggest that Paul is ascribing knowledge of the law to the Romans, because a large part of the world was under their rule and government. He is partly addressing the Jews or other strangers, and partly the common people and those in obscurity. Indeed, he is thinking particularly of the Jews, for he was involved in a dispute with them about the abrogation of the law. To prevent them, therefore, from supposing that he was dealing captiously with them, he shows that he was taking a common and universally known principle, which was quite familiar to those who had been brought up from their childhood in the teaching of the law.

2. *For the woman that hath a husband.* Paul's metaphor proves that we are freed from the law, in such a way that it no longer properly and by its own right retains any of its power over us. He could have proved this point in other ways, but since the example of marriage was very well suited to illustrate his subject, he introduced this metaphor instead of offering evidence to confirm his point. Readers may feel bewildered because the different parts of the sentence which are compared with each other do not altogether correspond. We should remember, however, that the apostle deliberately intended to avoid the rudeness of a stronger expression by making a minor change. To preserve the order of the metaphor he ought to have said that a woman after the death of her husband is freed from the bond of marriage. The law, which takes the place of a husband to us, is dead to us. We are, therefore, free from its power. Had Paul said that the law was dead, he might have offended the Jews by the harshness of his language. To prevent this offence, therefore, he turned his expression and said that *we are dead to the law.* Some scholars think that Paul is arguing from the less to the greater. I fear, however, that this interpretation is too forced, and so prefer the former, which is simpler. The whole argument, therefore, goes in this way—A woman is subject to her husband by the law while he is alive, so that she cannot become the wife of another. After the death of her husband, however, she is freed from the bond of the law, so that she may freely marry whom she pleases. The application of this then follows:

The law was our 'husband', under whose yoke we were held, until it became dead to us.

After the death of the law Christ took us to Himself, i.e. He freed us from the law and joined us to Himself.

Being, therefore, united to Christ who has been raised from the dead, we ought to cleave to Him alone.

And as the life of Christ is eternal after His resurrection, so hereafter we shall never be divorced from Him.

The word *law*, moreover, is not used here everywhere in the same

sense. In one place it means the mutual right of wedlock, in another
the authority of a husband to whom the wife is subject, and in another
the teaching of Moses. We must keep in mind that Paul is referring
here only to that part of the law which is proper to the ministry of
Moses. We must never imagine that the law is in any way abrogated
in regard to the Ten Commandments, in which God has taught us
what is right and has ordered our life, because the will of God must
stand for ever. The release here mentioned, we must carefully notice,
is not from the righteousness which is taught in the law, but from the
rigid demands of the law and from the curse which follows from its
demands. What is abrogated, therefore, is not the rule of good living
which the law prescribes, but that quality which is opposed to the
liberty which we have obtained through Christ, viz. the demand for
absolute perfection. Because we do not display this perfection it binds
us under the guilt of eternal death. Paul, however, had no wish to
determine here the true character of marriage rights, and so he was not
concerned to review the causes which make a woman free from her
husband. It would be wrong, therefore, to look for any sure doctrine
from this source.

4. *Through the body of Christ.* In the first place, Christ raised the
standard of His cross, and triumphed over sin. To do this, however, it
was necessary that the handwriting which held us bound should be
cancelled. This handwriting is the law, which, while it retains its
force, makes us debtors to sin. It is for this reason called the power of
sin. By the cancelling of this handwriting, therefore, we are delivered
in the body of Christ, even while it is fixed to the cross. The apostle,
however, goes farther and says that the bond of the law had been
destroyed, but not so that we may live according to our own will, like
a widow who lives as she pleases while she is unmarried. We have
now been bound to another husband. We have passed from one hand
to another, from the law to Christ. Paul, however, softens the harshness of the expression by saying that Christ has delivered us from the
yoke of the law, in order to ingraft us into His own body. Although
He subjected Himself voluntarily for a time to the law, it was not right
that the law should have dominion over Him. He conveys to His own
members also the liberty which is proper to Himself. We need not,
therefore, be surprised if He exempts from the yoke of the law those
whom He unites to Himself by a sacred bond (*sacro nexu*), in order that
they may become one body with Him.

Even to him who was raised. We have already said that Christ is put
in place of the law, so that no one should conceive of any freedom
apart from Him, or dare to effect a divorce from the law, if he is not
already dead to himself. Paul, however, has employed this paraphrase

to denote the eternity of that life which Christ has attained by His resurrection, in order that Christians may know that this union with Christ is to be perpetual. The spiritual marriage between Christ and His Church is more clearly described in Eph. 6.

That we might bring forth fruit to God. Paul always adds the final cause, lest anyone should use the pretext that Christ has delivered us from the bondage of the law as a licence for indulging the flesh and its lusts. Christ has offered us, together with Himself, as a sacrifice to the Father, and He regenerates us in order that we may bring forth fruit to God by the newness of our life. The fruits which our heavenly Father requires from us, as we know, are holiness and righteousness. If, however, we are servants of God, this does not detract from our liberty. Indeed, if we want to enjoy the great benefit which is to be found in Christ, our sole duty hereafter will be to consider how we are to promote the glory of God, for the sake of which Christ has taken us to Himself. Otherwise, we remain the bond-slaves not only of the law, but also of sin and death.

For when we were in the flesh, the sinful passions, which were through the law, wrought in our members to bring forth fruit unto death. But now we have been discharged from the law, having died to that wherein we were holden; so that we serve in the newness of the spirit, and not in oldness of the letter. (5-6)

5. *For when we were in the flesh.* Paul shows by contrast still more clearly how wrong the zealots of the law are to keep believers under its power. As long as the literal teaching of the law rules and is in force without connexion with the Spirit of Christ, the lust of the flesh is not restrained, but rather increases. It follows from this that the kingdom of righteousness is established only when Christ emancipates us from the law. At the same time Paul reminds us of the works which it becomes us to practise, when we are delivered from the law. As long, therefore, as a man is kept under the yoke of the law, he can procure nothing for himself but death by his constant sinning. If bondage to the law produces only sin, then freedom, the opposite of bondage, must tend to righteousness. If the former leads to death, then the latter leads to life. But let us consider the actual words of Paul.

In describing our condition during the time when we were subject to the dominion of the law, he states that we were *in the flesh.* We understand from this that the only benefit obtained by all those who are under the law is that their ears hear its external sound, but it does not produce any fruit or effect, since they are inwardly destitute of the Spirit of God. They must, therefore, remain altogether sinful and perverse, until a better remedy comes to heal their disease. Note, too, the common scriptural expression, *to be in the flesh*, which means to be endowed with the gifts of nature alone, without that peculiar grace with which God favours His chosen people. If this state of life is wholly sinful, it is evident that no part of our soul is pure by nature, and that the only power which our free will has is to send forth evil affections like darts into every part.

The sinful passions, which were through the law. That is, the law excited evil affections in us, which produced their effect in every part of us. There was no part which was not in bondage to our evil affections. The work of the law, in the absence of the Spirit, our inward Teacher (*interior Magister*), is to inflame our hearts still more, so that they burst forth into such lustful desires. It should be noted that Paul here compares the law with the corrupt nature of man, whose perversity and lust break forth with greater fury, the more they are held back by the restraints of righteousness. He adds again that as long as our carnal affections held sway under the law, they brought forth fruit to death. Paul thus proves that by itself the law was destructive. It follows that those who so greatly desire the bondage which issues in death are utter fools.

6. *But now we have been discharged from the law.* He pursues his argument from opposites. If the restraint of the law had so little effect in restraining the flesh that it aroused us rather to sin, then we must be loosed from the law, in order that we may cease to sin. If we are freed from the bondage of the law in order that we may serve God, those who derive their licence to sin from this fact are wrong, and those who teach us that in this way free rein is given to lust are also wrong. Note, therefore, that we are delivered from the law, when God looses us from its rigid demands and its curse, and endues us with His Spirit, in order that we may walk in His ways.

Having died to that wherein we were holden. This part is explanatory, or rather suggests how we have been made free. The law, as far as we are concerned, is abrogated, so that we are not oppressed with its intolerable burden, and do not find its inexorable rigour overwhelming us with its curse.

In newness of the spirit. Paul contrasts *spirit* and *letter*. Before our will has been formed according to the will of God by the Holy Spirit, we have nothing in the law but the outward letter. This, it is true, bridles our external actions, but it does not in the least restrain the fury of our lust. He ascribes our *newness* to the Spirit, because it succeeds the *old* man, just as the letter is called old, because it dies when it is renewed by the Spirit.

What shall we say then? Is the law sin? God forbid. Howbeit, I had

not known sin, except through the law: for I had not known coveting,
except the law had said, Thou shalt not covet: but sin, finding occasion,
wrought in me through the commandment all manner of coveting. (7-8)

7. *What shall we say then?* Since it was said that we must be freed
from the law, in order that we may serve God in newness of Spirit, the
fault of impelling us to sin, it seemed, was inherent in the law. But
since that would be absurd beyond measure, the apostle rightly undertook to disprove it. When he asks, *Is the law sin?*, he means, 'Does it
beget sin in such a way that the blame for sin is to be imputed to
the law?'

Howbeit, I had not known sin, except through the law. Sin, therefore,
dwells in us, and not in the law. Its cause is the corrupt desire of our
flesh, and we come to know it by our knowledge of the righteousness
of God which is declared to us in the law. We are not to understand
that there was no distinction at all between right and wrong without
the law, but that without the law we are either too dull to discern our
own depravity, or else we are made entirely devoid of sense through
self-flattery.

For I had not known coveting. This, then, is an explanation of the
previous sentence in which he shows that ignorance of sin, of which
he had spoken, consisted in the failure to perceive one's own lust. Paul
deliberately dwells on the one kind of sin, in which hypocrisy is
especially dominant, and which is always connected with weak self-
indulgence and false confidence. Men are never so deprived of judgment that they lose the distinction between external works. Indeed,
they are even compelled to condemn wicked counsels and similar
devices. This, however, they cannot do without bestowing due praise
on an upright mind. The sin of concupiscence is more secret and
deeply hidden. This is why men never take account of it, as long as
they judge according to their own feelings. Paul does not boast that
he had been free from concupiscence. He was not, however, so self-
indulgent as not to suppose that this sin was lurking in his heart.
Although he was deceived for a time, since he did not believe that his
righteousness was hindered by his concupiscence, yet he finally perceived that he was a sinner, when he saw that concupiscence, from
which no human being is free, was prohibited by the law.

Augustine says that Paul included the whole of the law in this
expression. This, if rightly understood, is true. When Moses shows
us what actions we must avoid to prevent doing wrong to our neighbour, he adds this prohibition concerning concupiscence which we are
to refer to all his prohibitions. It is quite certain that in the preceding
commandments Moses had condemned all the corrupt affections which

our hearts conceive. There is, however, a great difference between a deliberate purpose and the yearnings by which we are tempted. God, therefore, in this last commandment demands from us such integrity that no corrupt lust should move us to evil, however much we may withhold our consent. It was for this reason that I said that Paul's thought here goes beyond the capacity of ordinary men to understand. Civil laws avowedly punish intentions (*consilia*) and not events. Philosophers with greater refinement locate both vices and virtues in the mind (*in animo*). God, however, in this precept goes to the heart of our concupiscence, which, because it is more concealed than the will, is not reckoned as a vice. Not only was it pardoned by the philosophers, but at the present time the Papists fiercely maintain that in the regenerate it is not a sin. Paul, however, says that he had found the source of his sin in this hidden disease. It follows from this that those who are burdened by it have no excuse at all, except in so far as God pardons their fault. We are to observe in the meantime a distinction between depraved lusts which secure our consent, and concupiscence which tempts and affects our hearts in such a way that it stops in the midst of urging us to sin.

8. *But sin, finding occasion, wrought in me all manner of coveting.* All evil therefore proceeds from sin and the corruption of the flesh. The law is only the occasion of evil. Paul may seem to be speaking only of the excitement by which the law arouses our covetousness to burst into greater madness. I refer what he is saying, however, to the knowledge of sin which the law conveys, as if he had said, 'The law has revealed in me all my concupiscence which, while it lay concealed, seemed somehow not to exist.' I do not, however, deny that the flesh is more keenly stimulated to concupiscence by the law, and in this way also manifests itself. This may also have been the case with Paul. And yet I think that what I have said about the manifestation of sin suits the context better, for Paul immediately adds,

For apart from the law sin is dead. And I was alive apart from the law once: but when the commandment came, sin revived, and I died; and the commandment, which was unto life, this I found to be unto death: for sin, finding occasion, through the commandment beguiled me, and through it slew me. So that the law is holy, and the commandment holy, and righteous, and good. (8-12)

8. *For apart from the law sin is dead.* Paul expresses in the clearest terms the meaning of his words above. It is as if he had said that without the law the knowledge of sin is buried. This is a general observation to which he presently applies his own example. I wonder, therefore, what translators have meant by putting the passage in the

imperfect tense, as if Paul was speaking of himself. It is apparent that his purpose was to begin with a universal proposition, and afterwards to explain the subject by his own example.

9. *And I was alive.* Paul's intention is to imply that there had been a time when sin was dead to himself or in himself. We are not to understand that he had been at any time without the law. This phrase, *I was alive,* however, has a peculiar connotation. It was the absence of the law that was the reason for his being alive, that is, why, although he was inflated by confidence in his own righteousness, he claimed to have life when he was really dead. The sentence will be clearer if we state it thus, 'When at one time I was without the law, I was alive.' I have said that this expression is emphatic, for by feigning that he was righteous, he was also claiming to be alive. The meaning, therefore, is this: When I sinned by laying aside the knowledge of the law, my sin, which I failed to observe, was so lulled to sleep that it seemed to be almost dead. On the other hand, because I did not consider that I was a sinner, I was satisfied with myself, supposing that I had life.' The death of sin is the life of man, and again, the life of sin is the death of man.

The question is, when did Paul claim to be alive through his ignorance or (as he himself says) in the absence of the law? He had, it is certain, been instructed in the doctrine of the law from his childhood. That, however, was the 'theology of the letter', which does not humble its disciples. As he says elsewhere, a veil was interposed to prevent the Jews from seeing the light of life in the law (II Cor. 3.14). So too, in his own case, as long as his eyes were veiled while he lacked the Spirit of Christ, he was satisfied with the outward mask (*larva*) of righteousness. He refers, therefore, to the law as absent because, although it was before his eyes, it did not impress on him a serious sense of the judgment of the Lord. Thus the eyes of hypocrites are covered with a veil which prevents them from seeing how much is demanded of us by the precept which forbids us to covet.

But when the commandment came. Paul now refers to the law as *coming* on the other hand, when it has begun to be truly understood. It therefore 'awoke' sin from the dead, because it showed Paul how great was the depravity which abounded in the innermost parts of his heart, and at the same time it put him to death. Let us always remember that Paul is speaking of the intoxicating confidence in which hypocrites repose, while they flatter themselves because they take no notice of their sins.

This I found to be unto death. Paul states two things here: (1) The commandment shows us the way of life in the righteousness of God, and was given in order that we might obtain eternal life by observing the law of the Lord, unless prevented by the corruption which is in all of us. (2) None of us, however, obeys the law; rather, we plunge head over heels into the course of life from which the law recalls us. The law, therefore, can bring us nothing but death. We need to make this distinction between the nature of the law and our own wickedness. It follows from this that it is an accident that the law inflicts a mortal wound on us, just as if an incurable disease were rendered more acute by a healing remedy. The accident, I admit, is inseparable from the law, and for this reason the law, as compared with the Gospel, is elsewhere referred to as 'the ministration of death'. The point, however, holds good, that the law is not injurious to us by its own nature, but because our corruption provokes and draws upon us its curse.

11. *Sin, finding occasion, beguiled me.* It is true, even though the will of God is concealed from us and no doctrine lightens our path, that the whole of human life goes astray and abounds in error. Indeed, we are incapable of doing anything but err, until the law shows us the way of right living. But Paul is right in saying that we are led astray when sin is uncovered by the law, because only when the Lord has openly convicted us do we begin to be conscious of our error. The verb ἐξαπατᾷν, therefore, is to be understood not of the law itself, but of our knowledge of the law, because it reveals to us how much we have departed from the right course. We should, therefore, have translated the verb by *to lead out of the way*, for it is from the law that sinners, who previously went on their way without heed, learn to be disgusted at and dissatisfied with themselves, while seeing, when the law revealed the foulness of sin, that they had been hastening towards death. Paul again introduces the word *occasion*, so that we may know that the law does not of itself bring death, but that its connexion with death is adventitious and contigent upon other factors.

12. *So that the law is holy.* Some interpreters think that there is a duplication in the words *law* and *commandment*. I agree with them, for the purpose of showing that the words are emphatic. The law itself, and all that is commanded in the law, is *holy* in every way, and is therefore to be regarded with the highest honour. It is *just*, and cannot therefore have any unrighteousness laid to its charge. And it is *good*, and therefore pure and free from every fault. Paul thus defends the law against every accusation, to prevent anyone from daring to ascribe to it anything that is contrary to goodness, righteousness and holiness.

Did then that which is good become death unto me? God forbid. But sin, that it might be shewn to be sin, by working death to me through that which is good;—that through the commandment sin might become exceeding sinful. (13)

13. *Did then that which is good become death?* Paul has hitherto defended the law from all misrepresentations, but in such a manner that there still remained some doubt whether it was the cause of death. The human mind is perplexed by the problem of how it can be that the singular benefit of God brings us nothing but destruction. Paul, therefore, now answers this objection by denying that death arises from the law, although it is brought upon us by sin through the occasion of the law. This answer seems to contradict his previous statement that he had found that the commandment, which had been given for life, led to death. There is, however, no contradiction. In the former passage Paul meant that our depravity is the cause of our misusing the law to our destruction, in opposition to the nature of the law. But here he denies that the law is the material cause of death, so that death should be imputed to it. Paul speaks more freely of the law in II Cor. 3.7, where he calls it 'the dispensation of death'. He does so, however, in accordance with the usual practice in a matter of dispute, for he is not considering the nature of the law, but the false opinion of his opponents.

But sin. Without wishing to join issue with others, I am of the opinion that the passage should be read as I have rendered it. Accordingly the meaning is, 'Before it is uncovered by the law, sin is in some measure justified. When, however, it is revealed by the occasion of the law, then it truly is designated sin, and it appears the more wicked and "sinful", if I may use the expression, because it turns the universal goodness of the law to our destruction. Anything which renders harmful that which is otherwise healthful by nature must be very deadly.' The meaning is that it was necessary that the atrocity of sin should be detected by the law. If sin had not burst forth in enormous and indeed outrageous excess, it would not have been acknowledged as sin. This excess flows forth in a profusion of greater violence, while it converts life into death. The grounds for excuse, therefore, are then removed.

For we know that the law is spiritual: but I am carnal, sold under sin. For that which I do I know not: for not what I would, that I do practise; but what I hate, that I do. But if what I would not, that I do, I consent unto the law that it is good. So now it is no more I that do it, but sin which dwelleth in me. (14-17)

14. *For we know that the law is spiritual.* Paul begins now to make a closer comparison between the law and the nature of man, in order that the origin of the wickedness which leads to death may be more clearly understood. He then sets before us the example of a regenerate man, in whom the remains of the flesh dissent from the law of the Lord in

such a way that the spirit would gladly obey it. To begin with, however, Paul, as we have said, is making a simple comparison between nature and the law. Since there is no greater disagreement in matters relating to man than that which exists between spirit and flesh (for the law is spiritual and man carnal), what agreement therefore can there be between the nature of man and the law? The same as exists between darkness and light. Furthermore, by calling the law *spiritual*, not only does Paul mean that it requires the inward affections of the heart, as some interpreters explain, but by way of contrast, it also has the opposite meaning of the word *carnal*. Those interpreters whom we mentioned above explain *the law is spiritual* by saying that it not only binds the feet and hands, as far as external works are concerned, but it also applies to the affections of the heart, and requires the sincere fear of God.

The contrast between flesh and spirit is here expressed. It will be sufficiently clear from the context, and it has also in some measure already been shown, that the term flesh includes all that men bring from the womb. 'Flesh' is the designation applied to men at birth and for as long as they retain their natural character, because they are corrupt, and have no reputation for anything, nor do they desire anything, but what is gross and earthly. The spirit, on the other hand, is called the renewing of our corrupt nature, while God reforms us after His own image. Paul adopts this manner of speaking because the newness which is wrought in us is the gift of the Spirit.

The perfection of the doctrine of the law is therefore opposed here to the corrupt nature of man. The meaning is therefore, 'The law requires a heavenly and angelic righteousness, in which no spot appears, and which requires no addition to its cleanness. But I am a carnal man, and can do nothing but strive against it.' The interpretation of Origen, although it was formerly approved by many, is not worth refuting. He says that the law is called spiritual by Paul, because the Scripture is not to be understood in a literal sense. What has this to do with the present subject?

Sold under sin. By this expression Paul shows the strength which sin has in itself. By nature man is no less a slave to sin, than the bondmen whom their masters buy and ill-treat at will, as if they were oxen or asses. We are so completely driven by the power of sin, that our whole mind, our whole heart, and all our actions are inclined to sin. Compulsion I always exclude, for we sin of our own free will. It would not be sin if it were not voluntary. We are, however, so addicted to sin, that we can do nothing of our own accord but sin. The wickedness which holds sway within us drives us to it. This comparison does not therefore mean, as is said, a forced restraint, but a voluntary obedience, to which an inborn bondage inclines us.

15. *For that which I do I know not.* He now comes to a more particular example of a man who has already been regenerated. In this man the two objects of Paul's attention appear more clearly, viz. the great difference which exists between the law of God and the nature of man, and the impossibility of the law of itself producing death. Since carnal man rushes into the lust of sinning with the whole inclination of his mind, he appears to be sinning with as free a choice as if it were in his power to govern himself. This most pernicious opinion has been almost universally accepted—that man by his own natural powers can choose either course he pleases without the assistance of divine grace. But while the will of the believer is driven to good by the Spirit of God, the depravity of the nature which obstinately resists and strives against what is opposed to it, appears in him conspicuously. A regenerate man, therefore, affords the most suitable example to acquaint us with the extent of the disagreement between our nature and the righteousness of the law. His example also provides a more appropriate proof of the other clause than the mere consideration of human nature. The law, because it produces only death in the man who is wholly carnal, is more easily accused in that regard, since the source of the evil is doubtful. In a regenerate man the law produces wholesome fruits. This proves that it is the flesh alone which prevents the law from giving life. The law is far from producing death by itself.

For the purpose, therefore, of understanding the whole of this argument with more certainty and fidelity, it should be noted that this conflict mentioned by the apostle does not exist in man until he has been sanctified by the Spirit of God. When man is left to his own nature, he is completely borne away by his lust without any resistance. Although the ungodly are tormented by the stings of conscience, and cannot take such delight in their vices without having some taste of bitterness, yet we cannot deduce from this either that they hate evil or love good. The Lord thus permits them to endure such torments, in order to reveal his judgment to them in some way, but not to move them either with a love of righteousness or with a hatred of sin.

There is, therefore, this difference between them and believers. Believers are never so blinded and hardened in their minds as not to condemn their crimes when they are reminded of them in the judgment of their own conscience. Understanding is not utterly extinguished in them, but they retain a distinction between right and wrong. Sometimes, also, they are struck with horror on account of a sense of their sin, so that they bear a kind of condemnation even in this life. Nevertheless they approve of sin with all their heart, and therefore yield to it without any feeling of genuine repugnance. The stings of conscience by which they are afflicted proceed from a contradiction of judgment, rather than from the contrary affection of the will. Among the godly, on the other hand, the regeneration of God has been begun. They are so divided, however, that although they aspire to God with the special desire of their hearts, seek heavenly righteousness, and hate sin, they are drawn back again to the earth by the remnants of their flesh. Accordingly, in this state of distraction, they fight against their own nature and feel their own nature fighting against them. They condemn their sins, not only because they are compelled by the judgment of reason, but because they abhor them with genuine feeling of the heart and detest their conduct in committing sin. This is the Christian warfare between flesh and spirit, of which Paul speaks in Gal. 5.17.

It has, therefore, been well said that the carnal man plunges into sin with the consent and concurrence of his whole soul, but that a division at once begins as soon as he is called by the Lord and renewed by the Spirit. Regeneration only begins in this life. The remnants of the flesh that remain always follow their corrupt affections, and thus arouse the struggle against the Spirit.

The inexperienced, who do not take into consideration the subject with which the apostle is dealing or the plan which he is following, suppose it is human nature which he is here describing. It is true that among the philosophers we find such a description of human capacity. Scripture, however, is much more profound in its philosophy, for it sees that nothing but perversity has remained in the heart of man since Adam was deprived of the image of God. Thus, when the Sophists want to define free will, or to estimate the capacity of human nature, they seize this passage. But Paul, as I have already stated, is not here describing the bare nature of man, but is depicting in his own person the character and extent of the weakness of believers. For some time Augustine was involved in the same error, but after closer examination of the passage he not only retracted the false teaching which he had given, but in his first book to Boniface he proves by many powerful arguments that it can only be understood of the regenerate. We shall endeavour to make our readers see clearly that such is the case.

I know not. He means that he does not acknowledge as his own the works which he committed through the weakness of the flesh, since he hates them. Erasmus, therefore, has offered a tolerable translation by the word, *approve*, but because this might be ambiguous I have preferred to retain the word *understand*. We deduce from this that the doctrine of the law is so agreeable to right judgment that believers repudiate transgression of it as something sub-human. Since, however,

Paul seems to admit that his teaching differs from what the law prescribes, many interpreters have been deceived and have thought that he was speaking in a different character—hence the common error of maintaining that this whole chapter describes the nature of the unregenerate man. By 'transgression of the law', however, Paul understands all the lapses of the godly. But these do not deprive them either of the fear of God or the zeal to do well. Paul, therefore, denies that he is doing what the law demands, because he does not fulfil it in all its parts, but grows somewhat weary in his efforts.

For not what I would that do I practise. We are not to understand that Paul had always been incapable of doing good. He merely complains of his inability to do what he desired—to pursue goodness with due alacrity—because he was to some extent held bound. He also complains that he failed where he least wished to fail, because he stumbled through the weakness of his flesh. The godly heart, therefore, does not do the good that it wants to do, because it is not accompanied by the right exertion. It does the evil that it does not want to do because it desires to stand, and it falls, or at least it wavers. The expression to *want* and *not to want to do* are to be applied to the Spirit, which ought to hold the first place among believers. The flesh, of course, has its own will too, but by *will* Paul means that which he sought with the particular affection of his heart. That which contended against him he refers to as being contrary to his will.

We may deduce from this what we stated previously, that Paul is here speaking of believers. Some grace of the Spirit exists in them, which illustrates the agreement between a sound mind and the righteousness of the law, because the flesh does not hate sin.

16. *But if what I would not, that I do, I consent unto the law.* That is, 'While my heart acquiesces in the law, and enjoys its righteousness (and it assuredly does so when it hates the transgression of the law), it feels and acknowledges the goodness of the law in the fact of our being sufficiently convinced, when experience teaches us, that no evil is to be imputed to the law. Indeed, the law would bring salvation to men, if it were to encounter upright and pure hearts.' This consent is not to be taken in the sense in which it is used by unbelievers who say, 'I see the better course and approve of it; but I follow the worse', or again, 'I shall follow that which will be of hurt to me; and I shall avoid what I believe would be of profit.' These unbelievers act because they are compelled to, because they subscribe to the righteousness of God, although they are otherwise wholly estranged from it. The godly man, however, consents to the law seriously and with most eager desire of his heart, for his only desire is to go to heaven.

17. *So now it is no more I that do it.* This is not the entreaty of a man

who is excusing himself, as if he were blameless, like the many triflers who think that they have a just defence with which to cover up their acts of wickedness by ascribing it to the flesh. It is a declaration of the extent of the disagreement between his spiritual affection and his flesh, for believers are brought into obedience to God with such fervency of spirit that they deny their own flesh.

This passage also clearly proves that Paul is here discussing only the godly who have already been regenerated. As long as a man remains unchanged, whatever he may be like, he is rightly considered to be corrupt. But Paul denies here that he himself is wholly possessed by sin, indeed he exempts himself from bondage to it. Sin remains only in a part of his soul, as he strives for and aspires after the righteousness of God with the earnest affection of his heart, and proves in fact that he bears the law of God inscribed within himself.

For I know that in me, that is, in my flesh, dwelleth no good thing: for to will is present with me, but to do that which is good is not. For the good which I would I do not: but the evil which I would not, that I practise. But if what I would not, that I do, it is no more I that do it, but sin which dwelleth in me. (18-20)

18. *For I know.* He says that no good dwells in him as far as nature is concerned. *In me,* therefore, means, 'So far as I am concerned.' At the beginning of his discourse he condemns himself of being completely corrupt, when he confesses that no good dwells in him. He then adds a correction, lest he should insult the grace of God which also dwelt within him, but was no part of his flesh. Here again he confirms that he was not speaking of all mankind, but only of the believer who is divided in himself on account of the remnants of the flesh and the grace of the Spirit. What is the purpose of this correction, unless some part were exempt from depravity, and therefore not carnal? Under the term *flesh* Paul always includes all the endowments of human nature, and everything that is in man, except the sanctification of the Spirit. So, by the term *spirit,* which is usually contrasted with flesh, he means that part of the soul which the Spirit of God has purified from evil and so refashioned that the image of God shines forth within it. Both terms, therefore, *flesh* and *spirit,* are applicable to the soul. The one relates to that part which has been regenerated, and the other to that which still retains its natural affection.

To will is present. He does not mean that he has nothing but an ineffectual desire, but he denies that the efficacy of his work corresponds to his will, because the flesh hinders him from the exact performance of what he is doing. The words following, *the evil which I would not, that I practise,* should also be taken in this sense, because the flesh not only prevents believers from running swiftly, it also puts many obstacles in their way to trip them up. They do not, therefore, do what they ought, because they do not do it with the proper readiness. This *will*, therefore, which he mentions is the readiness of faith, when the Holy Spirit forms the godly, so that they are ready and eager to render their members obedient to God. Because, however, his ability is unequal to his desire, Paul says that he does not find what he wanted, viz. the accomplishment of the good which he desired.

19. The expression which follows next refers to the same point. He does not do the good which he wants, but the evil which he does not want, because however rightly believers may be influenced, they are still conscious of their own weakness, and regard no work that they do as being free from fault. Paul is not here dealing with a few of the errors of the godly, but is describing in general the whole course of their life. We conclude, therefore, that their best works are always corrupted by some mark of sin, so that no reward can be hoped for, except in so far as God pardons them.

Finally he repeats the statement that in so far as he is endowed with heavenly light, he is a true witness and subscriber to the righteousness of the law. It follows from this that if the integrity of our nature remained pure, the law would not bring death on us, nor oppose the man who is of a sound mind, and who shrinks from sin. Our health comes from the heavenly Physician.

I find then the law, that, to me would do good, evil is present. For I delight in the law of God after the inward man: but I see a different law in my members, warring against the law of my mind, and bringing me into captivity under the law of sin which is in my members. (21-23)

21. *I find then the law.* Paul holds here that there is a fourfold law. There is *the law of God*, which alone is properly so called, because it is the rule of righteousness by which our life is rightly formed. To this he adds *the law of the mind*. By this he designates the readiness of the faithful mind to obey the divine law. This is our conformity to the law of God. Opposed to this there is *the law of unrighteousness*. By this Paul means the power which iniquity exercises not only in a man who is not yet regenerate, but also in the flesh of the man who is. Even the laws of tyrants, however iniquitous they may be, are still called laws, however incorrectly. To this law of sin Paul makes *the law in his members* correspond, i.e. the concupiscence which resides in his members. He does so because of the agreement which exists between it and iniquity.

With regard to the first clause, many interpreters take the word *law* in its proper sense, and therefore κατά or διά is to be understood.

Thus Erasmus translates *by the law* as if Paul had said that he found that his fault was innate by the instruction and guidance of the law of God. The sentence will run better, however, without supplying any preposition: 'While believers strive after what is good, they find in themselves a tyrannical law, because a vicious tendency, which resists and is opposed to the law of God, is implanted in their bone and marrow.'

22. *For I delight in the law of God.* We see here, therefore, the nature of the division in godly minds, from which the struggle between the spirit and the flesh arises which Augustine somewhere calls 'the Christian struggle'. The law calls a man to the rule of righteousness; iniquity, which is the tyrannical law of Satan, arouses him to wickedness. The spirit leads him to render obedience to the divine law; the flesh draws him back in the opposite direction. Since he is distracted by various desires, man is now a twofold creature. But since his spirit ought to possess the sovereignty, he judges and estimates himself by that part particularly. Paul says that he is held captive by his flesh, because the fact that he is still tempted and incited by evil lusts is a constraint in regard to the spiritual desire which is entirely opposed to it.

We should notice carefully the meaning of *the inward man* and *members*. Many have gone astray by failing to understand these expressions. The *inward man*, therefore, does not simply mean the soul, but the spiritual part of the soul which has been regenerated by God. *Members* means the other remaining part. As the soul is the more excellent and the body the inferior part of man, so the spirit is superior to the flesh. The spirit takes the place of the soul in man, but the flesh, which is the corrupt and polluted soul, that of the body. For this reason, therefore, the former is termed *the inward man*, and the latter *the members*. The inward man is understood in a different sense in II Cor. 4.16, but the circumstances of the present passage require the interpretation which I have given. It is called the inward man *par excellence*, because it possesses the heart and the hidden affections, while the appetites of the flesh stray outside a man. It is like comparing heaven to earth, for Paul is using the word members by way of contempt to designate all that is evident in man, in order to show better that our secret renewal evades and is concealed from our senses, except in so far as it is apprehended by faith.

Since the *law of the mind* undoubtedly means an affection rightly ordered, it is clear that it is wrong to wrest this passage from its context to apply it to those who are not yet regenerate. Paul teaches us that these are devoid of understanding, because their soul has lost its reason (*anima a ratione degenerat*).

O wretched man that I am! who shall deliver me out of the body of this death? I thank God through Jesus Christ our Lord. So then I myself with the mind serve the law of God; but with the flesh the law of sin.
(24-25)

24. *O wretched man that I am!* He concludes his argument with a passionate exclamation, by which he teaches us that we are not only to struggle with our flesh, but also continually to lament and bewail within ourselves and in the presence of God our unhappy condition. He does not inquire who is to deliver him, as if he were in doubt, like the unbelievers, who do not understand that there is only one deliverer. His language is that of a man who is panting and almost fainting, because he sees that his help is not close enough. Paul, therefore, used the word *deliver*, in order to show that his deliverance required no ordinary power of God.

By *the body of death* he means the mass of sin, or the constituent parts from which the whole man is formed, except that in his case alone the remnants of sin were left, which held him captive. The pronoun τούτου, *this*, which I have followed Erasmus in applying to *body*, also agrees with death, but the general sense is the same. Paul wanted to teach us that the eyes of God's children are opened, so that they discern with prudence from the law of God the corruption of their nature and the death which proceeds from it. The word *body* means the same as *outward man* and *members*, because Paul notes that the origin of sin is that man has departed from the law of his creation, and thus become carnal and earthly. Although he still surpasses the brutes, his true excellence has been taken from him, and what remains is filled with innumerable corruptions, so that, in so far as his soul is degenerate, it may rightly be said to have changed into his body. Thus, too, God says in Gen. 6.3, 'My spirit shall not strive with man for ever, for that he also is flesh.' Man is here deprived of his spiritual excellence, and compared by way of reproach to the animals.

This passage of Paul's is noteworthy in that it serves to destroy all the glory of the flesh. It teaches us that even the most perfect are subject to misery as long as they dwell in the flesh, for they are liable to death. Indeed, when they examine themselves thoroughly, they find nothing in their own nature but wretchedness. Furthermore, Paul arouses them by his own example to anxious cries of distress, in order to prevent them from yielding to apathy, and bids them to seek death, as long as they remain on earth, as the only remedy for their evils. This is the right object in desiring death. Despair often drives the profane to the same wish, but they are wrong to seek death if it is because they loathe their present life, rather than because they are

wearied with their iniquity. We must add that although believers aim
at the true mark, they are not carried away by uncontrolled passion in
wishing for death, but submit to the will of God, to whom we ought
to live and die. For this reason they do not rage with indignation
against God, but humbly lay their anxieties in His bosom, for they do
not dwell on the thought of their misery without tempering their grief
with joy, as they recall the grace which they have received. We see
this from the following sentence.

25. *I thank God.* Paul, therefore, immediately adds this thanksgiving
to prevent anyone from thinking that he was stubbornly murmuring
against God in his complaint. We know how easy it is, even in grief
which we deserve, to fall into discontent or impatience. Therefore,
although Paul laments his state and sighs for his departure, at the same
time he confesses that he rests in the grace of God. In examining their
defects, the saints should not forget what they have already received
from God. Furthermore, the thought that they have been received
into the protection of God, so that they may never perish, and that they
have already been given the firstfruits of the Spirit, which make certain
their hope of the eternal inheritance, is sufficient to check impatience
and cherish peace of mind. Although they do not yet enjoy the
promised glory of heaven, yet, since they are content with the measure
which they have obtained, they are never without a reason for joy.

So then I myself with the mind serve the law of God. In this short
epilogue Paul teaches us that believers never reach the goal of righteousness as long as they dwell in the flesh, but that they continue in their
course until they put off the body. He again applies the word *mind*,
not to the rational part of the soul honoured by philosophers, but to
that part which is illuminated by the Spirit of God, so that it may
understand and will aright. Paul not only mentions understanding,
but also connects with it the earnest desire of the heart. With this
exception he confesses that he is devoted to God but in such a manner
that while he lives on the earth he is defiled with much corruption.
The passage is a notable one for condemning that most pernicious
dogma of the Purists (*Cathari*) which some turbulent spirits are
attempting to revive at the present time.

CHAPTER EIGHT

There is therefore now no condemnation to them that are in Christ Jesus.
For the law of the Spirit of life in Christ Jesus made me free from the
law of sin and of death. For what the law could not do, in that it was
weak through the flesh, God, sending His own Son in the likeness of
sinful flesh and as an offering *for sin, condemned sin in the flesh: that*
the ordinance of the law might be fulfilled in us, who walk not after the
flesh, but after the spirit. (1-4)

1. *There is therefore now no condemnation.* Having described the
struggle which the godly continually have with their own flesh, he
returns to the consolation which he had before mentioned, and which
was very necessary for them—although they are still beset by sin, yet
they are free from the power of death, and from every curse, provided
they live not in the flesh but in the Spirit. Paul connects these three
ideas together—the imperfection under which believers always labour;
the mercy of God in pardoning and forgiving it; and the regeneration
of the Spirit. This is mentioned last, lest any man should flatter himself
with a vain opinion, as if he were freed from the curse, while in the
meantime indulging his flesh without care. As the carnal man, therefore, flatters himself in vain, if, in no way concerned to amend his life,
he promises himself impunity under the pretext of this grace, so the
trembling consciences of the godly have an invincible defence. They
know that while they abide in Christ they are beyond every danger of
condemnation. It will now be worth while to consider the meaning
of the expressions.

By walking *after the Spirit*, Paul does not mean those who have
completely put off all the feelings of the flesh, so that their whole life
exhibits nothing but heavenly perfection, but those who diligently
labour to subdue and mortify the flesh, so that the earnest love of true
religion may appear to reign in them. Such believers, he declares, do
not walk according to the flesh, because wherever the sincere fear of
God flourishes, it deprives the flesh of its dominion, though it does not
abolish all its corruptions.

2. *For the law of the Spirit of life.* This is a proof of the former
sentence. We must note the meaning of the words in order to understand it. Paul improperly calls the Spirit of God the *law of the Spirit.*
This Spirit sprinkles our souls with the blood of Christ, not only to
cleanse us from the stain of sin in respect of our guilt, but also to

sanctify us to true purity. He adds that it is life-giving. The genitive case, according to Hebraic usage, is to be taken as an adjective. It follows from this that those who tie a man to the letter of the law make him subject to death. On the other hand, however, Paul calls the dominion of the flesh and the tyranny of death which follows from it *the law of sin and death*. The law of God is placed, as it were, in the middle. Although it teaches righteousness, it cannot confer it, but rather binds us in bondage to sin and to death by still stronger bonds.

The meaning of the sentence, therefore, is this: The law of God condemns men because as long as they remain under the obligation of the law, they are oppressed by the bondage of sin, and thus are guilty of death. The Spirit of Christ, however, abolishes the law of sin in us by correcting the inordinate desires of the flesh, and at the same time delivers us from the guilt of death. Someone may object that in this case the pardon, by which our offences are buried, depends on our regeneration. This is easily answered. Paul is not here assigning the reason, but merely specifying the manner, in which we are delivered from guilt. He denies that we obtain deliverance by the outward teaching of the law. In being renewed by the Spirit of God, however, we are at the same time also justified by a free pardon, so that the curse of sin may no longer lie upon us. The sentence, therefore, means the same as if Paul had said that the grace of regeneration is never separated from the imputation of righteousness.

I would not dare, with some interpreters, take *the law of sin and death* to mean the law of God. This seems too harsh an expression. Although by increasing sin the law may produce death, Paul has above deliberately declined to use this invidious expression. At the same time, however, I am no more in agreement with the opinion of those who explain *the law of sin* to mean the lust of the flesh, as if Paul had said that he had conquered it. It will, I think, soon be quite clear that Paul is speaking of unmerited absolution, which brings us undisturbed peace with God. I have preferred to retain the word *law*, rather than to render it, with Erasmus, *right* or *power*. Paul did not allude to the law of God without due consideration.

3. *For what the law could not do.* There follows now an elaboration or illustration of his proof—the Lord has justified us in Christ by his free mercy. This it was impossible for the law to do. But since this is a very notable sentence, let us examine each part of it.

We may infer from the last clause, where he adds, *who walk not after the flesh, but after the Spirit*, that Paul is here dealing with free justification, or the pardon by which God reconciles us to himself. If Paul intended to teach us that we are instructed by the Spirit of regeneration how to overcome sin, why did he add this phrase? It is, however, very appropriate that, having promised free remission to believers, Paul should confine this doctrine to those who join repentance to faith, and do not misuse the mercy of God by indulging the flesh. We must next consider the reason which is offered. The apostle teaches us how the grace of Christ absolves us from guilt. Now with regard to the expression, τὸ ἀδύνατον, the impossibility of the law, the words undoubtedly mean *defect* or *inability*, as if Paul had said that God had discovered a remedy by which the want of power on the part of the law was removed. Erasmus has rendered the particle, ἐν ᾧ, by *ea parte qua*—'in that part in which'. I think, however, that it is causal and therefore I have preferred to render it, *eo quod*—'because'. Although such a phrase does not perhaps occur among good authors in the Greek language, yet since the apostles are always making use of Hebraic phrases, this interpretation should not appear harsh. Perceptive readers will no doubt grant that what Paul has expressed here is the cause of the defect, as we shall shortly state again. Now although Erasmus supplies the principal verb, the text seems to me to run very well without it. The copulative καί, 'and', has led Erasmus astray and made him insert the verb *praestitit*—'has performed'. I think, however, that the copulative was put for the sake of amplification, unless perhaps some may approve of the conjecture of the Greek commentator, who joins the expression 'and for sin' with the preceding words, 'God sending His own Son in the likeness of sinful flesh and as an offering for sin.' I have, however, followed what I have thought to be the real meaning of Paul. I come now to the subject itself.

Paul clearly affirms that our sins were expiated by the death of Christ, because it was impossible for the law to confer righteousness upon us. It follows from this that more is commanded in the law than we are able to perform. If we were capable of fulfilling the law, there would have been no need to seek a remedy elsewhere. It is, therefore, absurd to measure human strength by the precepts of the law, as if God, in demanding what is just, had regarded the character and extent of our powers.

In that it was weak. Lest any should consider that he was irreverently accusing the law of weakness, or restrict it to ceremonial observances, Paul has expressly stated that this defect was not due to any fault in the law, but to the corruption of our flesh. It must be admitted that if anyone were to satisfy the divine law absolutely, he would be righteous in the presence of God. Paul does not, therefore, deny that the law is sufficient to justify us as far as doctrine is concerned, since it contains a perfect rule of righteousness. Since, however, our flesh does not attain that righteousness, the whole strength of the law fails and vanishes away. Thus the error, or rather the delusion, of those who imagine that Paul is depriving only ceremonies of the power to justify is refuted, since Paul expressly lays the blame on ourselves, and declares that he finds no fault in the doctrine of the law.

We are, moreover, to understand the *weakness* of the law in the sense in which the apostle usually takes the word ἀσθενείας, to mean not simply a slight weakness, but impotence. He adopts this meaning in order to signify that the law is of no consequence at all in bestowing righteousness. We see, therefore, that we are entirely excluded from the righteousness of Christ, because there can be no righteousness in ourselves. It is especially necessary to have this knowledge, because we shall never be clothed with the righteousness of Christ, unless we first know for certain that we have no righteousness of our own. The word *flesh* is always used in the same sense to mean ourselves. The corruption, therefore, of our nature renders the law of God of no use to us. Although it shows us the way of life, it does not bring us back from our headlong plunge into death.

God, sending His own Son. He now shows the manner in which our heavenly Father has restored righteousness to us by His Son. He condemned sin in the very flesh of Christ, i.e. by cancelling the handwriting He abolished the guilt which held us bound in the presence of God. The condemnation of sin has brought us into righteousness, for since our guilt has been done away with we are absolved, so that God regards us as righteous. In the first place, however, Paul states that Christ has been *sent*, in order to remind us that righteousness by no means resides in us, since it must be sought from him. Men trust in their own merits in vain, for they are righteous only at the pleasure of another, or borrow righteousness from the expiation which Christ fulfilled in His flesh. Christ, he says, came in *the likeness of sinful flesh.* Although the flesh of Christ was unpolluted by any stain, it had the appearance of being sinful, since it sustained the punishment due to our sins, and certainly death exerted every part of its power on the flesh of Christ as though it were subject to it. Because our High Priest had to learn by His own experience what it means to assist the weak, Christ was willing to undergo our infirmities, in order that He might be more inclined to sympathy. In this respect too there appeared in Him a certain resemblance (*imago*) to our sinful nature.

And as an offering for sin. I have just said that this is explained by some to be the cause or purpose for which God sent His son, viz. to give satisfaction for sin. Chrysostom and many after him understand this phrase in a slightly harsher sense—sin had been condemned on account of sin (*de peccato*), because it assailed Christ unjustly and contrary to what He deserved. I grant that the price of our redemption had been paid by this means, because a just and innocent man underwent punishment on behalf of sinners, but I cannot be induced to think that the word *sin* has been used here in any other sense than that of an expiatory victim, which is called אָשָׁם (*asham*), in Hebrew, just as the Greeks call a sacrifice on which a curse is laid κάθαρμα. Paul says the same thing in II Cor. 5.21: 'Him who knew no sin He made to be sin on our behalf; that we might become the righteousness of God in Him.' The preposition περί is here taken in a causal sense, as though he had said, '*Upon that sacrifice*, or *on account of the burden of sin laid on Christ*, sin was cast down from its power, in order that it may not now hold us in subjection to itself.' He says metaphorically that it was *condemned*, like those who lose their case, since God no longer reckons as guilty those who have obtained absolution through the sacrifice of Christ. If we say that the kingdom of sin, in which we were oppressed, has been destroyed, the meaning will be the same. Thus Christ took to Himself what was ours in order that He might transfer what was His to us, for He took upon Himself our curse, and has given us His blessing.

Paul adds here, *in the flesh*, in order to increase the certainty of our confidence when we see that sin has been conquered and abolished in our nature itself. Thus it follows that our nature is truly made partaker of His victory, as Paul presently also declares.

4. *That the ordinance of the law might be fulfilled.* The interpreters who understand that those who have been renewed by the Spirit of Christ fulfil the law, introduce a misrepresentation which is completely foreign to Paul's meaning. As long as believers sojourn in the world, they do not make such progress that the righteousness of the law is full or complete in them. We must, therefore, apply this phrase to forgiveness, for while the obedience of Christ is imparted to us, the law is satisfied, so that we are accounted just. The perfection which the law demands was exhibited in the flesh for this reason, that its rigorous demand should no longer have the power to condemn us. But because Christ communicates His righteousness only to those whom He joins to Himself by the bond of His Spirit, Paul mentions regeneration again, lest Christ should be thought to be the minister of sin. It is a common tendency to apply the doctrine of the fatherly indulgence of God to the lust of the flesh, while others maliciously slander this doctrine, as if it extinguished the pursuit of upright living.

For they that are after the flesh do mind the things of the flesh; but they that are after the spirit the things of the spirit. For the mind of the flesh is dead; but the mind of the spirit is life and peace: because the mind of the flesh is enmity against God; for it is not subject to the law of God, neither indeed can it be: and they that are in the flesh cannot please God.

(5-8)

5. *For they that are after the flesh.* Paul introduces this distinction between the flesh and the Spirit, not only to confirm his previous statement that the grace of Christ belongs only to those who, having been regenerated by the Spirit, strive after innocence of life, but also to raise up believers with a suitable consolation, so that they should not despair from a consciousness of their many infirmities. Since he had exempted from the curse only those who lead a spiritual life, it might have seemed that he was cutting off the hope of salvation from all mankind. Who will be found in this world adorned with angelic purity, so that he has nothing to do with the flesh? It was, therefore, necessary for Paul to add this definition of what it means *to be in the flesh* and *to walk after the flesh.* He does not at first make the distinction in such precise terms. As we shall see later on, however, his purpose is to inspire believers with good hope, although they are still bound to their flesh. They are not, however, to give rein to its lusts, but to entrust themselves to the direction of the Holy Spirit.

When he says that *carnal* men *care for,* or meditate upon, the things of the flesh, he declares that he does not regard as carnal those who aspire to heavenly righteousness, but those who are wholly addicted to the world. I have therefore rendered φρονοῦσιν by a word of broader meaning, 'mind' (*cogitant*), so that readers may understand that only those are excluded from the sons of God who have yielded themselves to the allurements of the flesh and apply their minds and zeal to corrupt desires. Now, in the second clause, he encourages believers to have good hope, if they feel that they are raised up to meditate upon righteousness by the Spirit. Wherever the Spirit reigns, it is a sign of the saving grace of God, just as the grace of God does not exist where the Spirit is extinguished and the kingdom of the flesh prevails. I will briefly repeat here the admonition which I have given before. To be *in the flesh,* or *after the flesh,* means the same as to be devoid of the gift of regeneration. All those who continue to live as 'natural men', to use the common expression are in such a state.

6. *The mind of the flesh is death.* Erasmus has 'affection' (*affectum*) for *cogitatio,* the Vulgate 'prudence' (*prudentiam*). Since, however, it is certain that Paul's τὸ φρόνημα is the same as that of Moses when he speaks of the imagination (*figmentum*) of the heart (Gen. 6.5), and that this word includes all the feelings of the soul from the reason and understanding to the affections, it seems to me that 'mind' (*cogitatio*) is better suited to the passage. Although Paul has used the particle γάρ, I am certain that this is confirmative, for there is a kind of concession here. Having given a brief definition of what it means *to be in the flesh,* he now adds the end which awaits all who have given themselves to the flesh. He thus proves by contrast that those who abide in the flesh

cannot be partakers of the grace of Christ, for throughout the whole course of their life they rush headlong towards death.

This passage is a notable one. We learn from it that in following the course of nature we plunge into death, for by ourselves we contrive nothing but destruction. Paul presently adds a contrasting clause, to teach us that if any part of us tends towards life, it is the Spirit which is displaying its power, since no spark of life proceeds from our flesh. Paul calls spiritual-mindedness life, because it is life-giving, or leads to life. By *peace* he means, according to Hebrew usage, all that belongs to well-being. Every action of the Spirit of God within us tends to our blessedness. There is, however, no reason for attributing salvation to works on this account, for although God begins our salvation, and finally completes it by renewing us after His image, yet the only cause of our salvation is His good pleasure, by which He makes us partakers of Christ.

7. *Because the mind of the flesh is enmity against God.* He adds a proof of the proposition which he had offered, that nothing but death proceeds from the labours of our flesh, because they are hostile to the will of God. Now the will of God is the rule of righteousness. It follows that whatever is contrary to it is unrighteous, and if it is unrighteous, it also brings death at the same time. We may look for life in vain if God is opposed to us and hostile, for death, which is the vengeance of His wrath, must of necessity immediately follow the wrath of God.

Let us observe here that the will of man is in all respects opposed to the divine will, for there must be as great a difference between us and God as there is between depravity and uprightness.

For it is not subject to the law of God. This is an interpretation of the previous sentence. It shows how all the meditations of the flesh are at war with the will of God, for the will of God can be sought only where He has revealed it. In the law God shows us what is pleasing to Him. Those, therefore, who wish to examine properly how far they agree with God, test all their purposes and practices by this standard. Although nothing is done in this world except by the secret governing providence of God, to use this as an excuse and say that nothing happens without His approbation is intolerable blasphemy. What foolishness it is to seek in a deep labyrinth for the distinction between right and wrong which the law has plainly and distinctly set before our eyes. The Lord, as I have said, does indeed have His own hidden counsel, by which He orders all things as He pleases; but because it is incomprehensible to us, we should know that we are debarred from a too curious investigation into it. For the meantime let this truth remain unalterable —only righteousness pleases God, and only by the law, in which He has faithfully testified what He approves or disapproves, can we form a right judgment of our works.

Neither indeed can it be. So much for the power of the freedom of the will which the Sophists cannot sufficiently extol. Paul is without doubt here explicitly affirming what they themselves openly detest, viz. that it is impossible for us to subject our affections to the law. They boast that the heart can turn either way, provided it is assisted by the influence of the Spirit, and that we have in our power the free choice of good or evil, if only the Spirit gives us help. Ours, however, is the choice or the refusal. They imagine, too, that there are good motions within us by which we are prepared of our own free will. Paul, on the other hand, declares that our heart is so swollen with hardness and unconquerable obstinacy that it is never moved to submit to the yoke of God naturally. He is not arguing about one or other of the affections, but uses an indefinite expression to cover all the emotions which arise within us. Let the Christian heart therefore drive far from itself the non-Christian philosophy of the freedom of the will, and let every one of us acknowledge himself to be, as in reality he is, the servant of sin, that he may be freed by the grace of Christ and set at liberty. It is the height of folly to boast of any other freedom.

8. *They that are in the flesh cannot please God.* I have purposely explained the adversative particle δέ as a causal one, for the apostle deduces from what has been said that all those who give themselves up to be driven by the lusts of the flesh are abominable to God. Paul has thus far confirmed the truth that all who do not walk according to the Spirit are alienated from Christ, because they lack the heavenly life.

> But ye are not in the flesh, but in the spirit, if so be that the Spirit of God dwelleth in you. But if any man hath not the Spirit of Christ, he is none of His. And if Christ is in you, the body is dead because of sin; but the spirit is life because of righteousness. But if the Spirit of Him that raised up Jesus from the dead dwelleth in you, He that raised up Christ Jesus from the dead shall quicken also your mortal bodies through His Spirit that dwelleth in you. (9-11)

9. *But ye are not in the flesh.* Paul applies hypothetically a general truth to those to whom he is writing, not merely to affect them more powerfully by directing his discourse particularly to them, but also that from the definition just given they may conclude for certain that they belonged to the number of those from whom Christ has removed the curse of the law. At the same time, however, Paul exhorts them to newness of life by explaining what power the Spirit of God has in the elect, and what fruits it produces.

If so be that the Spirit of God dwelleth in you. Paul adds an appropriate correction to arouse them to examine themselves more closely, in order that they may not make a vain pretence to the name of Christ. The most certain mark by which the sons of God are distinguished from the children of the world is their regeneration by the Spirit of God to innocence and holiness. His purpose, however, does not seem to have been so much to correct hypocrisy as to suggest reasons for glorying against the absurd zealots of the law, who regarded the dead letter as of more importance than the inward power of the Spirit, who gives life to the law.

This passage also teaches us that by the word *Spirit* Paul has not up to this point meant the *mind* or the *understanding*, which the advocates of free will call the superior part of the soul, but the gift of heaven. He explains that it is those whom God governs by His Spirit who are spiritual, and not those who obey reason on their own impulse. These, however, are not said to be 'after the Spirit' because they are filled with God's Spirit (which happens to no one today), but because they have the Spirit dwelling in them, even though they may find some remains of the flesh dwelling in them. The Spirit, however, cannot dwell in them without taking hold of the higher faculties. It is to be noted that man is designated from the principal part of his nature.

But if any man hath not the Spirit of Christ. He adds this in order to show how necessary it is for Christians to deny the flesh. The kingdom of the Spirit is the abolition of the flesh. Those in whom the Spirit does not reign do not belong to Christ; therefore those who serve the flesh are not Christians, for those who separate Christ from His Spirit make Him like a dead image or a corpse. We must always bear in mind the counsel of the apostle, that free remission of sins cannot be separated from the Spirit of regeneration. This would be, as it were, to rend Christ asunder.

If this is true, it is strange that we are accused of arrogance by the adversaries of the Gospel, because we dare to avow that the Spirit of Christ dwells in us. We must either deny Christ, or confess that we become Christians by His Spirit. It is dreadful indeed to hear that men have so departed from the Word of the Lord, that they not only boast that they are Christians without the Spirit of God, but also ridicule the faith of others. And yet this is the philosophy of the Papists.

Our readers should note here that the Spirit is sometimes referred to as the Spirit of God the Father, and sometimes as the Spirit of Christ without distinction. This is not only because His whole fulness was poured on Christ as our Mediator and Head, so that each one of us might receive from Him his own portion, but also because the same Spirit is common to the Father and the Son, who have one essence, and the same eternal deity. Because, however, we have no communication with God except by Christ, the apostle wisely descends from the Father, who seems to be at a greater distance, to Christ.

10. *And if Christ is in you.* Paul now applies his previous remarks concerning the Spirit to Christ, in order to signify the manner of Christ's dwelling in us. For as by the Spirit He consecrates us as temples to Himself, so by the same Spirit He dwells in us. He now explains more distinctly what we have already alluded to, that the sons of God are not reckoned spiritual, on the ground of a full and entire perfection, but only on account of the newness of life which has begun in them. He here anticipates a doubt, which might otherwise have caused us uneasiness; for although the Spirit possesses part of us, yet we see another part still being held by death. He therefore gives the answer that the power of quickening exists in the Spirit of Christ, which is able to absorb our mortality. He concludes from this that we must wait with patience until the remains of sin are entirely abolished.

Readers have already been reminded that the word *Spirit* does not mean the soul, but the Spirit of regeneration. Paul calls this Spirit of regeneration *life*, not only because He lives and flourishes in us, but also because He quickens us by His power, until He destroys our mortal flesh and at last renews us perfectly. So, on the other hand, the word *body* signifies the more stolid mass as yet unpurified by the Spirit of God from earthly defilements, which delight only in what is gross. It would be absurd otherwise to ascribe to the body the blame for sin. Again, the soul is so far from being life, that it does not even of itself have life. Paul's meaning, therefore, is that, although sin condemns us to death in so far as the corruption of our first nature still remains in us, yet the Spirit of God is victorious. It is no obstacle that only the first-fruits have been bestowed on us, for even even one spark of the Spirit is the seed of life.

11. *If the Spirit dwelleth in you.* Paul takes his confirmation of the last verse from the efficient cause, in the following manner: 'If Christ was raised by the power of the Spirit of God, and if the Spirit retains eternal power, He will also exert that power in us.' He takes it for granted that in the person of Christ there had been exhibited a specimen of the power which belongs to the whole body of the Church. Since He makes God the author of the resurrection, he attributes to Him the life-giving Spirit.

That raised up Christ Jesus. He describes God by a paraphrase which suited his present object better than if he had simply called Him by name. For the same reason he ascribes to the Father the glory of having raised up Christ. This offered a stronger proof of what he proposed to say than if he had attributed the resurrection to Christ Himself. The objection could have been made that Christ was able to raise Himself by a power which no man possesses. But when Paul says, 'God raised up Christ by His Spirit, whom He also communicated to you,' this cannot be contradicted, since God has thus made the hope of the resurrection certain for us. This does not in any way detract from the passage in John: 'I have power to lay it down, and I have power to take it again' (John 10.18). Christ certainly rose of Himself and through His own power, but as He usually ascribes to the Father what divine power He possesses, so the apostle has properly transferred to the Father that which was in Christ the proper work of His divinity.

By *mortal bodies* he means all in us that still remains subject to death. Paul's general practice is to apply this name to the grosser part of us. We conclude from this that he is not speaking of the last resurrection, which will take place in a moment, but of the continual operation of the Spirit, by which He gradually mortifies the remains of the flesh and renews in us the heavenly life.

So then, brethren, we are debtors, not to the flesh, to live after the flesh: for if ye live after the flesh, ye must die; but if by the Spirit ye mortify the deeds of the body, ye shall live. For as many as are led by the Spirit of God, these are sons of God. (12-14)

12. *So then, brethren, we are debtors.* This is the conclusion of the preceding remarks. If we are to renounce the flesh, we ought not to consent to it. If, again, the Spirit ought to reign in us, it is absurd not to attend to His bidding. Paul's sentence here is defective, for he omits the other part of his contrast, viz. that we are debtors to the Spirit. The meaning, however, is in no way obscure. This conclusion has the force of an exhortation, as Paul's custom is always to draw exhortation from doctrine. Thus in another passage he warns us, 'Grieve not the Holy Spirit of God, in whom ye were sealed unto the day of redemption '(Eph. 4.30). So also in Gal. 5.25, 'If we live by the Spirit, by the Spirit let us also walk.' This we do when we renounce carnal desires in order to devote ourselves to the righteousness of God as our bounden duty. This is the reasoning which we ought to follow, unlike the common practice of some blasphemers who idly declare that we need do nothing, because we have no power. But we are fighting against God, as it were, if we extinguish His grace which is offered to us by contempt and negligence.

13. *For if ye live after the flesh ye must die.* He adds a warning in order to shake off their sluggishness with greater severity. This also provides a useful refutation of those who boast of justification by faith without the Spirit of Christ. Their own conscience, however, more than sufficiently convicts them, since there is no confidence in God

where there is no love of righteousness. It is, indeed, true, that we are justified in Christ by the mercy of God alone, but it is equally true and certain, that all who are justified are called by the Lord to live worthy of their vocation. Let believers, therefore, learn to embrace Him, not only for justification, but also for sanctification, as He has been given to us for both these purposes, that they may not rend Him asunder by their own mutilated faith.

But if by the Spirit ye mortify the deeds of the body. Paul thus moderates his opinion, to prevent his making the godly, who are still conscious of much infirmity, feel in despair. Although we may still be subject to sin, nevertheless he still promises us life, provided we strive to mortify the flesh. He does not strictly require the destruction of the flesh, but only bids us make every exertion to subdue its lusts.

14. *For as many as are led by the Spirit of God, these are sons of God.* This is the proof of what has immediately gone before. Paul teaches us that only those are finally reckoned to be the sons of God who are ruled by His Spirit, since by this mark God acknowledges His own. This destroys the empty boast of hypocrites who usurp the title without the reality, and believers are thus aroused to undoubted confidence in their salvation. The substance of his remarks amounts to this, that all who are led by the Spirit of God are the sons of God; all the sons of God are heirs of eternal life; and therefore all who are led by the Spirit of God ought to feel assured of eternal life. The middle premise or assumption is omitted because it was axiomatic.

It is, however, appropriate to observe that the action of the Spirit is varied. There is its universal action by which all creatures are sustained and moved. There are also the actions of the Spirit which are peculiar to men, and these too are varying in their character. But by Spirit Paul here means *sanctification*, with which the Lord favours none but His elect, while He sets them apart for Himself as His sons.

For ye received not the spirit of bondage again unto fear; but ye received the spirit of adoption, whereby we cry, Abba, Father. The Spirit himself beareth witness with our spirit, that we are children of God: and if children, then heirs; heirs of God, and joint-heirs with Christ; if so be that we suffer with him, that we be also glorified with him. For I reckon that the sufferings of this present time are not worthy to be compared with the glory which shall be revealed to us-ward. (15-18)

15. Paul now confirms the certainty of that confidence in which he has recently bidden believers rest secure. He does so by mentioning the special effect produced by the Spirit. The Spirit has not been given to harass us with fear or torment us with anxiety, but rather to allay our disquiet, to bring our minds to a state of tranquillity, and to stir

us up to call on God with confidence and freedom. Paul, therefore, not only pursues the argument which he touched on before, but also dwells more on the other cause which he had connected with this at the same time, viz. that dealing with the fatherly indulgence of God, by which He forgives His people the infirmity of the flesh and the sins under which they still labour. Our confidence in this forbearance of God, Paul teaches us, is made certain by the Spirit of adoption, who would not bid us be bold in prayer without sealing to us free pardon. In order to make this more clear, Paul states that there are two spirits. One he calls *the spirit of bondage*, which we are able to derive from the law; and the other, *the spirit of adoption*, which proceeds from the Gospel. The first, he states, was formerly given to produce fear; the other is given now to afford assurance. The certainty of our salvation, which he wishes to confirm, appears, as we see, with greater clarity from such a comparison of opposites. The same comparison is used by the author of the Epistle to the Hebrews, when he says that we have not come to Mount Sinai, where all things were so terrible, that the people, terrified as if by the immediate declaration of death, implored that the word should not be spoken to them, and Moses himself confessed that he was filled with terror, 'but (we) are come unto mount Zion, and unto the city of the living God, the heavenly Jerusalem . . . and to Jesus the mediator of a new covenant' (Heb. 12.18ff).

From the adverb *again* we learn that Paul is here comparing the law with the Gospel. This is the inestimable benefit which the Son of God has brought us by His advent, that we should no longer be bound by the servile condition of the law. We are not, however, to infer from this either that no one was endowed with the Spirit of adoption before the coming of Christ, or that all who received the law were slaves and not sons. Paul compares the ministry of the law with the dispensation of the Gospel, rather than persons with persons. I admit that believers are here warned how much more liberally God has now dealt with them than He did formerly with the fathers under the Old Testament. He regards, however, the outward dispensation, and in this respect alone we excel them, for the faith of Abraham, Moses, and David, was more excellent than ours. Yet in so far as God kept them under a 'schoolmaster', they had not yet attained the liberty which has been disclosed to us.

We must, however, note at the same time that Paul is making a deliberate contrast because of false apostles between the literal disciples of the law and believers, whom Christ, their heavenly Master, not only addresses with the words of His mouth, but also teaches inwardly and effectually by His Spirit.

Although the covenant of grace is contained in the law, yet Paul removes it from there, for in opposing the Gospel to the law he regards only what was peculiar to the law itself, viz. command and prohibition, and the restraining of transgressors by the threat of death. He assigns to the law its own quality, by which it differs from the Gospel. The following statement, however, may be preferred: 'He sets forth only the law, in so far as God covenants with us in it with regard to works.' Our opinion, therefore, concerning persons should be as follows: 'When the law was published among the Jewish people, and also after it was published, the godly were enlightened by the same Spirit of faith. Thus the hope of eternal inheritance, of which the Spirit is the earnest and seal, was sealed on their hearts. The only difference is that the Spirit is more bountifully and abundantly poured out in the kingdom of Christ.' If, however, we regard the dispensation of doctrine itself, it will be seen that salvation was first revealed for certain when Christ was manifested in the flesh, so great was the obscurity in which all things were covered in the Old Testament, when compared with the clear light of the Gospel.

Finally, the law, considered in itself, can do nothing but bind those who are subject to its wretched bondage by the horror of death as well, for it promises no blessing except on condition, and pronounces death on all transgressors. As, therefore, under the law there was the spirit of bondage which oppressed the conscience with fear, so under the Gospel there is the spirit of adoption, which gladdens our souls with the testimony of our salvation. Note that Paul connects *fear* with bondage, since the law can do nothing but harass and torment our souls with wretched discontent as long as it exercises its dominion. There is, therefore, no other remedy for pacifying our souls than when God forgives us our sins, and deals kindly with us as a father with his children.

Whereby we cry, Abba, Father. Paul has altered the person in order to express the common lot of all the saints. 'You have', he is saying, 'received the Spirit, through whom you and all the rest of us believers cry. . . .' The imitation of the word used by a child of his father is very emphatic, because Paul uses the word *Father* in the person of believers. The repetition of the name by different words is for the sake of amplification. Paul means that the mercy of God has now been spread throughout the whole world to such an extent that, as Augustine observes, He is prayed to in all languages without distinction. Paul's object, therefore, was to express the consent which existed among all nations. It follows from this that there is now no difference between Jew and Greek, since they have grown together. The prophet Isaiah says something different when he declares that the language of Canaan would be common to all people (Isa. 19.18). The meaning, however, is the same. He is not referring to outward forms of speech, but to the harmony of the heart in worshipping God, and to the same simple zeal in professing His true and pure worship. The word *cry* is used to express confidence, as if he said, 'We do not pray in a doubtful way, but raise a loud voice to heaven without fear.'

Believers also called God Father under the law, but not with such free confidence, since the veil kept them far from the sanctuary. But now, when an entrance has been opened to us by the blood of Christ, we may glory with familiarity and in full voice that we are the sons of God. Hence arises this cry. The prophecy of Hosea is also thus fulfilled: 'I will say to them which were not my people, Thou art my people; and they shall say, *Thou art* my God' (Hos. 2.23). The more evident the promise is, the greater our freedom in prayer.

16. *The Spirit himself beareth witness.* He does not simply say that the Spirit of God is a witness to our spirit, but he uses a compound verb which could be translated into Latin by *contestatur* ('contests'), were it not that the Latin word *contestatio* has a different meaning. Paul means that the Spirit of God affords us such a testimony that our spirit is assured of the adoption of God, when He is our Guide and Teacher. Our mind would not of its own accord convey this assurance to us, unless the testimony of the Spirit preceded it. There is here also an explanation of the previous sentence, for while the Spirit testifies to us that we are the children of God, He at the same time pours this confidence into our hearts, so that we dare invoke God as our Father. And certainly, since the confidence of the heart alone opens our mouth, our tongues will be dumb to utter prayers, unless the Spirit bears testimony to our heart concerning the fatherly love of God. For we must always hold fast the principle that we do not pray to God properly unless we are persuaded for certain in our hearts that He is our Father, when we call Him such. The other principle, that our faith can be proved only by calling upon God, also corresponds to this. It is, therefore, not without reason that Paul recalls us to this test and shows that it is only when those who have embraced the promise of grace exercise themselves in prayers, that it is seen how serious is the faith of every believer.

The present passage is an excellent refutation of the shallow arguments of the Sophists concerning moral conjecture, which is nothing but uncertainty and anxiety of mind, or rather, wavering and delusion. An answer is given here at the same time to their objection, when they ask how a man can be fully assured of the will of God. This certainty, however, is not within the reach of man, but is the testimony of the Spirit of God, as Paul discusses more fully in the First Epistle to the Corinthians. This letter also provides a fuller explanation of the present passage. The proposition, therefore, remains—no one can be called a son of God who does not acknowledge himself to be such. This acknowledgment John terms *knowledge*, in order to denote its certainty (I John 5.19, 20).

17. *And if children, then heirs.* Paul proves from an argument derived from circumstances related to what he has said or which follow from it, that our salvation consists in having God as our Father. It is for children that the inheritance is appointed. When, therefore, God has adopted us as His children, He has at the same time also ordained an inheritance for us. Paul then indicates what sort of inheritance it is, viz. that it is heavenly, and therefore incorruptible and eternal, and such as has been manifested in Christ. By this manifestation not only is all uncertainty removed, but the excellence of this inheritance, which we share with the only-begotten Son of God, is also commended. Paul's purpose, however, as will presently appear more clearly, is to extol highly the inheritance which has been promised to us, so that we may be contented with it, despise with boldness the enticements of the world, and bear with patience whatever troubles may befall us in the world.

If so be that we suffer with him. There are various interpretations of this passage, but the sense which I favour before all others is this: 'We are fellow-heirs with Christ, provided we follow Him in the way in which He Himself has led us, in discerning our inheritance.' Paul made this mention of Christ, because he intended to pass on to this exhortation by these steps: 'The inheritance of God is ours, because we have been adopted by His grace as His sons. To remove any doubt, the possession of it has already been conferred on Christ, with whom we are made partakers. But Christ went to that inheritance by the cross. We, therefore, must go to it in the same way.' We are not to fear, as some do, that Paul is thus ascribing the cause of our eternal glory to our labours. This manner of speaking is usual in Scripture. He is, however, pointing out the order which the Lord follows in ministering salvation to us, rather than its cause. He has already sufficiently defended the free mercy of God against the merits of works. Now, while exhorting us to patience, he does not argue about the source of our salvation, but the manner in which God governs His people.

18. *For I reckon that the sufferings of this present time are not worthy to be compared.* Although it is quite appropriate to take this as a kind of correction, I prefer to regard it as an amplification of his exhortation, by way of anticipating an objection, in this sense: 'It should not trouble us if we have to pass to heavenly glory through various afflictions, since these, if compared with the greatness of that glory, are of very little importance.' Paul has put *the glory which shall be revealed* for

eternal glory, just as he refers to the sufferings of the world which pass away quickly as *the sufferings of this present time.*

It is clear from this that this passage was quite misunderstood by the schoolmen, who have derived from it their frivolous distinction between congruity and condignity. The apostle is not comparing the worth of each, but simply lightens the weight of the cross by comparing it with the greatness of glory, in order to confirm the minds of believers in patience.

For the earnest expectation of the creation waiteth for the revealing of the sons of God. For the creation was subjected to vanity, not of its own will, but by reason of him who subjected it, in hope that the creation itself also shall be delivered from the bondage of corruption into the liberty of the glory of the children of God. For we know that the whole creation groaneth and travaileth in pain together until now. (19-22)

19. *For the earnest expectation of the creation.* Paul instructs us that we have an example of the patience to which he had exhorted us even in dumb creatures themselves. Omitting the various interpretations of the passage, I understand it in this sense: 'There is no element and no part of the world which, touched with the knowledge of its present misery, is not intent on the hope of the resurrection.' Paul states two truths—all creatures labour, and yet are sustained by hope. From this too we see how immense is the price of eternal glory, which can excite and draw all things to desire it.

Further, the expression, *expectation waiteth for*, though somewhat unusual, has a most suitable meaning. Paul wanted to signify that the creatures, bound by great anxiety and held in suspense by a great longing, look for that day which will openly exhibit the glory of the sons of God. He calls it *the revealing of the sons of God*, when we shall be like God, as John says: 'Now are we children of God, and it is not yet made manifest what we shall be' (I John 3.2). I have retained Paul's words, because Erasmus' version, *Until the sons of God shall be made manifest*, was, I think, bolder than the passage allows, without sufficiently expressing the mind of the apostle. Paul does not mean that the sons of God shall be manifested in the last day, but that it shall then be made known how desirable and happy their condition is when they put off their corruption and put on heavenly glory. He ascribes hope to irrational creatures, so that believers may open their eyes to behold the invisible life, even though as yet it lies hidden beneath a humble garb.

20. *For the creation was subjected to vanity.* He declares the object of the expectation from its opposite. Since the creatures, which are subject to corruption, cannot be renewed until the sons of God are

wholly restored, while they seek for their renewal they look for the manifestation of the heavenly kingdom. He says that they have been *subjected to vanity*, because they do not remain firm and secure, but, being transitory and inconstant, pass swiftly away. Paul is undoubtedly contrasting vanity with natural perfection.

Not of its own will. Since there is no sense in such creatures, we must take *will* (*voluntas*) to mean natural inclination, according to which the whole nature of things tends to its own preservation and perfection. Everything, therefore, that is subject to corruption suffers violence against the purpose of nature and in opposition to it. By personification (κατὰ προσωποποίαν) Paul represents all the parts of the world as being endowed with sense, in order that we may feel more ashamed of our stupidity if we are not raised to a higher level by the uncertain fluctuation of this world which we see.

But by reason of him who subjected it. He sets before us an example of obedience in all creatures, and adds that it arises from *hope*. From hope comes the swiftness of the sun, the moon, and all the stars in their constant course, the continued obedience of the earth in producing its fruits, the unwearied motion of the air, and the ready power of the water to flow. God has given to each its proper task, and has not simply given a precise command to do His will, but has at the same time inwardly implanted the hope of renewal. The whole machinery of the world would fall out of gear at almost every moment and all its parts fail in the sorrowful confusion which followed the fall of Adam, were they not borne up from elsewhere by some hidden support. It would, therefore, he highly shameful for the earnest of the Spirit to produce less effect in the sons of God than hidden instinct does in the inanimate parts of creation. However much, therefore, created things may be inclined by nature to some other course, yet since it has been God's pleasure to make them subject to vanity, they obey His command, and because He has given them a hope of a better condition, they sustain themselves with this, and postpone their longing until the incorruption which has been promised to them is revealed. Paul ascribes *hope* to them by personification, just as before he ascribed will and refusal to them.

21. *In hope that the creation itself also shall be delivered.* He shows how the creature has been made subject to vanity *in hope*. But the time will come when it will one day be delivered, as Isaiah testifies and Peter still more clearly confirms.

We may, it is true, infer from this how dreadful is the curse which we have deserved, since all innocent creatures from earth to heaven are punished for our sins. It is our fault that they struggle in corruption. The condemnation of the human race is thus imprinted on the heavens, the earth, and all creatures. Again, this passage shows us to how great an excellence of glory the sons of God are to be exalted, and all creatures shall be renewed to magnify it and declare its splendour.

Paul does not mean that all creatures will be partakers of the same glory with the sons of God, but that they will share in their own manner in the better state, because God will restore the present fallen world to perfect condition at the same time as the human race. It is neither expedient nor right for us to inquire with greater curiosity into the perfection which will be evidenced by beasts, plants, and metals, because the main part of corruption is decay. Some shrewd but unbalanced commentators ask whether all kinds of animals will be immortal. If we give free rein to these speculations, where will they finally carry us? Let us, therefore, be content with this simple doctrine —their constitution will be such, and their order so complete, that no appearance either of deformity or of impermanence will be seen.

22. *For we know.* He repeats the same proposition in order to pass over to our own case, although what he now says has the effect and form of a conclusion. Because the creatures are subject to corruption, not through their natural desire, but by God's appointment, and also because they have a hope of being freed hereafter from corruption, it follows that they groan like a woman in labour until they have been delivered. This is a most appropriate comparison to inform us that the groaning of which he speaks will not be in vain or without effect. It will finally bring forth a joyful and happy fruit. In short, the creatures are not content with their present condition, and yet they are not so distressed as to pine away irremediably. They are, however, in labour, because they are waiting to be renewed to a better state. By saying that they *groan together*, he does not mean that they are bound together by common anxiety, but he connects them with us as our companions. The particle *until now*, or, *to this day*, serves to reduce the wearisome nature of the dullness which we experience each day. If the creatures have continued their groaning for so many ages, our softness or indolence will be inexcusable if we faint in the brief course of our shadowy life.

And not only so, but ourselves also, which have the firstfruits of the Spirit, even we ourselves groan within ourselves, waiting for our adoption, to wit, the redemption of our body. For by hope were we saved: but hope that is seen is not hope: for who hopeth for that which he seeth? But if we hope for that which we see not, then do we with patience wait for it. (23-25)

23. *And not only so, but ourselves also.* There are some who think that the apostle intended here to exaggerate the dignity of our future

blessedness, because all things, not simply the irrational parts of
creation, but we ourselves also who have been regenerated by the
Spirit of God, look for it with fervent desire. This view can be
defended, but Paul, it seems to me, is comparing the greater with the
less, as if he said, 'The excellence of our future glory is of such importance even to the very elements, which are devoid of sense and reason,
that they burn with desire for it. How much more should we, who
have been illuminated by the Spirit of God, aspire to and strive for the
attainment of so great a good both by the firmness of our hope and
the endeavours of our zeal.' Paul calls for two kinds of feelings in
believers. They are to *groan*, since they are burdened with a sense of
their present misery, and yet they are to *wait* patiently for their
deliverance. He wants them to be raised up by the expectation of
future blessedness, and to overcome all their present troubles by a mind
set above their immediate condition, so that they may not consider
their present character, but what they are to be.

Which have the firstfruits of the Spirit. I am not at all happy with the
interpretation of those who explain the word *firstfruits* (*primitias*) to
mean a rare and notable excellence. In order, therefore, to avoid
ambiguity, I have preferred to render the word as *beginnings* (*primordia*).
I do not consider the expression to have been applied to the apostles
alone, as these interpreters do, but to all believers who are sprinkled
in this world with only a few drops of the Spirit, or even those who
have made excellent progress, but who, even though they are endowed
with a sure measure of the Spirit, are still far from perfection.

These, then, for the apostle, are the beginnings or firstfruits, which
are contrasted with the complete ingathering. Since the fulness of the
Spirit has not yet been bestowed on us, it is not strange that we are
moved with unrest. Paul repeats *ourselves* and adds *in ourselves* for the
sake of emphasis, in order to express our desire more fervently. He
does not, however, call it simply a desire, but *groaning*, because where
there is a sense of our wretchedness, we also *groan*.

Waiting for our adoption. Paul improperly refers here to our *adoption*
as the enjoyment of the inheritance into which we have been adopted.
He has, however, very good reason for doing so, for he means that the
eternal decree of God would be void unless the promised resurrection,
which is the effect of that decree, were also certain. By this decree
God has chosen us as His sons before the foundation of the world, He
bears witness to us concerning it by the Gospel, and He seals the faith
of it on our hearts by His Spirit. Why is God our Father, if not that
we may receive a heavenly inheritance after we have finished our
earthly pilgrimage? The phrase which he presently adds, *the redemption
of our body*, has the same reference. The price of our redemption was

paid by Christ, but in such a way that death still holds us in its chains, and indeed, that we still carry it within us. It follows from this that the sacrifice of the death of Christ would be unfruitful and wasted, unless its fruit were to appear in our heavenly renewal.

24. *For by hope were we saved.* Paul confirms his exhortation by another argument, because our salvation cannot be separated from the appearance of death. He proves this from the nature of hope. Since hope extends to things which we have not yet experienced, and represents to our minds the image of things which are hidden and far remote, anything that is either openly seen or grasped by the hand cannot be hoped for. Paul takes for granted the undeniable truth that as long as we live in the world, our salvation resides in hope. It follows from this that hope is laid up with God far above our senses. By saying that hope which is seen is not hope, he uses a harsh expression, but it does not obscure the sense. He simply wishes to teach us, that since hope refers to a future and not a present good, it is never connected with the open possession. If, therefore, groaning is a burden to any, they are necessarily overthrowing the order which has been laid down by God, who does not call His people to triumph before He has exercised them in the warfare of suffering. But since it has pleased God to cherish our salvation close to His bosom, it is expedient for us to toil on earth, to be oppressed, to mourn, to be afflicted, indeed to lie as though half-dead, or like the dead. Those who seek a visible salvation reject it when they renounce hope, for hope has been appointed by God as the guardian of salvation.

25. *If we hope for that which we see not.* The argument is derived from what precedes to what follows, for patience necessarily follows hope. If it is burdensome to lack the good which one desires, we must faint from despair, unless we sustain and comfort ourselves by patience. Hope, therefore, always brings patience with it. Paul's conclusion is thus most appropriate—all that the Gospel promises concerning the glory of the resurrection vanishes away, unless we spend our present life in bearing with patience the cross and tribulations. If our life is invisible, we must have death before our eyes, but if our glory is invisible, then our present state is ignominy. If, therefore, we wish to sum up the whole of this passage in a few words, we may arrange Paul's arguments in this way, 'Salvation is laid up in hope for all the godly, but it is the peculiar quality of hope to be intent on future and absent benefits. The salvation of believers, therefore, is hidden. Now hope is sustained only by patience. The salvation of believers, therefore, is fulfilled only by patience.'

We have here, it may be added, a notable passage which shows that patience is the inseparable companion of faith. The reason for this is evident—while we comfort ourselves with the hope of a better condition, the sense of our present miseries is softened and mitigated, so that they are borne with less difficulty.

And in like manner the Spirit also helpeth our infirmity: for we know not how to pray as we ought; but the Spirit himself maketh intercession for us with groanings which cannot be uttered; and he that searcheth the hearts knoweth what is the mind of the Spirit, because he maketh intercession for the saints according to the will of God. (26-27)

26. *And in like manner the Spirit also helpeth our infirmity.* To prevent believers from objecting that they are too weak to be equal to bearing so many heavy burdens, he sets before them the aid of the Spirit, which is abundantly sufficient to overcome all difficulties. There is, therefore, no reason for any to complain that the bearing of the cross is beyond our strength, since we are strengthened by power from heaven. The Greek word συναντιλαμβάνεται is very strong. The Spirit itself takes part of the burden which oppresses our weakness, and not only gives us help and succour but lifts us up, as though it itself underwent the burden with us. The word *infirmities*[1] in the plural increases the force of the expression. Since experience shows us that unless we are supported by the hand of God, we are soon oppressed by innumerable evils, Paul admonishes us that, though we are weak in every part and various infirmities threaten our fall, there is sufficient protection in the Spirit of God to prevent us from ever being destroyed or being overwhelmed by any accumulation of evils. But these resources of the Spirit instruct us with greater certainty that it is by God's appointment that we strive with groanings and sighings for our redemption.

For we know not how to pray as we ought. Paul had spoken above of the testimony of the Spirit, by which we know that God is our Father, and in which we trust in daring to call on Him as our Father. He now repeats the second part relating to invocation and says that we are taught by the same Spirit how we are to pray to God, and what we are to ask of Him in our prayers. Paul has appropriately connected prayers with the anxious desires of the godly, because God does not afflict them with troubles in order that they may inwardly feed on hidden grief, but that they may unburden themselves by prayer, and thus exercise their faith.

Although there are, as I know, various explanations given of this passage, Paul, I think, simply means that we are blind in praying to God, because, although we feel our evils, our minds are too disturbed and confused to make the right choice of what suits us, or what is

[1] Thus Calvin's version, R.V. reads singular.

expedient for us. If anyone objects that we have a rule prescribed to us in the Word of God, my answer is that our affections remain oppressed with darkness in spite of this, until the Spirit guides them by His light.

But the Spirit Himself maketh intercession for us. Although it may not yet appear in fact that our prayers have been heard by God, Paul concludes that the presence of heavenly grace already shines forth in the very zeal for prayer, because no one of his own accord conceives devout and godly prayers. Unbelievers do indeed blurt out their prayers, but they merely mock God, because there is no sincerity or seriousness in them, or correctly ordered pattern. The Spirit, therefore, must prescribe the manner of our praying. Paul calls the groans into which we break forth by the impulse of the Spirit *unutterable*, because they far exceed the capacity of our intellect. The Spirit of God is said to *intercede*, not because He in fact humbles Himself as a suppliant to pray or groan, but because He stirs up in our hearts the prayers which it is proper for us to address to God. In the second place He affects our hearts in such a way that these prayers penetrate into heaven itself by their fervency. Paul has spoken in this way for the purpose of attributing the whole of prayer more significantly to the grace of the Spirit. We are bidden to knock. But no one of his own accord could premeditate a single syllable, unless God were to knock to gain admission to our souls by the secret impulse of His Spirit, and thus open our hearts to Himself.

27. *He that searcheth the hearts knoweth what is the mind of the Spirit.* The fact that we are heard by God while we pray through His Spirit is a notable reason for confirming our confidence, for He Himself is intimately acquainted with our prayers, as being the thoughts of His own Spirit. We should note here the propriety of the word *know*, which signifies that God does not take notice of those affections of the Spirit as being new and unaccustomed, nor reject them as unreasonable, but acknowledges them, and at the same time kindly receives them as being known to Himself. As, therefore, Paul had recently declared that God aids us while He leads us into His bosom, so now he adds another consolation. Our prayers which He regulates, will by no means be disappointed. Paul also gives the reason for this immediately, because in so doing He conforms us to His will. It follows from this that that which is agreeable to His will, by which all things are ruled, cannot be inefficacious. Let us also learn from this that the first part of prayer is consent to the will of the Lord, who is by no means bound to follow our desires. We must, therefore, pray to God to regulate our prayers according to His will, if we would have them accepted by Him.

And we know that to them that love God all things work together for good, even to them that are called according to his purpose. For whom He foreknew, He also foreordained to be conformed to the image of his Son, that he might be the firstborn among many brethren: and whom he foreordained, them he also called: and whom he called them he also justified: and whom he justified, them he also glorified. (28-30)

28. *And we know.* Paul now concludes from his statements above that the troubles of this life are so far from hindering our salvation that they rather assist it. His use of the illative particle presents no objection, for he is quite used to employing adverbs indiscriminately in this manner. His conclusion, however, at the same time includes his anticipation of an objection. The judgment of the flesh exclaims here that it does not at all appear that God hears our prayers, since our afflictions always continue in the same way. The apostle, therefore, anticipates this, and says that although God does not immediately succour His people, He does not desert them, for by a wonderful contrivance He turns their apparent losses in such a way as to promote their salvation. I have no objection if it is preferred to read this sentence by itself, as though Paul sought to prove by a fresh argument that it should not grieve or trouble us to have to bear adversities which assist our salvation. In the meantime, Paul's design is plain. Although the elect and the reprobate are exposed without distinction to similar evils, yet there is a great difference between them, for God instructs believers by afflictions, and procures their salvation.

We must, however, remember that Paul is speaking only of adversities, as though he had said, 'All that befalls the saints is so controlled by God that the final issue shows that what the world regards as harmful is to their advantage.' Augustine says that even the sins of the saints are so far from doing them harm by the ordaining providence of God, that they serve rather to advance their salvation. This statement, however, though true, does not relate to the present passage, which deals with the cross. It should be observed that Paul has included the whole of true religion in the love of God. The whole pursuit of righteousness, indeed, depends on this.

Even to them that are called according to his purpose. This clause seems to have been added by way of correction. No one is to think that, because believers love God, they obtain the advantage of deriving so much fruit from their adversities by their own merit. For we know that when salvation is under discussion, men gladly begin with themselves, and make preparations by which to anticipate the grace of God. Paul, therefore, instructs us that those whom he referred to as worshippers of God had been chosen by Him before. It is certain that Paul notes the order, so that we may know that the fact that everything happens to the saints for their salvation depends on the free adoption of God as the first cause. Indeed, Paul shows that believers do not love God before they are called by Him, as he reminds us in another place that the Galatians were known by God before they knew Him (Gal. 4.9). It is indeed true, as Paul says, that afflictions avail to the salvation only of those who love God; but the statement of John is no less true, that we begin to love God only when He first freely loves us.

Moreover, the calling of which Paul speaks here has a wide reference. It is not to be confined to the manifestation of election, which he will mention presently, but is simply opposed to the course pursued by men. 'Believers', Paul says, 'do not acquire godliness by their own efforts, but are rather led by the hand of God, since He has chosen them to be His peculiar people.' The word *purpose* distinctly excludes all that men imagine they reciprocate, as though Paul were denying that the causes of our election are to be sought in any other place than in the secret good pleasure of God. This appears more clearly in Eph. 1 and II Tim. 1, where the contrast between this purpose and human righteousness is also explicitly stated. There is no doubt, however, that Paul expressly stated here that our salvation is based on the selection of God, in order that he might pass from this to the subject which he immediately added, viz. that the afflictions which conform us to Christ have been determined for us by the same heavenly decree. Paul's purpose in doing this was to connect our salvation to the bearing of the cross as by a chain of necessity.

29. *For whom he foreknew, he also foreordained.* Paul shows, therefore, by the very order of election that all the afflictions of believers are simply the means by which they are conformed to Christ. He had previously declared the necessity for this. Affliction, therefore, is no reason why we should be grieved, bitter, or burdened, unless we also disapprove of the election of the Lord, by which we have been foreordained to life, and are unwilling to bear in our persons the image of the Son of God, by which we are prepared for the glory of heaven.

The foreknowledge of God here mentioned by Paul is not mere prescience, as some inexperienced people foolishly imagine, but adoption, by which He has always distinguished His children from the reprobate. In this sense Peter says that believers had been elected to the sanctification of the Spirit according to the foreknowledge of God. Those, therefore, to whom I have referred foolishly conclude that God has elected none but those whom He foresaw would be worthy of His grace. Peter does not flatter believers as though they were all elected for their individual merits, but by recalling them to the eternal counsel of God declares that they are entirely void of any worthiness. In this passage also Paul repeats in other words the remarks which he had just made concerning God's purpose. It follows from this that this knowledge depends on God's good pleasure, because in adopting those whom He would, God had no foreknowledge of anything outside Himself, but simply marked out those whom He purposed to elect.

The verb προορίζειν which is translated *predestinate*, refers to the circumstances of the present passage. Paul meant only that God had determined that all whom He has adopted should bear the image of Christ. He did not simply say that they should be conformed to Christ, but *to the image of Christ*, in order to teach us that in Christ there is a living and conspicuous example which is set before all the sons of God for their imitation. The sum of the passage is that free adoption, in which our salvation consists, is inseparable from this other decree, viz. that He had appointed us to bear the cross. No one can be an heir of heaven who has not first been conformed to the only-begotten Son of God.

That he may (or, *might*) *be the firstborn.* The Greek infinitive εἶναι may be rendered in either way, but I prefer the former. In calling Christ *firstborn* Paul meant simply to express that if Christ possesses the pre-eminence among all the sons of God, He was rightly given to us as an example, so that we should not refuse anything which He has been pleased to undergo. As, therefore, our heavenly Father testifies by every means to the authority and dignity which He has conferred upon His Son, He wants all those whom He adopts as the heirs of His kingdom to be conformed to His example.

Although the condition of the godly differs in appearance (just as there is a difference between the members of the human body), yet there is a connexion between each individual and his head. As, therefore, the firstborn bears the name of the family, so Christ is placed in a state of pre-eminence, not only that He should excel in honour among believers, but also that He should include all believers within Himself under the common mark of brotherhood.

30. *And whom He foreordained, them He also called.* Paul now employs a climax in order to confirm by a clearer demonstration how true it is that our conformity to the humility of Christ effects our salvation. In this he teaches us that our participation in the cross is so connected with our vocation, justification, and finally our glory, that they cannot in any way be separated.

In order that readers may better understand the meaning of the apostle, it is well that they should recall my previous statement that the word *predestine* does not refer to election, but to that purpose or decree of God by which He has ordained that His people are to bear the cross. By teaching us that they are now *called*, Paul means that God does not conceal what He has determined to do with them, but has disclosed it, in order that they may bear with equanimity and patience the condition laid upon them. *Calling* is here distinguished from secret election as being inferior to it. The objection might be made that no one has any knowledge at all of the condition which God has appointed for each man. To prevent this, therefore, the apostle says that God by His calling openly testifies of His hidden purpose. This testimony, however, does not consist in external preaching alone, but has the power of the Spirit connected with it, for Paul is dealing with the elect whom God not only constrains by His spoken Word, but also draws inwardly.

Justification might quite well be extended to include the continuation of the divine favour from the time of the calling of the believer to his death. But because Paul uses this word throughout the Epistle for the unmerited imputation of righteousness, there is no necessity for us to depart from this meaning. Paul's design is to show that the compensation which is offered to us is too precious to permit us to avoid affliction. What is more desirable than to be reconciled to God, so that our miseries should no longer be signs of His curse, or lead to our destruction?

Paul adds that those who are now oppressed by the cross shall be *glorified*, so that their troubles and reproaches are not to bring them any loss. Although glorification has as yet been exhibited only in our Head, yet, because we now perceive in Him the inheritance of eternal life, His glory brings to us such assurance of our own glory, that our hope may justly be compared to a present possession.

It should be added that Paul has employed a Hebraism and used the past tense instead of the present in his verbs. What is meant is almost certainly a continued act, thus: 'Those whom God now exercises under the cross according to His counsel, He calls and justifies at the same time to a hope of salvation, so that they should lose nothing of their glory in their humiliation. Although their present troubles deform it before the world, yet before God and the angels it always shines in perfection.' What Paul therefore intends to show by this climax is that the afflictions of believers, which cause their present humiliation, are intended solely that they may obtain the glory of the kingdom of heaven and reach the glory of the resurrection of Christ, with whom they are now crucified.

What then shall we say to these things? If God is for us, who is against us? He that spared not his own Son, but delivered him up for us all, how shall he not also with him freely give us all things? Who shall lay anything to the charge of God's elect? It is God that justifieth. (31-33)

31. *What then shall we say?* Having sufficiently proved his point, Paul now breaks into a series of exclamations, by which he expresses the greatness of soul which believers ought to possess while adversity urges them to despair. He teaches us by these words that the invincible courage which overcomes all temptations resides in the fatherly favour of God. The only way by which our judgment of the love or hatred of God is customarily formed is, as we know, by a consideration of our present state. Hence when things go wrong, sorrow takes possession of our minds, and drives away all confidence and consolation. Paul, however, cries out that a deeper principle is to be sought for, and that therefore those who confine themselves to gazing at the sorrowful spectacle of our warfare are wrong. I admit that the scourges of God are rightly reckoned in themselves to be the signs of God's wrath, but since they are consecrated in Christ, Paul bids the saints lay hold on the fatherly love of God before all things, so that, by relying on this shield, they may confidently triumph over all evil. It is a bronze wall for us that when God is favourable to us we shall be secure against all danger. Paul, however, does not mean that we shall have no opposition, but he promises us victory over every kind of enemy.

If God is for us, who is against us? This is the chief and therefore the only support to sustain us in every temptation. If God is not propitious to us, no sure confidence can be conceived, even though everything should smile upon us. On the other hand, however, His favour alone is a sufficiently great consolation for every sorrow, and a sufficiently strong protection against all the storms of misfortune. There are many testimonies of Scripture which refer to this truth, where the saints, relying on the power of God alone, dare to despise every adversity which they encounter in the world. 'Yea, though I walk through the valley of the shadow of death, I will fear no evil; for thou art with me' (Ps. 23.4). 'In God have I put my trust, I will not be afraid; what can man do unto me?' (Ps. 56.11). 'I will not be afraid of ten thousands of the people, that have set themselves against me round about' (Ps. 3.6).

There is no power under heaven or above it which can resist the arm of God. If, therefore, we have Him as our defender, we need fear no harm whatever. That man alone displays true confidence in God who is content with His protection, and had no fear sufficient to make him despair. Believers are certainly often shaken, but are never utterly cast down. In short, the apostle's object was to show that the godly soul ought to stand on the inward testimony of the Holy Spirit, and not to depend on external things.

32. *He that spared not His own Son.* Since it is of very great importance to us to be so thoroughly persuaded of the fatherly love of God, that we continue to glory in it without fear, Paul cites the price of our

reconciliation in order to confirm God's favours towards us. It is a notable and shining proof of His inestimable love that the Father did not hesitate to bestow His Son for our salvation. Paul therefore draws his argument from the greater to the less—since He had nothing dearer, more precious, or more excellent than His Son, He will neglect nothing which He foresees will be profitable to us.

This passage ought to admonish and arouse us to consider what Christ brings to us with Himself, for as He is a pledge of God's boundless love towards us, so He has not been sent to us void of blessings or empty-handed, but filled with all heavenly treasures, so that those who possess Him may not want anything that is necessary for their complete happiness. To *deliver us* here means to expose to death.

33. *Who shall lay anything to the charge of God's elect?* The first and chief consolation of the godly in adversity is to be persuaded for certain of the fatherly kindness of God. From this comes both the certainty of their salvation, and the calm security of soul by which adversities are sweetened, or, at least, the bitterness of sorrow is mitigated. There is, therefore, hardly any more appropriate exhortation to patience which can be brought than when we understand that God is propitious to us. And so Paul makes this confidence the beginning of the consolation, by which believers ought to be strengthened against all evils. Since man's salvation is assailed first by accusation, and then overthrown by condemnation, Paul first removes the danger of accusation, for there is only one God at whose tribunal we must stand. Seeing, therefore, that it is He who justifies us, there is no place for accusation. The contrasted clauses do not seem to be arranged exactly. The two parts which Paul ought to have contrasted are, 'Who shall accuse?' and, 'It is Christ who intercedes.' He ought then to have added the other two clauses, 'Who shall condemn us? It is God who justifies.' God's absolution corresponds to condemnation, and Christ's defence to accusation. But Paul had a reason for his transposition, since he wished to arm the sons of God from top to bottom with the confidence which wards off anxieties and fears. His conclusion, therefore, that the children of God are not liable to accusation because God justifies, is more emphatic than if he had said that Christ is our advocate, for it expresses more clearly that the way to judgment is completely shut off when the judge pronounces that he is wholly exempting from guilt the prisoner whose accuser would drag him to punishment.

The same argument also applies to the second clause. Paul shows us that believers are in no danger of undergoing condemnation, since Christ, by expiating their sins, has anticipated the judgment of God, and by His intercession not only abolishes death, but also covers our sins in oblivion, so that no account is taken of them.

The substance of the argument is that we are not only freed from terror by available remedies when we come to the judgment-seat of God, but that God comes to our aid beforehand, so that He may better provide for our confidence.

We must, however, note here what we have stated constantly before, that according to Paul, to be *justified* means simply to be accounted just by having been absolved from the sentence of God. There is no difficulty in proving this in the present passage, in which Paul argues from the basis of one proposition in order to nullify its opposite. To absolve and to accuse are opposites, and therefore God will not admit any accusation against us, because He has absolved us from all blame. The devil, to be sure, accuses all the godly; and the law of God itself and their own conscience also reprove them. But none of these have any influence upon the judge who justifies them. No adversary, therefore, can shake, much less destroy, our salvation.

Paul also refers to them as *elect*, in such a way as to have no doubt of his being in their number. He had that knowledge not, as some sophists falsely state, by special revelation, but by a perception common to all the godly. The statement, therefore, here used of the elect may, according to the example of Paul, be applied by all the godly to themselves. Otherwise, had he buried election in the secret counsel of God, this would have been a doctrine not only lacking in warmth, but completely lifeless. But since we know that Paul is here deliberately introducing something that all the godly ought to apply to themselves, there is no doubt that we are all being led to examine our calling, in order that we may determine that we are the children of God.

34. *Who is he that shall condemn?* As no one can succeed in his accusation when the judge absolves, so there remains no condemnation, when the laws have been satisfied and the penalty already paid. Christ is the One who once suffered the punishment due to us, and thereby professed that He took our place in order to deliver us. Anyone, therefore, who desires to condemn us after this must kill Christ Himself again. But Christ has not only died, He has also come forth as conqueror of death, and triumphed over its power by His resurrection.

Paul adds still more—Christ, he states, now sits at the right hand of the Father. By this he means that He obtains dominion over heaven and earth, and full power and rule over all things, as he states in Eph. 1.20. Lastly, he teaches us that Christ is seated in this way in order to be a perpetual advocate and intercessor in the defence of our salvation. It follows from this that if any one wishes to condemn us, he not only renders void the death of Christ, but also fights against the incomparable power with which the Father has honoured Him, and with such power conferred on Him supreme authority. This great security which dares to triumph over the devil, death, sin and the gates of hell, ought to be deeply implanted in all godly hearts, for our faith is nothing, unless we are persuaded for certain that Christ is ours, and that the Father is propitious to us in Him. There is, therefore, no more pernicious or destructive conception than the scholastic dogma of the uncertainty of salvation.

Who maketh intercession for us. Paul required to make this explicit addition, to prevent the divine Majesty of Christ from terrifying us. Although, therefore, Christ holds all things in subjection under His feet from His lofty throne, Paul represents Him as a Mediator, whose presence it would be absurd for us to dread, since He not only invites us to Himself in a kindly manner, but also appears for us before the Father as Intercessor. We are not to measure this intercession by our carnal judgment, for we must not think of Him as humbly supplicating the Father on bended knee and with outstretched hands. Christ, however, is justly said to intercede for us, because He appears continually before the Father in His death and resurrection, which takes the place of eternal intercession, and to have the efficacy of lively prayer for reconciling the Father and making Him ready to listen to us.

Who shall separate us from the love of Christ? shall tribulation, or anguish, or persecution, or famine, or nakedness, or peril, or sword? Even as it is written, For Thy sake we are killed all the day long: We were accounted as sheep for the slaughter. Nay, in all these things we are more than conquerors through Him that loved us. (35-37)

35. *Who shall separate us from the love of Christ?* Paul now extends this security more widely to inferior beings. Those who are persuaded of the divine benevolence towards them are able to stand firm in the most pressing afflictions. These usually torment men to such an extent, either because they do not consider that these things happen by the providence of God, or because they interpret them as signs of the wrath of God, or because they think that they have been forsaken by God, or because they see no end to them, or do not meditate on a better life, or for other similar reasons. But when the mind is purged from errors of this kind, it will easily subside and grow calm. The meaning of the words is that whatever may happen, we must stand firm in the belief that God, who once in His love embraced us, never ceases to care for us. Paul does not simply say that there is nothing which separates God from His love for us, but desires that the knowledge and lively sense of the love to which he bears witness should flourish in our hearts, in such a way that it always shines in the darkness of our affliction. As clouds, though they obscure the clear view of the sun, do not wholly deprive us of its light, so in our adversity God sends us the rays of His

grace through the darkness, lest any temptation should overwhelm us with despair. Indeed, our faith should be borne up on wings by the promises of God, and penetrate to heaven through all the intervening obstacles. Adversity, it is true, considered by itself, is a sign of God's wrath, but when pardon and reconciliation have preceded it, we should be resolved that, though God chastises us, He never forgets His mercy. Paul reminds us of what we have deserved, but while urging us to repentance he testifies no less that our salvation is the object of God's care.

He speaks of the love of Christ, because the Father has thus in some measure revealed His compassion to us. Since, therefore, the love of God is not to be sought out of Christ, Paul rightly recalls us to this truth, so that our faith may behold the serene countenance of the Father in the rays of the grace of Christ.

In short, no adversity ought to undermine our belief that when God is propitious, nothing is against us. Some take the love of Christ in a passive sense for the love by which we love Him, as if Paul would arm us for invincible courage. But this misinterpretation is easily disproved from the whole of the context, and Paul will also presently remove all doubt by a clearer definition of this love.

Shall tribulation, or anguish, or persecution? The masculine pronoun which Paul has just used has a hidden emphasis. When he might have said in the neuter gender, 'What shall separate us?' he preferred to personify inanimate beings in order to send us into the contest with as many champions as there are different kinds of temptations to shake our faith.

These three temptations differ in this way—*tribulation* included every kind of trouble or loss, but *anguish* is the inward feeling, when difficulties reduce us to not knowing what course to follow. Such was the anxiety of Abraham and of Lot, when the one was constrained to expose his wife to prostitution and the other his daughters, because in their difficulty and perplexity they had no way of escape. *Persecution* properly denotes the tyrannical violence by which the children of God are undeservedly tormented by the ungodly. Although in II Cor. 4.8 Paul denies that the children of God are στενοχωρούμενοι ('straitened'), he does not contradict himself, for he does not simply make them immune from anxious care, but means that they are delivered from it, as the example of Abraham and Lot also reveal.

36. *Even as it is written.* This quotation is of great importance in regard to the subject being discussed. Paul hints that the terror of death is so far from being a reason for our falling away, that it is almost always the lot of the servants of God to have death in front of their eyes. It is probable that this Psalm describes the miserable oppression of the

people under the tyranny of Antiochus, for it is expressly stated that he acted with such cruelty towards the worshippers of God for no other reason than his hatred of true religion. The glorious affirmation is also added that even so they did not depart from the covenant of God. It was this in particular, I think, that Paul had in view. It is no objection that the saints in this psalm complain of the calamity with which they were then afflicted beyond their accustomed sufferings. Since they have first affirmed their innocence, and show they are burdened by so many evils, we can fittingly argue from this that there is nothing new in the Lord permitting the saints to be exposed undeservedly to the cruelty of the ungodly. But it is evident that this takes place only for their good, since Scripture teaches us that it is inconsistent with the righteousness of God for Him to destroy the righteous with the wicked (Gen. 18.23). It is proper, rather, that He should repay affliction to those who afflict, and rest to those who are afflicted (II Thess. 1.6, 9). They then affirm that they suffer for the Lord, and Christ pronounces them blessed who suffer for righteousness' sake (Matt. 5.10). To say that they *are killed all the day long* means that death threatens them in such a way that there is little difference between such a life and death.

37. *We are more than conquerors.* i.e. we always struggle and yet emerge. I have retained the word used by Paul though it is infrequently used in Latin (*supervincimus*). It sometimes happens that believers seem to have been overcome and to be bowed down in utter weariness, so greatly does the Lord not only harass but also humiliate them. This issue, however, is always granted to them, that they obtain the victory.

In order, however, that they may recognize the source of this invincible power, he again repeats his previous affirmation. He not only teaches us that, because God loves us, He lends His hand to support us, but he also confirms his same affirmation concerning the love of Christ. This one word more than sufficiently proves that the apostle is not speaking here of the fervour of the love with which we are drawn to God, but of the fatherly benevolence of God or Christ towards us. The assurance of this, fixed deep in our hearts, will always draw us from hell to the light of life, and will be of sufficient strength to support us.

For I am persuaded, that neither death, nor life, nor angels, nor principalities, nor things present, nor things to come, nor powers, nor height nor depth, nor any other creature shall be able to separate us from the love of God, which is in Christ Jesus our Lord. (38-39)

38. To confirm us more strongly in the things which we experience, Paul now also bursts into hyperbole. Should anything in life or death,

he says, seem able to tear us away from God, it will not do so. Indeed, the very angels themselves, were they to attempt to overthrow this foundation, will do us no harm. It is no objection that angels are ministering spirits, appointed for the salvation of the elect (Heb. 1.14), for Paul argues here from that which cannot possibly happen, as in Gal. 1.8. We may note in this respect how worthless all things ought to appear in our sight when compared with the glory of God, since it is lawful to dishonour even angels themselves for the purpose of asserting His truth. By *principalities* and *powers* are also meant angels, who are so termed because they are the primary instruments of the divine power. These two words were added so that, if the word *angels* sounded too insignificant, something more might be expressed. The interpretation, 'Neither angels, nor any other high powers there may be,' may be preferred. This is our manner of speaking when we are referring to things which are unknown to us, and exceed our comprehension.

Nor things present, nor things to come. Although Paul is speaking in hyperbolical language, he in fact asserts that no length of time can separate us from the grace of the Lord. It was necessary to add this, since we have not only to struggle with the sorrow which we feel from present evils, but also with fear and anxiety with which impending dangers may harass us. The meaning, therefore, is that we are not to fear that our faith in our adoption will be destroyed by the continuance of evils, however long it may be.

This passage clearly contradicts the schoolmen, who foolishly maintain that no one is certain of final perseverance, except by the favour of a special revelation, and this, they hold, is very rare. Such a dogma wholly destroys faith, and faith is certainly nothing if it does not extend to death and beyond. On the contrary, however, we are to have confidence that He who has begun a good work in us, will accomplish it until the day of the Lord Jesus.

39. *Which is in Christ Jesus.* i.e., of which Christ is the bond. He is the beloved Son in whom the Father is well pleased (Matt. 3.17). If, therefore, we cleave to God by Him, we are assured of God's inflexible and unwearied kindness towards us. Paul now speaks here more plainly than above, placing the fountain of love in the Father, and affirming that it flows to us from Christ.

CHAPTER NINE

*I say the truth in Christ, I lie not, my conscience bearing witness with
me in the Holy Ghost, that I have great sorrow and unceasing pain in
my heart. For I could wish that I myself were anathema from Christ
for my brethren's sake, my kinsmen according to the flesh: who are
Israelites; whose is the adoption, and the glory, and the covenants, and
the giving of the law, and the service of God, and the promises; whose
are the fathers, and of whom is Christ as concerning the flesh, who is
over all, God blessed for ever. Amen.* (1-5)

In this chapter Paul begins to meet the offences which might have
turned men's minds away from Christ, for the Jews, for whom He was
appointed by the covenant of the law, not only rejected, or despised,
but for the most part detested him. From this, one of two conclusions
seemed to follow—either that there is no truth in the divine promise,
or that Jesus, whom Paul preached, is not the Lord's Christ who had
been peculiarly promised to the Jews. In his subsequent remarks Paul
gives an excellent solution to both these difficulties. He deals with this
subject, however, in such a way as to refrain from all bitterness towards
the Jews, so that he might not embitter them. And yet he does not
yield an inch to them, if it means damaging the Gospel, for he grants
them their privileges in such a way that he does not detract from Christ
in any respect. But He passes to a discussion of the present subject so
abruptly that there appears to be no connexion in his discourse, and
yet he commences his new exposition as if he had already touched on it
previously. His reason for such a course is this. He has completed the
treatment of the doctrine which he was discussing, and when he turns
his attention to the Jews, he is astonished at their unbelief as if it were
something unnatural, and suddenly bursts into protest, as if he were
dealing with a subject which he had previously treated. There was no
one who would not automatically entertain the thought, 'If this is the
doctrine of the law and the prophets, how does it happen that the
Jews so obstinately reject it?' There was also the well-known fact that
the Jews had too great a hatred for all that Paul had said up to this point
concerning the law of Moses and the grace of Christ to assist the faith
of the Gentiles by agreeing with him. The removal of this stumbling-
block was therefore necessary, lest it should impede the course of the
Gospel.

1. *I say the truth in Christ.* Since it was assumed for the most part

that Paul was the sworn enemy of his own nation, so that to some extent he was suspected of teaching them to forsake Moses, even by the household of faith, he prepares the minds of his readers by employing a preface, before entering into dispute concerning his proposed subject. In this preface he disentangles himself from the false suspicion of hostility towards the Jews. Since the subject merited an oath, and since he saw that his affirmation would otherwise scarcely be credited in face of this already conceived prejudice, he swears that he is speaking the truth.

This and similar examples (as I have reminded my readers in the first chapter) ought to teach us which oaths are lawful, viz. those which render credible any truth, the knowledge of which is of profit, and which otherwise would not be believed.

The expression, *in Christ*, means *according to Christ*. By adding *I lie not*, he signifies that he is speaking without falsehood or disguise. *My conscience bearing witness with me*. By these words he summons his conscience before the judgment-seat of God, because he calls the Spirit to witness to his meaning. He inserted the name of the Spirit for the purpose of testifying more fully that he was free and clear of any corrupt feeling of contention, and that he was pleading the cause of Christ under the guidance and direction of the Spirit of God. Being blinded by the affections of the flesh, men may frequently obscure the light of truth knowingly and wilfully, though they may not deceive. To swear by the name of God, in the proper sense of the word, is to call Him as a witness to confirm that which is doubtful, and at the same time to subject ourselves to His judgment if what we say is false.

2. *That I have great sorrow*. Paul's abrupt termination of his discussion before expressing his subject is skilful. It was not yet opportune to mention openly the destruction of the Jewish nation. It may also be added that in so doing he is suggesting a greater degree of sorrow, since elliptical expressions generally indicate compassion. But he will presently state the cause of his grief, when he has more fully confirmed his sincerity.

The agony which Paul felt so greatly at the destruction of the Jews, which he knew had to come to pass by the will and providence of God, teaches us that the obedience which we render to the providence of God does not prevent us from grieving at the fall of profligate men, though we know that they are doomed to this fall by the just judgment of God. The same mind is capable of experiencing these two feelings, so that in looking to God, it can willingly bear the ruin of those whom He has determined to destroy, but when it turns its thoughts to men, it condoles with them in their evils. Those, therefore, who demand of the godly a stoical indifference to suffering and insensibility to pain, ἀπάθειαν καὶ ἀναλγησίαν, lest they should resist the decree of God, are greatly in error.

3. *For I could wish that I myself were anathema.* Paul could not have expressed his love with greater vehemence than by his present affirmation. This is perfect love, which does not refuse even death for the salvation of a friend. But the word which Paul has added, *anathema,* shows that he is speaking not only of temporal but of eternal death. He explains its meaning when he says, *from Christ,* for *anathema* refers to separation. And does not separation from Christ simply mean to be excluded from all hope of salvation? It was, therefore, a proof of the most fervent love that Paul did not hesitate to call on himself the condemnation which he saw hanging over the Jews, in order that he might deliver them. It is no objection that he knew that his salvation was founded on the election of God, which cannot by any means fail. The more passionate emotions plunge impetuously on, without heed or regard for anything but the object on which they are fixed. Paul, therefore, did not add the election of God to his prayer, but put it out of mind, and gave all his attention on the salvation of the Jews.

The doubt of many whether this was a legitimate desire can be settled in this way—'This is the unending boundary of love, that it goes on even unto death.' If, therefore, we love in God and not out of God, our love will never be too much. Such was Paul's love, for while he saw his own race endowed with so many of God's benefits, he embraced the gifts of God in them, and them for the sake of God's gifts. It was also a matter of the greatest sorrow to him that these gifts should perish, and for this reason he burst into this extreme prayer in the confused state of his mind.

I do not thus accept the opinion of those who think that Paul spoke these words from a regard to God alone and not men. Nor, again, do I agree with others, who say that he had regard only to the love of men without any consideration for God, but I connect the love of men with zeal for the glory of God.

I have not yet, however, explained what Paul's principal point was, viz. that the Jews are here regarded as being adorned with their own distinguishing characteristics which marked them off from the rest of the human race. God by His covenant had so highly exalted them, that if they fell, the faithfulness and truth of God Himself would also fail in the world. The covenant would have been made void, which would, it is said, stand firm forever, as long as the sun and moon shall shine in heaven (Ps. 72.7). Thus the abolition of the covenant would be more strange than the upheaval of the whole world in a dire and distressing upheaval. Paul, therefore, is not making a simple and bare comparison between men, for, although it were better for one member to perish than the whole body, Paul has a high regard for the Jews, because he endows them with the character and quality of a chosen people. This will appear more evident from the context, as we shall soon see in the proper place. Although the words *my kinsmen according to the flesh* signify nothing new, they contribute very greatly to amplifying the meaning of the passage. In the first place, to prevent anyone from thinking that Paul was willingly or instinctively looking for an opportunity of quarrelling with the Jews, he intimates that he had not put off the feeling of humanity in such a way as not to be affected by this horrifying destruction of his own flesh. In the second place, since it was necessary that the Gospel, of which he was the preacher, should come out of Sion, he does not press his commendation of his race at length to no effect. The qualifying expression, *according to the flesh*, is not, in my view, added for the sake of disparaging the Jews, but rather for creating confidence in himself. Although the Jews had disowned Paul, he does not conceal the fact that his origin is from that nation, whose election continued vigorous in the root, even though the branches had withered. Budaeus's interpretation of the word *anathema* contradicts Chrysostom, who confuses ἀνάθεμα with ἀνάθημα.

4. *Who are Israelites.* Paul now explains why the destruction of his people caused him so much distress that he was prepared to redeem them by his own death. They were *Israelites.* The relative pronoun is put in place of a causal adverb. This anxiety likewise distressed Moses when he desired to be blotted out of the book of life, lest the holy and elect race of Abraham should be reduced to nothing (Exod. 32.32). Paul, therefore, assigns other and even higher reasons also, besides human affection, which ought to have made him favourable to the Jews. The Lord had given them the exalted privilege of being separated from the common order of mankind. These high praises for their dignity are proofs of his love. We generally speak in such kindly terms only of those whom we love. Although their ingratitude rendered them unworthy of esteem on account of these gifts of God, Paul does not cease to give them due respect. By this he teaches us that the ungodly cannot spoil the good gifts of God in such a way as to prevent them from being always deservedly worthy of being praised and held in esteem, even though those who abuse them derive nothing from them but greater disrepute. Just as we are not to despise the gifts of God in the ungodly from hatred towards them, so on the contrary we are to use prudence lest our kind esteem and regard for them should inflame them with pride, and much more lest our praises should have the appearance of flattery. Let us imitate Paul, who granted the Jews their privileges in such a way that afterwards he declares that without

Christ nothing is of any worth. His inclusion among their commendations of the fact that they were Israelites is not, moreover, without
effect, for Jacob had prayed that, rather than the greatest blessing, they
should be called by his name (Gen. 48.16).

Whose is the adoption. The intention of the whole of Paul's discourse
is that, although the Jews had blasphemously separated themselves
from God by their defection, yet the light of the grace of God had not
wholly been extinguished among them, as he has said in Rom. 3.3.
Although they were unbelievers and had broken His covenant, yet
their perfidy had not rendered the faithfulness of God void, not only
because He preserved for Himself some seed as a remnant from the
whole multitude, but also because the name of a church still continued
among them by the right of inheritance.

The Jews had now stripped themselves of all these privileges, so that
it was of no advantage to them to be called the children of Abraham.
Nevertheless, because there was a danger the Gentiles should depreciate
the majesty of the Gospel through their faith, Paul does not consider
what they deserved, but covers their foulness and dishonourable conduct by casting many veils over them, until the Gentiles were fully
persuaded that the Gospel had flowed to them from a heavenly
fountain, from the sanctuary of God, and from a chosen nation. For
the Lord had passed by all other nations, and selected them as a people
peculiar to Himself, and had adopted them as His children, as He often
testifies by Moses and the prophets. And not content simply to name
them sons, He sometimes calls them His first-begotten, and sometimes
His beloved. Thus the Lord says in Exod. 4.22f, 'Israel is my son, my
firstborn: and I have said unto thee, Let my son go, that he may serve
me'; 'For I am a father to Israel, and Ephraim is my firstborn' (Jer.
31.9); and again, 'Is Ephraim my dear son? is he a pleasant child? for as
often as I speak against him, I do earnestly remember him still: therefore my bowels are troubled for him; I will surely have mercy upon
him, saith the Lord' (Jer. 31.20).

By these expressions he intends not only to commend his indulgence
towards Israel, but rather to display the power of adoption, in which
the promise of the heavenly inheritance is contained.

Glory means the excellence into which the Lord had exalted that
people above all other nations, both by many various means and also
by dwelling in the midst of them. Besides many signs of His Presence,
He formerly exhibited a singular proof of it in the ark, from which
He both gave answers and heard His people, in order to put forth His
power in helping them. For this reason it was termed 'the glory of
God' (I Sam. 4.22).

Since Paul has distinguished here between *covenants* and *promises*, we may note that there is this difference. A covenant is that which is conceived in express and solemn words, and contains a mutual obligation, for instance, the covenant which was made with Abraham. But the promises are found in various places in Scripture. For when God had once made a covenant with His ancient people, He did not cease to offer them His grace from time to time by new promises. It follows that promises are related to the covenant as their only source, in the same way as the special help, by which God declares His love to believers, flows from the one and only fountain of election. And since the law was simply the renewal of that covenant, to ensure that it was remembered more fully, it seems that *the giving of the law* ought here to be restricted particularly to the things which the law decreed. It is the singular honour conferred on the Jewish people that they have God as their lawgiver. If others boast of their Solons and Lycurguses, how much better reason is there for glorying in the law? We read of this in Deut. 4.32. By *service* Paul means that part of the law in which the lawful manner of worshipping God is prescribed, such as rites and ceremonies. These should have been regarded as lawful on account of God's appointment, without which every invention of men is nothing but a profanation of religion.

5. *Whose are the fathers.* It is also of some importance to be descended from saints and men loved by God, since God has promised the godly fathers mercy towards their children, even to a thousand generations, particularly in the words addressed to Abraham, Isaac, and Jacob (Gen. 17.4) and elsewhere. It makes no difference that, if this descent is separated from the fear of God and holiness of life, it is vain and unprofitable in itself, for we see the very same thing also in worship and the glorifying of God, as passages throughout the prophets, but especially Isa. 1.11, 60.1, and also Jer. 7.4, show. Since, however, God respects these things when they are joined to the pursuit of godliness with some degree of honour, Paul has properly regarded them as among the privileges of the Jews. They are called the heirs of the promises because they had descended from the fathers (Acts 3.25).

Of whom is Christ. There is no reason for referring this descent to the fathers, as if Paul intended only to say that Christ had descended from the fathers. His object was to conclude his account of the pre-eminence of the Jews by stating in praise that Christ had proceeded from them. It is no empty honour to be united by a natural kinship with the Redeemer of the world. If He honoured the whole human race when He connected himself with us by sharing our nature, much more did He honour the Jews, with whom He desired to have a close bond of affinity. We must, however, always hold that if this relationship established by grace is separated from godliness, it is so far from being advantageous that it leads rather to greater condemnation.

We have here a notable passage. Paul distinguishes the two natures in Christ in such a way as to unite them at the same time in His very person. By saying that Christ had descended from the Jews, Paul declares his true humanity. The words which are added, *as concerning the flesh*, denote that Christ possessed something superior to flesh. Paul seems to be making here a clear distinction between humanity and divinity, but he finally connects both together when he says that Christ Himself, who was born of the Jews according to the flesh, is God blessed for ever.

We must observe further that this ascription of praise belongs only to the one eternal God. In another passage (I Tim. 1.17) Paul states that there is one God to whom honour and glory are due. To separate this clause from the rest of the context for the purpose of depriving Christ of this clear witness to His divinity, is an audacious attempt to create darkness where there is full light. The words are quite plain, 'Christ, who is from the Jews according to the flesh, is God blessed for ever.' I am in no doubt that Paul, who experienced difficulty in dealing with the stumbling-block that lay against him, deliberately raised his thoughts to the eternal glory of Christ, not so much for his own sake as for the purpose of encouraging others by his example to raise up their thoughts.

> *But it is not as though the word of God hath come to nought. For they are not all Israel, which are of Israel: neither, because they are Abraham's seed, are they all children: but, In Isaac shall thy seed be called. That is, it is not the children of the flesh that are children of God; but the children of the promise are reckoned for a seed. For this is a word of promise, According to this season will I come, and Sarah shall have a son.* (6-9)

6. *It is not as though the word of God hath come to nought.* Paul had been brought into a state of great emotion by the intensity of his prayer. Being now desirous, therefore, of returning to his task of instruction, he adds what may be regarded as a qualifying statement, as though to restrain himself from excessive anguish. His deploring of the destruction of his people seemed to produce the absurd position that the covenant which God had made with Abraham had failed (for the favour of God could not fail the Israelites without abolishing the covenant). He takes the opportunity, therefore, of anticipating this absurdity, and shows how nonetheless the grace of God would constantly remain among the Jewish people, however great their blindness, so that the truth of the covenant might stand firm.

Some read, 'But it is not possible . . .' as though in Greek it were οἷόν τε. But since this reading is not found in any manuscript, I prefer the common reading, 'Not that it had failed', in the following sense: 'That I deplore the destruction of my nation does not mean that I think that the promise of God formerly given to Abraham is now disannulled or abolished.'

For they are not all Israel. Paul's proposition is that the promise was given to Abraham and to his seed, but in such a way that his inheritance does not relate to all of his descendants without distinction. It will follow that the defection of some does not prevent the covenant from remaining firm and steadfast.

In order, however, that it may be more evident on what condition the Lord adopted the posterity of Abraham as a people peculiar to Himself, two points should here be considered. First, the promise of salvation, given to Abraham, belongs to all who trace their natural descent to him, because it is offered to all without exception. For this reason they are rightly termed the heirs and successors of the covenant made with Abraham, or, as Scripture states, the children of the promise. Since it was the will of the Lord that His covenant should be sealed, as much in Ishmael and Esau as in Isaac and Jacob, it appears that they were not altogether estranged from Him, unless perhaps one disregards the circumcision, which was communicated to them by God's command. But we cannot maintain this position without dishonouring God. The apostle stated before that the covenants belonged to them, even though they did not believe (3.3). In Acts 3.25, Peter calls them *the sons of the covenant*, because they were the descendants of the prophets. The second point to be considered is that the appellation 'children of the promise' properly belongs to those in whom its power and efficacy is found. On this account Paul here asserts that not all the children of Abraham are the children of God, although the Lord had entered into a covenant with them, because few continued firm in the faith of the covenant. God Himself, however, testifies in Ezek. 16, that they are all His children. When, in short, the whole people are called the inheritance and the peculiar people of God, what is meant is that they have been chosen by the Lord when the promise of salvation has been offered to them and confirmed by the symbol of circumcision. Since, however, many of them reject this adoption by their ingratitude, and thus in no degree enjoy its benefits, another difference arises among them with regard to the fulfilment of the promise. To prevent anyone from thinking it strange that this fulfilment of the promise was not evident in very many of the Jews, Paul therefore denies that they were included in the true election of God.

We may, if it is preferred, put it in a different way: 'The general election of the people of Israel does not prevent God from choosing for Himself by His secret counsel those whom He pleases.' God's condescension in making a covenant of life with a single nation is indeed a remarkable illustration of undeserved mercy, but His hidden grace is more evident in the second election, which is restricted to a part of the nation only.

When Paul says that *they are not all Israel, which are of Israel*, and that *because they are Abraham's seed* they are not all children, he is using a figure of speech known as paronomasia. In the first clause he includes all the descendants, in the second he refers only to the true sons, who have not fallen from their position.

7. *But, In Isaac shall thy seed be called.* Paul discusses this in order to show that the secret election of God overrules the outward calling. It is by no means opposed to this calling, but rather tends to confirm and complete it. In order, therefore, to prove both propositions, he assumes in the first place that the election of God is not confined to the natural descendants of Abraham, nor included in the conditions of the covenant. To confirm this he now employs a most apt illustration. If there ought to have been any genuine descendants of Abraham who did not fall away from the covenant, it should have been those who first obtained the privilege. But when we find that one of the first two sons of Abraham was separated from the line of descent, even while Abraham was still alive and the promise new, how much more might this have taken place in his far descendants? This prophecy is taken from Gen. 17.20, where the Lord says in answer to Abraham that He had heard his prayer for Ishmael, but that there would be another on whom the promised blessing would rest. It follows that certain men are elected from the chosen people by special privilege, and in these the common adoption becomes efficacious and valid.

8. *That is, it is not the children of the flesh that are children of God.* He now deduces from the prophecy a statement which includes the whole of what he proposed to prove. If the seed is called in Isaac and not in Ishmael, and Isaac is no less the son of Abraham and Ishmael, it must be that not all natural sons are to be regarded as the seed, but that the promise is fulfilled in a special way only in some, and does not belong equally and in common to all. Those who have no greater virtue than natural descent, Paul calls *children of the flesh*, just as those who are peculiarly sealed by the Lord are called children of the promise.

9. *For this is a word of promise.* He adds another testimony from Scripture, in the application of which we may see the amount of care and skill with which he handles Scripture. When the Lord said that He would come, and that a son would be born to Abraham of Sarah, He intimated that His blessing was not yet conferred, but was still to come. But Ishmael was already born when He said this. God's blessing, therefore, had no reference to Ishmael. We may also observe

in passing the great caution with which Paul proceeds here, to prevent exasperating the Jews. He first, therefore, simply states the facts, but conceals the reason. He will then disclose the source.

And not only so; but Rebecca also having conceived by one, even by our father Isaac—for the children being not yet born, neither having done anything good or bad, that the purpose of God according to election might stand, not of works, but of him that calleth, it was said unto her, The elder shall serve the younger. Even as it is written, Jacob I loved, but Esau I hated. (10-13)

10. *And not only so.* In this chapter some sentences are cut short, for example, *but Rebecca also having conceived by one, even our father Isaac.* Paul leaves off in the middle before he comes to the principal verb. The meaning, however, is that not only may this difference as far as the inheritance of the promise is concerned be seen in the children of Abraham, but that there is also a much clearer example in Jacob and Esau. In the case of the former, some might allege that their condition was unequal, since one was the son of a handmaid. But Jacob and Esau were born of the same mother. They were twins in fact. Yet one is rejected, and the other chosen by the Lord. It is clear from this that the promise is not fulfilled in all the children of the flesh without distinction.

Since Paul is referring to those persons to whom God made His counsel known, I prefer to understand a masculine pronoun rather than a neuter, as Erasmus does. The meaning is that God's special election had been revealed not only to Abraham, but afterwards also to Rebecca, while she carried twins in her womb.

11. *For the children being not yet born.* He now begins to rise higher, in order to show the reason for this difference, which he informs us is to be found in the election of God alone. He had previously noted briefly that there was a difference between the natural children of Abraham, viz. that although by circumcision all were adopted into participation in the covenant, yet the grace of God was not effectual in them all. Those, therefore, who enjoy the benefits of God are the children of the promise. Paul, however, had either passed over in silence or at least made a veiled allusion to the cause of this occurrence. But now he plainly refers the whole cause to the unmerited election of God, which in no way depends on men. In the salvation of the godly we are to look for no higher cause than the goodness of God, and no higher cause in the destruction of the reprobate than His just severity.

Paul's first proposition, therefore, is as follows: 'As the blessing of the covenant separates the people of Israel from all other nations, so also the election of God makes a distinction between men in that nation, while He predestinates some to salvation, and others to eternal condemnation.' The second proposition is, 'There is no other basis for this election than the goodness of God alone, and also His mercy since the fall of Adam, which embraces those whom He pleases, without any regard whatever to their works.' The third is, 'The Lord in His unmerited election is free and exempt from the necessity of bestowing equally the same grace on all. Rather, He passes by those whom He wills, and chooses whom He wills.' Paul briefly includes all these propositions in one clause, and will afterwards consider the remaining points.

By saying, *the children being not yet born, neither having done anything good or bad,* he shows that God, in making the difference between them, could not have paid any regard to works which did not yet exist. Those who argue to the contrary that this is no reason why the election of God should not make a difference between men according to the merits of their works (for God foresees from the works which they are to do who will be worthy or undeserving of His grace) are not more clear-sighted than Paul, but are offended by the first principle of theology, which ought to be well known to all Christians, viz. that God can see nothing in the corrupt nature of man, as displayed by Esau and Jacob, to induce Him to show His favour. When, therefore, Paul says that neither of them had at that time done any good or evil, we must add at the same time his assumption that they were both the children of Adam, sinners by nature, and not possessed of a single particle of righteousness.

I do not dwell on the explanation of these points, because the meaning of the apostle is obscure. Because, however, the sophists are not content with Paul's simple statement, and attempt to evade it by lightly-considered distinctions, I have desired to show that Paul was by no means unacquainted with the arguments which they allege, but that they themselves are blind to the first principles of faith.

Besides, even though the corruption which is diffused through the whole human race is of itself sufficient to cause damnation before it shows its nature in deed or act, it follows from this that Esau deserved to be rejected, for he was by nature a child of wrath. In order, however, to prevent any doubt from remaining, as though Esau's condition had been worse because of some vice or fault, it was expedient for Paul to exclude sins no less than virtues. It is true that the immediate cause of reprobation is the curse which we all inherit from Adam. Nevertheless, Paul withdraws us from this view, so that we may learn to rest in the bare and simple good pleasure of God, until he has established the doctrine that God has a sufficiently just cause for election and reprobation in His own will.

That the purpose of God according to election might stand. In almost every word he urges on his readers the free election of God. If works had any place, he would have had to say, 'so that remuneration may be related to works'. Paul, however, sets in opposition to works the purpose of God, which is contained in His own good pleasure alone. So that no ground of dispute on the subject might remain, he removed all doubt by adding another clause, *according to election,* and then a third, *not of works, but of him that calleth.* Let us, therefore, now consider the context more closely. If the purpose of God according to election is established because, before the brothers were born and had done either good or evil, one is rejected and the other chosen, therefore to desire to attribute the cause of the difference between them to their works is to subvert the purpose of God. By adding, *not of works, but of him that calleth,* he means not on account of works, but of the calling alone. Paul wishes to exclude all consideration of works. The constancy of our election is wholly comprehended in the purpose of God alone. Merits are of no avail here, for they issue only in death. Worthiness is disregarded, for there is none, but the goodness of God reigns alone. The doctrine that God either elects or reprobates as He foresees each to be worthy or unworthy of His favour, is false, therefore, and contrary to the Word of God.

12. *The elder shall serve the younger.* Note how the Lord distinguishes between the sons of Isaac, while they are still in their mother's womb. The oracle of God thus answers Jacob. It followed from this that God's will was to show to the younger son a peculiar favour, which He denied to the elder. Although this promise had reference to the right of primogeniture, yet God declared His will in it as the type of something greater. We may see this clearly if we consider what little advantage with regard to the flesh Jacob derived from his birthright. He was exposed on account of it to great danger, obliged, in order to escape from it, to quit his home and his country, and treated in a most inhuman way in his exile. On his return, tremblingly and uncertain of his life, he prostrated himself at the feet of his brother, humbly asked forgiveness for his offence, and escaped death only through the pardon offered to him by Esau. Where do we find Jacob's dominion over his brother, from whom he was compelled to seek his life by entreaty? There was, therefore, something greater than the birthright promised in the answer given by the Lord.

13. *As it is written, Jacob I loved.* Paul confirms by still stronger testimony how much the promise given to Rebecca relates to his present subject. The spiritual condition of Jacob was witnessed to by

his dominion, and that of Esau by his bondage. Jacob also obtained this favour through the kindness of God, and not by his own merit. This declaration of the prophet, therefore, shows why the Lord conferred the birthright on Jacob. It is taken from Mal. 1, where the Lord declares His kindness to the Jews, before reproaching them for their ingratitude. 'I have loved you', He says. He then adds the source from which His love sprang. 'Was not Esau Jacob's brother?' as if to say, 'What privilege had he, that I should prefer him to his brother? None at all. Their right was equal, except that the younger ought by the law of nature to have been subject to the older. Yet I chose Jacob and rejected Esau, induced to this course by my mercy alone, and not by any worthiness in his works. And now I had adopted you to be my people, so that I might show the same kindness towards the seed of Jacob. But I had rejected the Edomites, the descendants of Esau. You, therefore, are so much the worse, since the recollection of this great favour cannot arouse you to adore my majesty.' Although Malachi also mentions the earthly blessings which God had bestowed on the Israelites, they are not to be taken in any other sense than as symbols of His benevolence. Where the wrath of God is found, death follows. But where His love is found, there is life.

What shall we say then? Is there unrighteousness with God? God forbid. For he saith to Moses, I will have mercy on whom I have mercy, and I will have compassion on whom I have compassion. So then it is not of him that willeth, nor of him that runneth, but of God that hath mercy. For the scripture saith unto Pharaoh, For this very purpose did I raise thee up, that I might shew in thee my power, and that my name might be published abroad in all the earth. So then he hath mercy on whom he will, and whom he will he hardeneth. (14-18)

14. *What shall we say then?* The flesh cannot hear the wisdom of God without being at once disturbed by perplexing questions, and it struggles to call God by some means to account. Hence we find the apostle, whenever he deals with some high mystery, answering the many absurdities with which he knew the human mind would otherwise be occupied. Men stumble at many trifling difficulties, particularly when they hear what Scripture teaches concerning predestination.

The predestination of God is truly a labyrinth from which the mind of man is wholly incapable of extricating itself. But the curiosity of man is so insistent that the more dangerous it is to inquire into a subject, the more boldly he rushes to do so. Thus when predestination is being discussed, because he cannot keep himself within proper limits, he immediately plunges into the depths of the sea by his impetuosity. What remedy then will there be for the godly? Must they avoid every

thought of predestination? Not at all. Since the Holy Spirit has taught
us nothing but what it is to our interest to know, this knowled¬ ¸ will
undoubtedly be useful to us, provided we shall confir ¿ it to the Word
of God. Let this, therefore, be our sacred rule, not to seek to know
anything about it except what Scripture teaches us. Where the Lord
closes His holy mouth, let us also stop our minds from going on
further. Since, however, these foolish questions will come naturally
to us, being what we are, let us hear from Paul how they are to be met.

Is there any unrighteousness with God? The madness of the human
mind is certainly immense, in that it is more disposed to accuse God of
unrighteousness than to blame itself for its blindness. Paul had no wish
to go out of his way to seek a subject by which to upset his readers, but
took up for discussion the irreverent doubt which steals into the thought
of many as soon as they hear that God determines the condition of
every individual according to His will. The type of injustice which
the flesh imagines is that God has regard for one man, while passing
another by.

In order to remove this difficulty, Paul divides the whole subject
into two parts. In the first he deals with the elect, and in the second the
reprobate. In the case of the elect he would have us contemplate the
mercy of God, but in the case of the reprobate acknowledge His
righteous judgment. In the first place, therefore, he answers that the
idea that there is injustice in God is detestable. He then shows that
there can be no injustice at all either to the elect or the reprobate.

Before we proceed further, however, this objection clearly proves
that the reason why God elects some and rejects others is to be found
in His purpose alone. If the difference between the two had been
based on a regard for their works, Paul would have discussed this
question of the unrighteousness of God to no purpose, for no suspicion
of unrighteousness can arise when God deals with every one according
to his merit. It is worth noticing also, in the second place, that although
Paul saw that this part of the doctrine could not be discussed without
immediately arousing blustering contradictions and fearful blasphemies,
yet he introduced it frankly and without dissimulation. Indeed, he
does not conceal how great an occasion for stormy and agitated anger
it affords us on our learning that before men are born their lot is
assigned to each of them by the secret will of God. Nevertheless he
continues, and declares without equivocation what he has learned from
the Holy Spirit. It follows that the delicacy of those who affect an
appearance of greater prudence than the Holy Spirit in removing or
resolving offences, is quite intolerable. Lest God should be accused of
any fault, it is a matter of faith for them simply to confess that the
salvation or the destruction of men depends on His free election. Were

they to restrain their minds from irreverent curiosity, and bridle their tongues from unrestrained licence, their modesty and sobriety would be worthy of approbation. But what audacity to check the Holy Spirit and Paul! May there flourish, therefore, sufficient greatness of soul in the Church of God to prevent its godly teachers from being ashamed of the simple profession of true doctrine, however hated it may be, and to refute whatever reproaches the ungodly may pour forth.

15. *For He saith to Moses.* As far as the elect are concerned, God cannot be charged with any unrighteousness, for He favours them with His mercy according to His good pleasure. Here too, however, the flesh finds reasons for complaint, for it cannot allow God to show favour to one and not to another, unless the cause be made evident. Because it seems absurd, therefore, that some men should be preferred to others without merit, human effrontery enters into controversy with God, as if He showed more respect to some persons than was right. We must now see how Paul defends the righteousness of God.

In the first place, he does not by any means obscure or conceal what he saw was disliked, but persists in asserting it with unswerving constancy. In the second place, he takes no trouble to find reasons to soften its harshness, but is content to restrain offensive and petulant objections by the testimonies of Scripture.

Paul's defence that God is not indeed unjust, because He is merciful to whom He pleases, might appear to be lacking in warmth. But because God regards His own authority alone as sufficient, so that He needs the defence of no other, Paul was content that God should be the vindicator of His own right. Paul here brings forward the answer which Moses received from the Lord, when he prayed for the salvation of the whole people. 'I will be gracious,' God replies, 'to whom I will be gracious, and will shew mercy on whom I will shew mercy' (Exod. 33.19). By this assertion the Lord declared that He is a debtor to no man, and that everything bestowed on them comes from His free goodness. Secondly, this kindness is free, so that He may confer it on whom He pleases. And finally, no reason higher than His own will can be conceived why He should do good and show favour to some, but not to all. The words really mean, 'I will never take my mercy away from the man to whom I have once purposed to show it, and I will bestow continual kindness on the man to whom I have determined to be kind.' God thus assigns the highest cause for bestowing grace to His own voluntary purpose, and at the same time intimates that He has appointed His mercy peculiarly for some. The precise language used here excludes all outward causes, as when, in claiming for ourselves freedom of action, we say, 'I shall do what I intend to do.' The relative pronoun expressly denotes that mercy will not be extended indiscriminately to all. We are deprived of this freedom when we restrict God's election to external causes.

The only true cause of salvation is expressed in the two words used by Moses. חָנַן means to favour, or to show kindness freely and bountifully; רָחַם is to be treated with mercy. Paul thus establishes what he intended to prove, viz. that because the mercy of God is free, it is not bound, but turns wherever it pleases.

16. *It is not of him that willeth.* Paul deduces from this statement the incontrovertible conclusion that our election is to be attributed neither to our diligence, zeal, nor efforts, but is to be ascribed entirely to the counsel of God. Let no one think that those who are elected are chosen because they are deserving, or because they have in any way won for themselves the favour of God, or even because they possessed a grain of worthiness by which God might be moved to act. The simple view which we are to take is that our being counted among the elect is independent either of our will or our efforts (Paul has put 'running' for 'striving' or 'endeavour'). It is rather to be attributed wholly to the divine goodness, which freely takes those who neither will to achieve, nor strive for, nor even think of such a thing. The arguments of those who reason from this passage that we have the capacity to strive for election, but that it effects nothing of itself without the help of God's mercy, are foolish. The apostle is not showing the capacity which we have, but excludes all our efforts. To say that we *will* or *run* to achieve it, therefore, is a mere cavil, because Paul denies that the man who wills or runs is capable of achieving election. He meant simply that neither willing nor running can achieve anything.

Those, however, who continue on the other hand to be idle and inactive on the pretence of allowing the grace of God freedom of action, are to be condemned. Although our own striving accomplishes nothing, yet the effort which is inspired by God is not without effect. We do not, therefore, say this for the purpose of letting our capriciousness and indolence smother the Spirit of God as He instils sparks into us, but so that we may understand that everything we have is from Him. We are, therefore, to learn to ask and hope for all things from Him, and to ascribe all things to Him, while wholeheartedly pursuing our salvation with fear and trembling.

Pelagius has attempted to evade this assertion of Paul by another quibbling and quite worthless objection. He has maintained that our election does not depend on willing and running alone, since the mercy of God assists us. Augustine, however, has refuted him both effectively and astutely. If it is denied that the will of man is the cause of election, because it is a partial and not the sole cause, so we may also say on the other hand that election is not dependent on God's mercy, but on willing and running. Where there is mutual co-operation there will also be reciprocal praise. But this latter proposition falls incontrovertibly by its own absurdity. Let us, therefore, determine to ascribe to His mercy the salvation of those whom God is pleased to save, in such a way as to leave nothing to the industry of man.

Some interpreters would have it that these words are spoken in the person of the ungodly, but this is no more plausible. Is it consistent to twist passages of Scripture in which the righteousness of God is proclaimed for the purpose of reproaching Him with tyranny? Again, is it probable that Paul would have allowed the Scriptures to be treated with gross contempt, when he could readily and easily have refuted his opponents? But these are means of escape seized on by those who measured this incomparable mystery of God by their own wrong judgment. To their delicate and tender ears this doctrine was too harsh to be considered worthy of the apostle. It would have been more seemly for them to bend their stubbornness to the obedience of the Spirit, that they might not be so greatly addicted to their own gross lies.

17. *For the scripture saith.* Paul now comes to the second part, the rejection of the ungodly. Since there appears to be some less reasonable factor in this, he endeavours all the more to make it plain how God, in rejecting whom He wills, is not only without blame, but is wonderful in His wisdom and fairness. Paul, therefore, takes his proof-text from Exod. 9.16, where the Lord declares that it was He who raised up Pharaoh for this end, for the purpose of proving by his defect and subjugation, while he obstinately strove to oppose the divine power, how invincible is the arm of God. No human strength is capable of bearing this, much less of breaking it. Note the example which the Lord desired to give in the case of Pharaoh.

We are accordingly to take two points into consideration here, first, Pharaoh's predestination to destruction, which refers to the just but secret counsel of God, and second, the purpose of this predestination, which is to proclaim the name of God. It is on this that Paul particularly dwells. If this hardening of Pharaoh's heart is such as to be the cause of God's name being made known, it is blasphemous to accuse Him of any unrighteousness.

Since many interpreters also destroy the meaning of this passage in attempting to minimize its harshness, we must note first that in Hebrew the expression *I did raise* is *I have appointed thee.* God is here desirous to show that Pharaoh's obstinacy would not prevent Him from delivering His people. He affirms not only that He had foreseen Pharaoh's violence, and had means at hand for restraining it, but that He had so ordained it on purpose, with the express design of providing a more notable demonstration of His power. It is, therefore, a misinterpretation to render the passage, as some scholars do, to mean that Pharaoh had been preserved for a period of time, since the discussion here is rather of what took place at the beginning. Since many accidents may befall men from various quarters to retard their purposes and impede the course of their actions, God says that Pharaoh had proceeded from Him, and that his character was given to him by God. The words *I have raised up* suit this interpretation very well. In order, however, that no one should imagine that Pharaoh had been divinely compelled by some universal and confused impulse to rush headlong into that violent conduct, Paul notes the specific cause or design of his action. God had known what Pharaoh was going to do, but had deliberately appointed him for this purpose. It follows that it is profitless to dispute with God, as if He were bound to give a reason since He comes forward of His own accord, and anticipates this objection by declaring that the reprobate, in whom He desires His name to be made known, proceed from the secret fountain of His providence.

18. *So then he hath mercy on whom he will.* The consequence in regard both to the elect and the reprobate is here given. We are to understand this as being the conclusion of the apostle alone, for he promptly enters into discussion with his opponent, and begins to bring forward the objections which might have been offered on the other side. There is, therefore, no doubt at all that, as we have just suggested, Paul is speaking his own views here in saying that God favours with His mercy those whom He pleases according to His own will, and unsheaths the severity of His judgment against any person whom He pleases. Paul's purpose is to make us accept the fact that it has seemed good to God to enlighten some in order that they may be saved, and blind others in order that they may be destroyed, so that we may be satisfied in our minds with the difference which is evident between the elect and the reprobate, and not inquire for any cause higher than His will. We ought to notice these words, *on whom He will*, and *whom He will*, in particular. Paul does not allow us to go beyond this.

The word *harden*, when applied to God in Scripture, implies not only permission (as some weak exegetes would interpret it), but also the action of the divine wrath. All external circumstances which contribute to the blinding of the reprobate are the instruments of His wrath. Satan himself, who works inwardly with compelling power, is God's minister in such a way that he acts only by His command. The trivial evasion held by the schoolmen in regard to foreknowledge falls therefore to the ground. Paul does not inform us that the ruin of the ungodly is foreseen by the Lord, but that it is ordained by His counsel and will. Solomon also teaches us that not only was the des-

truction of the ungodly foreknown, but the ungodly themselves have
been created for the specific purpose of perishing (Prov. 16.4).

*Thou wilt say then unto me, Why doth he still find fault? For who
withstandeth his will? Nay but, O man, who art thou that repliest
against God? Shall the thing formed say to him that formed it, Why didst
thou make me thus? Or hath not the potter a right over the clay, from the
same lump to make one part a vessel unto honour, and another unto
dishonour?* (19-21)

19. *Thou wilt say then.* At this point in particular the flesh rages
when it hears that the predestination to death of those who perish is
referred to the will of God. The apostle, therefore, undertakes again
to anticipate the objections of his opponents, since he saw that the
mouths of the ungodly could not be restrained from assailing the
righteousness of God with noisy cries. He expresses their feelings
admirably, too. Not being content with defending themselves, they
make God guilty in their place. Then, having laid on Him the blame
of their own condemnation, they express indignation at His great
power. They are forced, it is true, to yield, but they do so in resent-
ment, because they are unable to resist Him, and while they attribute
the dominion to Him, they accuse Him of tyranny. So also the Sophists
in their schools talk nonsense about what they call His absolute justice,
as if God would forget His own righteousness and test His authority
by throwing everything into confusion. The ungodly, therefore, are
speaking to this effect in the present passage: 'What cause has God to be
angry with us, since He has made us as we are, and leads us where He
pleases at His will? What does He achieve by destroying us, except to
inflict punishment upon his own workmanship in us? It is not our part
to contend with Him, for however much we should resist Him, He
will still gain the upper hand. If, therefore, He condemns us, His
judgment will be unjust, and the power which He now misuses against
us had no restraint.' What answer does Paul have to this?

20. *Nay but, O man, who art thou?* Since there is a participle in the
Greek, we may also read in the present tense, *who disputest*, or *con-
tendest*, or *strivest* in *opposition to God?* The Greek expression has the
meaning, 'Who art thou, that thou enterest into a dispute with God?,'
but the sense is not greatly different. In this first answer Paul simply
restrains the irreverence of the blasphemy by arguing from the condition of man. He will presently give another answer by which he
will vindicate the righteousness of God from every accusation.

It is clear that Paul advances no higher cause than the will of God.
The obvious solution to the problem was that there are just grounds
for the difference. Why, then, did he not make use of this short

answer, but assign the highest place to the will of God, so that it alone should be sufficient for us, rather than any other cause? If the objection that God reprobates or elects according to His will those whom He does not honour with His favour, or towards whom He shows unmerited love—if this objection had been false, Paul would not have omitted to refute it. The ungodly object that men are exempted from guilt if the will of God has the first place in their salvation or in their destruction. Does Paul deny this? He does not, and by his answer he confirms that God determines to deal with men as He pleases. Yet men rise up in their wrath to contend with Him, but to no avail, because He assigns whatever fate He pleases to His creatures by His own right.

Those who say that Paul's failure to offer a reason for this led him to reprove God, grievously slander the Holy Spirit. To begin with, Paul was unwilling to introduce arguments which he could have used, and which were calculated to vindicate God's justice, because they would not have been understood. Indeed, he will qualify his second argument in such a way as to avoid undertaking a full defence, but so that he may thus prove the righteousness of God to those of us who consider it with humility and reverence. He took, therefore, the most appropriate course of admonishing man of his own condition, saying, 'Since thou art man, thou acknowledgest thyself to be dust and ashes. Why then dost thou contend with the Lord concerning that which thou art by no means able to understand?' In short, the apostle did not introduce into his discussion what he could have said, but what our ignorance would accept. Conceited men are resentful, because, in admitting that men are rejected or chosen by the secret counsel of God, Paul offers no explanation, as though the Spirit of God were silent for want of reason, and does not rather warn us by His silence—a mystery which our minds do not comprehend, but which we ought to adore with reverence. In this way he curbs the perversity of human curiosity. Let us know, therefore, that God refrains from speaking to us for no other reason than that He sees that His boundless wisdom cannot be comprehended in our small measure. Thus having pity on our frailty, He summons us to moderation and sobriety.

Shall the thing formed? Paul, we see, continues to insist on our considering the will of God to be just, although the reason for this may be concealed from us. He shows that God is robbed of His right, if He is not free to deal with His creatures as He sees fit. This appears to be harsh to many people. There are some, too, who allege that God is greatly dishonoured if such arbitrary power is bestowed on Him. But does their distaste make them better theologians than Paul, who has laid it down as the rule of humility for the believers, that they should look up to the sovereignty of God and not evaluate it by their own judgment?

He represses this arrogance of contending with God by a most appropriate metaphor, in which his allusion seems to have been to Isa. 45.9 rather than Jer. 18.6. The one truth which we learn from Jeremiah is that Israel is in the hand of the Lord, so that, on account of its sins, God may break it wholly in pieces, as a potter does his vessel of clay. But Isaiah goes further. 'Woe unto him', he says, 'that striveth with his maker', viz. the pot that strives with the potter. 'Shall the clay say to him that fashioneth it, What makest thou?' There is surely no reason why mortal man should think himself better than an earthen vessel, when compared with God. We are not, however, to be over-particular in applying this quotation to our present subject, since Paul meant to allude to the words of the prophet only in order that his metaphor might have more significance.

21. *Hath not the potter a right over the clay?* The reason why the thing formed ought not to strive with its maker is that the maker merely acts according to his own rights. The word *right* does not mean that the maker has power or strength to do what he pleases, but that this power to act rightly belongs to him. Paul does not want to claim for God an inordinate power, but the power which He should rightly be given.

In applying the metaphor we should further consider that as the potter takes nothing from the clay, whatever form he may have given it, so God takes nothing from man, whatever the condition in which He may have created him. We must simply remember this, that God is deprived of part of His honour if He is not allowed authority to be arbiter of life and death over men.

What if God, willing to shew his wrath, and to make his power known, endured with much longsuffering vessels of wrath fitted unto destruction: and that he might make known the riches of his glory upon vessels of mercy, which he afore prepared unto glory? (22-23)

22. *What if God endured with much longsuffering vessels of wrath?* Paul's second answer shows briefly that, although the counsel of God is incomprehensible in regard to predestination, yet His unimpeachable equity is to be seen as clearly in the destruction of the reprobate as in the salvation of the elect. He does not offer a reason for the divine election to explain why one should be chosen and another rejected. It was unfitting that the things which are contained in the secret counsel of God should come under the censure of men. That mystery would not be explained. He therefore keeps us from inquisitively examining those matters which elude human comprehension. In the meantime,

however, he shows that as far as God's predestination manifests itself, it reveals true righteousness.

I take the particle εἰ δέ, which Paul used, to mean *What if?*, in order to make the whole of this sentence a question. The meaning will appear more clearly if we read the particle in this way. Paul's expression is elliptical, and has the implication, 'Who then can accuse God of unrighteousness, or arraign Him? For nothing but the most perfect rule of righteousness is here to be seen.'

If we wish to understand Paul's meaning, we must examine almost every word. He argues in the following way. There are vessels prepared for destruction, i.e. appointed and destined for destruction. There are also vessels of wrath, i.e. made and formed for the purpose of being proofs of the vengenance and displeasure of God. If the Lord bears patiently with them for a time by not destroying them at the earliest opportunity, but postponing the judgment prepared for them, and if He does so in order to demonstrate the decrees of His severity (so that the others may be stricken with terror at such fearful examples) and likewise to make known His power, to which He makes them submit in many ways, and also so that this may make the extent of His mercy toward the elect better known and shine with greater clarity, is there anything reprehensible in this dispensation? Paul's failure to explain why vessels are made ready for destruction is not surprising, for he assumes from what he has said above that the reason is hidden in the eternal and inexplicable counsel of God, whose righteousness is worthy of our worship rather than our scrutiny.

Paul has used the word *vessels* in a general sense to mean *instruments*. The performance by any creature of any act is its administration of the divine power. We, therefore, who are believers are for very good reasons called *the vessels of mercy*, for the Lord uses us as instruments for the exhibition of His mercy. The reprobate, however, are *the vessels of wrath*, since they serve to display the judgment of God.

23. *That he might make known the riches of his glory.* There is, I am persuaded, a transposition of grammatical order in the two particles καί and ἵνα. I have, therefore, translated by, *that he might also make known*, in order that the present clause may harmonize better with the previous one. This is the second reason why God's glory is revealed in the destruction of the reprobate. The fulness of the divine mercy towards the elect is more clearly confirmed by this. The elect differ from the reprobate only in the fact of their deliverance from the same gulf of destruction. This, moreover, is by no merit of their own, but by the free goodness of God. It must, therefore, be true that the infinite mercy of God towards the elect will gain our increasing praise, when we see how wretched are all those who do not escape His wrath.

I interpret the word *glory*, which is twice repeated here, to mean, by metonymy, the mercy of God. God's chief praise consists in acts of kindness. Thus, in Eph. 1.13, having taught us that we have been adopted by God to the praise of the glory of His grace, he adds that we are sealed by the Spirit of our inheritance to the praise of His glory. The word *grace* is omitted. His meaning, therefore, was that the elect are instruments or organs, by whom God exercises His mercy for the purpose of glorifying His name among them.

Although Paul is more explicit in this second clause in stating that it is God who prepares the elect for glory, when before he had simply said that the reprobate were vessels prepared for destruction, there is no doubt that the preparation of both is dependent on the secret counsel of God. Otherwise Paul would have said that the reprobate yield or cast themselves into destruction. Now, however, he means that their lot is already assigned to them before their birth.

> Even *us, whom he also called, not from the Jews only, but also from the Gentiles? As he saith also in Hosea, I will call that my people, which was not my people; and her beloved, which was not beloved. And it shall be, that in the place where it was said unto them, Ye are not my people, there shall they be called sons of the living God. And Isaiah crieth concerning Israel, If the number of the children of Israel be as the sand of the sea, it is the remnant that shall be saved: for the Lord will execute his word upon the earth, finishing it and cutting it short. And, as Isaiah hath said before, Except the Lord of Sabaoth had left us a seed, we had become as Sodom, and had been made like unto Gomorrah.* (24-29)

24. *Whom he also called.* From the dispute in which Paul has been engaged up to this point concerning the freedom of divine election, two consequences follow. First, the grace of God is not so limited to the Jewish people that it cannot also flow to other nations, and spread over the whole world. Second, it is not so restricted to the Jews as to come to all the children of Abraham according to the flesh without exception. If the election of God is founded on His good pleasure alone, it exists wherever He has willed it to be. The way is now open for Paul, having established election, to proceed to those observations which he has designed to make with regard both to the calling of the Gentiles and the rejection of the Jews. The former of these seemed absurd on account of its novelty, and the latter quite unworthy. Since, however, the latter had more in it to offend, he deals first with that article which was less offensive. He says, therefore, that the vessels of God's mercy, which He has chosen for the glory of His name, are taken from all peoples, from the Gentiles no less than from the Jews. Although in using the relative *whom* Paul does not strictly observe the

rules of grammar, he meant to add by making a transition that we are the vessels of the glory of God, who have been taken partly from the Jews and partly from the Gentiles. Paul proves here from the calling of God, that there is no difference of nationality in election. If our descent from the Gentiles did not prevent God from calling us, it is evident that the Gentiles are by no means to be excluded from the kingdom of God and the covenant of eternal salvation.

25. *As he saith also in Hosea.* He now shows that the calling of the Gentiles should not seem to be anything strange, since it had long before been foretold by the prophet. The meaning is clear, but there is some difficulty in the application of the prophecy, for it will not be denied that the prophet is referring to the Israelites in that passage. Offended by their crimes, the Lord declares that they are no longer His people. He afterwards says in consolation that He will make those whom He does not love His beloved, and those who are not a people His people. Paul endeavours to apply to the Gentiles this prophecy which is explicitly addressed to the Jews.

It had been held by those who have hitherto offered the best explanation of this difficulty that Paul intended to argue in this way—the impediment which might appear to prevent the Gentiles from becoming partakers of salvation has also existed among the Jewish people. As, therefore, God formerly received into His favour the Jews whom He had rejected and exiled, so also now He displays the same kindness towards the Gentiles. Although this interpretation can be supported, it seems to me a little forced. The reader must consider whether it would not be more suitable to regard the consolation offered by the prophet as having been given not only for the Jews, but also for the Gentiles. When the prophets had pronounced the vengeance of God on the Jews on account of their iniquities, it was not strange or unusual for them to direct their attention to the kingdom of Christ, which was to be spread throughout the whole world. They did so with good reason, for when the Jews provoked the wrath of God by their sins, in such a way as to merit His rejection of them, no hope of salvation remained except in their turning to Christ, through whom the covenant of grace is restored. As it was founded on Him, so it is restored in Him, now that it is destroyed. Since also Christ is without doubt the only refuge in our desperate plight, no sound comfort can be brought to wretched sinners and to those who see the wrath of God hanging over them, unless Christ is set before their eyes. It is usual for the prophets, as we have observed, having humbled the people by threatening them with divine vengeance, to recall them to Christ, the only place of refuge for those who are in desperate plight. Where the kingdom of Christ is raised, there also is lifted up that heavenly Jerusalem, into which the inhabitants of every part of the world are gathered. This is the particular emphasis in the present prophecy. When the Jews were banished from the family of God, they were thereby reduced to a common level with the Gentiles. The distinction between Jew and Gentile has been removed, and the mercy of God now extends indiscriminately to all the Gentiles. We can see from this that the prediction of the prophets applies well to the present subject. In this prophecy God declares that when He has put the Gentiles on a level with the Jews, He will gather a Church for Himself from among strangers, so that those who were not a people would begin to be His people.

I will call that my people, which was not my people. This is said in regard to God's separation of Himself from His people. He had already accomplished this by depriving them of all their dignity, so that they did not surpass the other nations. Although those whom God in His eternal counsel has destined for Himself as sons are His sons and will always be so, yet Scripture frequently counts as God's children only those whose election has been proved by their calling. By this we are taught not to form a judgment, much less to pronounce an opinion, concerning the election of God, except in so far as it reveals itself by its own evidence. Thus when Paul had shown the Ephesians that their election and adoption had been determined by God before the creation of the world, he shortly afterwards declares that they had at one time been estranged from God (Eph. 2.12), viz. during the period when the Lord had not yet shown His love towards them, although He had embraced them with His eternal mercy. In this passage, therefore, those to whom God declares His wrath rather than His love are said to be *not beloved*. We know that God's wrath lies upon all mankind, until men are reconciled to Him by adoption.

The feminine gender of the participle is derived from the text of Hosea, who had said that a daughter had been born to him, and he had given this name, *not beloved*, to her, in order that the people might know by this sign that they were hated by God. As their rejection by God was the reason for hatred, so the prophet teaches us that God's adoption of those who for a time had been strangers is the beginning of love.

27. *And Isaiah crieth concerning Israel.* Paul now proceeds to the second part of his subject. He was, however, unwilling to begin his discussion of it, in case he should over-exasperate the minds of his countrymen. His description of Isaiah as *exclaiming*, and not speaking, is deliberately intended to arouse greater attention. The words of the prophet are plainly designed to prevent the Jews from boasting excessively in the flesh. It is a terrible thing to learn that only a small

number out of an incalculable multitude shall obtain salvation. Although the prophet, after his description of the destruction of the people, declares that there is some hope of grace remaining in order to prevent believers from thinking that the covenant of God was wholly wiped out, yet he restricts it to a few. Since, however, he had made the prediction concerning his own time, we must see how Paul duly adapts it to suit his purpose. The meaning must be that, when the Lord willed to deliver His people from their captivity in Babylon, His desire was that the benefit of His deliverance should be extended to a very few only of that vast multitude, who might deservedly be said to be the remnant of the destruction, when compared with the great number of people whom He permitted to perish in exile. That physical restoration of the Jews prefigured the true renovation of the Church of God which is accomplished in Christ, and indeed was only its beginning. What took place then is now to be fulfilled with much greater certainty in the development and completion of that deliverance.

28. *Finishing it and cutting it short.* I shall omit the various interpretations and state what I believe to be the appropriate meaning of this passage. The Lord will so reduce and cut off His people, that the remnant will look as though it has been consumed, i.e. it will have the appearance or show signs of a mighty downfall. The few, however, who will remain from the devastation will be the work of the righteousness of the Lord, or, rather, serve to testify to the righteousness of God throughout the world. Since *word* in Scripture generally means a *thing*, Paul uses *finished word* to mean *completion (consummatio)*. Many interpreters, anxious to employ over-subtle arguments, have laboured under a gross misapprehension here, for they have imagined that the doctrine of the Gospel is termed 'completion', because, when the ceremonies have been abrogated, it is a brief summary of the law. It should, however, rather have been called the 'destruction' (*consumptio*) of the law. It is not only here that the Septuagint has erred, but also in Isa. 10.22, 23, 28.22 and Ezek. 11.13, where we read, 'Ah Lord God! wilt thou make a full end of the remnant of Israel?' For the prophets mean, 'Wilt thou bring even the remnant to utter destruction?' This misinterpretation has arisen through the ambiguity of the Hebrew word. The word בָּלָה means to finish and to perfect, as well as to

consume. This distinction, however, has not been sufficiently noticed in the passages in which it occurs. Isaiah did not use this single verb, but two substantives ('consumption', and 'consummation, and that determined'), so that the mistranslation of the Hebrew in the Septuagint is strikingly inept. What purpose was there in obscuring a sentence, quite clear in itself, in ambiguous language? We may also add that Isaiah is here speaking hyperbolically, meaning by 'consumption' the kind of diminution which frequently occurs at the time of some memorable slaughter.

29. *And as Isaiah hath said before.* Paul introduces another quotation from the first chapter, where the prophet bewails the devastation of Israel in his own lifetime. This devastation of the Jews is not without precedent, for the people of Israel have no privilege but what they have derived from their ancestors. These, however, had been treated in such a manner that the prophet complains that their afflictions had been such as to reduce them almost to the destruction of Sodom and Gomorrah. There was, however, this difference. A few were preserved as seed to raise up the name of Israel, so that it might not wholly perish, or be wiped out by eternal oblivion. It behoved God to be ever mindful of His promise, so as to manifest His mercy in the midst of His severest judgments.

What shall we say then? That the Gentiles, which followed not after righteousness, attained to righteousness, even the righteousness which is of faith: but Israel, following after a law of righteousness, did not arrive at that law. Wherefore? Because they sought it not by faith, but as it were by works. They stumbled at the stone of stumbling; even as it is written, Behold, I lay in Zion a stone of stumbling and a rock of offence: and he that believeth on him shall not be put to shame. (30-33)

30. *What shall we say then?* In order to leave the Jews with no occasion for complaining against God, he now begins to explain in a way comprehensible to human intelligence why the Jewish nation has been thus rejected. Those who attempt to establish and exalt those causes above the secret predestination of God (which ought, as Paul has already taught us, to be considered as the highest cause), are lying under an error and reversing God's order. But as the secret predestination of God is above every other cause, so the corruption and wickedness of the ungodly affords a ground and provides the occasion for the judgments of God. Since Paul's subject was a difficult one, he confers with his readers and, as though in doubt, asks what he can say here.

That the Gentiles, which followed not after righteousness. There was nothing, it seemed, more absurd or inconsistent than that the Gentiles, who wallowed in the lusts of their flesh without any regard for righteousness, should be invited to share salvation and obtain righteousness, while the Jews, on the other hand, who had devoted themselves assiduously to the work of the law, should be driven from all the rewards of righteousness. Paul introduces this singular paradox without further explanation, in such a way as to mitigate any harshness in it by adding in explanation that the righteousness which the Gentiles attained consists in faith. It depends, therefore, on the mercy of the Lord and not on any peculiar worth in man. The zeal for the law, by which the Jews were actuated, was absurd, since they were seeking to be justified by works, and thus were striving to attain to a position which no man can reach. They were, moreover, offended at Christ, through whom alone we have access to the attainment of righteousness.

In this first clause, however, it was the object of the apostle to exalt the pure grace of God, so that no other cause might be sought for in the calling of the Gentiles than His deigning to embrace those who were unworthy of His favour.

Paul speaks expressly of righteousness, without which there can be no salvation; but in saying that the righteousness of the Gentiles proceeds from faith, he denotes that it is based on free reconciliation. If we imagine that the Gentiles are justified because they have obtained the Spirit of regeneration by faith, we greatly misinterpret the meaning of Paul. It would not have been true that they had attained what they were not seeking, unless God had freely embraced them while they were erring and straying, and offered them a righteousness for which they could have had no desire, since it was unknown to them. We should also note that the Gentiles obtained righteousness by faith only because God anticipated their faith by His grace. Had they first aspired to righteousness by means of faith, they would still have been pursuing it. Faith itself, therefore, is a part of grace.

31. *But Israel, following after a law of righteousness.* Paul frankly makes the incredible statement that it is not strange that the Jews have accomplished nothing by their strenuous pursuit of righteousness, because by running out of the way they have wearied themselves to no purpose. In the first part of the verse he has, I think, put *law of righteousness* by hypallage to mean *righteousness of the law,* and when he repeats the phrase in the second clause, he has understood it in a different sense to mean the form or rule of righteousness. The whole verse, therefore, means that although Israel depends on the righteousness of the law, it has not obtained the true method of justification, viz. that which is prescribed in the law. Paul's use of contrasted expressions is striking, when he informs us that legal righteousness was the reason why Israel fell from the law of righteousness.

32. *Not by faith, but as it were by works.* It is commonly regarded as justified to excuse excessive zeal. Paul, therefore, shows that those who endeavour to obtain salvation by trusting in their works are justly rejected, for they are doing everything in their power to destroy faith, without which no salvation can be hoped for. Should they, therefore, achieve what they desire, such success would mean the annihilation of true righteousness. We see also how faith and the merits of works are

contrasted, as being entirely contrary to each other. Since, therefore, trust in works is the chief obstacle to our attainment of righteousness, it is necessary that we should renounce it, in order that we may put our trust in the goodness of God alone. This example of the Jews should inspire with fear all those who strive to obtain the kingdom of God by works. By the works of the law Paul does not mean ceremonial observances, as we have already shown, but the merits of works to which faith is opposed—faith which, to use the phrase, looks with both eyes to the mercy of God alone, without regarding any worthiness of its own.

They stumbled at the stone of stumbling. Paul confirms his previous sentence by an excellent argument. There is nothing more absurd than that those who strive to destroy righteousness should obtain it. Christ has been given to us for righteousness; anyone who obtrudes the righteousness of works on God strives to deprive Christ of His office. It is clear from this that whenever men rely on the confidence of works under the empty pretence of being zealous for righteousness, they are waging war with God in their raging madness.

It is easy to realize how those who trust in their works are offended by Christ. If we do not acknowledge ourselves to be sinners who are void and destitute of any righteousness of our own, we obscure the dignity of Christ, which consists in His being light, salvation, life, resurrection, righteousness, and healing to all of us. Why is He all these things, but to give sight to the blind, restore the condemned, quicken the dead, raise up those who are brought to nothing, cleanse those who are full of filth, and cure and heal those who are infected with diseases? Indeed, if we claim any righteousness for ourselves, we are in some measure struggling with the power of Christ, since His office consists as much in breaking down all the pride of the flesh as in relieving and comforting those who labour and are heavy laden.

The passage (Isa. 3.14) is properly quoted. God there declares that He would be to the people of Judah and of Israel a rock of offence, at which they would stumble and fall. Since Christ Himself is the very God who spoke by the prophet, it is not strange that this too is now fulfilled in Him. By referring to Christ as the *stone of stumbling*, he tells us that we are not to be surprised if those who have stumbled at the rock of offence by their own perverse obstinacy, when God had shown them the easy way, have made no progress in the way of righteousness. We must, however, note that Christ is not properly and in His own person a stone of stumbling, but is such rather in consequence of human wickedness, as we see from what follows.

33. *And he that believeth on him shall not be put to shame.* Paul added this quotation taken from another part of Isaiah for the consolation of

the godly, as if to say, 'There is no reason why we should be afraid of Him because Christ is called the stone of stumbling, or entertain fear instead of confidence, for He is appointed for the ruin of the unbelieving, but for the life and resurrection of the godly.' As, therefore, the former prophecy, concerning the stumbling and offence, is fulfilled in the rebellious and the unbelievers, so there is another which is intended for the godly, viz. that He is a firm stone, precious, a corner-stone, most firmly fixed, and whoever has relied on Him shall never fail. Paul's expression *shall not be put to shame* rather than *shall not hasten* or *fall*, has been taken from the Septuagint. It is certain that in that passage the Lord intended to confirm the hope of His people. When the Lord bids us to entertain good hope, it follows that we cannot be ashamed. See the similar passage in I Pet. 2.10.

CHAPTER TEN

Brethren, my heart's desire and my supplication to God is for them, that they may be saved. For I bear them witness that they have a zeal for God, but not according to knowledge. For being ignorant of God's righteousness, and seeking to establish their own, they did not subject themselves to the righteousness of God. For Christ is the end of the law unto righteousness to everyone that believeth. (1-4)

1. We see from this how anxiously the man of God had guarded against giving offence. To mitigate any harshness which there was in his interpretation of the rejection of the Jews, he continues as before to affirm his goodwill towards them. He proves this by its effect, viz. that their salvation was a matter of concern to him before the Lord. Such affection arises only from unfeigned love. He was also under the necessity of affirming, perhaps for another reason, his love towards the nation from which he was descended, for his doctrine would have never been received by the Jews had they considered him to be their avowed enemy. His defection would also have been suspected by the Gentiles, for they would have thought, as we mentioned in the last chapter, that his apostasy from the law proceeded from his hatred of men.

2. *For I bear them witness.* The object of this verse was to secure confidence in his affection. There was a good reason why he should regard them with compassion rather than hatred, since he perceived that they fell only through ignorance, and not through wickedness of mind, and especially since he saw that they were induced to persecute the kingdom of Christ only by some affection for God. But let us learn from this where our good intentions may impel us, if we yield to them. For a man to pretend, when he is rebuked, that he meant no harm, is commonly held to be an excellent and very proper excuse. Very many people at the present time are prevented by this pretext from giving their whole efforts to searching out the truth of God, because they think that any wrong that they have committed through ignorance, without designed malice, and indeed with good intentions, will be excused. And yet none of us can excuse the Jews for having crucified Christ, treated the apostles with barbarous cruelty, and for having attempted to destroy and extinguish the Gospel, although they have the same defence as the one in which we confidently glory. Away then with those empty equivocations about good intention. If we

seek God from the heart, let us follow the way by which alone we have access to Him. It is better, as Augustine says, to limp in the right way than to run with all our might out of the way. If we would be really religious, let us remember the truth taught us by Lactantius—the only true religion is that which is connected with the Word of God. On the other hand, however, when we see those who wander in darkness perish, even though they wander with good intention, let us reflect that we well deserve a thousand deaths, if having been enlightened by God, we wander knowingly and willingly from His way.

3. *For being ignorant of God's righteousness.* Notice how they went astray through their unconsidered zeal. They wanted to set up a righteousness of their own, and their foolish confidence proceeded from their ignorance of God's righteousness. Observe the contrast between the righteousness of God and that of men. We see, first, that they are opposed to one another, and cannot stand together. It follows that the righteousness of God is overthrown as soon as men set up their own righteousness. Again, in order to provide a correspondence between the two types of righteousness, Paul calls the righteousness which is His gift *God's righteousness*, while on the other hand that which men seek from themselves or believe that they bring to God he calls human righteousness. Those, therefore, who desire to be justified in themselves do not submit to the righteousness of God, for the first step to obtaining the righteousness of God is to renounce our own righteousness. Why do we seek for righteousness from another source, except that our lack of it compels us to do so?

We have stated elsewhere how men put on the righteousness of God by faith. Christ's righteousness is imputed to them. Paul inveighs strongly against the pride which puffs up the hypocrites, although they conceal it under the specious disguise of zeal, when he says that by shaking off God's yoke, they are all opposed to and in revolt against the righteousness of God.

4. *For Christ is the end of the law.* The word *completion,* or *perfection,* as Erasmus has translated it, is, I think, quite appropriate in this passage. Since, however, the other reading has received almost universal approval, and is also quite suitable, I leave it to my readers to retain it.

The apostle here refutes the objection which might have been made against him. The Jews might have appeared to have pursued the right path, because they had devoted themselves to the righteousness of the law. It was necessary for Paul to disprove this false opinion. He does this here by showing that those who seek to be justified by their own works are false interpreters of the law, because the law has been given to lead us by the hand to another righteousness. Indeed, every doctrine of the law, every command, every promise, always points to Christ.

We are, therefore, to apply all its parts to Him. But we cannot do this, unless we are stripped of all righteousness, are overwhelmed by the knowledge of our sin, and seek unmerited righteousness from him alone. The gross abuse of the law by the Jews, who in their evil-doing made a stumbling-block of what was to be their help, is in consequence rightly censured. Indeed, it is evident that they had shamefully mutilated the law of God, for they rejected its soul and snatched at the dead body of the letter. The law promises a reward to those who observe it. Now, however, that it has proved all men guilty, it has substituted a new righteousness in Christ, which is not acquired by the merits of our works, but being freely given is received by faith. Thus the righteousness of faith (as we saw in the first chapter), is witnessed to by the law. This remarkable passage declares that the law in all its parts has reference to Christ, and therefore no one will be able to understand it correctly who does not constantly strive to attain this mark.

For Moses writeth that the man that doeth the righteousness which is of the law shall live thereby. But the righteousness which is of faith saith thus, Say not in thy heart, Who shall ascend into heaven? (that is, to bring Christ down:) or, Who shall descend into the abyss? (that is, to bring Christ up from the dead.) But what saith it? The word is nigh thee, in thy mouth, and in thy heart: that is, the word of faith, which we preach: because if thou shalt confess with thy mouth Jesus as Lord, and shalt believe in thy heart that God raised Him from the dead, thou shalt be saved: for with the heart man believeth unto righteousness; and with the mouth confession is made unto salvation. (5-10)

Paul now compares the righteousness of faith and the righteousness of works in order to make it clear how greatly they are at variance. The difference which exists between opposites is seen more clearly by a comparison between them. He is not referring to the writings of the prophets, but to the testimony of Moses, and for this reason alone, that the Jews might understand that the law had not been given by Moses in order to maintain their confidence in their works, but rather to lead them to Christ. Although Paul might have cited the prophets as witnesses of his assertion, this difficulty still remained. Why should the law prescribe another form of righteousness? He therefore removes this difficulty very satisfactorily when he establishes the righteousness of faith by the teaching of the law itself.

We must understand the reason why Paul makes the law agree with faith, and yet sets the righteousness of the law in opposition to the righteousness of faith. The word law is used in a twofold sense. At times it means the whole of the doctrine taught by Moses, and at times that part of it which belonged peculiarly to his ministry, and is contained in its precepts, rewards and punishments. The universal office which Moses had was the instruction of the people in the true rule of godliness. If this is true, it was his duty to preach repentance and faith. But faith is not taught without offering the promises, the free promises, of the divine mercy. Paul, therefore, was obliged to be a preacher of the Gospel, and it is clear from many passages that he performed this office with fidelity. In order to teach the people repentance, it was necessary for him to instruct them in the manner of life which was acceptable to God. He included this in the precepts of the law. In order to instil in the minds of the people a love of righteousness, and implant also a hatred of iniquity, he had to add promises and threats to declare the rewards which were laid up for the just, and the awful punishments for sinners. The duty now to be performed by the people was to consider in how many ways they were accursed, and how far they were from being able to earn anything from God by their works. Being thus led to despair of attaining any righteousness of their own they were to flee to the haven of divine goodness—to Christ Himself. This was the purpose of the ministry of Moses.

The promises of the Gospel, however, are found only here and there in the writings of Moses, and these are somewhat obscure, while the precepts and rewards, appointed for those who observe the law, frequently occur. The function, therefore, of teaching the character of true righteousness of works is, with justification, properly and peculiarly attributed to Moses, as is also the function of showing the nature of the remuneration which awaits those who observe it, and what punishment awaits those who transgress it. For this reason Moses himself is contrasted with Christ by John, when he says, 'The law was given by Moses; grace and truth came by Jesus Christ' (John 1.17). Whenever the word *law* is used in this restricted sense, Moses is implicitly contrasted with Christ. We are then to see what the law contains in itself when separated from the Gospel. I must, therefore, refer what I say here of the righteousness of the law not to the whole office of Moses, but to that part of it which was peculiarly entrusted to him. I now come to Paul's actual words.

For Moses writeth. Paul has γράφει, 'writes', but the verb is to be taken with the prefix as ἐπιγράφει, 'describes'. The passage is taken from Lev. 18.5, where the Lord promises eternal life to those who will keep His law. We see that Paul has also taken the passage in this sense, and not of temporal life only, as some hold. Paul reasons thus from the passage in Leviticus: 'Since no man attains the righteousness prescribed by the law, unless he has exactly fulfilled every part of it, and since all men have always come far short of this perfection, it is in vain for any one to strive for salvation in this way. Israel, therefore, was quite wrong in hoping to be able to obtain the righteousness of the law, for we are all excluded from this.' We should observe how he argues from the promise itself that the law is of no use to us because of the impossible condition. To quote the promises of the law in order to establish the righteousness of works is quite empty subtlety. We are so far from attaining salvation from them that if we trust in them, a sure curse awaits us. The stupidity of the Papists, who count it sufficient to lay hold of empty promises to prove merits, is the more detestable. 'God', they say, 'has not in vain promised life to those who worship Him.' But at the same time they fail to see that the promise of life was given in order that the sense of their transgressions might strike them all with the fear of death, and that being thus compelled by their own need, they might learn to take refuge in Christ.

6. *But the righteousness which is of faith saith thus.* This passage may for two reasons cause considerable difficulty to the reader. Paul seems to have not only distorted the proper sense of the passage, but also to have changed the words to a different meaning. We shall later consider the interpretation of the words, but first let us give our attention to the application. The passage is taken from Deut. 30.12, where Moses, as in the former quotation, is speaking of the doctrine of the law, which Paul applies to the promises of the Gospel. This difficulty may easily be removed in the following way: Moses in that passage is showing how easy an access the Jews had to life, since the will of God is no longer hidden or far isolated from them, but is placed before their eyes. Had Paul spoken only of the law, his argument would have been illogical, since it is no easier to keep the law of God when it is set before one's eyes than when it is at a great distance. Moses, therefore, does not mean the law alone but the whole doctrine of God in general, which includes the Gospel. The word of the law is never of itself in our heart, not even the least syllable of it, until it is ingrafted in us by the faith of the Gospel. In the second place, even after regeneration the Word of the law cannot properly be said to be in our hearts, because it requires a perfection, from which even believers themselves are far distant. But the Word of the Gospel, though it does not fill our heart, has its dwelling there, for it offers pardon for imperfection and defect. Throughout that chapter (as also in the fourth) Moses endeavours to commend God's great kindness to His people, because He had taken them under His discipline and government. This commendation could not have applied merely to the law. It is no objection that Moses is speaking there of forming their lives in accordance with the rule of the law, for he connects the spirit of regeneration with the free righteousness of faith. He therefore infers one from the other, for the observance of

the law springs from faith in Christ. It is certain, too, that this verse depends on the truth, 'The Lord shall circumcise thine heart', which he had stated shortly before in the same chapter. It is, therefore, simple to disprove those who say that Moses in this passage is dealing with good works. I admit that this is the case, but I maintain that there is nothing illogical in deriving the observance of the law from its source, i.e. the righteousness of faith. We must now seek the explanation of the words.

Say not in thy heart, Who shall ascend? Moses uses the words *heaven* and *the abyss*, to suggest places which are fairly remote and difficult for man to reach. Paul applies these words to the death and resurrection of Christ, as if some spiritual mystery lay beneath them. If it is alleged that this interpretation is too forced and subtle, we should understand that the object of the Apostle was not to explain this passage exactly, but only to apply it to his treatment of the subject in hand. He does not, therefore, repeat what Moses has said syllable by syllable, but employs a gloss, by which he adapts the testimony of Moses more closely to his own purpose. Moses had spoken of inaccessible places; Paul mentioned those which are most hidden from our sight and yet are visible to our faith. If, therefore, we take these statements of Paul as having been made by way of amplification or as a gloss, we shall not be able to say that he has done violence to or distorted the words of Moses. We shall, rather, acknowledge that his allusion to the words *heaven* and *abyss* is elegant without any loss of meaning.

Let us, therefore, now give a simple explanation of the words of Paul: 'The assurance of our salvation lies on two foundations, viz. our realization that life has been gained for us, and death has been conquered.' Paul, therefore, teaches us that our faith is supported by both of these through the Word of the Gospel, for Christ has swallowed up death by dying, and by rising again He received life into His power. The benefit of Christ's death and resurrection is now communicated to us by the Gospel. There is, therefore, no reason for us to seek for anything farther. And so, in order that the righteousness of faith may be clearly seen to be abundantly sufficient for our salvation, Paul teaches us that these two parts, which alone are necessary for salvation, are included in it. *Who shall ascend into heaven?* is equivalent to saying, 'Who knows whether that inheritance of eternal and heavenly life awaits us?' And, *Who shall descend into the deep?* means 'Who knows whether the everlasting destruction of the soul accompanies the death of the body?' Paul teaches us that both of these doubts are removed by the righteousness of faith. The first doubt would draw Christ down from heaven, and the other would bring Him back again from death. Christ's ascension into heaven ought to

establish our faith in eternal life in such a way that to doubt whether
the inheritance of heaven is prepared for believers, in whose name and
for whose sake Christ has entered heaven, is almost to drag Him
down from this possession of heaven. In the same way, since He
underwent the horrors of hell in order to deliver us from them, to
doubt whether believers are still exposed to this misery is to make His
death void, and indeed to deny it.

8. *But what saith it?* The negative statements which Paul has used
up to this point are concerned with the removal of the obstacles to
faith. It remains, therefore, for him to recount the means of obtaining
righteousness, and to this end he adds a positive affirmation. The
introduction of a question, when he might have summarized all his
remarks in a single statement, was designed to arouse attention. At the
same time he desired to inform his readers of the great difference which
exists between the righteousness of the law and that of the Gospel.
The former presents itself at a distance, and prevents the whole human
race from approaching it, while the latter, encountering us close at
hand, invites us warmly to enjoy its gifts.

The word is nigh thee. We should note, first, that to prevent men's
minds from being reduced to ambiguities and straying from salvation,
Paul prescribes for them the limits of the Word (*verbi metas*) within
which they are to keep themselves. It is as if he were bidding them be
content with the Word alone, and informing them that the secrets of
heaven, which would dazzle their eyes by their brightness, astonish
their ears, and stun their very mind with wonder, are to be contemplated in this mirror.

Believers, therefore, derive notable consolation from this passage
with regard to the certainty of the Word. For they may rest in it with
as great security as they would in what they saw to be actually present.
We are also to notice that Moses sets forth the Word, on which we
base our firm and calm confidence in salvation.

That is, the word of faith. Paul is justified in taking this as *word of faith*,
for the doctrine of the law by no means calms or quietens the conscience
nor supplies it with what should satisfy it. He does not, however, in
the meantime exclude the other parts of the Word of Scripture, and in
particular the precepts of the law. He wants, however, to make
righteousness equivalent to the remission of sins, even apart from the
exact obedience which the law requires. The Word of the Gospel,
therefore, which commands us not to earn righteousness by works, but
to embrace it when freely offered by faith, is sufficient to give peace to
men's minds and establish their salvation.

The *word of faith* is put by metonymy for *the word of promise*, i.e. for
the Gospel itself, since it is related to faith. The contrast between law

and Gospel is to be understood, and from this distinction we deduce that, just as the law demands work, the Gospel requires only that men should bring faith in order to receive the grace of God. The phrase *which we preach* is added to prevent any suspicion that Paul differed from Moses. Paul declares that in the ministry of the Gospel there was complete agreement between him and Moses, since Moses too has placed our happiness in the free promise of divine grace alone.

9. *Because if thou shalt confess with thy mouth.* Here too Paul is making an allusion, rather than a true and proper translation, for it is likely that Moses used the word *mouth* by synecdoche to mean face or sight. The apostle's allusion to the word *mouth* in this manner was appropriate. When the Lord sets His Word before our face, He is without doubt calling us to make confession of it. The Word of the Lord ought to bring forth fruit wherever it exists, and our confession of the Word is the fruit of the mouth.

To put *confession* before *faith* is an inversion of order quite common in Scripture. The order would have been better if the faith of the heart had been put first, and the confession of the mouth, which arises from it, had followed. But he makes a true confession of Jesus as Lord, who adorns Him with His own power, acknowledging Him as the one who was given by the Father and is described in the Gospel.

Paul's express mention of Christ's resurrection alone is not to be taken to imply that His death was of no importance, but because by His resurrection He completed the whole work of our salvation. Even though our redemption and satisfaction, by which we are reconciled to God, were accomplished by His death, yet the victory over sin, death, and Satan was procured by His resurrection. From this also came righteousness, newness of life, and the hope of a blessed immortality. For this reason Christ's resurrection alone is often set before us to confirm our assurance of salvation, not in order to distract our attention from his death, but because it testifies to the effect and fruit of His death. In short, the resurrection of Christ includes His death. We have made some mention of this subject in the sixth chapter.

Furthermore, Paul requires not merely a historical faith, but includes within the resurrection itself the design of Christ's rising. We must remember the purpose for which Christ rose again. It was the Father's design in raising Him to restore us all to life. Although Christ had the power of getting His life back by Himself, this work is generally in Scripture ascribed to God the Father.

10. *For with the heart man believeth unto righteousness.* This passage may assist us in understanding justification by faith. It shows that we obtain righteousness by embracing the goodness of God offered to us in the Gospel. We are, therefore, justified by our believing that God

is gracious to us in Christ. But let us note that the seat of faith is not in the head but in the heart. I am not going to argue about the part of the body in which faith is located, but since the word *heart* generally means a serious and sincere affection, I maintain that faith is a firm and effectual confidence, and not just a bare idea.

With the mouth confession is made unto salvation. It may appear strange that Paul now ascribes part of our salvation to faith, after having declared so frequently on previous occasions that we are saved by faith alone. We should not, however, conclude from this that our confession is the cause of our salvation. Paul's desire was solely to show how God accomplishes our salvation, viz. by making faith, which He has put into our hearts, show itself by confession. Indeed, he simply wanted to point out the nature of true faith, from which this fruit springs, lest any one should hold out the empty title of faith for faith itself. True faith ought to kindle the heart with zeal for God's glory in such a way that it pours forth its own flame. And certainly those who are justified are already in possession of salvation, and therefore believe as much with the heart unto salvation as make confession with the mouth. Paul, we see, has made a distinction in such a way as to refer the cause of justification to faith, and also to show what is required to complete salvation. No one can believe with the heart without confessing with the mouth. There is laid on us as a perpetual consequence of faith the necessity of confession with the mouth, but this is not to ascribe salvation to confession.

Those of our day who proudly boast to us of an imaginary faith, which, being content with the secrecy of the heart, neglects the confession of the mouth as being a superfluous and empty thing, must see what answer they are to give to Paul. It is quite nonsensical to insist that there is fire, when there is neither flame nor heat.

For the scripture saith, Whosoever believeth on him shall not be put to shame. For there is no distinction between Jew and Greek: for the same Lord is Lord of all, and is rich unto all that call upon him: for, Whosoever shall call upon the name of the Lord shall be saved. (11-13)

11. *For the scripture saith.* Having stated the reasons why God had justly rejected the Jews, he returns to affirm the calling of the Gentiles. This is the other part of the question which he is now discussing. Since, therefore, Paul had pointed out the way by which men obtain salvation, a way which is as common and accessible to the Gentiles as to the Jews, he now openly extends it to the Gentiles, adding first an expression to include all, and then invites them to it by name. He repeats the passage from Isaiah which he had already quoted, in order

to give more authority to his view, and also to show how well the prophecies spoken concerning Christ agree with the law.

12. *For there is no distinction.* If confidence alone is required, the goodness of God will manifest itself unto salvation wherever it is found. In this case, therefore, there will be no distinction of race or nation. Paul adds the strongest of reasons. If the One who is the Creator and Maker of the whole world is the God of all mankind, He will display His kindness to all by whom He has been invoked and acknowledged as their God. Since His mercy is infinite, it must necessarily extend to all who have sought it.

Rich is here used in an active sense, and means kind and beneficent. The riches of our Father are not, we should note, diminished by His liberality. We are not, therefore, deprived of any, however much He may enrich others with the manifold abundance of His grace. There is therefore no reason why some should envy the blessings of others, as if they lost anything thereby.

Although this argument was sufficiently strong, Paul confirms it by the testimony of the prophet Joel. This quotation, since Joel has used a general term, includes all men equally. Readers, however, will see much better from the context that Joel's declaration accords with the present passage, not only because he is prophesying there of the kingdom of Christ, but also because, having prophesied that the wrath of God would burn terribly, he promises salvation, even in the midst of God's anger, to all who shall have called on the name of the Lord. It follows that the grace of God penetrates to the very abyss of death, if only men seek it from there, so that it is not by any means to be withheld from the Gentiles.

How then shall they call on him in whom they have not believed? and how shall they believe in him whom they have not heard? and how shall they hear without a preacher? and how shall they preach, except they be sent? even as it is written, How beautiful are the feet of them that bring glad tidings of good things! But they did not all hearken to the glad tidings. For Isaiah saith, Lord, who hath believed our report? So belief cometh of hearing, and hearing by the word of Christ. (14-17)

I shall not detain the reader long here in recounting and disproving the opinions of others. I shall state my own view freely, but each must form his own judgment. To understand the point of this rhetorical climax, we must first bear in mind that there was a mutual connexion between the calling of the Gentiles and the ministry which Paul exercised among them, so that the esteem in which the one was held depended on the approbation accorded to the other. It was now necessary for Paul to establish beyond doubt the calling of the Gentiles, and, at the same time, to give a reason for his own industry, lest he should seem to be dissipating the grace of God by withholding from the children the bread intended for them by God, and giving it to dogs. Paul, therefore, establishes both these points at the same time. But until each part has been recounted in order, we shall not fully understand how he connects the threads of his discourse. His climax means in effect that both Jews and Gentiles, by the very fact of their calling upon the name of God, declare their belief in Him. There can be no true invoking of God's name unless such invocation has been preceded by a correct knowledge of Him. Moreover, faith arises from the Word of God. But wherever the Word of God is preached, it is only by the special providence and appointment of God (*speciali Dei providentia et ordinatione*). Faith, therefore, exists where God is invoked; where there is faith, it has been preceded by the seed of the Word; and where there is preaching, there is the calling of God. There is a clear and undoubted sign of the divine goodness where His calling is thus efficacious and productive of fruit. It will finally be established from this that the Gentiles, whom God has admitted to participation in His salvation, are not to be excluded from the kingdom of God. For as the preaching of the Gospel is the cause of faith among them, so the mission of God, by which it pleased Him to provide for their salvation in this manner, is the cause of preaching. Let us now consider separately the rest of the passage.

14. *How then shall they call on Him?* Paul's purpose here is to connect the invocation of God with faith, since there is a very close relationship between these two things. He who calls upon God enters the only haven of salvation, and the most secure refuge, as a son commits himself to the bosom of a perfect and most loving father, to be protected by his care, cherished by his gentleness and love, sustained by his kindness, and strengthened by his power. This attainment is possible only for the man whose mind has previously been so greatly persuaded of the fatherly kindness of God towards him that he dares to hope for any kind of blessing from Him.

It is, therefore, necessary that those who call upon God should believe that in Him they have protection, for Paul is speaking here of that calling upon God which is approved by Him. Hypocrites also pray to God, but not to their salvation, since they invoke Him without any sense of faith. This demonstrates the foolishness of all the schoolmen who present themselves before God with doubts, unsustained by any confidence. Paul's attitude is far different, for he assumes it as axiomatic that we cannot rightly pray unless we are persuaded for certain of success. He is not here referring to implicit faith, but that certainty which our minds conceive of His fatherly kindness, when He reconciles us to Himself by the Gospel and adopts us as His children. By this confidence alone we have access to Him, as we are also taught in Eph. 3.12.

On the other hand, we learn that the only true faith is that which brings forth prayer to God. It is impossible for a believer who has tasted the goodness of God ever to cease to aspire to that goodness in all his prayers.

How shall they believe in Him? The point is that we are dumb until the promise of God opens our mouth to pray. This is also the order which we see in the prophet Zechariah: 'I will say, It is my people; and they shall say, The Lord is my God' (Zech. 13.9). It is not for us to form any God we please. The proper knowledge of God, therefore, which we ought to possess is that which is set forth in His Word. If anyone forms a conception of God as good which is derived from his own opinion, it will be no sure and genuine faith which he has, but an unstable and fleeting imagination. The Word, accordingly, is required for a true knowledge of God. But it is the preached Word alone which Paul has here described, for this is the normal mode which the Lord has appointed for imparting His Word (*ordinaria ratio dispensandi*). If it is contended from this that God can instil a knowledge of Himself among men only by means of preaching, we shall deny that this was the meaning of the apostle. Paul was referring only to the ordinary dispensation of God (*ordinarium Dei dispensandi*), and had no desire to prescribe a law to His grace.

15. *How shall they preach, except they be sent?* Paul's meaning is that when any nation is favoured with the preaching of the Gospel, it is a pledge and proof of the divine love. There is no preacher of the Gospel who has not been raised up by God in His special providence. It is certain, therefore, that God visits that nation in which the Gospel is proclaimed. Since, however, Paul is not dealing at all here with the lawful call of any individual, it would be unnecessary to enter into a more protracted discussion of that matter at this point. It is enough to bear this fact alone in mind, that the Gospel does not fall from the clouds like rain, by accident, but is brought by the hands of men to where God has sent it.

As it is written, How beautiful are the feet. We are to apply this passage in the following manner to our present subject. The Lord, intending to give hope of deliverance to His people, acclaims with high praise the coming of those who bring the glad tidings of this deliverance. By this very statement, therefore, he has made it clear that the apostolic ministry (*apostolicum ministerium*), by which the message of eternal life is brought to us, is valued equally with the Word. It follows from this that this ministry is from God, since there is nothing in the world to

be desired or which is worthy of praise, which does not proceed from
His hand.

We also learn from this, however, how much the preaching of the
Gospel is to be desired by all good men, and how much they ought to
value it, since it is thus commended by the mouth of the Lord. Without question God bestows the highest praise on the incomparable value
of this treasure to awaken the minds of all men to desire it eagerly.
Feet, by metonymy, means arrival.

16. *But they did not all hearken.* This bears no relation to the argument
which Paul proposed to follow in this rhetorical climax, and therefore
he does not repeat it in the conclusion which follows immediately. It
suited Paul, however, to introduce the sentence here, by way of
meeting the objection of any who might base their argument on what
he had said, viz. that the Word always precedes faith as the seed comes
before the corn, and draw the conclusion that faith follows wherever
the Word is preached. Israel, which had never been without the Word,
might have made a boast of this kind. It was, therefore, necessary for
Paul to demonstrate in passing that there are many called who are
not chosen.

The passage which he quotes is taken from Isa. 53.1, where the
prophet, before giving his famous prophecy of the death and the
kingdom of Christ, speaks with wonderment of the small number of
believers, a number which appeared to his mind to be so small as to
compel him to cry out, 'Who hath believed our report?' (Isa. 53.1),
i.e. the Word which we preach. Although in Hebrew the term
שְׁמוּעָה means discourse, *sermonem*, in a passive sense, the Septuagint
has rendered it ἀκοήν, and the Vulgate *auditum*, but the sense is clear.

We now see why Isaiah admitted this objection in passing, i.e. to
prevent anyone from supposing that faith necessarily follows where
there is preaching. He does, however, point out the reason later when
he adds, 'To whom hath the arm of the Lord been revealed?' By this
he means that only when God shines in us by the light of His Spirit is
there any profit from the Word. Thus the inward calling, which alone
is effectual and peculiar to the elect, is distinguished from the outward
voice of men. This clearly proves the stupidity of the argument of
certain interpreters who maintain that all are elected without distinction, because the doctrine of salvation is universal, and because God
invites all men to Himself without distinction (*promiscue*). The general
nature of the promises does not alone and of itself make salvation
common to all. Rather, the peculiar revelation which the prophet
has mentioned restricts it to the elect.

17. *So belief cometh of hearing.* We see from the conclusion what
Paul had in view in framing his rhetorical climax, viz. to show that

wherever faith exists, God has already afforded a sign of His election. In the second place, He has poured out His blessing by the ministry of the Gospel in order to enlighten the minds of men by faith, and thereby also instruct them to call upon His name, by which salvation is promised to all men. He has thus declared that the Gentiles are admitted to a share of the eternal inheritance. This is a noteworthy passage on the efficacy of preaching, for Paul declares that faith is produced by preaching. He has just stated that by itself preaching is profitless, but when the Lord is pleased to work, it is the instrument of His power. Certainly the human voice cannot by its own power penetrate into the soul. Too much honour would be paid to a mere mortal if it were said that he had power to regenerate us. The light of faith also is too exalted to be able to be conferred by man. But all these things do not prevent God from acting effectually by the voice of man, so as to create faith in us by his ministry.

It must further be noted that faith has no other foundation than the doctrine of God. Paul does not state that faith arises from any kind of doctrine, but expressly limits it to the Word of God. This restriction would have been absurd if faith could rest on the opinions of men. All human inventions must therefore cease when we are dealing with the certainty of faith. Hereby also the popish spectre of implicit faith which separates faith from the Word is destroyed, and much more the detestable blasphemy that faith in the Word remains uncertain until the authority of the Church supports it.

But I say, Did they not hear? Yea, verily, Their sound went out into all the earth, And their words unto the ends of the world. But I say, Did Israel not know? First Moses saith, I will provoke you to jealousy with that which is no nation, With a nation void of understanding will I anger you. And Isaiah is very bold, and saith, I was found of them that sought me not; I became manifest unto them that asked not of me. But as to Israel he saith, All the day long did I spread out my hands unto a disobedient and gainsaying people. (18-21)

18. *But I say, Did they not hear?* Since preaching imbues the minds of men with the knowledge of God, which of itself leads them to call on God, the question remained whether the truth of God had been proclaimed to the Gentiles. The Jews were greatly offended at the unusual step which Paul had taken in going to the Gentiles. He therefore asks the question whether God had ever before directed His Voice to the Gentiles, and performed the office of Teacher to the whole world. For the purpose of showing that the school into which God might gather scholars to Himself from every part of the world is open to all, he also cites the testimony of the psalmist from Ps. 19.4.

This seems to have little connexion with the subject. The psalmist is not speaking in that passage of apostles, but of the voiceless works of God, in which, he says, the glory of God shines forth so manifestly that they may be said to have a tongue of their own to declare the acts of God's power.

Ancient interpreters, followed by later writers, have been led by this passage of Paul to explain the whole of the Psalm in allegorical terms. Thus the sun going forth as a bridegroom from his chamber without question was Christ, while the apostles were the heavens. Those who were more reverent and proceeded more modestly in their interpretation of Scripture are of the opinion that Paul has transferred to the apostles what the psalmist had properly said of the architecture of heaven. But since I notice that the servants of the Lord have universally treated the Scriptures with greater respect, and have not been so free in twisting their meaning, I cannot be persuaded that Paul has misconstrued this passage in this way. I therefore take his quotation in the true and proper sense of the psalmist. The argument is this— from the very beginning of the world God has displayed His divinity to the Gentiles by the testimony of His creation, if not by the preaching of men. Although the Gospel was not heard at that time among the Gentiles, yet the whole workmanship of heaven and earth spoke and proclaimed its Author by its preaching. It is, therefore, clear that, even during the time in which the Lord confined the favour of His covenant to Israel, He did not withdraw the knowledge of Himself from the Gentiles, without continually inflaming some spark of it among them. He did indeed manifest Himself more closely at that time to His chosen people, so that the Jews might justifiably have been compared to domestic hearers, who were taught intimately by His holy mouth. Since, however, He also spoke to the Gentiles at a distance by the voice of the heavens, this prelude revealed His desire to make Himself known at length to them also.

I do not know why the Septuagint has translated the Hebrew word קַו by φθόγγον. The Hebrew means a *line*, sometimes in building, and sometimes in writing. It is probable, I think, that since the same word is twice repeated in this passage, the heavens are introduced as proclaiming the power of God to all mankind both in writing and in speech. The psalmist reminds us by the words *going forth* that this doctrine proclaimed by the heavens is not confined to the narrow limits of a single land, but sounds to the furthest regions of the world.

19. *But I say, did Israel not know?* This objection from the opposite side is taken from a comparison between the less and the greater. Paul has argued that the Gentiles are not to be excluded from the knowledge

of God, since He has manifested Himself to them from the beginning, although only in an obscure way and through shadows, or at least has given them some taste of His truth. What then is to be said of Israel, which had been enlightened by a very different light of doctrine? How is it that strangers and non-Jews should run to the light held up to their view afar off, while the holy race of Abraham reject the light which they have seen close at hand? We must always bear in mind the distinction which we find in Deut. 4.7, 8: 'What great nation is there, that hath a god so nigh unto them, as the Lord our God is whensoever we call upon him?' It is, therefore, not irrelevant to ask why the knowledge of God did not follow the doctrine of the law with which Israel was endowed.

First Moses saith. Paul proves from the statement of Moses that there is nothing irrational in God's preferring the Gentiles to the Jews. The passage is taken from the celebrated song of praise in which God upbraids the Jews for their unfaithfulness, and threatens to take the revenge on them of provoking them to jealousy by taking the Gentiles into His covenant, because they had gone over to false gods. 'By despising and rejecting me,' He says, 'you have transferred my right and honour to idols. To avenge this wrong, I in turn will put the Gentiles in your place, and make over to them what I have hitherto given you.' This, however, could not have been done without repudiating the Jewish people. The jealousy mentioned by Moses arose from God's appointing for Himself a nation from those who were not a nation, and raising up from nothing a new people, who were to occupy the place from which the Jews had been driven, since they had forsaken the true God and whored after idols. It is no excuse for the Jews that, at the coming of Christ, they had not gone over to that gross external idolatry, since they had profaned the whole worship of God by their inventions, and indeed finally denied that God the Father was revealed to them in Christ, His only-begotten Son. This is the ultimate form of godlessness.

Note that *a nation void of understanding* and *no nation* mean the same thing, for without the hope of eternal life men strictly have no existence. Furthermore, the beginning and origin of life arise from the light of faith. Spiritual existence, therefore, flows from the new creation. In this sense Paul calls believers the work of God, through whom they have been regenerated by His Spirit and renewed after His image. The word *foolish* informs us that apart from the Word of God all human wisdom is mere vanity.

20. *And Isaiah is very bold, and saith.* Since this prophecy is a little more clear, Paul states that it is expressed with much confidence in order to arouse greater attention. The prophet, he says, had not spoken

figuratively nor ambiguously, but in plain, clear words had affirmed
the calling of the Gentiles. Paul has here separated by a few intervening
words what we find in Isa. 65.1 in a single connected passage, where
the Lord declares that the time would come when He would turn His
favour to the Gentiles. He immediately adds as His reason His weariness with the obstinacy of Israel, which had become intolerable to Him
through its excessive length of duration. He therefore speaks in this
way: 'Those who did not inquire of me before, and neglected my
name, have now sought me' (Isaiah uses the past tense for the future to
denote the certainty of the prophecy), 'and those who did not seek me
have found me beyond their hope and desiring.'

I know that this whole passage is misconstrued by some Jewish
teachers to mean that God promised that He would make the Jews
come back from their defection. It is, however, quite certain that He
is speaking of strangers, for there presently follows in the text the words,
'I said, Behold me, I am come unto a nation that was not called by
my name' (Isa. 65.1). Without any question, therefore, the prophet
foretells that those who had formerly been strangers would be received
into the household of God by a new adoption. This, therefore, is the
calling of the Gentiles, but in this we see the general type of the calling
of all believers. There is no man who anticipates the Lord, but we are
all without exception delivered from the deepest pit of death by His
free mercy, even when there is no knowledge of Him, no desire for
worshipping Him, and indeed no perception of His truth.

21. *But as to Israel he saith.* Paul repeats the reason why God passes
over to the Gentiles. It is because He sees that His grace is treated with
contempt by the Jews. In order, however, that his readers may better
understand that in the second clause Isaiah is pointing out the blindness
of the people, Paul expressly reminds us that it is the chosen people
who are being reproached for their wickedness. Literally the words
are, 'He says *to* Israel', but Paul has imitated the Hebrew idiom, for ל
is often put for מן. God says that He stretched forth His hands to
Israel, whom He constantly called to Himself by His Word, and did
not cease to allure by every kind of favour. These are the two methods
which God employs to call men, for in this way He proves His good
will to them. In particular, however, He has complained of the
contempt shown to His doctrine. This contempt is all the more
detestable the more strikingly God reveals His fatherly care in calling
men to Himself by His Word.

The expression *spread out my hands* is very emphatic. In procuring
our salvation by the ministers of His Word, God stretches forth His
hands to us exactly as a father stretches forth his arms, ready to receive

his son lovingly into his bosom. He says *all the day*, in order that no one might think it strange that God should be wearied in showing kindness to the Jews, although His unceasing care for them has no effect. We find the same figure of speech in Jer. 7.13 and 11.7, where He says that He rose up early in the morning to warn them.

Their unbelief is also designated by two most appropriate terms. Although the participle ἀπειθοῦντα may be translated *stubborn* or *rebellious*, the translation of Erasmus and the Vulgate, which I have placed in the margin, is quite satisfactory. But since the prophet is accusing the people of obstinacy and then adds that they were wandering in ways which were not good, I am convinced that the Septuagint intended to express the Hebrew סוֹרֵר by two words, referring to them first as disobedient or rebellious, and also as contradictory. Their stubbornness was revealed in the fact that the people obstinately rejected the sacred warnings of the prophets with uninhibited pride and bitterness.

CHAPTER ELEVEN

I say then, Did God cast off his people? God forbid. For I also am an Israelite, of the seed of Abraham, of the tribe of Benjamin. God did not cast off his people which he foreknew. Or wot ye not what the scripture saith of Elijah? how he pleadeth with God against Israel, Lord, they have killed thy prophets, they have digged down thine altars; and I am left alone, and they seek my life. But what saith the answer of God unto him? I have left for myself seven thousand men, who have not bowed the knee to Baal. Even so then at this present time also there is a remnant according to the election of grace. But if it is by grace, it is no more of works: otherwise grace is no more grace. (1-6)

1. *I say then, Did God cast off his people?* The tenor of Paul's remarks up to this point concerning the blindness and obstinacy of the Jews might have seemed to suggest that at His coming Christ had deprived the Jews of all hope of salvation and removed the promises to another people. It is this objection, therefore, which he anticipates in the present passage. He qualifies what he had previously stated concerning the repudiation of the Jews in such a way as to prevent any from supposing that the covenant which had formerly been made with Abraham was now abrogated, or that God had so forgotten it that the Jews were now completely estranged from His kingdom, as the Gentiles were before the coming of Christ. Paul denies this, in order that he may shortly prove that it was untrue. But the question is not whether God has rejected the people justly or unjustly. It was proved in the last chapter that when the people had rejected the righteousness of God through misplaced zeal, they were justly punished for their pride, deserved to be blinded, and were finally cut off from the covenant.

The cause of their rejection, therefore, is not now in dispute, but the question at issue concerns a different matter, viz. whether the covenant which God formerly made with the fathers was abolished, even though they deserved such punishment from God. That the covenant should be destroyed by any human unfaithfulness was absurd, for Paul maintains the principle that since adoption is free and founded on God alone and not on men, it stands firm and inviolable, however great may be the incredulity which conspires to overthrow it. This difficulty must be resolved, lest the truth and election of God should be believed to be dependent on human worthiness.

For I also am an Israelite. Before entering on the subject under discussion, he proves in passing from his own example how absurd it is to think that that nation has been forsaken by God. Paul himself was an Israelite by origin, and not a proselyte, or one newly admitted to the commonwealth of Israel. Since, therefore, he deserved to be reckoned as one of God's most chosen servants, this was proof that God's grace rested on Israel. Paul, therefore, takes the conclusion as proved, but he will give a sufficient explanation of it afterwards.

His purpose in referring to himself, in addition to the designation of Israelite, as the seed of Abraham, and in also mentioning his own tribe, is that he may be regarded as a true Israelite; cf. also Phil. 3.4. It seems forced and far-fetched to hold, as some interpreters do, that Paul's derivation of his descent from the tribe of Benjamin, which had almost been exterminated, is able to commend the mercy of God.

2. *God did not cast off his people.* Paul's answer is negative and qualified. If the apostle had absolutely denied that the people were rejected, he would have contradicted himself. By inserting a correction, however, he shows that the rejection of the Jews is not of such a character as to render void the promise of God. Thus his answer is divided into two parts. God has by no means rejected the whole race of Abraham, by acting contrary to the trustworthiness of His covenant. The effect, however, of His adoption is not found in all the children of the flesh, because His secret election precedes adoption. Thus the general rejection was not able to prevent some seed from being saved, for the visible body of the people was rejected in such a way that no member of the spiritual body of Christ was lost.

If we ask whether circumcision was not a common symbol of the grace of God to all the Jews, so that they should have been counted as His people, the obvious answer is that, because outward calling by itself is ineffectual without faith, the honour which the unbelieving refuse when it is offered to them is justly taken from them. Thus there remains a special people, in whom God exhibits proof of His constancy. Paul derives the origin of God's steadfastness from His secret election. He does not say here that God has regard to faith, but that He stands by His purpose not to reject the people whom He has foreknown.

My previous suggestion must here again be noted, that the verb *foreknown* does not mean some mere glimpsing, by which God foresaw the character of each human being who was to come, but means the good pleasure by which He has chosen for His children those who, since they had not yet been born, could not have been able to work their way into His favour. Thus he tells the Galatians that they had been known by God (Gal. 4.9), because He anticipated them with His favour, in order to call them to a knowledge of Christ. We now understand that, although universal calling may not produce fruit, yet the faithfulness of God does not fail, but always He preserves His Church as long as the elect remain. Although God invites all the people to Himself without distinction, He does not inwardly draw any except those whom He knows to be His own and has given to His Son, and whom He will also keep faithfully to the very end.

Or wot ye not what the scripture saith? Since there were so few of the Jews who had believed in Christ, it was hardly possible for any other conclusion to be drawn from this small number than that the whole race of Abraham was rejected. The thought might occur that no sign of God's grace existed in so terrible a loss. Since adoption was the sacred bond by which the children of Abraham were bound together in faith to God, it was quite unlikely that the Jewish people would be miserably and wretchedly scattered, unless the faithfulness of God had ceased to be. In order to obviate this stumbling-block, Paul employs the very suitable example of Elijah, in whose time, he recalls, there had been such a desolation that there no longer remained any appearance of a Church. And yet when no trace of the grace of God was visible, the Church of God was as it were hidden in a tomb, and in this way was marvellously preserved.

It follows, therefore, that those who evaluate the Church on the basis of their own opinions are in error. And indeed if that distinguished prophet who was so endowed with the light of the Spirit was deceived in this way when he desired to reckon the number of God's people by his own judgment, what will be the case with us, for our highest discernment, when compared with his, is nothing but dullness? Let us, therefore, form no rash decision on this point, but rather let this truth remain fixed in our hearts, that the Church, which may not appear as anything to our sight, is nourished by the secret providence of God. Let us also remember that those who calculate the number of the elect by the measure of their own senses are acting in folly and arrogance, for God has a way, accessible to Himself but concealed from us, by which He wonderfully preserves His elect, even when all seems lost.

The reader should note that the careful comparison which Paul makes both here and elsewhere between his own time and the ancient condition of the Church greatly serves to confirm our faith, when we reflect that nothing happens to us at the present day which was not experienced by the holy fathers of old. Anything new, as we know, greatly disturbs weak minds.

With regard to the expression, *of Elijah*, I have retained Paul's phrase, for it may mean either *in the history of* or *in the things done by* Elijah. It seems to me more likely, however, that Paul has used a Hebrew idiom; for בְּ, which corresponds to ἐν in Greek, is often used in Hebrew to mean *of*.

How he pleadeth with God. It was a proof of how much Elijah honoured the Lord that he did not hesitate to oppose his own nation for the glory of God, and to pray for its utter destruction, because he thought that the religion and worship of God had perished in Israel. His error, however, lay in condemning the whole nation except for himself on account of the impiety for which he wanted them to be so severely punished. In this passage which Paul quotes, moreover, there is no imprecation, but merely a complaint. But since his complaint is such that he despairs of the whole people, it is quite clear that in so doing he gives them up to destruction. Let us, therefore, note what it was that Elijah preached, viz. that since ungodliness had universally prevailed and had taken possession of almost the whole of the land, he considered that he alone was left.

4. *I have left for myself seven thousand men*. Although we may take the definite for an indefinite number, it was quite certainly the will of the Lord to specify a great multitude. Since, therefore, the grace of God prevails so greatly even in the most deplorable circumstances, do not let us lightly assign to the devil all those whose godliness we do not openly see. We should at the same time also have this truth stamped deeply within us, that however ungodliness may abound in every part of the world, and fearful confusion press us on all sides, yet the salvation of many remains secure under the seal of God. To prevent anyone, however, from using this pretext as an excuse for laziness, just as most men seek to hide their faults from the secret oversight of God, we should again observe that only those who remain sound and undefiled in the faith of God are said to be saved. There is also this circumstance in the case which we ought to note. Only those who did not prostitute their body to the worship of idols, even by an outward act of pretence, remain unharmed. The writer of the passage grants not only that they have purity of mind, but also that they had kept their body undefiled by any uncleanness or superstition.

5. *Even so then at this present time*. Paul applies the example to his own period, and to make the points of resemblance complete, calls them a *remnant* in comparison with the great number whose eyes were set on ungodliness. Although he alludes at the same time to the prophecy which he had previously quoted from Isaiah, he shows that faith in God still shines forth even in a dismal and confused desolation, because a remnant is still left. To confirm this with greater certainty he expressly refers to them as a remnant, because they testify by their survival through the grace of God that His election is unchangeable, even as the Lord said to Elijah, when the whole people had fallen into idolatry, that He had preserved seven thousand. We deduce from this that it was by His kindness that the people had been delivered from

destruction. Paul is not here speaking simply of grace, but recalls us now to election, in order that we may learn to regard with reverence the secret counsel of God. One of Paul's propositions, therefore, is that few are saved in comparison with the great number of those who assume the name of the people of God. The other is that those whom God has chosen without any regard to merit are saved by His power. *Election of grace* is a Hebrew idiom for free election.

6. *If it is by grace, it is no more of works.* Paul amplifies his statement from a comparison of opposites. The grace of God and the merit of works are so opposed to one another that if we establish one we destroy the other. If, then, we cannot allow any consideration of works in election without obscuring the unmerited goodness of God, which Paul so greatly desired to commend to us in election, those fanatics, who make the worthiness which God foresees in us the cause of our election, must consider what answer they are to give to Paul. Whether it is past or future works which we are considering, Paul's statement that grace leaves no room for works will always resound in our ears. He is not speaking here only of our reconciliation with God, or of the means or immediate causes of our salvation, but goes higher and asks why God chose only some and passed by others before the foundation of the world. He states that God was led to make this distinction for no other reason than His own good pleasure, and contends that any concession given to works detracts to that extent from grace.

It follows from this that it is wrong to confuse foreknowledge of works with election. If God chooses some and rejects others according to His foreknowledge of whether they will be worthy or unworthy of salvation, then the reward of works has already been established, and the grace of God will not bear sole sway, but will be only a half part of our election. Just as Paul has previously argued in the case of Abraham's justification that where a reward is paid, grace is not freely bestowed, so now he draws his argument from the same source and states that if works are taken into consideration when God adopts a certain number of men to salvation, it is a matter of reward being due, and therefore salvation will not be a free gift.

Paul is speaking here of election. Since, however, the reasoning which he uses is universal, we ought to extend it to the whole of the argument concerning our salvation. We are to understand that whenever we attribute our salvation to the grace of God, we are stating that there is no merit in works, or rather we are to believe that whenever we mention grace we are destroying the righteousness of works.

What then? That which Israel seeketh for, that he obtained not; but the election obtained it, and the rest were hardened: according as it is written, God gave them a spirit of stupor, eyes that they should not see, and ears that they should not hear, unto this very day. *And David saith, Let their table be made a snare, and a trap, And a stumblingblock, and a recompense unto them: Let their eyes be darkened that they may not see, And bow thou down their back alway.* (7-10)

7. *What then? That which Israel seeketh for.* Since the matter with which he is here dealing is difficult, he hesitates in putting his question. His desire, however, was to give a more certain answer by expressing this doubt. The answer follows presently, and Paul suggests that only one answer can be given. This is that Israel has laboured in vain in seeking for salvation, because it strove for it with misplaced zeal. Although he does not here mention the reason, yet, since he had previously expressed it, he certainly meant it to be understood in this passage also. His words mean that it should not now seem strange that Israel had made no progress in struggling after righteousness. From this there follows logically the statement which he has added immediately next on election. If Israel has obtained nothing by merit, what have others obtained whose case or condition was no better? What is the source of so great a distinction between equals? Who does not here see that it is election alone which makes the difference?

The meaning of this word is uncertain. Some think that it is to be taken collectively for the elect themselves, so that the two parts of the comparison may correspond. I do not disapprove of this view, provided it is admitted at the same time that there is more in the word *election* than would have been implied by his using the words *the elect*, viz. his suggestion that the only reason for our having obtained righteousness was *election*. It is as though he were saying that righteousness is not obtained by those who rely on merit in striving for it, but by those whose salvation depends on the unmerited election of God. He briefly compares the remnant who were saved by the grace of God with the whole of Israel, or the whole body of the people. The conclusion is that the cause of salvation does not reside in men, but depends on the mere good pleasure of God.

And the rest were hardened. As the elect alone are delivered from destruction by the grace of God, so all who are not elect must necessarily remain in blindness. Paul's meaning in regard to the reprobate is that their ruin and condemnation stem from the fact of their having been forsaken by God.

Although the passages which he quotes are taken from various parts of Scripture rather than from a single passage, they all seem to contradict his purpose, if we examine them more closely in their contexts. Each passage shows us that blindness and hardness of heart are referred

243

to as scourges, by which God punishes the wicked deeds already committed by the ungodly. Paul, however, attempts to prove here that it is not those whose wickedness has earned it who are blinded, but those who were rejected by God before the foundation of the world.

We may solve this difficulty briefly in the following way. It is the perversity of our nature when forsaken by God that is the source of the ungodliness which thus provokes His fury. In speaking, therefore, of eternal reprobation, Paul has intentionally referred to the consequences which proceed from it as fruit from the tree or the river from its source. The ungodly are indeed punished with blindness for their sins by the just judgment of God. If, however, we inquire into the source of their ruin, we must conclude that, since they are cursed by God, there is nothing but a curse which all their deeds, sayings, and purposes can bring or store up for them. Indeed, the cause of eternal reprobation is so hidden from us, that we can do nothing else but wonder at the incomprehensible counsel of God, as we shall see at length from Paul's conclusion. It is foolishness to try to conceal beneath the garb of immediate causes, as soon as we hear them mentioned, this first cause which is hidden from our notice, as though God had not freely determined before the fall of Adam to do what He thought best with the whole human race. It is foolishness, because He condemns its corrupt and depraved seed, and also because He repays to individuals the reward which their sins have deserved.

8. *God gave them a spirit of stupor.* The passage here quoted from Isaiah is, I am certain, that which Luke refers to in Acts as having been taken from Isaiah, although the words are slightly altered. He does not repeat here the words used by the prophet, but merely takes from him the conclusion that God has given them the spirit of bitterness, so that they remain dull of sight and hearing. The prophet is indeed bidden to harden the heart of the people, but Paul gets to the very centre of the matter when he states that a brutal insensibility takes hold of all the senses when men have been given up to this folly, so that they bitterly attack the truth. When the bitterness of gall displays itself, and indeed even madness in rejecting truth, Paul does not call it merely the spirit of dizziness, but of remorse. He declares that the reprobate are so driven out of their mind by the secret judgment of God, that they are lost in amazement and are incapable of forming any judgment at all. The expression, *seeing they see not* denotes the dullness of their senses.

Paul adds his own words *unto this very day* to prevent the objection that this prophecy had been fulfilled long ago, and that it was therefore false to apply it to the period of the preaching of the Gospel. He anticipates this objection by suggesting that the blindness which is described in that passage did not last merely a single day, but had continued with the incurable obstinacy of the people until the coming of Christ.

9. *And David saith.* In this quotation from David there has also been some change in the words, but it does not alter the meaning. David says, 'Let their table before them become a snare, and when they are in peace, let it become a trap' (Ps. 69.22). There is no mention of recompense, but there is sufficient agreement on the main point. The psalmist is praying that all these things in life which in other respects are desirable and blessed—and this is what he means by *table* and *prosperity*—may be turned to the ruin and destruction of the ungodly. He then gives them up to blindness of spirit and loss of strength, indicating the former by the darkening of their eyes, and the latter by the bowing down of their back. We need not be surprised that this should extend to almost the whole of the nation, for we know that not only were the chief men hostile to David, but the common people also were opposed to him. We see clearly, therefore, that what we read in the passage applies not just to a few but to a great number. Indeed, if we consider who it was whom David prefigured, it will also be easy to see the allusion in the opposite clause. Since, therefore, this curse awaits all Christ's enemies, so that their food shall be turned into poison (just as we see that the Gospel is the savour of death unto death for them), let us embrace the grace of God with humility and trembling. David, moreover, is speaking of the Israelites who were descended from Abraham according to the flesh, and who at that period held the first place in the kingdom. Paul, therefore, appropriately applies David's testimony to his present subject, so that the blindness of a great part of the people should not seem strange or unusual.

I say then, Did they stumble that they might fall? God forbid: but by their fall salvation is come unto the Gentiles, for to provoke them to jealousy. Now if their fall is the riches of the world, and their loss the riches of the Gentiles; how much more their fulness? But I speak to you that are Gentiles. Inasmuch then as I am an apostle of Gentiles, I glorify my ministry: if by any means I may provoke to jealousy them that are my flesh, and may save some of them. For if the casting away of them is the reconciling of the world, what shall the receiving of them be, but life from the dead? (11-15)

11. *Did they stumble that they might fall?* We shall be greatly hindered in understanding this argument unless we observe that the apostle is speaking at one time of the whole of the Jewish nation, and at another of individuals. This explains the fact that at times he says that the Jews have been banished from the kingdom of God, cut off from the tree,

and cast into headlong destruction by the judgment of God, while on other occasions he denies that they have fallen from grace. They remain rather in possession of the covenant, he maintains, and have their place in the Church of God.

Paul, therefore, now speaks with this distinction in mind. Since the majority of the Jews were opposed to Christ, so that almost the whole nation was gripped by this perversity, and few among them seemed to have a sound understanding, he asks whether the Jewish nation had been offended by Christ in such a way that their destruction was universal, with no hope of repentance remaining. He rightly denies here that the salvation of the Jews was to be despaired of, or that they were so rejected by God that there was no restoration to come, or that the covenant of grace, which God had made with them once, was completely abolished, since there always continued to remain in the nation the seed of blessing. That we are to understand Paul's meaning in this way is evident from the fact that whereas previously he connected certain ruin with the blindness of the Jews, he now gives them a hope of rising again. These two ideas are quite contradictory. Those, therefore, who have obstinately been offended by Christ have stumbled and fallen into destruction. The nation itself, however, has not so fallen that one who is a Jew must necessarily perish, or be estranged from God.

But by their fall salvation is come unto the Gentiles. The apostle states two truths in this passage. The fall of the Jews had resulted in the salvation of the Gentiles. It had, however, this purpose, that the Jews should be stirred up by jealousy and thus turn their minds to repentance. Paul had no doubt considered the testimony of Moses, which he had already quoted, where the Lord threatens Israel that as He had been provoked to jealousy by Israel's false gods, so by the law of retaliation He would also provoke the Jews because they were a foolish nation.

The word παραζηλῶσαι here used denotes the feeling of envy or jealousy which consumes us when we see another preferred to us. If, therefore, the design of the Lord is to provoke to envy, the Jews had not fallen in order to be cast into eternal destruction, but so that the blessing of God which they despised might reach to the Gentiles, in order that the Jews too might finally be roused to seek the Lord from whom they had fallen away.

There is, however, no reason for readers to weary themselves greatly in the application of this testimony. Paul does not press the proper meaning of the word, but alludes only to a common and well-known practice. As envy rouses a wife who has been rejected by her husband through her own fault to strive to be reconciled, so now it may be, he says, that the Jews, having seen the Gentiles put in their place, may be

touched with grief at their rejection, and seek after reconciliation.
12. *Now if their fall is the riches of the world.* Paul had taught that the
Gentiles had entered into the place of the Jews after they had been
rejected, in order not to make the salvation of the Jews offensive to the
Gentiles, as though their salvation rested on the destruction of the Jews.
He therefore anticipates this false view and states in contradiction that
nothing could contribute more to the promotion of the salvation of
the Gentiles than that the grace of God should flourish and thrive
among the Jews to the greatest extent. To prove this point he uses an
argument from the less to the greater. If the fall of the Jews could raise
up the Gentiles, and their diminution enrich them, how much more
would their fulness? The former took place contrary to nature, but
the latter would come to pass naturally. It is no contradiction of this
argument that the Word of God extended to the Gentiles after the
Jews had rejected it and cast it from them. Had they received it, their
faith would have brought forth much more fruit than their unbelief
then occasioned. The truth of God would have been confirmed by
the evident fact of its fulfilment among them, and they themselves
would have prevailed upon many by their teaching. It was these
whom they now turned away by their obstinacy.

Paul would have been more correct if he had contrasted the rising
of the Gentiles with the fall of the Jews. I make this point to prevent
anyone from looking here for ornate language, or taking offence at
this bluntness of speech. Paul's writings were not intended to turn the
tongue to eloquence but to mould the heart.

13. *But I speak to you that are Gentiles.* He uses a very strong argument to confirm that the Gentiles lose no benefit if the Jews return
again into favour with God, for he shows that the salvation of the
Gentiles is so annexed to the salvation of the Jews that the same means
is able to advance both. He addresses the Gentiles in the following way.
'I am peculiarly destined to be your apostle. It is therefore my duty
to procure your salvation with especial zeal (for this is committed to
my charge), and to omit every other task and attend to that one only.
I shall, however, be faithfully performing my duty if I shall win to
Christ any of my own nation, and this will be for the glory of my
ministry and so for your own good.' Anything that served to advance
Paul's ministry was to the advantage of the Gentiles, for their salvation
was the object of his ministry.

Here also he uses the verb παραζηλῶσαι, 'to provoke to envy', to
make the Gentiles seek the accomplishment of Moses' prophecy as he
describes it, when they have understood that it would be to their
benefit (Deut. 32.22).

14. *And may save some of them.* Note here that the minister of the

Word may be said to save in his own way those whom he brings to the obedience of faith. We are to regulate the dispensation of our salvation in such a way that we know that all its worth and efficacy are in the power of God, and bestow on Him the praise He deserves. Let us, however, understand that preaching is an instrument for effecting the salvation of believers. Although it can accomplish nothing without the Spirit of God, yet through the inward working of the Spirit it reveals His action most powerfully.

15. *For if the casting away of them is the reconciling of the world.* This passage is considered obscure by many and badly misinterpreted by some. It should in my view be understood as another argument derived from a comparison between less and greater, in the following sense. If the rejection of the Jews has been able to occasion the reconciliation of the Gentiles, will not their reception be much more powerful, and should it not raise them even from the dead? Paul always insists that the Gentiles have no cause for envy, as though their condition would be worse if the Jews had been restored to favour. Since, therefore, God has marvellously brought life out of death and light out of darkness, how much more, he reasons, ought we to hope that the resurrection of a people virtually dead will bring the Gentiles to life. It is no difficulty, as some maintain, that reconciliation is not different from resurrection. We understand resurrection here to mean the act by which we are transferred from the kingdom of death to the kingdom of life. Although the subject is one and the same, each word has its different emphasis, and this affords sufficient cogency to the argument.

And if the firstfruit is holy, so is the lump: and if the root is holy, so are the branches. But if some of the branches were broken off, and thou, being a wild olive, wast grafted in among them, and didst become partaker with them of the root of the fatness of the olive tree; glory not over the branches: but if thou gloriest, it is not thou that bearest the root, but the root thee. Thou wilt say then, Branches were broken off, that I might be grafted in. Well: by their unbelief they were broken off, and thou standest by thy faith. Be not highminded, but fear: for if God spared not the natural branches, neither will He spare thee. (16-21)

16. *And if the firstfruit is holy.* By comparing the worthiness of the Jews and the Gentiles, he now deprives the latter of pride, and endeavours to appease the former as best he can. He shows that, if the Gentiles allege that there is any privilege of their own which brings them honour, they in no way excel the Jews, and indeed if it came to a contest, they would be left far behind. Let us remember that in this comparison Paul is contrasting nation with nation, not man with man.

If, therefore, we compare them, we shall find that they are equal because both are the children of Adam. The only difference is that the Jews had been separated from the Gentiles, in order that they might become a people peculiar to the Lord.

They were, therefore, sanctified by a holy covenant and adorned by a peculiar honour of which God did not at that time deem the Gentiles worthy. Since, however, the covenant seemed at that period to display little vitality, Paul bids us look back upon Abraham and the patriarchs, with whom the blessing of God was certainly neither empty nor inefficacious. He concludes, therefore, that a hereditary holiness had passed from them to all their posterity. This conclusion would not have been valid had he been dealing only with persons, and not rather taken the promise into account. Because a father is just, he does not immediately transfer his integrity to his son. But because the Lord sanctified Abraham to Himself on condition that his seed also should be holy, and therefore bestowed holiness not only upon the person of Abraham, but also upon his whole race, Paul rightly argues from this that all the Jews have been sanctified in their father Abraham.

To confirm this view he introduces two metaphors, one taken from the ceremonies of the law and the other from nature. The firstfruits which were offered sanctified the whole lump. Similarly the goodness of the juice is spread from the root to the branches. Descendants have the same relationship to their parents from whom they spring as the lump has to the firstfruits or the branches to the tree. It is not surprising, therefore, that the Jews are sanctified in their father.

There will be no difficulty here if we understand holiness to mean simply the spiritual nobility of the race, which was not peculiar to their nature, but originated from the covenant. It will, I admit, be maintained with some truth that the Jews are naturally holy, because their adoption is hereditary, but I am speaking now of our first nature, according to which we are all, as we know, accursed in Adam. The dignity, therefore, of an elect people is properly speaking a supernatural privilege.

17. *But if some of the branches were broken off.* He now touches on the present dignity of the Gentiles. This is the dignity which will be possessed by any branches which are taken and grafted into some noble tree. The Gentiles sprang from a wild, unfruitful olive-tree, because they found nothing but a curse in their whole race. Any glory, therefore, that they possess comes from their new ingrafting, not from their old stock. The Gentiles, therefore, have no cause for boasting of any dignity of their own in comparison with the Jews. Paul shows some wisdom, moreover, in lessening the harshness of his expression by saying that some of the branches were broken, not that the whole of

the top of the tree was cut off, even as God also took some of the Gentiles from different places to ingraft into the sacred and blessed trunk.

18. *But if thou gloriest, it is not thou that bearest the root.* The Gentiles cannot vie with the Jews concerning the excellence of their race without contending against Abraham himself. To do so would have been quite outrageous, since he is like the root which bears them and gives them life. It would have been as absurd for the Gentiles to boast against the Jews, as far as the excellence of their race is concerned, as for the branches to vaunt against their roots. Paul would ever have us consider the origin of our salvation. We know that when Christ pulled down the wall of partition by His coming, the whole world was imbued with the grace which God had previously conferred on the chosen people. It follows that the calling of the Gentiles resembled an ingrafting, and that they grew together into the people of God only as they struck root in the stock of Abraham.

19. *Thou wilt say then.* In the person of the Gentiles Paul cites all the excuses which they could have brought forward for themselves. These excuses were so far from filling them with pride, that they rather afforded them cause for humility. If the Jews were cut off on account of their unbelief, and the Gentiles ingrafted by faith, they have no other course than to recall to mind the grace of God, and thereby dispose themselves to modesty and submission. The natural consequence and inherent property of faith is to produce in us self-abasement and fear. But this does not mean a fear which in any way is opposed to the assurance of faith. Paul would not have our faith vacillate, or alternate between assurance and doubt, much less have us alarmed or anxious.

What then will be the nature of this fear? As the Lord bids us take two matters into our consideration, so this must produce a double state of mind. He desires that we should constantly have in mind the wretched condition of our nature. This can produce nothing but dread, weariness, anxiety, and despair. Thus it is truly to our advantage that we should be completely laid low and bruised in order that we may at last cry to Him. But this dread, which is conceived from self-examination, does not prevent our minds from relying on His goodness and remaining calm. This weariness does not hinder us from enjoying full consolation in Him, nor do this anxiety and despair debar us from obtaining sure joy and hope in Him. This fear, therefore, of which he speaks is set up as an antidote to proud contempt, because as all men claim more for themselves than is right, become too off-hand, and in the end grow insolent towards others, so we ought to that extent to be fearful lest our heart should be inflated with pride and exalt itself.

Paul seems to cast some doubts on our salvation, when he urges the

Gentiles to take heed lest they too should not be spared. My answer is that since this exhortation refers to the subduing of the flesh, which is always insolent even in the children of God, it in no way detracts from the certainty of faith. We ought particularly to notice and recall what I have just stated, that Paul's remarks are directed not so much to individuals as to the whole body of the Gentiles. Among these there might have been many who were inflated without cause, professing faith rather than possessing it. On account of these Paul threatens the Gentiles with being cut off, and not without reason, as we shall see again afterwards.

21. *For if God spared not the natural branches.* This is a most powerful argument for repressing all over-confidence. We should never think of the rejection of the Jews without being struck with dread and terror. The one thing which caused their ruin was their despising of the divine judgment through their negligent disregard of the dignity which they had obtained. They were not spared, though they were natural branches. What then will become of us who are wild and alien branches, if we become excessively insolent? But this reflection leads us to distrust ourselves, and makes us cling with greater boldness and tenacity to the goodness of God.

This proves again more clearly that Paul is speaking generally to the body of the Gentiles, for the breaking off which he mentions could not apply to individuals, whose election is unchangeable, since it is based on the eternal purpose of God. Paul therefore declares to the Gentiles, that they will pay the price for their pride if they insult the Jews, because God will again reconcile to Himself His former people whom He has divorced.

Behold then the goodness and severity of God: toward them that fell, severity; but toward thee, God's goodness, if thou continue in his goodness: otherwise thou also shalt be cut off. And they also, if they continue not in their unbelief, shall be grafted in: for God is able to graft them in again. For if thou wast cut out of that which is by nature a wild olive tree, and wast grafted contrary to nature into a good olive tree: how much more shall these, which are the natural branches, be grafted into their own olive tree? (22-24)

22. *Behold then the goodness and severity of God.* By placing the matter before his readers' view, Paul confirms more clearly and confidently that the Gentiles have no occasion to be proud. They see in the Jews an example of God's severity which ought to frighten them thoroughly. In themselves, however, they have a proof of His grace and goodness, which ought to arouse them to thankfulness alone and to extolling the

Lord and not themselves. These words, therefore, convey this meaning: 'If you scoff at their calamity, think first what you have been.
For you were threatened with the same severity of God, had you not
been delivered by His unmerited gentleness. Consider also what you
are even now, for your salvation will be guaranteed only by your
acknowledging God's mercy with humility. But if you forget yourself, and vaunt insolently over the Jews, the same ruin into which they
fell awaits you. It is not enough to have embraced only once the grace
of God, unless during the whole course of your life you follow His
call. Those who have been enlightened by the Lord must always turn
their minds to perseverance, for those who having responded to the
call of God for some time finally begin to despise the kingdom of
heaven, by no means continue in the goodness of God, and thus by
their ingratitude deserve to be blinded again.'

Paul does not address each of the godly separately (as we have said
before), but compares the Gentiles and the Jews. It is true that each of
the Jews individually received the reward due to his unbelief when
they were banished from the kingdom of God, and that all of the
Gentiles who were called were vessels of God's mercy. In the meantime, however, we must bear in mind Paul's purpose, for he was
desirous that the Gentiles should depend upon the eternal covenant of
God, in order that they might connect their own salvation with that of
the elect people. Then, lest the rejection of the Jews should be a cause
of stumbling, as though their ancient adoption were disannulled, he
desired that the example of punishment inflicted on the Jews should
fill them with terror, so that they might lift their thoughts in reverence
to the judgment of God. It is our general neglect of these matters
which ought rightly to have instructed us in humility that is the source
of our great license in posing inquisitive arguments.

Paul adds the condition, *if thou continued in His goodness*, because he is
not arguing about individuals who are elected, but about the whole
body. I grant that as soon as any one abuses the goodness of God, he
deserves to be deprived of the grace which is offered to him. It would,
however, be improper to say in particular of any of the godly that God
had mercy on him when He chose him, on condition that he should
continue in His mercy. The perseverance of faith, which perfects the
effect of God's grace in us, flows from election itself. Paul teaches us,
therefore, that the Gentiles were admitted into the hope of eternal life
on condition that they would retain possession of it by their gratitude.
Certainly, the fearful defection of the whole of the world which
afterwards took place gives clear evidence of how necessary this
admonition was. When God had watered the whole of the world
with his grace in but a moment, so that religion flourished universally,

the truth of the Gospel shortly afterwards vanished, and the treasure of salvation was taken away. The only explanation of so sudden a change is that the Gentiles fell away from their calling.

Otherwise thou shalt also be cut off. We now understand in what sense Paul threatens with being cut off those whom he has previously admitted to have been ingrafted into the hope of life by the election of God. Although in the first place this cannot happen to the elect, they have need of such warning, in order to subdue the pride of the flesh which, as it is in fact opposed to their salvation, ought to be terror-stricken through fear of damnation. In so far, therefore, as Christians are enlightened by faith, they learn to their assurance that the calling of God is without repentance. But in so far as they carry about with them the flesh which wantonly resists the grace of God, they are taught humility by this word, 'Take heed lest thou be cut off.'

We should, however, bear in mind the solution which I have mentioned, that Paul is not discussing here the special election of each individual, but is setting the Gentiles and Jews in opposition to one another. He is, therefore, not so much addressing the elect as those who falsely boasted that they had taken the place of the Jews. Indeed he addresses the Gentiles at the same time, and speaks to the whole body in common. Among these there were many believers and members of Christ in name only.

But if in regard to individuals you ask how anyone can be cut off after being grafted in, and how, after being cut off, he can be grafted in again, conceive of three modes of ingrafting and two of cutting off (*formam insitionis triplicem, exsectionis duplicem*). The children of believers, to whom the promise is due according to the covenant made with their fathers, are grafted in. So are these who received the seed of the Gospel, which either strikes no root, or is choked before it comes to bear fruit. Thirdly, the elect are grafted in, and they are illuminated unto eternal life by the immutable purpose of God. The first are cut off when they reject the promise given to their fathers, or at other times do not receive it through ingratitude. The second are cut off when the seed is withered and destroyed; and since the danger of this evil threatens all as far as their nature is concerned, we must acknowledge that this warning used by Paul relates in some measure to believers, lest they should indulge themselves in the sloth of the flesh. With regard to the present passage, it should be enough for us that God threatens the Gentiles with the same punishment as He had inflicted on the Jews, if they become like them.

23. *For God is able to graft them in again.* This argument would mean nothing to the profane. Although they may concede that God is powerful, they take a distant view of His power as though it were shut

up in heaven, and therefore for the most part they deprive it of its effect. Since, however, believers regard God's power as being actually present wherever they hear it mentioned, Paul thought that this reason was sufficient to impress them. He assumes it moreover, as axiomatic that God has punished the unbelief of His people, but not, however, in such a way as to have forgotten His mercy, just as He has often at other times restored the Jews after He had apparently banished them from His kingdom. At the same time Paul shows by a comparison how much easier it would be to reverse the present state of things than it would have been to create them, i.e. how much easier it is for the natural branches to derive their substance from their own root, if they are restored to the place from which they had been cut off, than for the wild and unfruitful ones to do so from a different stock. This was the relationship between the Jews and the Gentiles.

For I would not, brethren, have you ignorant of this mystery, lest ye be wise in your own conceits, that a hardening in part hath befallen Israel, until the fulness of the Gentiles be come in; and so all Israel shall be saved; even as it is written, There shall come out of Zion the Deliverer; He shall turn away ungodliness from Jacob: And this is my covenant unto them, When I shall take away their sins. (25-27)

25. *I would not, brethren, have you ignorant.* He arouses his readers at this point to greater attention by saying that he will tell them a secret. He does so deliberately, for he wants to end this very intricate subject by a short, clear statement. Yet the statement which he makes is quite unexpected. The causal particle *lest* indicates his present purpose, which is to restrain the insolence of the Gentiles and keep them from exulting over the Jews. This warning was very necessary to prevent the revolt of that people from causing excessive disturbance to the weak, as though they had all for ever lost any hope of salvation. The same warning is no less profitable for us at the present day, so that we may know that the salvation of the remnant (whom the Lord will finally gather to Himself) is hidden beneath the seal of God's ring. Whenever a long delay casts us into despair, let us remember this word *mystery*. By this Paul clearly instructs us that the manner of their conversion will be unique and unprecedented, and that therefore those who attempt to measure it by their own judgment will be in error. There is nothing more perverse than to regard as incredible something that we do not see. Paul calls it a mystery, because it is incomprehensible until the time of its revelation. It has, however, been disclosed to us, as it was to the Romans, in order that our faith may be content with the Word, and bear us up with hope, until the event itself becomes a fact.

A hardening in part hath befallen Israel. The words *in part* do not, I believe, refer simply to time or number, but have been used, as I interpret it, to mean *in a measure*. Paul wanted, I think, merely to qualify a word which in itself was otherwise harsh, *Until* does not suggest the course or order of time, but means rather, '*In order that* the fulness of the Gentiles. . . .' The meaning, therefore, will be that God in some measure has blinded Israel in such a way that while they reject the light of the Gospel, it is transferred to the Gentiles, and these may seize the vacant possession. And so this blindness of the Jews serves the providence of God in accomplishing the salvation of the Gentiles which He had ordained. The *fulness of the Gentiles* means a great number, for proselytes did not then, as they had done before, connect themselves with the Jews in small numbers, but there was such a change that the Gentiles formed almost the entire body of the Church.

26. *And so all Israel shall be saved.* Many understand this of the Jewish people, as if Paul were saying that religion was to be restored to them again as before. But I extend the word *Israel* to include all the people of God, in this sense, 'When the Gentiles have come in, the Jews will at the same time return from their defection to the obedience of faith. The salvation of the whole Israel of God, which must be drawn from both, will thus be completed, and yet in such a way that the Jews, as the first born in the family of God, may obtain the first place.' I have thought that this interpretation is the more suitable, because Paul wanted here to point to the consummation of the kingdom of Christ, which is by no means confined to the Jews, but includes the whole world. In the same way, in Gal. 6.16, he calls the Church, which was composed equally of Jews and Gentiles, the Israel of God, setting the people, thus collected from their dispersion, in opposition to the carnal children of Abraham who had fallen away from faith.

As it is written. He does not confirm the whole sentence by this passage from Isaiah (Isa. 59:20), but only the one clause which states that the children of Abraham share in the redemption. If we take the view that Christ had been promised and offered to them, but that they had been deprived of His grace because they had rejected Him, the words of the prophet express more, viz. that there would still be a remnant, who, after having repented, will enjoy the grace of deliverance.

Paul, however, does not quote the passage in Isaiah word for word. The original reads, 'A redeemer shall come to Zion, and unto them that turn from transgression in Jacob, saith the Lord' (Isa. 59.20). We need not worry ourselves unduly on this matter, for the point which we are to consider is how appropriately the apostles adapt to their purpose the proofs which they adduce from the Old Testament. They desire only to point to the passages, in order to direct their readers to the fountain itself.

Furthermore, although in this prophecy deliverance is promised to the spiritual people of God, among whom the Gentiles also are included, yet because the Jews are the firstborn, it was necessary that what the prophet declares should be fulfilled particularly in them. The fact that Scripture calls all the people of God Israelites is ascribed to the excellence of that nation, which God preferred to all others. Isaiah then states that the One who will redeem will come to Zion, because He has regard to the ancient covenant. He adds also that those who have repented of their transgression will be redeemed in Jacob. By these words God explicitly claims some seed for Himself, so that His redemption may be effectual in His chosen and peculiar nation.

Although the expression used by the prophet, 'shall come to Zion' (Isa. 59.20), suited his purpose better, Paul felt no scruple in following the commonly accepted translation which reads, 'A redeemer shall come out of Zion.' The same thing is true in regard to the second part, which in Paul's version is, 'He shall turn away ungodliness from Jacob.' Paul held that, because it is the peculiar office of Christ to reconcile an apostate people who broke their covenant, it was sufficient to consider this one fact, that some conversion was undoubtedly to be hoped for, lest they should all perish together.

27. *And this is my covenant unto them.* Although Paul had briefly touched in the last prophecy quoted from Isaiah on the office of the Messiah, in order to advise the Jews of what they were chiefly to hope for from Him, he deliberately added these few words from Jeremiah for the same purpose. The words which he adds do not appear in the former passage. This fact is related also to his confirmation of the subject under discussion. His statements concerning the conversion of the people might have seemed incredible, for the people were so stubborn and obstinate. He therefore removes this obstacle by declaring that the new covenant consisted in the free remission of sins. We may gather from the words of the prophet that God will have nothing more to do with His apostate people, except in as far as He shall remit the offence of treachery as well as their other sins.

As touching the gospel, they are enemies for your sake: but as touching the election, they are beloved for the fathers' sake. For the gifts and the calling of God are without repentance. For as ye in time past were disobedient to God, but now have obtained mercy by their disobedience, even so have these also now been disobedient that by the mercy shewn to you they also may now obtain mercy. For God hath shut up all unto disobedience, that he might have mercy upon all. (28-32)

28. *As touching the gospel.* He shows that the worst feature in the Jews does not mean that they are on that account to be despised by the Gentiles. Their chief crime was unbelief. Paul teaches us that they had been thus blinded for a time by the providence of God, in order that a way might be made for the Gospel to come to the Gentiles. They were not, however, perpetually excluded from the grace of God. Paul, therefore, admits that for the present they were alienated from God on account of the Gospel, in order that in this way the salvation, which before h ¹ been entrusted to them, might come to the Gentiles. God, however, was not unmindful of the covenant which He made with the fathers, and by which He testified that He had embraced that nation with His love by His eternal counsel. Paul confirms this by the notable assertion that the grace of the divine calling cannot be rendered void. This is the meaning of the words which follow.

29. *The gifts and the calling of God are without repentance.* Gifts and calling mean by hypallage the benefits of calling. This is not to be understood of any calling, but of that calling by which God has adopted the offspring of Abraham into His covenant. This was the particular matter under dispute, just as shortly before Paul had used the word *election* to denote the secret counsel of God by which the Jews were formerly distinguished from the Gentiles. He is not, we must remember, dealing now with the private election of any individual, but the common adoption of a whole nation, which to outward appearances might have seemed to have fallen for a time, but which has not been cut off by the roots. Because the Jews had fallen from their privilege and the salvation promised to them, Paul contends, in order that some hope for the remnant may continue, that the counsel of God, by which He had once condescended to choose them for Himself as a peculiar nation, stands firm and immutable. If, therefore, it is completely impossible for the Lord to depart from the covenant which He made with Abraham in the words, 'I will be a God unto . . . thy seed' (Gen. 17.7), then He has not wholly turned His kindness away from the Jewish nation.

Paul does not contrast Gospel with election, as though there were any disagreement between them, for God calls those whom He has chosen. Since, however, the Gospel was preached to the Gentiles contrary to the expectation of the world, he rightly compares this grace with the ancient election of the Jews, which had been manifested so many ages before. Election therefore derives its name from its antiquity, for God had passed by the rest of the world and chosen one people for Himself.

Paul says *on account of the fathers*, not because they gave any reason to be loved, but because the grace of God had descended from them to their posterity, according to the form of the covenant, 'Thy God and the God of thy seed.' It has already been stated how the Gentiles obtained mercy through the unbelief of the Jews. God, in anger with the Jews for their unbelief, had turned His kindness to the Gentiles. The statement which follows immediately after, that they have been made unbelievers through the mercy which was shown to the Gentiles, is a little too harsh, and yet it contains nothing unreasonable, because Paul is not explaining their blindness, but simply means that the Jews had been deprived of the blessing which God transferred to the Gentiles. Lest, however, they should imagine that they had attained by the merit of their faith what the Jews had lost through unbelief, Paul mentions only mercy. The sum, therefore, is that because God desired to have pity on the Gentiles, the Jews were for this reason deprived of the light of faith.

32. *For God hath shut up all unto disobedience.* This striking conclusion of Paul's shows that there is no reason why those who have some hope of salvation should despair of others. Whatever they may now be, they have been like all others. If, by the mercy of God alone, they have emerged from unbelief, they ought to leave room for that mercy to operate among others also. Paul makes the Jews equal in guilt to the Gentiles, in order that both may understand that access to salvation lies open to others as much as to themselves. It is the mercy of God alone which saves, and which may be bestowed on both. This view, therefore, corresponds with the prophecy of Hosea quoted above, 'I will say to them which were not my people, Thou art my people' (Hos. 2.23). Paul does not mean that God blinds all men in such a way that their unbelief is to be imputed to Him, but that He has so disposed things by His providence that all men are guilty of unbelief. His purpose in doing this is to have them subject to His judgment, so that all merit may be buried, and salvation depend on His goodness alone.

Paul, therefore, makes two points here. There is nothing in any man, apart from the mere grace of God, in virtue of which he is preferred before others. And God in the dispensation of His grace is not hindered from bestowing it on whom He has pleased. The word *mercy* is emphatic. It means that God is bound to none, and that therefore He saves all freely, because all are equally lost. Those who conclude from this that all men will be saved are speaking utter nonsense. Paul simply means that both Jews and Gentiles obtain salvation from no other source than the mercy of God, that he may not leave anyone grounds for complaint. It is true that this mercy is offered to all without exception, but they must have sought it by faith.

O the depth of the riches both of the wisdom and the knowledge of God!

how unsearchable are his judgments, and his ways past tracing out! For who hath known the mind of the Lord? or who hath been his counsellor? or who hath first given to him, and it shall be recompensed unto him again? For of him, and through him, and unto him, are all things. To him be the glory for ever. Amen. (33-36)

33. *O the depth of the riches!* The apostle here first breaks into language which arises spontaneously from a devout consideration of God's dealings with the faithful. He then in passing restrains the effrontery of the godlessness which habitually cries out against the judgment of God. When, therefore, we hear the words *O the depth,* we are unable to express how much power this declaration of wonder should have in repressing the heedlessness of the flesh. After having spoken out of the Word and Spirit of the Lord, and overcome at last by the sublimity of so great a mystery, Paul can do nothing but wonder and exclaim that the riches of the wisdom of God are too deep for our reason to be able to penetrate them. If, therefore, we enter at any time on a discourse concerning the eternal counsels of God, we must always restrain both our language and manner of thinking, so that when we have spoken soberly and within the limits of the Word of God, our argument may finally end in an expression of astonishment. We ought not to be ashamed if our wisdom does not surpass his who, having been borne into the third heaven, had seen mysteries unutterable to man. And yet he had been able to find no other purpose here than that he should humble himself in this way.

Some render the words of Paul in this way: 'O the deep riches, and wisdom, and knowledge of God!' as if the word βάθος had been used simply as an adjective, while by *riches* they mean liberality. This, however, seems to me to be forced. Paul, therefore, I am certain, is extolling the deep riches of wisdom and knowledge in God.

How unsearchable are his judgments. He expresses the same theme in different words by a repetition familiar in Hebrew. Having spoken of judgments, Paul adds *ways* to mean God's ordinances or the manner of His activity or government. He still continues with his exclamation, in which the more he exalts the divine mystery, the more he deters us from the curiosity of our investigation. Let us then learn not to make inquiries concerning the Lord, except so far as He has revealed them by Scripture. Otherwise we enter a labyrinth from which retreat will not be easy. We must note that Paul is not here discussing all the mysteries of God, but those which are hidden with God, and which He desires us only to admire and adore.

34. *Who hath known the mind of the Lord?* He begins here to restrain human presumption by laying hold of it, lest men should murmur

against the judgments of God. He has two means of so restraining them: first, by maintaining that all human beings are wholly prevented by their blindness from examining the predestination of God by their own judgment (for to argue about a matter which is unknown is presumptuous and wrong); and second, by stating that we can have no cause for complaining of God, since there is no man who can boast that God is a debtor to him. On the contrary, all are under obligation to His kindness.

We must all, therefore, remember to keep our minds within this limit, lest in investigating predestination, we go beyond the oracles of God, while we learn that in this matter men can discern no more than a blind man in darkness. This, however, has very little bearing on the undermining of our faith, which arises not from the acumen of the human intellect, but from the illumination of the Spirit alone. Even Paul himself states elsewhere that all the mysteries of God far exceed the comprehension of our natural capacity, and goes on to add that believers comprehend the mind of the Lord, because they have not received the spirit of this world, but the Spirit who has been given to them by God and by whom they learn of His otherwise incomprehensible goodness.

As, therefore, we are quite unable by our own powers to investigate the secrets of God, so we come to clear and certain knowledge of them by the grace of the Holy Spirit. Now if it is our duty to follow the guidance of the Spirit we must stop and take our stand where He has left us. If anyone affects to know more than the Spirit has revealed, he will be overwhelmed with the immeasurable brightness of that unapproachable light. We must bear in mind the distinction, which I have just mentioned, between the secret counsel of God and His will revealed in Scripture. Although the whole doctrine of Scripture surpasses in its sublimity the intellect of man, yet believers who follow the Spirit as their Guide with reverence and circumspection are not forbidden access to God's will. It is different, however, with His hidden counsel, the depth and height of which we cannot reach by investigation.

35. *Who hath first given to him?* This is another argument by which Paul very powerfully defends the righteousness of God against all the accusations of the ungodly. If no one has God under obligation to himself by his merits, no one can justly expostulate with Him because he does not receive a reward. The man who desires to compel someone to do him a kindness must do the service by which he merits that person's kindness. The meaning, therefore, of Paul's words is that God cannot be accused of unrighteousness, unless it is stated that He does not render to every man his due. But it is evident that God

deprives no one of his rights, since He is under obligation to none. Who can boast of any work of his own by which he has merited God's favour?

In this noteworthy passage we are taught not that it is in our power to provoke God to bestow salvation upon us by our good works, but that He anticipates the undeserving by His unmerited goodness. Paul shows us not only what men are in the habit of doing, but also what they are able to do. If we desire to make an honest examination of ourselves we shall find not only that God is in no way our debtor, but also that we are all answerable to His judgment. Not only do we deserve no favour from Him, but we are more than worthy of eternal death. Paul concludes that God owes us nothing on account of our corrupt and depraved nature, and also asserts that, even if man were perfect, he could bring nothing to God by which to procure His favour, because as soon as man begins his existence, he is already by the very law of creation so bound to his Maker that he has nothing of his own. We shall, therefore, fail if we endeavour to deprive God of His right to do freely what He pleases with the creatures whom He has made, as though it were a matter of mutual debt and credit.

36. *For of him, and through him, and unto him, are all things.* This is a confirmation of the preceding sentence. Paul shows that we are far from being able to boast in any good of our own against God, since we ourselves have been created by Him from nothing, and now our very being depends upon Him. He concludes from this that it is right that our being should be directed to His glory. How absurd it would be that the creatures, whom He has formed and sustains, should have any other purpose than to show forth His glory! I am aware that the phrase εἰς αὐτόν, *unto Him,* is sometimes used to mean ἐν αὐτῷ, *in* or *by Him,* but this is an improper usage. Since, however, the proper meaning suits the present argument better, it is preferable to retain it than to have recourse to an incorrect usage. The sum of the argument is that the whole order of nature would be inverted unless the same God, who is the beginning of all things, is also the end.

To him be the glory for ever. He now confidently assumes as proved for certain the proposition that the glory of the Lord is to remain everywhere unalterable. The sentence will lack point if we take it in a general sense. Its emphasis depends on the context, which states that God justly claims for Himself absolute authority, and that nothing beyond His glory is to be sought in the state of mankind and of the whole world. It follows that any views which tend to detract from His glory are absurd, irrational, and indeed insane.

CHAPTER TWELVE

*I beseech you therefore, brethren, by the mercies of God, to present your
bodies a living sacrifice, holy, acceptable to God, which is your reasonable service. And be not fashioned according to this world: but be ye
transformed by the renewing of your mind, that ye may prove what is
the good and acceptable and perfect will of God.* (1-2)

Paul has dealt with those matters from which it was necessary for
him to begin in raising up the kingdom of God. We are to seek for
righteousness only from God; we are to look for our salvation from
His mercy alone; and the sum of all our blessings is laid up for us, and
daily offered to us, in none but Christ. He now proceeds to the
regulation of our moral actions by a very well-ordered arrangement
(*optimo ordine*). Since the soul is regenerated into a heavenly life by
that saving knowledge of God and of Christ, and our life itself is formed
and regulated by holy exhortations and precepts, we display our
enthusiasm for ordering our life in vain, if we have not first shown
that the origin of all righteousness for men is to be found in God and
Christ. This is what it means to raise men from the dead.

This is the main difference between the Gospel and philosophy.
Although the philosophers speak on the subject of morals splendidly
and with praiseworthy ability, yet all the embellishment which shines
forth in their precepts is nothing more than a beautiful superstructure
without a foundation, for by omitting principles, they propound a
mutilated doctrine, like a body without a head. The manner of teaching among the Roman Catholics is much the same. Although they
speak incidentally of faith in Christ and the grace of the Holy Spirit, it
is quite clear how much nearer they are to pagan philosophers than to
Christ and His apostles.

Just as the philosophers, before they legislate concerning morals,
discuss the end of goodness and inquire into the sources of the virtues
from which they later draw out and derive all duties, so Paul here lays
down the principle from which all the parts of holiness flow. This is
that we are redeemed by the Lord for the purpose of consecrating
ourselves and all our members to Him. It is worth while examining
each of Paul's remarks.

1. *I beseech you therefore, brethren, by the mercies of God.* We know
that impure men greedily lay hold of all that Scripture proclaims
concerning the infinite goodness of God for the purpose of indulging

the flesh. Hypocrites, on the other hand, maliciously obscure their knowledge of His goodness as far as they can, as though the grace of God would extinguish their zeal for a godly life, and open a door for boldness in sinning. Paul's entreaty teaches us that men will never worship God with a sincere heart, or be roused to fear and obey Him with sufficient zeal, until they properly understand how much they are indebted to His mercy. The Papists count it enough if they extort some kind of forced obedience by fear. Paul, however, in order to bind us to God not by servile fear but by a voluntary and cheerful love of righteousness, attracts us by the sweetness of that grace in which our salvation consists. At the same time he reproaches us with ingratitude if, having had experience of so kind and liberal a father, we do not in return strive to dedicate ourselves wholly to Him.

Paul's emphasis in thus exhorting us is the more powerful as he excels all others in setting forth the grace of God. The heart must be harder than iron which is not kindled by the above-mentioned doctrine into a love for God, whose kindness towards itself it feels to be so profuse. Where then are those who think that all exhortations to an honourable life are taken away if we set men's salvation in the grace of God alone? A godly mind is not formed to obey God by precepts or sanctions so much as by a serious meditation upon the divine goodness towards itself.

We may observe here at the same time the gentleness of the apostle's spirit, because he preferred to deal with believers by admonitions and friendly entreaties rather than by strict commands. He knew that in this way he would accomplish more among those who were willing to be taught.

To present your bodies a living sacrifice. The knowledge that we are consecrated to the Lord is, therefore, the beginning of the true course for attaining good works. It follows that we must cease to live to ourselves, in order that we may devote all the actions of our life to His service.

There are then two points to be considered here. First, we are the Lord's, and second, we ought for this very reason to be holy, for it is an affront to God's holiness to offer Him anything which has not first been consecrated. On this assumption it follows at the same time that we ought to meditate on holiness throughout the whole of our life, and that it is a kind of sacrilege if we relapse into uncleanness, for this is nothing but to profane what was sanctified.

Paul maintains throughout great propriety in what he says. He states, first, that our *body* is to be offered as a sacrifice to God. By this he implies that we are no longer in our own power, but have passed entirely into the power of God. This, however, cannot be, unless we renounce ourselves, and thus deny ourselves. He then declares by the adjectives which he adds what kind of sacrifice this ought to be. By calling it *living* he means that we are sacrificed to the Lord in order that our former life may be destroyed in us, and that we may be raised up to a new life. By the term *holy* he denotes, as we have already mentioned, the true nature of a sacrificial act. The object to be sacrificed is approved for immolation only when it has previously been sanctified. The third epithet reminds us that our life is correctly ordered when we regulate this sacrifice of ourselves in accordance with the will of God. It also brings us no ordinary consolation, for it instructs us that our labours are pleasing and acceptable to God when we devote ourselves to uprightness and holiness.

By *bodies* he means not only our skin and bones, but the totality of which we are composed. He has used this word to denote by synecdoche all our parts, for the members of the body are the instruments by which we perform our actions. He also requires of us blamelessness not only of body but also of soul and spirit, as in I Thess. 5.23. In bidding us to *present* ourselves, Paul is alluding to the Mosaic sacrifices which were presented at the altar as in the sight of God. He is also, however, making a striking reference to the readiness which we ought to show in receiving the commands of God, so that we should obey them without delay.

We deduce from this that all who do not propose to worship God merely err and stray in a miserable condition. We see now also the sacrifices which Paul commends to the Christian Church. Since we have been reconciled to God through Christ by His one true sacrifice, we are all by His grace made priests in order that we may dedicate ourselves and all we have to the glory of God. No sacrifice of expiation remains to be offered, and cannot be offered without great dishonour to the cross of Christ.

Your reasonable service. In my opinion this clause was added to give a better explanation and confirmation of the preceding exhortation. It is as though he had said, 'Present yourselves a sacrifice to God, if you are minded to worship Him, for this is the proper way of serving God, and, if any depart from it, they are false worshippers.' If God is properly worshipped only when we regulate all our actions according to His command, let us have done with all devised forms of worship, which He justly abominates, since He values obedience more than sacrifice. Men are pleased with their own inventions and (as Paul says elsewhere) display an empty show of wisdom, but we learn what the heavenly Judge declares in opposition to this by the mouth of Paul. By calling it a *reasonable* service which God commands, he dismisses all that we attempt contrary to the rule of His Word as foolish, insipid, and rashly undertaken.

2. *And be not fashioned according to this world.* Although the term *world* has several meanings, here it means human character and conduct. It is to this, and not without reason, that Paul forbids us to be conformed. Since the whole world lies in the power of the evil one, we must put off all that is of man, if we would truly put on Christ. To remove any doubt, he explains what he means by its opposite, when he bids us to be transformed to a renewing of our mind. These contrasts are frequent in Scripture, and explain a subject with greater clarity.

We must note here the renewal which is demanded of us. It is not that of the flesh only, as the teachers in the Sorbonne explain this word to mean the lower part of the soul, but of the mind, which is our most excellent part, and to which philosophers ascribe the pre-eminence. They call it τὸ ἡγεμονικόν, the regulative principle, and maintain that reason is a queen of utmost wisdom. Paul, however, pulls her down from her throne, and does away with her by teaching us that we must be renewed in *mind.* However much we may flatter ourselves, Christ's words are still true, that the whole man must be born again if he wishes to enter into the kingdom of God, for in both mind and heart we are entirely alienated from the righteousness of God.

That ye may prove. We have here the purpose for which we ought to put on a new mind. It is to dismiss our own counsels and desires, and those of all men, and be attentive to the will of God alone. The knowledge of God's will is true wisdom. But if the renewal of our mind is necessary for the purpose of proving what the will of God is, it is clear from this how hostile the mind is to God.

The epithets which Paul adds are used to commend the will of God, so that we may seek to know it with greater eagerness. It is, of course, true that if our obstinacy is to be brought into order we must ascribe the true praise of righteousness and perfection to the will of God. The world persuades itself that the works which it has devised are good. Paul exclaims that good and right are to be determined according to the commandments of God. The world is pleased with its own inventions and takes delight in them. Paul affirms that the only thing which pleases God is that which He has commanded. The world, in order to find perfection, escapes from the Word of God to new inventions. Paul holds that perfection lies in the will of God, and shows that if anyone transgresses this limit he is deluded by a false imagination.

For I say, through the grace that was given me, to every man that is among you, not to think of himself more highly than he ought to think;

but so to think as to think soberly, according as God hath dealt to each man a measure of faith. (3)

3. *For I say, through the grace that was given me.* If the causal particle is not considered superfluous, this verse will agree with the former. Since Paul now wanted our whole study to be directed to an investigation of the will of God, his next task was to draw us away from empty curiosity. The causal particle, however, is frequently redundant in Paul, and therefore the verse may be taken as a simple affirmation. The meaning will thus be quite consistent.

Before he gives any command, he reminds them of the authority which he had been given, so that they might listen to his voice as they would to the voice of God Himself. His meaning is, 'I do not speak of myself, but as God's ambassador I bring you the commands with which He has charged me.' He refers to this apostleship as grace, as he did before, in order that he may commend the goodness of God in it. At the same time he intimates that he had not forced his way into the apostleship by any temerity of his own, but had been accepted by the calling of God. In establishing his authority, therefore, by this preface to his remarks, he binds the Romans by the necessity of obedience, unless they are willing to despise God in the person of His minister.

Then follows the command by which he draws us away from the study of those matters which can bring nothing but mental torment without edification. Paul forbids anyone to take upon himself more than his capacity and calling may bear. At the same time he admonishes us to think and meditate only on those matters which will be able to make us sober-minded and unassuming. I prefer this interpretation of the passage to the translation of Erasmus, 'Let no one think proudly of himself.' This sense bears too little relation to the words, while the other is more in agreement with the context. The clause, *more highly than he ought to think*, shows what he meant by the previous word ὑπερφρονεῖν, viz. that we go beyond the bounds of wisdom if we engage in those subjects about which it is improper for us to be anxious. *To think soberly* is to be attentive to those studies by which we feel that we are instructed and educated in moderation.

According as God hath dealt to each man. Paul has here inverted the words, and means *as to each man God hath dealt.* He is here expressing the reason for the sober wisdom of which he is speaking. Since there is a varied distribution of graces, each man has determined upon the best manner for becoming wise, while keeping himself within the limits of the grace of faith which is conferred upon him by the Lord. When, therefore, we pay no regard to what we have been given, but go beyond the limits of our knowledge in our heedlessness and temerity, we are displaying affectation of wisdom not only in matters which are unnecessary, and which it is of no profit to us to know, but also in matters which it is otherwise useful for us to know. God does not permit this insolence to go unpunished. We often see how those, who through foolish ambition go beyond the bounds which are set for them, are led astray by their folly.

The main point is that it is part of our reasonable sacrifice for us all to present ourselves to be ruled and guided by God in a gentle and teachable spirit. In setting up faith in opposition to human judgment, Paul restrains us from our own opinions, and at the same time purposely sets a limit for believers, so that they may humbly keep themselves within the bounds of their own defects also.

For even as we have many members in one body, and all the members have not the same office: so we, who are many, are one body in Christ, and severally members one of another. And having gifts differing according to the grace that was given to us, whether prophecy, let us prophesy according to the proportion of our faith; or ministry, let us give ourselves to our ministry; or he that teacheth, to his teaching; or he that exhorteth, to his exhorting: he that giveth, let him do it with liberality; he that ruleth, with diligence; he that sheweth mercy, with cheerfulness. (4-8)

4. *For even as we have many members.* Paul now confirms by a reference to the calling of all believers the proposition which he had stated concerning the limitation of the wisdom of each believer according to the measure of his faith (*secundum fidei mensuram*). We are called on condition that we unite together in one body, since Christ has established among all those who believe in Him the association and organic union which exists between the members of the human body. And since men could not come into such a unity by themselves, He Himself became the bond of that union. Because, therefore, the relation which exists in the human body ought also to exist in the fellowship of believers, Paul proves by the application of this metaphor how necessary it is for each individual to consider what is appropriate to his nature, capacity and calling. Although this metaphor has various aspects, it is chiefly to be applied to our present subject in the following manner. As the members of the one body have distinct powers, and all the members are distinct, since no member possesses all powers at the same time or assumes the offices of the others, so also God has dispensed various gifts to us. By this distinction He has determined the order which He desired us to maintain, so that each should regulate himself according to the measure of his ability, and not thrust himself into the duties which belong to others. No one should seek to have

all things at one time, but should be content with his lot, and willingly
refrain from usurping the offices of others. When, however, Paul
expressly points out the fellowship which exists among us, he also
intimates at the same time how zealous we ought to be in appropriating
to the common good of the body the powers possessed by individuals.

6. *Having gifts differing according to the grace that was given to us.* Paul
does not now speak simply of cherishing brotherly love among ourselves, but commends humility as the best means of regulating our
whole life. All men desire to have enough to prevent them from
needing help from their brethren. But there is a bond of fellowship
when no one has sufficient for himself, but is forced to borrow from
others. I admit, therefore, that the fellowship of the godly exists only
when each one is content with his own measure, and imparts to his
brethren the gifts which he has received, and in turn allows himself to
be assisted by the gifts of others.

Paul especially desired to repress the pride which he knew to be
innate in men. To prevent anyone from being grieved that he has not
been given everything, he reminds us that each individual has his own
responsibility assigned to him by the good purpose of God, because
it is expedient for the common salvation of the body that no individual
should be so furnished with the fulness of gifts as to despise his brethren
with impunity. We have here, therefore, the main object which the
apostle has in view. All things are not appropriate for all men, but the
gifts of God are so distributed that each has a limited portion. Each
individual ought to be so intent upon bestowing his own gifts for the
edification of the Church, that no one may relinquish his own function,
and trespass on that of another. The safety of the Church is preserved
by this most excellent order and symmetry, when every individual of
himself imparts to the common good what he has received from the
Lord without preventing others from doing so. To invert this order
is to fight with God, by whose ordination it was appointed. The
difference of gifts arises not from the will of man, but because it has
pleased the Lord to dispense His grace in this manner.

Whether prophecy let us prophesy. By citing some special examples,
he now shows how every man ought to be employed in exercising his
powers or maintaining his position. All gifts have their own appointed
limits, and to depart from them is to spoil the gifts themselves. The
passage is a little confused, but we may arrange it so that the conclusion
may begin at this point: 'Let the man, therefore, who has prophecy
test it by the analogy of faith, and the man who has ministry use it for
ministering, or doctrine for teaching, etc. Those who have this object
in view will keep themselves properly within their limits.'

This passage, however, is understood in various senses. Some interpreters mean by *prophecy* the power of predicting, which flourished in the Church about the time when the Gospel began, as the Lord was at that time desirous to commend the dignity and excellence of His kingdom by every means. They hold that the additional words, *according to the proportion of our faith* (*secundum analogiam fidei*), are to be referred to all the clauses. I prefer, however, to follow those who understand the word in a wider sense to mean the peculiar gift of revelation by which a man performs the office of interpreter with skill and dexterity in expounding the will of God. In the Christian Church, therefore, prophecy at the present day is simply the right understanding of Scripture and the particular gift of expounding it, since all the ancient prophecies and all the oracles of God have been concluded in Christ and His Gospel. Paul understood it in this sense when he said, 'I would have you all speak with tongues, but rather that ye should prophesy' (I Cor. 14.5), and 'We know in part and we prophesy in part' (I Cor. 13.9). It is not clear that he intended here to consider only those wonderful graces by which Christ adorned His Gospel at the beginning. We see rather that he is referring simply to ordinary gifts which remain perpetually in the Church.

It is not, I think, a sufficiently valid objection to maintain that the apostle would have addressed these words in vain to those who, because they had the Spirit of God, were unable to call Christ accursed. In another passage (I Cor. 14.32), he declares that the spirit of the prophets is given to the prophets, and orders the first speaker to be silent if any revelation has been given to anyone sitting by. He may, therefore, for the same reason here be admonishing those who prophesy in the Church to conform their prophecies to the rule of faith, lest at any point they should wander or deviate from the straight line. By the word *faith* he means the first principles of religion, and any doctrine that has been found not to correspond with these is condemned as false.

There is less difficulty in the other clauses. Let him who is ordained as a minister, he says, exercise his office in ministering, and let him not imagine that he was admitted to that honour for himself, but for others. Paul is saying, 'Let him fulfil his office by ministering aright, that he may answer to his name.' Thus under the term *doctrine* he commends sound edification to teachers, and means: 'Let him that excels in doctrine know that his object is that the Church should be truly taught, and let him have this one study only, to render the Church more learned by his doctrine.' A teacher (*doctor*) is one who forms and instructs the Church by the Word of truth. Let him that excels in the gift of exhortation regard it as his object to exhort with efficacy.

These offices have a close relationship to and connexion with each other. They do not, however, cease on this account to be different.

No one can exhort without doctrine; yet he who teaches is not at once endowed with the gift of exhortation. No one prophesies, teaches, or exhorts without ministering. It is, however, sufficient if we preserve the distinction which we see in the gifts of God and also know to be suitable for Church order.

8. *He that giveth, let him do it with liberality.*[1] We see clearly from these latter clauses that we are here being shown what is the legitimate use of God's gifts. When Paul speaks here of givers (μεταδιδοῦντας), he does not mean those who give their own possessions, but technically the deacons who are charged with the distribution of the public property of the Church. When he speaks of those who show mercy (ἐλεοῦντας), he means widows and other ministers, who were appointed to take care of the sick, according to the custom of the ancient Church. The functions of providing what is necessary for the poor, and of devoting care to their attention, are different. On the former he impresses *simplicity*, by which they are to administer faithfully what was entrusted to them without fraud or respect of persons. From the latter he desires a display of compliance with *cheerfulness*, that they may not, as very often happens, spoil the services which they render by their morose attitude. As nothing affords more consolation to the sick or to anyone otherwise distressed than the sight of helpers eagerly and readily disposed to afford him help, so if he observes gloominess on the face of those who help him, he will take it as an affront.

When he speaks of those who *rule* (προισταμένους), Paul is properly referring to those to whom the government of the Church was committed. These were the elders (*seniores*), who presided over and ruled the other members and exercised discipline. What he says of these, however, may be extended to include every kind of ruler. Great care is required from those who are charged with the security of all, and great diligence from those who are in duty bound to keep watch day and night for the safety of all. The circumstances of that period, however, prove that Paul was not speaking of rulers in general (for at that time there were no godly magistrates) but of the elders who were the judges of morals (*morum censores*).

Let love be without hypocrisy. Abhor that which is evil; cleave to that which is good. In love of the brethren be tenderly affectioned one to another; in honour preferring one another; in diligence not slothful; fervent in spirit; serving the Lord[2]*; rejoicing in hope; patient in tribulation; continuing stedfastly in prayer; communicating to the necessities of the saints; given to hospitality.* (9-13)

---

[1] Calvin's version reads 'simplicity', *simplicitate.*
[2] Calvin's version reads, 'serving the time', *tempori servientes.*

9. *Let love be without hypocrisy.* Proposing now to address us concerning particular duties, he begins appropriately with love, which is the bond of perfection. In this regard he enjoins the very necessary principle that all dissimulation is to be removed, and that love is to arise from pure sincerity of mind. It is difficult to express how ingenious almost all men are in counterfeiting a love which they do not really possess. They deceive not only others, but also themselves, while they persuade themselves that they have a true love for those whom they not only treat with neglect, but also in fact reject. Paul declares here, therefore, that the only real love is that which is free from all dissimulation. Any man can easily judge whether he has anything in the recesses of his heart which is contrary to love. The words *good* and *evil*, which follow immediately in the text do not have a general meaning. *Evil* means the malicious injustice which does injury to men, and *good* the kindness which assists them. It is a familiar contrast in Scripture to have vices first forbidden and then virtues commended.

I have followed neither Erasmus nor the Vulgate in rendering the particle ἀποστυγοῦντες by 'hating'. Paul in my opinion desired to express something more, and the force of the term 'turning away' corresponds better to the opposite clause, where he bids us not only to take care to do well, but also to continue to do so.

10. *In love of the brethren be tenderly affectioned.* There are no words sufficient for Paul by which to express the ardour of the affection with which we ought to embrace one another. He refers to it as brotherly love, and says that it produces a tender affection, στοργή, which in Latin means the loving respect which exists among kinsfolk. This should indeed be the kind of love that we bestow upon the children of God. For this purpose he adds a precept which is most necessary if good will is to be maintained. Each is to prefer his brethren in honour. There is no poison more effective in alienating the affections than the thought that one is despised. I have no great objections if readers choose to understand by *honour* kindness of every sort, but I prefer the former interpretation. As there is nothing more opposed to brotherly concord than the contempt which arises from pride, while each esteems others less and exalts himself, so modesty, by which each comes to honour others, best nourishes love.

11. *In diligence not slothful.* This precept is given to us not only because a Christian life ought to be active, but because it is proper that we should frequently disregard our own advantage and bestow our labours upon our brethren, and not always upon those who are good, but often upon those who are most ungrateful and worthless. In short, because we ought to forget ourselves in very many of our duties, we shall never be properly prepared to obey Christ, unless we urge

ourselves forward and strive diligently to shake off all our laziness.
By adding *fervent in spirit*, he shows how we are to attain this. Our
flesh, like the ass, is forever lazy, and therefore needs to be spurred on.
It is the fervour of the Spirit alone which corrects our indolence.
Diligence in well-doing, therefore, requires the zeal which the Spirit
of God has kindled in our hearts. Why, then, someone may say, does
Paul exhort us to this fervour? My answer is that, although this zeal
is the gift of God, these duties are laid upon believers in order that they
may shake off their listlessness and take to themselves the flame which
God has kindled. It usually happens that we stifle or extinguish the
Spirit by our own fault.

The third counsel, *serving the time*, refers to the same thing. Since
the course of our life is short, our opportunity for doing good soon
passes away. We ought, therefore, to be more eager in the performance
of our duty. So Paul in another passage bids us to redeem the time,
because the days are evil (Eph. 5.16). The meaning may also be that
we should know how to apply ourselves to the time, for there is great
importance in doing this. Paul, however, I think, is contrasting his
command to serve the time with idleness. The reading in many old
manuscripts is κυρίῳ. I hesitate to reject this reading outright, although
at first sight it may seem unrelated to the context. If, however, it is
acceptable, I believe that Paul desired to relate to the worship of God
the duties which we discharge for our brethren and everything that
serves to strengthen love, in order to give greater encouragement to
believers.

12. *Rejoicing in hope*. These three counsels are connected, and seem
somehow to refer to *serving the time*. The man who puts his joy in the
hope of a future life, and bears his tribulations with patience best
applies himself to the time, and avails himself of the opportunity of
pursuing his course with vigour. Whatever may be the case (for it
does not make much difference whether the phrases are related or not),
Paul first forbids us to remain content with our present blessings, or to
set our joy on earth and on earthly things, as if our happiness were
located there. He bids us rather raise our minds to heaven, that we
may enjoy full and solid joy. If our joy rests on the hope of a future
life, this will give birth to patience in adversity, because no feelings of
sorrow will be able to overwhelm that joy. These two things are
therefore related to one another—the joy which is conceived from
hope, and patience in adversity. Only the man who has learnt to seek
his happiness beyond this world, in order to lessen and alleviate the
bitterness of the cross with the consolation of hope, will calmly and
quietly submit to bearing the cross.

Since, however, both of these things are far above our strength, we must be instant in prayer, and continuously call upon God, that He may not allow our hearts to faint and fall to the ground, or be broken by calamities. Furthermore, Paul not only stimulates us to prayer, but expressly calls for perseverance, because our warfare is unceasing and various assaults arise daily. Even the strongest are unable to bear these without frequent acquisition of new vigour. But diligence in prayer is the best remedy to prevent our being wearied.

13. *Communicating to the necessities of the saints.* He returns to the duties of love, and the chief of these is to do good to those from whom we expect the least recompense. It generally happens that those who are more weighed down by poverty than others and stand in need of help are treated with greatest contempt, because benefits conferred on them are regarded as lost. God, therefore, commends these very persons to us in a special manner. It is only when we relieve our needy brethren, for no other reason than that of exercising our kindness, that we truly prove our love. Now *hospitality,* i.e. the friendliness and generosity which are shown to strangers, is not the lowest sort of love, for these are the most destitute of all, since they are far away from their own kindred. For this reason Paul expressly commends us to be hospitable. We see, therefore, that the more a man is disregarded, the more attentive we ought to be to his wants. Note, too, how appropriate are Paul's remarks, when he says that we are to *communicate* to the necessities of the saints. By this he suggests that we are to relieve the wants of our brethren, as though we were aiding ourselves. He particularly commands us to assist the *saints.* Although our love ought to extend to the whole human race, it should embrace with particular affection those who are of the household of faith, for they are connected to us by a closer bond.

Bless them that persecute you; bless, and curse not. Rejoice with them that rejoice; weep with them that weep. Be of the same mind one toward another. Set not your mind on high things, but condescend to things that are lowly. Be not wise in your own conceits. (14-16)

14. *Bless them that persecute you.* I wish to urge the reader once and for all not to look over-anxiously for a precise order in the individual precepts. Let us rather be content at this point to have a few brief precepts by which to be wholly conformed to a holy life. These are derived from the principle laid down by the apostle at the beginning of the chapter.

He will immediately give us precepts against retaliating when injuries are inflicted upon us. But here he calls for conduct even more difficult. We are not to call down any evil upon our enemies, but to wish for them every prosperity, and pray that God may grant them this, however much they may harass us and treat us discourteously. The more difficult it is for us to practice this gentleness, the more intensely we ought to strive for it. The Lord gives us no command in which He does not call for our obedience. Nor are we allowed any excuse, if we lack that disposition by which the Lord would have us differ from the ungodly and the children of the world.

I grant that this is hard and quite contrary to human nature, but there is nothing so arduous that it cannot be overcome by the power of God and this we shall never lack, provided we do not neglect to pray for it. Although there is hardly any who has made such advance in the law of the Lord that he fulfils this precept, no one can boast that he is the child of God, or glory in the name of a Christian, who has not partially undertaken this course, and does not struggle daily to resist the will to do the opposite.

I have said that this is more difficult than to forego revenge when one has been injured. There may be some who keep their hands from violence and are not driven by a desire to do injury, but they would still like destruction or loss to befall their enemies from some other source. Even if they are so much at peace as to wish them no evil, there is hardly one person in a hundred who desires to do good to anyone from whom he has received injury. Indeed, most men start cursing without any sense of shame. God, however, not only restrains our hands from doing wrong by His Word, but also subdues the bitter feelings in our minds. Not only so, He would also have us be concerned for the well-being of those who bring destruction on themselves by wrongfully injuring us.

Erasmus was mistaken in his understanding of the meaning of the verb εὐλογεῖν, which he failed to see was the opposite of cursing and abuse. In both instances Paul would have God bear witness to our patience, that we may not merely bridge the passion of our anger in our prayers, but by praying for their forgiveness may also show our sorrow for our enemies, while they perish of their own free choice.

15. *Rejoice with them that rejoice.* In the third place Paul states the general truth that believers are to embrace each other with mutual affection, and to regard the fortunes of each as being shared in common by all. He first recounts and specifies our responsibilities. We are to *rejoice with them that rejoice* and *weep with them that weep.* The nature of true love is such that each one prefers to grieve with his brother than to look from a distance on his grief through fastidiousness or unwillingness to act. In short, therefore, we should adapt ourselves to one another as far as possible, and whatever our circumstances may be, each should enter into the feelings of the other, whether to sorrow with him in adversity or to rejoice in prosperity. Not to welcome a

brother's happiness with joy is a mark of envy; and not to grieve at his misfortune is inhumanity. Let us, therefore, have the compassion for one another by which we may be conformed to every state of mind.

16. *Be not wise in your own conceits.* What the apostle says in the Greek is more significant and appropriate to the comparison: 'Do not ponder on high things.' By this he means that a Christian ought not to aspire ambitiously to those attainments in which he excels others, nor to have feelings of superiority, but should rather study discretion and meekness. It is in these that we excel in the presence of the Lord, and not in pride or contempt of the brethren. Paul adds an appropriate command to what he has said above, for nothing does more to break the unity which he has mentioned than when we exalt ourselves and aspire to a higher course, so that we may raise ourselves up to more elevated position. I take the word *lowly* in the neuter, in order to complete the comparison. Every ambition and elation of mind, therefore, which hides within the name of magnanimity is here condemned. The chief virtue of believers is moderation, or rather, submission, which always prefers to yield honour to others than to take it away from them.

Paul's other statement is closely connected to this. Nothing inflates the mind more than a high opinion of our own wisdom. He wants us, therefore, to put this opinion aside, listen to others, and submit to their counsels. Erasmus has translated φρονίμους by *arrogantes*, 'arrogant', but the rendering is forced and meaningless. Paul in this case would be repeating the same word twice without any emphasis. The most fitting remedy for curing arrogance is not to have too high an opinion of our own wisdom.

Render to no man evil for evil. Take thought for things honourable in the sight of all men. If it be possible, as much as in you lieth, be at peace with all men. Avenge not yourselves, beloved, but give place unto wrath: for it is written, Vengeance belongeth unto me; I will recompense, saith the Lord. (17-19)

17. *Render to no man evil for evil.* There is hardly any difference between this precept and that which follows a little later, except that revenge implies more than the kind of recompense with which he is now dealing. Sometimes we render evil for evil, even when we do not exact punishment equivalent to the injury sustained, as when we treat with unkindness those who impart no benefit to us. We usually estimate the benefit which each individual can be to ourselves, or at least their capacity for being benefited by us, so that we bestow our services on those who have already obliged us, or from whom we expect a favour. Again, if anyone has denied us help when we needed

it, by returning like for like (as the saying is) we shall afford him no more in time of need than we received of him. There are other examples also of the same kind in which we return evil for evil without obvious revenge.

Take thought for things honourable. I am quite satisfied with the rendering of Erasmus, 'Prepare, therefore,' but I have chosen to translate it literally. Since every man is more attentive to his own advantage or more careful to avoid loss than is just, Paul seems to call for a different care and attention. His point is that we ought to give unremitting attention so that all men may be edified by our honesty. Just as we must have innocence of conscience before God, so we should not neglect to have an honourable reputation before men. If it is proper that God should be glorified in our good works, then He loses this amount of glory when men see nothing in us that is worthy of praise. And not only is the glory of God obscured, but He is also insulted, for all the sins that we commit are brought forward by the ignorant for the purpose of dishonouring the Gospel.

When, however, we are bidden to *take thought for things honourable in the sight of all men*, we must notice at the same time the purpose of this command. This is not that men may admire and praise us, for this is a desire which Christ carefully guards us from entertaining when He bids us to exclude all men and admit God alone as the witness of our good deeds. The purpose of this command is rather that men may lift up their minds to God and give Him the praise, so that our example may arouse them to the pursuit of righteousness, and finally that they may sense the fair and pleasant fragrance from our own lives which may draw them to the love of God. If we are slandered on account of the name of Christ, even then we do not cease to *take thought for things honourable in the sight of men*. But when we are slandered, that saying is then fulfilled 'as deceivers, and yet true' (II Cor. 6.8).

18. *If it be possible.* Peace of mind and a way of life so ordered as to make us beloved by all is no common endowment in a Christian man. If we will devote ourselves to this attainment, we must be endowed not only with the utmost fairness, but also with the highest courteousness and good nature, so as to win not only the just and good, but also change the hearts of the ungodly.

Two words, however, must here be stated in warning. We are not to strive to attain the favour of men in such a way that we refuse to incur the hatred of any for the sake of Christ, as often as this may be necessary. There are, it is true, some who, though deserving of universal admiration on account of their pleasant manner and peace of mind, are nonetheless hated even by their nearest relations on account of the Gospel. The second caution is that good nature should not degenerate into compliance, so that for the sake of preserving peace we are complaisant to men's sins. Since, therefore, it is not always possible for us to be at peace with all men, he has added two exceptive phrases, *if it be possible*, and *as much in you lieth*. We shall have to determine what the exception is on the basis of the duty required by godliness and love, so that we may not violate peace, unless compelled by one or other of these two causes. It is fitting that we should tolerate much, forgive offences, and willingly pardon the extreme rigour of the law for the sake of cherishing peace, provided that we are prepared, as often as necessity requires, to fight courageously. The soldiers of Christ cannot have lasting peace with the world, which is ruled by Satan.

19. *Avenge not yourselves.* The evil which he here corrects is, as we have suggested, more serious than the one which he has just mentioned above. And yet both arise from the same source, viz. an inordinate love of self and an innate pride, which makes us very indulgent to our own faults while being ruthless to those of others. Since, therefore, this disease creates in almost all men a frenzied desire for revenge when they have suffered even the slightest injury, he commands us here not to seek revenge, however grievously we may have been hurt, but to commit revenge to the Lord. And because those who have once been seized by this unruly passion cannot easily be bridled, he restrains us by referring to us in persuasive terms as *beloved*.

The precept, then, is that we should not revenge nor seek to revenge injuries which have been done to us, because we are to *give place unto wrath*. To give place to wrath is to entrust the Lord with the power of judgment. Those who attempt revenge deprive Him of this power. If, therefore, it is wrong to usurp the office of God, we are not allowed to exact revenge either, because in so doing we anticipate the judgment of God, who has willed to reserve this office for Himself. At the same time Paul intimates that those who wait patiently for His help will have God to vindicate them, while those who anticipate His vengeance leave no place for His help.

Paul prohibits us here not only from taking revenge with our own hands, but also from allowing our hearts to be tempted by such a desire. To make a distinction here between public and private revenge is therefore superfluous. The man who seeks the aid of a magistrate with a heart that is malevolent and desirous of revenge is no more to be excused than if he devises means for taking revenge by himself. Indeed, as we shall see presently, we are not even always to ask God to avenge us. If our petitions arise from personal feelings and not from the pure zeal of the Spirit, we do not make God our judge so much as the servant of our corrupt desire.

We *give place* to wrath, therefore, only when we wait patiently for

the proper time for our deliverance, praying in the meantime that those
who now trouble us may repent and become our friends.

For it is written, Vengeance belongeth unto me. Paul takes his proof
from the song of Moses, Deut. 32.35, where the Lord declares that He
will avenge His enemies. God's enemies are all those who oppress His
servants without any cause. 'He who touches you', He says, 'touches
the apple of mine eye.' Let us, therefore, be content with the consolation that those who cause us trouble when we do not deserve it will not
escape unpunished, nor shall we make ourselves more liable or exposed
to the injuries of the wicked by enduring them. We shall, rather,
provide the Lord, who is our only judge and deliverer, with the
opportunity of bringing us help.

Although we ought not to pray to God to avenge our enemies, but
should pray for their conversion, so that they may become our friends,
yet if they continue in their wickedness, the same thing will happen to
them as will happen to all the others who despise God. Paul, however,
does not quote this passage as though it were right for us to burn with
anger as soon as we are injured, and demand in our prayers that God
should avenge our injuries in proportion to the urgings of our flesh.
He teaches us, first, that it is not our task to exact revenge, unless we
want to usurp the responsibility of God. And second, he intimates that
we are not to fear that the wicked may rage with greater ferocity when
they see us bearing our sufferings with patience, for God does not take
upon Himself the office of exacting vengeance in vain.

*But if thine enemy hunger, feed him; if he thirst, give him to drink: for
in so doing thou shalt heap coals of fire upon his head. Be not overcome
of evil, but overcome evil with good.* (20-21)

20. *But if thine enemy hunger, feed him.* He now shows how we may
truly fulfil the precepts against taking revenge and returning evil for
evil. We are not only to refrain from doing injury but also to do good
to those who have done wrong to us. There is a kind of indirect
retaliation when we fail to treat with kindness those who have injured
us. By the words *food* and *drink* we are to understand kindness of every
sort. According, therefore, to our ability we are to help our enemy in
any matter in which he shall stand in need of either our resources,
advice or efforts. By *enemy* he does not mean those whom we treat
with hatred, but those who entertain enmity towards us. If they are to
be helped in their bodily needs, much less ought we to oppose their
salvation by invoking evil on them.

Thou shalt heap coals of fire upon his head. Paul shows the benefit
which we may derive from treating our enemies with acts of courtesy,
because we do not willingly squander our time and trouble in vain.

Some interpret *coals* to mean the destruction which is heaped on the head of our enemy, if we treat the unworthy with kindness and act differently towards him than he has deserved at our hands. We shall thus double his guilt. Others prefer to take the view that when our enemy sees himself so kindly treated, his mind is drawn to love us in return. I take the simpler view. His mind will be torn in one of two ways. Either our enemy will be softened by kindness, or, if he is so ferocious that nothing may assuage him, he will be stung and tormented by the testimony of his conscience, which will feel itself overwhelmed by our kindness.

21. *Be not overcome of evil.* This sentence seems to have been written by way of confirmation. In this life our whole struggle is against wickedness. If we try to retaliate, we admit that we have been defeated by it. But if, on the other hand, we return good for evil, we display by that very act an invincible constancy of mind. And this is truly the most glorious kind of victory, and its reward is not just imagined, but really experienced, while the Lord grants greater success to their patience than any they could wish for. On the other hand, anyone who attempts to overcome evil with evil will perhaps surpass his enemy in doing harm, but it will be to his own ruin, for by so acting he is fighting the devil's battle.

CHAPTER THIRTEEN

Let every soul be in subjection to the higher powers: for there is no power but of God; and the powers that be are ordained of God. Therefore he that resisteth the power, withstandeth the ordinance of God, and they that withstand shall receive to themselves judgment. (1-2)

1. *Let every soul be in subjection.* Paul's careful treatment of this passage in his instructions concerning the Christian life seems to have been forced on him by some great necessity, which the preaching of the Gospel was able to occasion in that age in particular, although at all times this is involved in it. There are always some restless spirits who believe that the kingdom of Christ is properly exalted only when all earthly powers are abolished, and that they can enjoy the liberty which He has given them only if they have shaken off every yoke of human slavery. This error, however, possessed the minds of the Jews more than others, for they thought it a disgrace that the offspring of Abraham, whose kingdom had flourished greatly before the coming of the Redeemer, should continue in bondage after His appearing. There was another thing, too, which alienated the Jews as much as the Gentiles from their rulers. These rulers not only all detested true godliness, but also persecuted religion with feelings of utmost hostility. It seemed absurd, therefore, to acknowledge as lawful masters and rulers those who were contriving to snatch the kingdom from Christ, the only Lord of heaven and earth. It is probable that these reasons led Paul to establish the authority of the magistrates with the greater care. He first of all lays down a general precept which briefly summarizes what he intends to say, and then adds further statements which help to explain and prove the precept.

He calls them *higher powers*, because they excel other men, rather than *supreme*, as though they possess the highest authority. Magistrates, therefore, are so called in relation to those who are subject to them, and not from any comparison between them. By using this expression Paul intended, I think, to remove the empty curiosity of those who often ask by what right those who are in authority came by their power. It ought really to be sufficient for us that they rule. They have not attained this high position by their own strength, but have been placed there by the hand of the Lord. By mentioning *every soul* Paul removes every exception, lest any should claim to be immune from the common submission to obedience.

For there is no power but of God. The reason why we ought to be subject to magistrates is that they have been appointed by God's ordination. If it is the will of God to govern the world in this manner, any who despise His power are striving to overturn the order of God, and are therefore resisting God Himself, since to despise the providence of the One who is the Author of civil government (*iuris politici*) is to wage war against Him. We should understand, furthermore, that the powers of magistrates are from God, not as pestilence, famine, war, and other punishments for sin are said to be from Him, but because He has appointed them for the just and lawful government of the world. Although dictatorships and unjust authorities are not ordained governments, yet the right of government is ordained by God for the well-being of mankind. Since, therefore, it is lawful to prevent war and to seek remedies for other evils, the apostle commands us freely and of our own account to respect and honour the right and authority of magistrates as being useful for mankind. The punishments which God inflicts on the sins of men may not properly be termed ordinances, but are the means which He purposely appoints for the preservation of legitimate order.

2. *He that resisteth the power.* Because no one can resist God without causing his own ruin, Paul warns that those who in this respect oppose the providence of God will not go unpunished. We must, therefore, take heed lest we incur this condemnation. By the word *judgment* I understand not merely the punishment which is inflicted by the magistrate, as if Paul had intended to say that those who resist authority would be justly punished, but also every act of God's vengeance, however He may exact it. Paul gives us a general picture of the end which awaits those who strive against God.

For rulers are not a terror to the good work, but to the evil. And wouldest thou have no fear of the power? do that which is good, and thou shalt have praise from the same: for he is a minister of God to thee for good. But if thou do that which is evil, be afraid; for he beareth not the sword in vain: for he is a minister of God, an avenger for wrath to him that doeth evil. (3-4)

3. *For rulers are not a terror to the good work.* He now commends us to obey rulers on the grounds of their usefulness. The causative γάρ must therefore refer to the first proposition, and not to the last verse. The usefulness of rulers is that the Lord has designed by this means to provide for the peace of the good, and to restrain the waywardness of the wicked. In these two ways the safety of mankind is secured. Unless the fury of the wicked is opposed and the innocent protected from their wilfulness, there will be universal destruction. If this,

therefore, is the only remedy by which mankind can be protected from destruction, we ought to preserve it with care, unless we want to admit that we are the public enemies of the human race.

The words which Paul adds *wouldest thou have no fear of the power? do that which is good*, mean that we have no reason for fearing the magistrate if we are good. Indeed, he says, the very desire to shake off or remove this yoke from oneself is tacit proof of an evil conscience that is plotting some mischief. Paul, however, is here speaking of the true and natural duty of the magistrate, and although those who hold power often depart from this, we must still render them the obedience which is due to rulers. If a wicked ruler is the Lord's scourge to punish the sins of the people, let us reflect that it is our own fault that this excellent blessing of God is turned into a curse.

Let us, then, continue to honour the good ordinance of God. This is easy to do, provided we impute to ourselves any evil which may accompany it. Paul, therefore, teaches us here the purpose for which the Lord has appointed magistrates. The effects of this will always be felt, unless this excellent and beneficial institution is corrupted through our own fault. Rulers, however, never abuse their power by harassing the good and the innocent without retaining in their despotic rule some semblance of just government. No tyranny, therefore, can exist which does not in some respect assist in protecting human society.

Paul has also noted here the two parts considered by philosophers also to constitute the well-ordered administration of a state, viz. the rewards given to the virtuous and the punishment inflicted upon the wicked. The word *praise*, according to Hebrew usage, is to be taken here in an extended sense.

4. *For he is a minister of God to thee for good.* Magistrates may learn from this the nature of their calling. They are not to rule on their own account, but for the public good. Nor do they have unbridled power, but power that is restricted to the welfare of their subjects. In short, they are responsible to God and to men in the exercise of their rule. Since they have been chosen by God and do His business, they are answerable to Him. But the ministry which God has committed to them has reference to their subjects. They have also therefore an obligation to them. Paul instructs individuals that it is by the divine kindness that they are defended by the sword of rulers against the injuries of the wicked.

For he beareth not the sword in vain. A second part of the function of magistrates is their duty to repress by force the insolent behaviour of the wicked, who do not willingly allow themselves to be governed by laws, and to inflict punishment on their offences as God's judgment requires. Paul explicitly declares that magistrates are armed with the sword not just for empty show, but in order to smite evildoers. *An avenger for wrath* means one who executes God's wrath. Paul proves this from the use of the sword, which the Lord has delivered into his hand. This is a noteworthy passage for proving the right of the sword. If by arming the magistrate the Lord has also committed to him the use of the sword, then whenever he punishes the guilty by death, he is obeying God's commands by exercising His vengeance. Those, therefore, who consider that it is wrong to shed the blood of the guilty are contending against God.

Wherefore ye must needs be in subjection, not only because of the wrath, but also for conscience sake. For for this cause we pay tribute also; for they are ministers of God's service, attending continually upon this very thing. Render to all their dues: tribute to whom tribute is due; custom to whom custom; fear to whom fear; honour to whom honour. (5-7)

5. *Wherefore ye must needs be in subjection.* Paul now repeats briefly the command which he had given at the beginning concerning obedience to magistrates, but with this refinement, that they are to be obeyed not only on the grounds of human necessity, but also in order that we may obey God. By *wrath* he means the vengeance which magistrates can exact for contempt shown to their dignity. 'We must not', he says, 'be obedient because we may not resist those who are armed and have greater power without being punished, in the same way as we generally bear injuries which we are unable to repel. Rather, we must voluntarily take upon ourselves the submission to which our conscience is bound by the Word of God.' Even, therefore, if the magistrate were unarmed and it were lawful to provoke and despise him with impunity, we should no more attempt to do this than if we saw the threat of punishment hanging immediately over us. The individual does not have the right to deprive of his authority the one who is set in power over us by the Lord. The whole of this discussion concerns civil government (*de civilibus praefecturis*). Those, therefore, who bear rule over men's consciences attempt to establish their blasphemous tyranny from this passage in vain.

6. *For this cause ye pay tribute also.* Paul takes the opportunity of mentioning tributes, and he bases his reason for paying tribute on the office of the magistrates. If it is their responsibility to defend and preserve uninjured the peace of the upright and to resist the impious attempts of the wicked, they cannot do this unless they are assisted by force and strong protection. Tributes, therefore, are paid by law to support such necessary expenses. This is not the proper place to enter into a fuller discussion concerning the manner of paying taxes or tributes, nor is it our concern either to prescribe to rulers how much

they ought to spend for individual purposes, or to call them to account. It is right, however, that they should remember that all that they receive from the people is public property, and not a means of satisfying private lust and luxury. We see the uses for which Paul appoints the tributes which are paid, viz. that heads of state may be furnished with assistance for the defence of their subjects.

7. *Render to all their dues*. It seems that the apostle's intention here is to summarize the particulars in which subjects have obligations to magistrates. They are to hold them in regard and honour, to obey their edicts, laws and judgments, and to pay tribute and taxes. By the word *fear* he means obedience, and by *custom* and *tribute* not simply customs duties and imposts, but other revenues also.

This passage confirms his previous statement that we ought to obey kings and all other governors, not because we are compelled, but because this is an obedience acceptable to God. He wants them not only to be feared, but also to be honoured by a respect which is freely offered.

Owe no man any thing, save to love one another: for he that loveth his neighbour hath fulfilled the law. For this, Thou shalt not commit adultery, Thou shalt not kill, Thou shalt not steal, Thou shalt not covet, and if there be any other commandment, it is summed up in this word, namely, Thou shalt love thy neighbour as thyself. Love worketh no ill to his neighbour: love therefore is the fulfilment of the law. (8-10)

8. *Owe no man anything*. There are some who think that this remark is ironical, as though Paul were answering the objection of those who contended that Christians were burdened by having other precepts than that of love enjoined on them. I do not deny that it may be taken ironically, as though he conceded to the demand of those who admit no other law than that of love, but in a different sense. I prefer, however, to take the words in the simple sense, for I think that Paul meant to refer the precept concerning the power of magistrates to the law of love, so that no one might consider it weak. It is as though he had said, 'When I request you to obey rulers, I require only what all believers ought to perform by the law of love. If you wish the good to prosper (and not to wish this would be inhuman), you ought to strive to make the laws and judgments prevail, in order that the people may be obedient to the defenders of the laws, for these men enable us to enjoy peace.' To introduce anarchy, therefore, is to violate charity, for the immediate consequence of anarchy is the disturbance of the whole state.

For he that loveth his neighbour hath fulfilled the law. Paul's design is to reduce all the precepts of the law to love, so that we may know that we are duly obeying the commandments when we are maintaining love, and doing so in such a way that we are prepared to endure any burden which may help to preserve charity. He thus fully confirms the precept which he has given concerning the obedience which we are to render to magistrates. This obedience constitutes not the least part of love.

Some, however, feel a difficulty in this passage from which they cannot quite escape. This is Paul's teaching that the law is fulfilled if we love our neighbour. He makes no mention here, however, of the worship of God, although he should not have omitted this. But Paul is not referring to the whole of the law. He is speaking simply of the duties which the law requires from us in regard to our neighbour. It is true, of course, that the whole law is fulfilled when we love our neighbours, for true love to men flows only from the love of God, and is the evidence and effect of this love. But Paul here mentions only the second table, for his inquiry related only to that. It is as if he had said, 'He who loves his neighbour as himself has performed his duty towards the whole world.' The objection of the sophists, who attempt to find justification by works in this verse, is futile. Paul is not stating what men do or fail to do, but speaks of circumstances which we will nowhere find to have been fulfilled. When we say that men are not justified by works, we do not deny that the observance of the law is true righteousness. But since no one performs the law, or has ever performed it, we maintain that all men are excluded from it, and that therefore our only refuge is in the grace of Christ.

9. *For this, Thou shalt not commit adultery.* We cannot infer from this passage what precepts are contained in the second table, since he also adds at the end, *and if there be any other commandments.* He has omitted the command which enjoins the honouring of parents. It may seem absurd that he should have disregarded a point which had the closest reference to his subject. But may the apostle not have passed it over in silence to avoid obscuring his argument? I would hesitate to assert this, however, for I see that he has stated all that he intended to prove, viz. that if by all His commandments God had no other purpose than to instruct us in the duty of love, we ought to strive to attain it in every way. The reader, however, who seeks no quarrel will readily acknowledge that by passages such as these Paul was desirous to prove that the object of the whole law is to encourage us to cultivate love for one another. We must supply what he passed over in silence, viz. that obedience to magistrates is not the least important way by which to cherish peace and preserve brotherly love.

10. *Love worketh no ill to his neighbour.* He proves from its effect that the word love contains the teachings which we are given in all of

these commandments. Those who are endowed with true love will never think of injuring their brethren. The whole law forbids only one thing—doing any harm to our neighbour. This, however, should be related to Paul's present purpose. Since magistrates are the guardians of peace and equity, those who desire that every individual should preserve his rights, and that all men may live free from injury, must defend to the utmost of their power the order of magistrates. It is the enemies of government who reveal their desire to do harm. Paul's repetition of the statement that love is the fulfilment of the law is to be understood, as before, of that part of the law which refers to human society. There is no allusion at all here to the first table of the law, which deals with the worship of God.

And this, knowing the season, that now it is high time for you to awake out of sleep: for now is salvation nearer to us than when we first believed. The night is far spent, and the day is at hand: let us therefore cast off the works of darkness, and let us put on the armour of light. Let us walk honestly, as in the day; not in revelling and drunkenness, not in chambering and wantonness, not in strife and jealousy. But put ye on the Lord Jesus Christ, and make not provision for the flesh, to fulfil the lusts thereof. (11-14)

11. *And this, knowing the season.* He now begins another form of exhortation. Since the rays of heavenly life have begun to shine upon us at the dawn of day, we ought to do what those who are in the public gaze are in the habit of doing. These take great care not to do any base or dishonourable action, for if they have committed any offence, they see that they will be answerable to too many witnesses. Much more should we avoid all uncleanness, since we ourselves always stand in the sight of God and His angels, and are invited by Christ, the true Sun of righteousness, to behold His face.

In brief, therefore, the words mean this: 'Since we know that the proper time has now come in which to awake from sleep, let us cast aside all that belongs to the night. Let us shake off all the works of darkness, for the darkness itself has now been dispersed, and let us attend to the works of light, and walk as we should in the day.' The intervening words are to be put in parenthesis. They are metaphorical, however, and therefore it is worth while noting the meaning of each part. By *night* Paul means ignorance of God, and all who are held in this ignorance wander and sleep as in the night. Unbelievers labour under the two evils of being blind and stupid. This stupidity Paul designates a little later by *sleep*, which is the image, he says, of death. By *light* he means the revelation of divine truth, by which Christ the Sun of righteousness arises on us. By *awaking out of sleep* he means that we are to be armed and ready to do what the Lord requires of us. The *works of darkness* are shameful and wicked acts, for the night, he says, is without shame. The *armour of light* means honourable, sober, and chaste actions, which are usually done in the day. Paul says, *armour* rather than works, because we are to fight in the service of the Lord. The words at the beginning, *And this*, are to be read by themselves. They are dependent upon Paul's previous doctrine, and mean, like the Latin *adhaec* or *praeterea*, 'besides', or 'furthermore'. The *time*, he says, is known to believers, because the calling of God and the day of visitation require new life and behaviour. He then adds in explanation that it was *high time* to awake. Καιρός rather than χρόνος denotes the right moment or opportunity.

For now is salvation nearer to us. This passage is variously misinterpreted. Many refer the word *believed* to the time of the law, as if Paul were saying that the Jews had believed before Christ appeared. I reject this view, however, as harsh and strained. It would surely be absurd to apply a general truth to a small part of the Church. There were very few Jews in the whole of the group to which he wrote. This language, therefore, would not be appropriate to the Romans. Also, his comparison between night and day in my opinion removes this difficulty. The statement, therefore, seems to me to be perfectly straightforward —'our salvation is now nearer than when we began to believe'—and refers to the time which preceded their faith. Since the adverb has an indefinite sense, this statement of the apostle's is much more appropriate, as we see from what follows.

12. *The night is far spent, and the day is at hand.* This is the occasion which he has just mentioned. Although believers were not yet received into the full light, he rightly compares our knowledge of a future life which shines upon us by the Gospel to the dawn of day. *Day* does not here mean, as elsewhere, the light of faith (otherwise he would not have said that it was only approaching, but that it was present, and indeed now shining in the middle of its course). It means rather that blessed splendour of the heavenly life, the beginnings of which we now see in the Gospel. What he is saying in brief is that as soon as God begins to call us, we ought to direct our attention to the coming of Christ, just as we conclude from the first rising of the day that the full light of the sun is at hand.

He says that the *night* is far spent, because we are not covered with thick darkness as the unbelievers, who see no spark of life. The hope of resurrection is set before our eyes by the Gospel. Indeed, the light of faith, by which we learn that the full brightness of heavenly glory is at hand, ought to arouse us and keep us from taking our ease while we are on earth. Shortly afterwards, however, when he bids us to walk in the light as in the day, he does not continue the same metaphor, for he compares our present state, in which Christ shines on us, to the day. Paul wanted in various ways to exhort us at times to meditate on our future life, and at other times to regard God with reverence.

13. *Not in revelling and drunkenness.* He mentions here three kinds of vices, each of which he has referred to by two names—intemperance and excess, carnal lust and the impure conduct which is connected with it, and envy and contention. If these actions are so shameful that even carnal men are ashamed to commit them before the eyes of their fellow men, we, who walk in the light of God, ought at all times to refrain from them, even when we are withdrawn from men's sight. Although he mentions strife before jealousy in the third group, Paul undoubtedly meant to instruct us that dispute and contests arise from this source, for when anyone seeks the pre-eminence, there is envy of one another. Ambition is the cause of both evils.

14. *But put ye on the Lord Jesus Christ.* This metaphor occurs very frequently in Scripture in regard to what adorns or disfigures a man. Both are seen in his clothing. A filthy and torn garment disgraces a man, while a clean and attractive one secures him much esteem. *To put on* Christ means here to be defended on every side by the power of His Spirit, and thus rendered fit to discharge all the duties of holiness. In this way the image of God, which is the only true ornament of the soul, is renewed in us. Paul has in view the purpose of our calling, since God, by adopting us, ingrafts us into the body of His only-begotten Son with this requirement, that we renounce our former life and become new men in Him. For this reason he also states in another passage that believers *put on Christ* in baptism (Gal. 3.27).

And make not provision for the flesh. As long as we carry our flesh with us, we cannot entirely neglect it, for although our conversation is in heaven, yet we are pilgrims on earth. We must therefore pay attention to the things that relate to the body, but only as affording us help in our pilgrimage, and not that they may make us forget our homeland. Even the heathen have said that nature is contented with a little, while the appetites of men are insatiable. Everyone, therefore, who desires to satisfy the longings of the flesh must not only be profligate, but also immersed in the very depths of lustfulness.

Paul curbs our desires and reminds us that the cause of all intemperance is discontent with the sober or lawful use of our possessions. He has therefore laid down this rule, that we are to provide for the wants of our flesh, but not to indulge its lusts. It is in this way that we shall use this world without abusing it.

CHAPTER FOURTEEN

But him that is weak in faith receive ye, yet not to doubtful disputations.
One man hath faith to eat all things: but he that is weak eateth herbs.
Let not him that eateth set at nought him that eateth not; and let not him
that eateth not judge him that eateth: for God hath received him. Who
art thou that judgest the servant of another: to his own lord he standeth
or falleth. Yea, he shall be made to stand; for the Lord hath power to
make him stand. (1-4)

1. *But him that is weak in the faith.* He now passes to a precept
particularly necessary for the instruction of the Church. Those who
have made greater progress in Christian doctrine are to accommodate
themselves to the less experienced, and bestow their strength to sustain
the weakness of these persons. There are some of God's people who
are weaker than others, and who, if they are not treated with great
tenderness and forbearance, are disheartened and finally become alienated from religion. It is probable that this happened in that age in
particular, for the Churches were formed of both Jews and Gentiles.
Some of these had for long been accustomed to the ritual observances
of the Mosaic law, and nurtured in them from childhood, and did not
easily relinquish them. There were others who had never learned such
things, and therefore refused a yoke to which they had not been
accustomed.

Men are readily inclined to slide from a difference of opinion into
dispute and controversy. The apostle, therefore, shows how those
who are of different opinions may live together without disagreement.
He prescribes the best way of doing this. Those who have the greater
strength are to spend their labour in assisting the weak, while those
who have made the greater progress are to bear with the inexperienced.
If God makes us stronger than others, He does not give us our strength
to enable us to oppress the weak. Nor is it the part of Christian wisdom
to be insolent beyond measure and to despise others. In this way,
therefore, he addresses his remarks to the more experienced and those
already confirmed. These are under a greater obligation to help their
neighbours, because they have received more grace from the Lord.

Not to doubtful disputations. The sentence is incomplete, since the
word which is necessary to complete the sense is wanting. It is clear,
however, that Paul meant simply that the weak should not be wearied
with troublesome disputes. We must, however, remember the hypo-

thesis with which he is now dealing. Although many of the Jews still adhered to the shadows of the law, they were, he admits, wrong to do so. He asks, however, that they should be excused for a short time, for pressing them with greater severity would have meant undermining their faith. Paul refers to questions which disturb minds not yet sufficiently established, or which entangle them in doubts, as contentious. We may, however, widen this phrase to include any thorny and difficult questions which cause disquiet and disturbance to weak consciences without edifying them. We must, therefore, consider what questions each is able to bear, and accommodate our doctrine to the capacity of the individual.

2. *One man hath faith.* I do not see which of the various readings Erasmus has followed. He has mutilated the sentence, although it is complete in Paul's words, and instead of using the relative article he has incorrectly put 'Another, indeed, believes.' It should not seem harsh or strained if I take the infinitive for the imperative, for Paul very frequently adopts this manner of speaking. He therefore refers to those who are assured in their conscience as believers, and grants them the use of all things without any difference. In the meantime the weak man eats herbs and abstains from what he considers to be prohibited to him. If the common version is preferred, the meaning will then be that it is wrong for one who freely eats all things, because he believes that he may, to demand the same rule of those who are still immature and weak in the faith. To translate the word as *sick* as some have done, is absurd.

3. *Let not him that eateth set at nought him that eateth not.* Paul meets the defects on both sides in a wise and appropriate manner. Those who are stronger have this fault. They despise and even ridicule those who are entangled by petty scruples, because they are full of stupid superstitions. The latter, on the other hand, can scarcely avoid making hasty judgments without condemning what they do not understand. All that they see done contrary to their own view they consider to be evil. Paul, therefore, warns the former to refrain from contempt, and the latter not to be over-scrupulous. The reason which he adds, since it applies to both groups, should be applied to the two clauses. 'When', he says, 'you see a man enlightened by the knowledge of God, you have sufficient proof that he has been received by the Lord. But if you despise or condemn him you reject one whom God has embraced.'

4. *Who art thou that judgest the servant of another?* Just as you would be acting with discourtesy and indeed arrogance, if you were to compel another man's servant to obey your laws, and to measure all his deeds by your own rule of judgment, so you take too much for granted if you condemn a servant of God for something because it does not please

you. It is not your responsibility to prescribe what he should or should not do, nor need he live according to your regulation.

When Paul deprives us of the right to judge, it is to both person and act that he is referring. There is, however, a great difference between these. In regard to the man, we must leave him, whoever he is, to the judgment of God. In regard to his deeds, we are not to pass judgment according to our own opinion, but according to the word of God. The judgment which we take from God's Word is neither human nor strange. At this point, therefore, Paul wants to keep us from forming any rash judgment. This is the error into which we fall if we dare to pronounce judgment on human conduct apart from the word of God.

To his own lord he standeth or falleth. This means that the Lord properly has the power either to disapprove or to accept the action of His servant. Those who attempt to seize this power to themselves are offending against Him. By adding *Yea, he shall be made to stand,* Paul not only bids us refrain from condemning, but also exhorts us to mercy and kindness, so that we may always entertain good hopes of those in whom we see something that belongs to God. The Lord has given us cause to hope that He will fully confirm and lead to perfection those in whom He has begun the work of His grace.

Paul does not simply argue from the power of God, as if he were saying that God can do this if He wants, but in the usual manner of Scripture connects God's will with His power. He is not, however, speaking here of any permanent obligation, as if those whom God has once raised up must stand firm to the end, but simply exhorts us to entertain good hopes and to let our judgments incline in this direction. So also he teaches us in another passage, 'He which began a good work in you will perfect it until the day of Jesus Christ' (Phil. 1.6). In short, Paul shows us how those in whom love is strong should pass judgment.

One man esteemeth one day above another; another esteemeth every day alike. Let each man be fully assured in his own mind. He that regardeth the day, regardeth it unto the Lord: and he that eateth, eateth unto the Lord, for he giveth God thanks; and he that eateth not, unto the Lord he eateth not, and giveth God thanks. (5-6)

5. *One man esteemeth one day above another.* Paul had just spoken of scruples in the choice of meats. He now adds another example with regard to distinction between days. Both were derived from Judaism. Now the Lord distinguishes in the law between meats, and pronounces some unclean and prohibits their use. He also appoints festival and solemn days and commands them to be observed. The Jews, therefore, who had been brought up from their childhood in the doctrine of the

law, could not lay aside the reverence for days which they had received
from the beginning, and to which they had been accustomed through
the whole of their lives. Nor did they dare to touch meats from which
they had abstained for so long a period. It was a mark of their weakness
that they held such opinions. Had they possessed a clear and certain
knowledge of Christian liberty, they would have had different views.
But it was a mark of piety for them to abstain from what they thought
was lawful, just as it would have been a mark of presumption and
contempt to have done anything contrary to their conscience.

The apostle, therefore, gives us very wise guidance here when he
commands every man to be certain of his own purpose. He means by
this that Christians ought to study obedience with such care that they
do nothing which they do not think, or rather are not certain, is pleasing to God. We must constantly remember that the principle of true
living is that men should depend on the will of God, and not allow
themselves to move even a finger if they are uncertain or vacillating in
their mind. Thoughtlessness will speedily become arrogance when we
dare to go further than our conviction allows us. Should it be objected
that there is always the difficulty of error, and that therefore the certainty which Paul requires cannot be found in the weak, the answer is
easy. Such persons are to be pardoned, provided they keep themselves
within their own limits. Paul's only desire was to restrain the undue
licence by which many became involved, as if by accident, in matters
of doubt and uncertainty. He therefore requires us to choose so that
the will of God may come first in all our actions.

6. *He that regardeth the day regardeth it unto the Lord.* Since Paul knew
for certain that the observance of days proceeds from ignorance of
Christ, we cannot believe that he would give his wholehearted defence
to such a corruption. And yet his words seem to imply that those who
observe days are committing no offence, for God can accept only what
is good. It is necessary, therefore, if we are to understand his purpose,
to distinguish between the opinion entertained by anyone concerning
the days to be observed, and the observance itself to which he is bound.
The opinion is superstitious, and Paul does not deny this. He has
already condemned it by calling it weakness, and will at once do so
again more openly. If someone who is bound by this superstition
hesitates to violate the solemnity of a day, God approves of this in him,
because he hesitates to do anything with a doubtful conscience. Could
a Jew do anything if he had not yet succeeded in being delivered from
the superstitious observance of days? He has the Word of the Lord in
which the observance of days is commended. The necessity of observance is imposed on him by the law, and he still does not see that it has
been abrogated. There is nothing, therefore, for him to do but wait

for a fuller revelation, and restrict himself to the limits of his own capacity, nor may he enjoy the blessing of liberty before he has embraced it by faith.

We are to form the same opinion also of those who refrain from unclean meats. If they ate in a state of uncertainty, that would not have meant receiving a blessing from God's hand, but laying hold of what is forbidden. Let them, therefore, make use of other things which they think are permitted, and follow the measure of their own understanding. They will thus give thanks to the Lord, which they could not do were they not convinced that they had been fed by the kindness of God. We are not to despise them on this account, as though they offend the Lord by this continence and devout restraint. Nor is there any absurdity in saying that the self-restraint of the weak is approved by God, but this is not because the Father is indulgent to them.

Paul has just called for certainty of mind, lest anyone should rashly maintain some observance or other by his own judgment. We must, therefore, consider whether in the present passage he is exhorting rather than affirming. The sentence will read more easily if we understand it as follows: 'Let every man know the reason for what he does, for he must give account of it before the judgment-seat of heaven. For whether a man eats meat or abstains, he must in both have regard to God.' Certainly nothing is better calculated both to curb arbitrary freedom in judging, and to correct superstition, than our summons to the judgment-seat of God. For this reason Paul wisely sets before each individual the Judge to whose will they are to refer all that they do. The affirmative form of the sentence does not stand against this interpretation, for Paul adds immediately afterwards, *none of us liveth to himself, and none dieth to himself.* He is not discussing here what men may do, but tells them what they ought to do.

Note too what he says—when we eat to the Lord or abstain from eating, we *give* Him *thanks.* Hence eating is impure and abstinence is impure where there is no giving of thanks. It is the name of God alone, when we call upon Him, that sanctifies us and all our actions.

For none of us liveth to himself, and none dieth to himself. For whether we live, we live unto the Lord; or whether we die, we die unto the Lord: whether we live therefore, or die, we are the Lord's. For to this end Christ died, and lived again, that he might be Lord of both the dead and the living. (7-9)

7. *For none of us liveth to himself.* He now confirms the previous sentence by arguing from the whole to a part. We need not be surprised that the particular actions of our life are to be referred to the Lord, since life itself ought to be wholly devoted to His glory. The

life of a Christian is properly ordered only when it has the will of God as its object. But if all our actions are to be referred to His will, it is quite wrong to attempt anything which we consider is displeasing to Him, indeed which we are not convinced will please Him.

8. *We live unto the Lord.* This does not mean here as in 6.11, to be made *alive unto God* by His Spirit, but to be conformed to His will and pleasure, and to order all things to His glory. Nor are we only to *live unto the Lord,* but also *to die unto the Lord,* i.e. both our death and our life are to be given up to His will. Paul gives us the best of reasons for this—*whether we live or die we are the Lord's.* It follows from this that He has power over our life and death. The application of this doctrine is very wide. God claims such power over life and death that every individual is to bear his own condition in life as a yoke laid on him by God. It is just that God should assign to every man his station and course in life. In this way we are not only forbidden to attempt to do anything hastily without a command from God, but we are also commanded to be patient in all trouble and loss. If, therefore, the flesh at any time shrinks from adversity, let us remember that a man who is not free and master of himself perverts law and order if he does not depend on the will of his Lord. Thus too we are taught the rule by which to live and die, so that if He lengthens our life in the midst of continual sorrow and weariness, we are not to seek to depart before our time. But if He should suddenly recall us in the prime of our life, we must always be ready for our departure.

9. *For to this end Christ died.* This is a confirmation of the argument which has just been given. To prove that we must live and die to the Lord, Paul had said that *whether we live or die* we are in the power of Christ. He now shows how rightly Christ claims this power over us, since He has acquired it at so great a price. By undergoing death for our salvation, He has acquired a dominion for Himself which could not be destroyed by death, and by rising again, He has received our whole life as His own property. By His death and resurrection, therefore, He has enabled us to serve the glory of His name both in death and in life. The words *lived again* mean that a new state of life was procured for Him by His resurrection, and, because the life which He now lives is not subject to change, that His dominion over us is also eternal.

But thou, why dost thou judge thy brother? or thou again, why dost thou set at nought thy brother? for we shall all stand before the judgment-seat of God. For it is written, As I live, saith the Lord, to me every knee shall bow, And every tongue shall confess to God. So then each one of us shall give account of himself to God. Let us not therefore

judge one another any more: but judge ye this rather, that no man put a
stumblingblock in his brother's way, or an occasion of falling. (10-13)

10. *But thou, why dost thou judge thy brother?* Having related the life
and death of all of us to Christ, he passes on from this to describe the
judgment which the Father has conferred on Him together with His
dominion over heaven and earth. Paul concludes from this that it is
impudent and presumptuous for anyone to usurp the power to judge
his brother, for by taking such a liberty he robs Christ our Lord of the
power which He alone has received from the Father.

In the first place, by using the word *brother* he restrains this desire
to pass judgment. If the Lord has ordained among us a society of
brothers, equality must be observed. Anyone, therefore, who assumes
the part of a judge is behaving insolently. Secondly, he recalls us to
the only true Judge, whose power none can remove and whose
tribunal none can escape. It would, therefore, be as absurd for a
Christian to take to himself the liberty of judging the conscience of his
brother, as it would be for a criminal, who ought to lie at the footstool
of the judge, to occupy the judgment-seat. James argues in almost the
same terms when he says, 'He that judgeth his brother judgeth the
law', and, 'if thou judgest the law, thou art not a doer of the law, but a
judge'. Again he says, 'One only is the lawgiver and judge, even he
who is able to save and to destroy' (Jas. 4.11f). The *judgment-seat* which
Paul assigns to Christ means His power of judgment, just as the voice
of the archangel, by which we shall be summoned, is elsewhere called
the *trump* (I Thess. 4.16), because its awful sound will pierce the minds
and ears of all.

11. *For it is written, As I live, saith the Lord.* Paul seems to have
quoted this passage from the prophet not so much to prove what he
had said about the judgment of Christ, for this was not a matter of
dispute among Christians, as to show that all must await it with
humility and submission. This is the sense of the passage. Paul,
therefore, has first stated in his own words that the judgment of all
men is in the power of Christ alone. He now shows from the words
of the prophet that all flesh should be humbled by the expectation of
that judgment. This is what bowing the knee means. The Lord
predicts in this passage from Isaiah that His glory will be made known
among all nations, and His majesty shine forth in every part of the
world, although at that time it lay concealed among a very few people,
as in some obscure corner of the earth. If, however, we look into the
matter more closely, it is evident that the fulfilment of this prophecy
is not yet a fact, and never has been in this world, nor are we to hope
for it in time to come. At the present time God rules in the world

only by His Gospel, and His Majesty is rightly honoured only when it is made known by the preaching of his Word and revered. But the Word of God has always had its enemies who have obstinately opposed it, and its scorners who have treated it with ridicule, as though it were a mere fable and object of mockery. There are many such at the present time, and there always will be. It is clear from this that this prophecy begins in the present life, but will not reach its fulfilment until the day of the last resurrection has shone, when Christ's enemies shall all be laid low to become His footstool. But this will not come about unless the Lord sits in judgment. Paul, therefore, has rightly applied this prophecy to the judgment-seat of Christ.

The passage is also a notable one for confirming our faith in the eternal divinity of Christ. It is God who speaks here, the God who has once and for all declared that He will not give His glory to another (Isa. 42.8). Now if what He claims for Himself alone is fulfilled in Christ, it is beyond question that He reveals Himself in Christ. The truth, indeed, of this prophecy was openly revealed when Christ gathered a people to Himself from the whole world, and restored them to the worship of His Majesty and the obedience of His Gospel. It was to this that Paul referred in Phil. 2.9,10, when he said that God has given Christ a name at which every knee should bow. This will be fully revealed when He shall ascend His judgment-seat to judge the living and the dead, even as all judgment in heaven and earth has been given to Him by the Father.

The words of the prophet are, 'Unto me . . . every tongue shall swear', but since an oath is a form of divine worship, the words which Paul uses, *shall confess*, convey the same meaning. The Lord desired simply to state that all men would not only acknowledge His majesty, but also confess their obedience to Him both by mouth and the outward gesture of the body which he has designated by the bowing of the knee.

12. *Each one of us shall give account*. This conclusion recalls us to humility and lowliness of mind. Paul immediately concludes from this that we are not to judge one another. We are not allowed to usurp the office of judgment, for we ourselves must submit to judgment and give account of ourselves.

The word *judge* has various meanings, and Paul has felicitously used the word in opposite senses. In the first place he forbids us to judge by condemning. In the second place he commands us to apply all our judgment of reason to avoid giving offence. Indirectly he reproves those malignant fault-finders who employ all their cunning in discovering something in the life of their brethren with which to find fault. He therefore bids them rather to exercise caution, because by their neglect they often cast their brethren down or put some stumbling-block in their way.

I know, and am persuaded in the Lord Jesus, that nothing is unclean of itself: save that to him who accounteth anything to be unclean, to him it is unclean. For if because of meat thy brother is grieved, thou walkest no longer in love. Destroy not with thy meat him for whom Christ died. Let not then your good be evil spoken of: for the kingdom of God is not eating and drinking, but righteousness and peace and joy in the Holy Ghost. For he that herein serveth Christ is well-pleasing to God, and approved of men. (14-18)

14. *I know that nothing is unclean of itself.* In order to anticipate the objection of those who had made such progress in the Gospel of Christ that they made no distinction between foods, he first shows us what opinion we are to form of foods when considered in themselves. He then adds how we may sin in using them. He declares, therefore, that no food is impure to a right and pure conscience, and that the only obstacle to making a pure use of foods arises from ignorance and error. If anyone imagines that there is any uncleanness in his food, he cannot use it freely. He adds soon afterwards, however, that we are to have regard not just to the foods themselves, but to our brethren also in whose presence we eat. We ought not to treat the use of God's blessing with such indifference that our use of them is not subject to love. The words, therefore, mean, 'I know that all foods are clean, and therefore I leave them to you to use freely. I allow your conscience to be free from all scruples. In short, I do not simply keep you from the foods themselves, but desire that you should lay aside all thought of them, and not neglect your neighbour.'

Unclean here means that which is profane and used indiscriminately by the ungodly. It is opposed to those things which had been peculiarly sanctified for the use of the faithful people. Paul says that he knows and is fully persuaded that all food is pure, in order to remove all doubts about its purity. He adds *in the Lord Jesus*, because it is by His grace and favour that all the creatures which were otherwise cursed in Adam, are blessed to us by the Lord. He desired, however, at the same time to set the liberty given by Christ in opposition to the bondage of the law, so that they might not think that they were bound by an observance from which Christ had made them free. The exception which Paul makes teaches us that there is nothing so pure that it may not be contaminated by a corrupt conscience. It is faith alone and godliness which sanctify all things to us. Since unbelievers are inwardly unclean, they defile everything that they touch (Titus 1.15).

15. *For if because of meat thy brother is grieved.* Paul now shows in

how many ways the offence which we cause our brethren may spoil the use of things that are good. The first reason is that love is violated if our brother is made to grieve for so slight a reason, for it is contrary to love to cause anyone distress. The second is that the price of the blood of Christ is wasted when a weak conscience is wounded, for the most contemptible brother has been redeemed by the blood of Christ. It is intolerable, therefore, that he should be destroyed for the gratification of the belly. We are given up to our lusts with shame beyond measure if we prefer food, a quite worthless thing, to Christ. The third reason is that if the liberty which Christ has attained for us is good, we ought to see that men do not slander it and rightly disparage it when we abuse the gifts of God. These reasons should keep us from incurring offence heedlessly by our liberty.

17. *For the kingdom of God is not eating and drinking.* Paul now teaches us, on the other hand, that we may abstain without loss from the use of our liberty, because the kingdom of God does not consist in these things. Whatever offence may result, we must not by any means omit those duties which relate either to the setting up or the preservation of the kingdom of God. If for love's sake we may abstain from the use of meats without doing dishonour to God, harm to Christ's kingdom, or offence to godliness, we cannot tolerate those who disturb the Church for the sake of meat. Paul uses similar arguments in his First Epistle to the Corinthians: 'Meats for the belly, and the belly for meats: but God shall bring to nought both it and them. But the body is not for fornication, but for the Lord; and the Lord for the body' (I Cor. 6.13). And again, 'But meat will not commend us to God: neither, if we eat not, are we the worse; nor, if we eat, are we the better' (I Cor. 8.8). Paul wants to show us by this that meat and drink are of too little value to be the cause of hindering the course of the Gospel.

But righteousness and peace and joy in the Holy Ghost. Paul has not contrasted these with food and drink in the course of his argument for the purpose of enumerating all that constitutes the kingdom of Christ, but of showing that it consists of spiritual things. He has, however, summed up in a few words all that the Gospel means, viz. consciousness of moral goodness, peace with God, and the possession of true joy of conscience through the Holy Spirit dwelling in us. As I have said, he has applied these few attributes to his present argument. Those who have become partakers of true righteousness enjoy a most excellent and inestimable blessing, viz. the quiet joy of conscience. What more do those who have peace with God desire?

By connecting *peace* with *joy*, he is expressing, I think, the mode of this spiritual joy, for however listless or buoyed up the reprobate may be, the conscience is made glad and cheerful only when it feels God to be reconciled and favourable to it. Only this peace provides true joy. Although it was in Paul's interest to declare, when he mentioned these great gifts, that the Spirit was the author of them, in this passage he wanted to suggest the contrast which existed between the Spirit and outward blessings, so that we should know that we may enjoy all the gifts which belong to the kingdom of God without the use of food.

18. *For he that herein serveth Christ.* Paul draws his argument from its effect. When anyone has been accepted by God and approved by men, the kingdom of God cannot but thrive and flourish perfectly in him. Those who serve Christ in righteousness with a quiet and peaceable conscience commend themselves both to God and man. Wherever therefore, there is righteousness, peace, and spiritual joy, the kingdom of God is complete in all its parts. It does not, therefore, consist of material things. He who obeys God's will, says Paul, is acceptable to God, and, he declares, he is approved by men, because they cannot but bear testimony to the virtue which they see with their eyes. This is not because the wicked always spare the children of God. Indeed, even when there is no occasion, they often heap many insults upon them and slander the innocent with false statements. In a word, they turn good actions into faults by their malicious interpretation. Paul, however, is speaking here of upright judgment, and this is free from bad temper, hatred, or superstition.

So then let us follow after things which make for peace, and things whereby we may edify one another. Overthrow not for meat's sake the work of God. All things indeed are clean; howbeit it is evil for that man who eateth with offence. It is good not to eat flesh, nor to drink wine, nor to do anything whereby thy brother stumbleth. (19-21)

19. *So then let us follow after things which make for peace.* Paul does what he can to recall us from the mere consideration of meats to those higher attainments which ought to have the first place in all our actions, and therefore have precedence over them. We must eat to live; but we must live to serve the Lord. That man serves the Lord who edifies his neighbour by kindness and courtesy. In these two things, harmony and edification, almost all the duties of love consist. To prevent this from being held of little importance, Paul repeats the opinion which he had given before, that corruptible meat is of too little worth to be the cause of destroying the building of the Lord. Wherever there is even a spark of godliness we may discern the work of God, and those who disturb a conscience which is still weak by their unfeeling conduct demolish this work of God.

We are to notice that Paul connects edification with peace, because occasionally those who are too generous in making allowance for one another do very much harm by their compliance. We must, therefore, in our zeal for complying with one another, exercise discrimination and consider the advantages, so that we may gladly give our brother all that serves to further his salvation. So Paul admonishes us in another passage: 'All things are lawful; but all things are not expedient', and immediately gives the reason, 'but all things edify not' (I Cor. 10.23f).

20. Paul effectively repeats the idea of *overthrow not for meat's sake the work of God*, and means by this that he is not calling for abstinence if it involves any detriment to godliness, as he has just said. Although we do not eat anything we please, but abstain from the use of meats for the sake of our brethren, yet the kingdom of God remains entire.

All things indeed are clean. Paul grants that all things are pure, but he makes an exception by adding, *howbeit it is evil for that man who eateth with offence.* It is as if he said, 'Meat indeed is good, but the offence which it may cause is bad.' Food has been given to us to eat, provided we do not offend love. To violate love, therefore, in the eating of meat spoils our enjoyment of pure meat. He concludes from this that it is good to abstain from anything that may give offence to our brethren.

The faith which thou hast, have thou to thyself before God. Happy is he that judgeth not himself in that which he approveth. But he that doubteth is condemned if he eat, because he eateth not of faith; and whatsoever is not of faith is sin. (22-23)

22. *The faith which thou hast.* To draw his discussion to an end, Paul shows what constitutes the advantage of Christian liberty. In doing so he makes clear that those who do not know how to govern themselves in the use of it are making a false boast of freedom. He says, therefore, that since our knowledge of liberty arises from faith, it properly looks to God. Those, therefore, who possess certainty of this kind ought to be content with peace of conscience before God. It is not necessary for them to prove to men that they possess it. It follows, therefore, that if we offend our weak brethren by eating flesh, we do so by evil caprice, because we are not compelled by any necessity to do so. We can easily see how this passage is misinterpreted by some commentators who deduce from it that it does not matter how a man may behave in observing foolish and superstitious ceremonies, provided one's conscience remains pure before God. As the context itself shows, Paul had no such intention. Ceremonies are appointed for the worship of God, and are also a part of our confession. Those who separate faith from confession rob the sun of its heat. Paul, however, is not

dealing with this question here, but is arguing only about our liberty in using meat and drink.

Happy is he that judgeth not himself. Paul desires to teach us here, first, how we may lawfully use the gifts of God, and second, how great a barrier ignorance is when it keeps us from urging the inexperienced beyond the limits of their weakness. The general truth which he states is, 'The man who is not conscious of wrongdoing is happy, since he duly examines what he does.' This applies to all that we do. Many commit the worst of crimes without any scruple of conscience, but they do so because they shut their eyes and plunge heedlessly on, wherever the blind, raging intemperance of the flesh leads them. There is a great difference between stupidity and discernment. The man, therefore, who discriminates in what he does is *happy*, so long as he is not stung by an accusing conscience when he has honestly weighed and considered what he is doing. This is the only security which can make our works pleasing to God. In this way Paul removes the empty excuse, which many put forward from ignorance, since their error stems from laziness and negligence. If good intention (as it is called) were sufficient, the examination by which the Spirit of God weighs men's work in this matter would not be necessary.

23. *But he that doubteth is condemned.* Paul uses a single well-chosen word to express the state of a mind which wavers and is uncertain of the necessary course of action. To *doubt* means to change from one position to another, and to be held in suspense between various plans of action without knowing which way to turn. The main thing in good works is the certainty and calm assurance of a mind which is conscious of being right before God. Nothing, therefore, is more opposed to the approval of our works than confused alarm. Would to God that this truth were securely implanted in men's minds. We are to attempt only what the mind is convinced is acceptable to God. Men would not then be so confused in many parts of their lives, nor waver, nor plunge onward with blind impulse, wherever their imagination drives them. For if we are restricted in our mode of living to such moderation that no one is to touch a scrap of bread with a doubting conscience, how much greater caution ought we to exercise in matters of the greatest importance?

And whatsoever is not of faith is sin. The reason for this condemnation is that any work, however excellent or distinguished it may appear to be, is reckoned a sin unless it is founded on a right conscience. God does not regard outward show, but the inward obedience of the heart. On this alone depends the value of our works. What kind of obedience is it if someone undertakes a task which he is not persuaded is approved by God? Where such doubt exists, therefore, anyone who goes against the testimony of his conscience is rightly accused of prevarication.

The word *faith* here means a constant persuasion of the mind and an unshaken certainty—and not just any certainty, but that which is derived from the truth of God. Confusion, therefore, and uncertainty spoil all our actions, however fair they may otherwise be. Now since a God-fearing mind can never find sure rest in anything but the Word of God, all man-made forms of worship, and all works that originate in the minds of men here disappear. To condemn all that is not of faith is to reject all that is not supported and approved by the Word of God. And yet it is not even enough that our actions are approved by the word of God, unless our mind, dependent on this conclusion, prepares itself eagerly for the work it has to do. The first principle, therefore, of upright living, if our minds are not to be in continual uncertainty, is to rest with confidence on the Word of God, and go wherever it calls us.

CHAPTER FIFTEEN

Now we that are strong ought to bear the infirmities of the weak, and not to please ourselves. Let each one of us please his neighbour for that which is good, unto edifying. For Christ also pleased not himself; but as it is written, The reproaches of them that reproached thee fell upon me. (1-3)

1. *Now we that are strong ought to bear the infirmities of the weak.* To prevent those who had made more progress than others in the knowledge of God from thinking it unfair that a greater burden should be laid upon them, Paul shows that the strength by which they excel the others is bestowed on them for the purpose of sustaining the weak and keeping them from falling. Just as God appoints those to whom He has given superior learning to instruct the ignorant, so He commits to those whom He makes strong the duty of supporting the weak by their strength. All the gifts of grace are thus to be communicated among the members of Christ. The stronger we are in Christ, therefore, the more we are bound to support the weak.

When he says that a Christian ought not to study his own pleasure, Paul means that he should not devote his efforts to his own satisfaction, as is usually the case with those who are contented with their own judgment and show no concern for others. This admonition is very appropriate to the present subject. Nothing does more to hinder or delay our service of other people than the excessive self-concern which leads us to neglect them, and to follow our own plans and desires.

2. *Let each one of us please his neighbour.* He teaches us here that we are under obligation to others, and therefore that it is our duty to render them satisfaction and to comply with them. There is no exception, and we must comply with the needs of our brethren when we are able to do so according to the Word of God to their edification.

There are two propositions stated here. (i) We are not to be content with our own judgment, nor to acquiesce in our own desires, but must on all occasions labour and strive to satisfy our brethren. (ii) When we desire to comply with the needs of our brethren, we must look to God, so that our object may be their edification. Most men can be appeased only by indulging their desires. But if we want to do a favour to many of them, we must not be concerned with their salvation so much as bear with their folly. We must not, therefore, regard what is expedient for them, but what they seek to their ruin, nor must we strive to please those whose only pleasure is evil.

3. *For Christ also pleased not himself.* If it is the duty of a servant to refuse nothing that his master takes upon himself, it would be quite absurd for us to wish to exempt ourselves from the necessity of bearing another's weakness, for Christ, in whom we glory as our Lord and King, submitted Himself to this. He laid aside all regard for Himself and devoted Himself wholly to this task. He is the true fulfilment of the words of the Psalmist in Ps. 69.9 where, among other things, he says, 'the zeal of thine house hath eaten me up; and the reproaches of them that reproach thee are fallen upon me'. By this he means that he had burned with such passion for the glory of God, and was seized by such a desire to advance His kingdom, that he forgot himself and was absorbed in this one thought. He had so devoted himself to the Lord that he was grieved in his heart whenever he beheld God's holy name exposed to the slander of the ungodly.

The second part of the verse which mentions 'the reproaches of God' may be understood in two ways. It may mean either that Christ was as much affected by the reproaches which were heaped on God as if He Himself had endured them in His own person. Or it may mean that He felt as much grief when He saw the wrong done to God as he would have if He Himself had been responsible for it. But if Christ reigns in us, as He must reign in those who believe in Him, this feeling will also be strong in our own hearts, so that any dishonour done to the glory of God will torment us as much as if it were done to us. Away with those whose most earnest prayer is to obtain the greatest honour among those who treat the name of God with every slander, trample Christ under foot, and not only mutilate His Gospel with abuse but persecute it with fire and sword. It is not safe, surely, to receive such honour from those who not only despise Christ but also treat Him with abuse.

For whatsoever things were written aforetime were written for our learning, that through patience and through comfort of the scriptures we might have hope. Now the God of patience and of comfort grant you to be of the same mind one with another according to Christ Jesus: that with one accord ye may with one mouth glorify the God and Father of our Lord Jesus Christ. (4-6)

4. *For whatsoever things were written aforetime.* This is an application of his illustration. Paul's purpose is to prevent any of his readers from thinking that his exhortation to imitate Christ was too far-fetched. 'There is nothing', he says, 'in Scripture which may not contribute to your instruction and the training of your life.'

This notable passage shows us that the oracles of God contain nothing vain or unprofitable. At the same time also it instructs us that it is by the reading of the Scripture that we make progress in godliness and holiness of life. We ought, therefore, to strive to learn all that is delivered to us in Scripture. It would be an insult to the Holy Spirit to imagine that He had taught us anything which it is of no advantage to know. Let us also know that all that we learn from Scripture is conducive to the advancement of godliness. Although Paul is speaking of the Old Testament, we are to hold the same view of the writings of the apostles. If the Spirit of Christ is everywhere the same, it is quite certain that He has accommodated His teaching to the edification of His people at the present time by the apostles, as He formerly did by the prophets. This passage also provides an excellent refutation of the fanatics who maintain that the Old Testament is abolished, and that it has no relevance at all to Christians. Are they to have the impertinence to turn Christians from those books which, as Paul testifies, have been appointed by God for their salvation?

When he adds *that through patience and through comfort of the scriptures we might have hope*, he does not include the whole of that benefit which is to be derived from the Word of God, but briefly points to its main object. The particular service of the Scriptures is to raise those who are prepared by patience and strengthened by consolation to the hope of eternal life, and to keep their thoughts fixed upon it. Some translate the word *consolation* by *exhortation*. I have no objection to this, except that consolation suits patience better, because patience arises from consolation. It is only when God tempers our hardships with consolation that we are ready to endure them with patience. The patience of believers is not that hardihood which philosophers enjoin, but the meekness by which we willingly submit to God when the taste of His goodness and fatherly love renders all things sweet to us. This patience cherishes and sustains unceasing hope in us.

5. *Now the God of patience and of comfort grant you to be of the same mind.* God is designated from the effect which He produces. Paul previously attributed this effect to the Scriptures, but for a different reason. God alone is the author of patience and of consolation, because He inspires both these attributes in our hearts by His Spirit, and yet He uses His Word as the instrument for accomplishing this object. He first teaches us what true consolation and patience are, and then inspires and implants this teaching in our hearts. Having exhorted and admonished those at Rome to the performance of their duty, Paul now turns to prayer. He knew quite well that any discussion of the duty of the individual would accomplish nothing unless God should accomplish inwardly by His Spirit what He spoke by a human voice. The chief point of his prayer is to bring their minds to true concord and

to make them truly agree with one another. He also shows at the same time what the bond of this unity is by saying that he wants them to agree together *according to Christ*. Any agreement which is made apart from God is worthless, and by 'apart from God' I mean that which alienates us from His truth. To make our union in Christ still more commendable, Paul teaches us how necessary it is, since we do not truly glorify God unless the hearts of all believers are united in His praise, and their tongues too join in harmony. There is no reason, therefore, for anyone to boast that he will glorify God in his own way, for God sets so high a store on the unity of His servants that He will not allow His glory to be sounded amid discord and controversy. This one thought ought to be sufficient to subdue the excess of dispute and controversy which occupies the minds of many at the present time.

Wherefore receive ye one another, even as Christ also received you, to the glory of God. For I say that Christ hath been made a minister of the circumcision for the truth of God, that he might confirm the promises given unto the fathers, and that the Gentiles might glorify God for his mercy; as it is written, Therefore will I give praise unto thee among the Gentiles, and sing unto thy name. And again he saith, Rejoice, ye Gentiles, with his people. And again, Praise the Lord, all ye Gentiles; and let all the peoples praise him. And again, Isaiah saith, There shall be the root of Jesse, and he that ariseth to rule over the Gentiles; On him shall the Gentiles hope. (7–12)

7. *Wherefore receive ye one another.* Paul returns to his exhortation. To confirm this he continues to retain the example of Christ, who embraced not one or two of us, but all of us together, and has united us in such a way that we ought to cherish one another if we desire to remain in His bosom. We shall, therefore, confirm our calling only if we do not separate ourselves from those to whom the Lord has bound us.

The phrase *to the glory of God* may refer to us only, or to Christ, or to both Christ and ourselves together. I prefer the last sense, meaning, 'As Christ has made known the glory of the Father in receiving us all into His grace when we stood in need of mercy, so we ought to establish and confirm this union which we have in Christ, in order to make known also the glory of God.'

8. *For I say that Christ hath been made a minister.* He now shows how Christ has embraced us all, by making no difference between the Jews and the Gentiles, except that He was promised in the first place to the Jewish nation and peculiarly destined to them before He was revealed to the Gentiles. But Paul shows that there was no difference between them in what was the source of all their disputes, for Christ had

gathered both of them from their pitiable scattered state, and having gathered them, brought them into the kingdom of His Father, to form one flock in one sheepfold, under one shepherd. It is right, therefore, Paul declares, that they should continue to be united together, and not despise one another, since Christ despised neither of them.

He speaks first, therefore, of the Jews, and says that Christ was sent to them, in order to accomplish the truth of God by performing the promises given to the fathers. It is no little honour that Christ, the Lord of heaven and earth, put on flesh in order to procure their salvation. The more He humbled Himself for their sake, the greater was the honour He conferred on them. Paul assumes this as an undoubted fact, so that we have greater cause to be surprised at the appalling impudence of those fanatics who do not hesitate to regard the promises of the Old Testament as temporal, and to confine them to the present world. To prevent the Gentiles from claiming any excellence greater than that of the Jews, Paul expressly declares that the salvation which Christ has brought was the peculiar privilege of the Jews by the covenant, because by His coming He fulfilled the promise formerly given by the Father to Abraham, and thus became the servant of that people. It follows from this that the old covenant was in fact spiritual, although it was annexed to earthly types. The fulfilment of the promises, of which Paul is now speaking, must refer to eternal salvation. To prevent the objection that since the covenant was given to Abraham, salvation had been promised only to his descendants, Paul expressly confines the promises themselves to the fathers. The virtue of Christ is therefore to be confined to bodily blessings, or else the covenant made with Abraham extended beyond the things of this world.

9. *That the Gentiles might glorify God.* Paul spends longer in proving the second point, because it was a matter of dispute. His first quotation is from Ps. 18 (referred to in II Sam. 22), in which we undoubtedly have a prophecy of the kingdom of Christ. From this quotation Paul also proves the calling of the Gentiles, because the promise is given there that the glory of God will be confessed among the Gentiles. We cannot truly preach God except among those who hear us celebrating His praises. God's name, therefore, cannot be made known among the Gentiles, unless they are granted a knowledge of Him and come into fellowship with the people of God. Throughout Scripture we find that the praises of God cannot be proclaimed except in the assembly of the faithful, whose ears are capable of hearing His praise.

10. *Rejoice ye Gentiles, with his people.* I do not accept the general interpretation that this verse is taken from the Song of Moses. Moses' design in his song of triumph was to strike terror in the adversaries of

Israel by the greatness of God, rather than to invite them to share a common joy. I am therefore of the opinion that the verse is quoted from Ps. 67.5, in which the Psalmist says, 'Let the peoples praise thee, O God: let all the peoples praise thee.' Paul added *with his people* by way of explanation, for the Psalmist here connects the Gentiles with Israel, and invites both alike to rejoice. But there is no rejoicing without the knowledge of God.

11. *Praise the Lord, all ye Gentiles.* This quotation is highly appropriate. How could a people, ignorant of the greatness of God, praise Him? They could no more do this than call on His name when they did not know it. The prophecy, therefore, is a most appropriate one for proving the call of the Gentiles. This is made still more evident from the reason added by the Psalmist, who bids them in this passage give thanks for God's truth and mercy (Ps. 117.1).

12. *And again, Isaiah saith.* This is the most famous prophecy of all, for the prophet here comforts the small remnant of the faithful when things were almost past hope, by stating that a shoot would spring from the dry and dead trunk of the family of David, and a branch, which would restore the people of God to their former glory, would flourish from the despised root. It is clear from the description given in this passage that this shoot is Christ, the Redeemer of the world. The prophet then adds that He will be lifted up for a sign to the Gentiles, so that He may save them. Paul's words differ from the Hebrew text, which has *stand for a sign*, where we read *arise*. But the meaning is the same, viz. that Christ will be seen clearly, like a sign. The Hebrew has *seek* for *hope*. In the usual language of Scripture to seek God is simply to hope in Him.

The calling of the Gentiles is confirmed twice in this prophecy, first, when Christ, who reigns among believers alone, is said to be raised up as a sign to them, and second when it is said that they will have hope in Christ. But they cannot have hope without the preaching of the Word and the illumination of the Spirit. The Song of Simeon corresponds to this passage. Hope in Christ is a witness to His divinity.

Now the God of hope fill you with all joy and peace in believing, that ye may abound in hope, in the power of the Holy Ghost. And I myself also am persuaded of you, my brethren, that ye yourselves are full of goodness, filled with all knowledge, able also to admonish one another. But I write the more boldly unto you in some measure, as putting you again in remembrance, because of the grace that was given me of God, that I should be a minister of Christ Jesus unto the Gentiles, ministering the gospel of God, that the offering up of the Gentiles might be made acceptable, being sanctified by the Holy Ghost. (13-16)

13. *Now the God of hope fill you with all joy.* He now concludes the passage as before with a prayer in which he desires the Lord to give them all that He had commanded. From this we see that the Lord in no way measures His precepts according to our strength, or the power of free-will, nor does He instruct us in our duty, so that we may place reliance on our own powers and prepare ourselves to render obedience. Rather, the precepts which He gives us require the assistance of His grace to stimulate us to an assiduous desire for prayer. When he says *the God of hope,* he is referring to the last verse, and means, 'May the God in whom we all hope fill you with joy and gladness of conscience, and also with unity and concord in believing.' God will not approve our peace unless we are bound together by a pure and perfect faith. It may be preferred to take ἐν τῷ πιστεύειν as εἰς τὸ πιστεύειν, meaning that they were to devote their peace to believing. It is only when we embrace what we are taught calmly, gladly, and with one mind, that we are really prepared for faith. It is better, however, to connect faith with peace and joy, since faith is the bond of holy and lawful concord, and the strength of godly joy. Although the peace referred to may be that which all believers have inwardly with God, the context leads us rather to the former explanation. Paul adds also *that ye may abound in hope,* for hope is thus confirmed and increased in believers. The phrase *in the power of the Holy Ghost* means that all these things are gifts of the divine benevolence. The word *power* is intended to set forth emphatically the wonderful strength by which the Holy Spirit produces in us faith, hope, joy and peace.

14. *I myself also am persuaded.* Paul anticipates an objection, or rather makes a kind of concession, with a view to pacifying the Romans, in case they should consider that they were being censured by so many pressing admonitions, and thus were being unjustly treated. He therefore makes an excuse for having ventured to assume the character of a teacher and giver of exhortation among them. He had done this, he says, not because he had any doubts of their wisdom, kindness, or perseverance, but because his duty compelled him. In this way he removes all suspicion of presumption, which shows itself in particular when someone intrudes into another's business, or deals with matters which do not concern him. In Paul's case we can see the remarkable discretion of this holy man, who was quite content to be of no reputation, provided only the doctrine which he preached should retain its authority. The Romans had many airs, and the name of their city made even the humblest of their people proud. They were thus unwilling to accept a stranger, particularly if he was not of Latin origin and a Jew. Paul has no desire to contend with this pride in his own name, but subdues it by gentle flattery, declaring that he

was undertaking to address them in virtue of his office as an apostle.

Ye yourselves are full of goodness, filled with all knowledge. Two particular qualifications are required in a counsellor. There is *kindness*, which moves his heart to assist his brethren by his advice and disposes him to show friendliness in word and in expression. There is also *skill* or wisdom in affording advice which secures him authority, so that he is able to benefit the hearers whom he addresses. There is nothing more opposed to brotherly advice than ill-will and arrogance, which make us disdain and despise those who are in error, and choose to treat them with ridicule rather than to correct them. Harshness, too, whether in word or expression, deprives our advice of its effect. However we may excel in both kindliness and courtesy, we shall not be the proper persons to give advice, unless we have great wisdom and experience. Paul, therefore, attributes both of these qualifications to the Romans, and testifies that they themselves were quite capable of exhorting one another without the help of anyone else, for he admits that they were abundantly endowed both with kindness and experience. They were, therefore, quite able to offer encouragement.

15. *I write the more boldly unto you.* Paul now excuses his conduct, and to show his discretion grants the boldness of his action in having interposed in a matter which they were able to perform by themselves. He adds, however, that he chose this bold course by the necessity of his office, because he was a minister of the Gospel to the Gentiles, and could not therefore pass by those who belonged to the Gentiles. He thus humbles himself, however, in order to exalt the excellence of his office. By pointing to the grace of God, by which he had been raised to that high honour, he does not allow what he has done in virtue of his apostolic office to be despised. He states, furthermore, that he had not usurped the function of a teacher, but of a counsellor whose duty consists in recalling to mind facts already known.

16. *Consecrating the gospel.*[1] I prefer this translation to that adopted at first by Erasmus, *ministering the gospel.* Paul is undoubtedly referring to the sacred mysteries performed by the priest. The one who offers in sacrifice the people whom he obtains for God makes himself a priest or celebrant in the ministry of the Gospel. It is in this way that he performs the sacred mysteries of the Gospel. The priesthood of the Christian pastor is, as it were, to offer men in sacrifice to God, by bringing them to the obedience of the Gospel, and not, as the Papists have hitherto arrogantly boasted, by offering Christ to reconcile men to God. Paul does not, however, here refer to the pastors of the Church simply as priests, as though this were to be the title given to

---

[1] Calvin's version reads 'consecrating the gospel', *consecrans Evangelium*, which we have retained in the Commentary.

them in perpetuity, but has taken the opportunity of employing this metaphor, since he desired to commend the dignity and efficacy of the ministry. A preacher of the Gospel, therefore, must have as his end, in the performance of his office, the offering to God of souls purified by faith. Erasmus later corrected his version to read *sacrificing the gospel*. This is not only incorrect, but also obscures the sense, for the Gospel is more like the sword with which the minister offers men to God as sacrificial victims.

He adds that such sacrifices are *acceptable* to God, and thus not only commends the ministry, but also affords great consolation to those who give themselves up to be thus consecrated. Now as ancient sacrifices were dedicated to God by outward sanctifications and washings, so these 'sacrifices' are consecrated to the Lord by the Spirit of holiness, through the inward working of whose power they are separated from this world. Although purity of the soul arises from faith in the Word, yet because the voice of man can of itself accomplish nothing and is lifeless, the function of cleansing truly and properly belongs to the Spirit.

I have therefore my glorying in Christ Jesus in things pertaining to God. For I will not dare to speak of any things save those which Christ wrought through me, for the obedience of the Gentiles, by word and deed, in the power of signs and wonders, in the power of the Holy Ghost; so that from Jerusalem, and round about even unto Illyricum, I have fully preached the gospel of Christ; yea, making it my aim so to preach the gospel, not where Christ was already named, that I might not build upon another man's foundation; but, as it is written, They shall see, to whom no tidings of him came, and they who have not heard shall understand. (17-21)

17. *I have therefore my glorying in Christ Jesus.* Having given a general commendation of his own calling in order that the Romans might know that he was a true and undoubted apostle of Christ, he now adds statements to prove that he had not only undertaken the apostolic office which had been laid upon him by the appointment of God, but that he had also admirably adorned it. At the same time also he mentions the fidelity which he had exhibited in discharging his office. It is not enough that we have been ordained if we are not responsive to our calling and do not discharge our duties. Paul does not commend his calling from a desire to secure honour, but because no means of procuring favour for his doctrine and establishing its authority among those at Rome was to be neglected. He glories, therefore, in God and not in himself, for his one object is to return unbroken praise to God.

His purely negative statement is a sign of his unassuming character, but it serves to confirm the truth of what he wants to say. 'The truth itself', he says, 'provides me with so many occasions for glorying, that I have no need to seek false praise which belongs to others. I am content with what is true.' Perhaps too he desired to anticipate the unfavourable reports which he knew were being spread in various quaters by ill-intentioned opponents. He therefore states in advance that he would speak only on matters which were well known.

18. *For the obedience of the Gentiles.* This verse shows that Paul's object was to secure approval of his ministry among the Romans, so that his teaching might have some success. He proves, therefore, from *signs* that God by the presence of His power had attested his preaching, and set a seal to his apostleship, so that no one should now doubt that he was appointed and sent by the Lord. The *signs* that he mentions are *word*, *deed* and *miracles*. This shows that the word *deed* includes more than *miracles*. He uses the expression *in the power of the Holy Ghost* to conclude his list of signs, and means by it that the Spirit alone could have effected them. In short, he asserts that both in his teaching and in his actions the power and energy which he had displayed in preaching Christ revealed the wonderful power of God. But there were also miracles, he says, which were signs to render his evidence more conclusive.

He first mentions *word* and *deed*, and then particularly specifies the power of working miracles. The same order is also adopted in Luke when he says that Christ was mighty in Deed and Word (Luke 24.19), and in John when Christ Himself refers the Jews to His own works for a proof of His divinity (John 5.36). Paul does not mention simply miracles, but distinguishes them by two different expressions. Where Paul speaks here of 'the power of signs and wonders', Peter has 'mighty works and wonders and signs' (Acts 2.22). These are proofs of God's power to awaken men to marvel at Him and also to adore Him when they are struck with wonder at His power. The importance of miracles is that they arouse us to some particular truth about God.

This is a notable passage concerning the usefulness of miracles, which is to arouse among men a reverence for God and obedience to Him. Thus in Mark we read, 'They went forth, the Lord working with them, and confirming the word by the signs that followed' (Mark 16.20). So Luke says in Acts, 'The Lord bare witness unto the word of his grace, granting signs and wonders' (Acts 14.3). Any miracles, therefore, which seek to glorify the creature and not God, and which bolster up untruths and not the Word of God, are manifestly of the devil. I refer *the power of the Spirit* which Paul puts in the third place to both *word* and *deed*.

19. *So that from Jerusalem I have fully preached the gospel.* Paul proves his assertion by quoting the effects produced by the Spirit in his preaching, for the success which followed it surpassed all human power. Who could bring together so many churches for Christ without the assistance of the power of God? 'I have spread the Gospel', Paul says, 'from Jerusalem to Illyricum, and not by hurrying straight to my destination, but passing through all the intervening territory round about.' The Greek verb πεπληρωκέναι, which, following others, we have rendered *fully preached*, means both to perfect and to supply what is wanting. Hence πλήρωμα in Greek means perfection as well as a supplement. My interpretation would be that Paul spread the preaching of the Gospel by 'supplying' what was wanting. Others had begun to preach it before him, but he himself disseminated it still further.

20. *Making it my aim so to preach the gospel.* Because it was necessary for Paul not only to approve himself as a servant of Christ and a pastor of the Christian Church, but also to claim the character and office of an apostle, if he was to gain the attention of the Romans, he states here the proper and particular distinguishing mark of the apostleship. The duty of an apostle is to disseminate the Gospel where it has not yet been preached, according to our Lord's command, 'Go ye . . . and preach the gospel to the whole creation' (Mark 16.15). We must pay careful attention to this point, lest we make a general rule of what belongs particularly to the apostolic office. It is not to be regarded as a fault that a successor was appointed to fill the place of the apostle who established the Church. We may, therefore, regard the apostles as the founders of the Church, while the pastors who succeed them have the duty of protecting and also increasing the structure which they have erected. Paul refers to any foundation which has been laid by some other apostle as *another man's foundation*—Christ is the only stone on which the Church is founded (I Cor. 3.11; Eph. 2.20).

21. *But as it is written.* He uses the prophecy of Isaiah to confirm what he had said of the sign of his apostleship. Speaking of the kingdom of Messiah, Isaiah predicts (Isa. 52.15) among other things that this kingdom must be extended into the whole world, and that the knowledge of Christ must be brought to the Gentiles who had never before heard of His name. It is proper that this task should be performed by the apostles, for that command was specially given to them. The apostleship of Paul, therefore, is made evident in the fact that this prophecy is fulfilled in him.

Any attempt to apply this passage to the pastoral office is misplaced, for we know that the name of Christ must always continue to be preached in churches which are properly ordered. Paul, therefore,

preached Christ to those of other countries to whom He was unknown,
in order that pastors might daily proclaim the same doctrine in every
place after his departure. It is certain that the prophet is speaking of
the beginning of the kingdom of Christ.

*Wherefore also I was hindered these many times from coming to you:
but now, having no more any place in these regions, and having these
many years a longing to come unto you, whensoever I go unto Spain
(for I hope to see you in my journey, and to be brought on my way
thitherward by you, if first in some measure I shall have been satisfied
with your company) (22-24)*

22. *Wherefore also I was hindered.* Paul now applies the remarks
which he had made about his apostleship to a different subject, in order
to excuse his conduct for never having come to them, although he had
been appointed for them as well as for others. He therefore mentions
in passing that in propagating the Gospel from Judaea to Illyricum he
had completed a course which had been laid upon him by the Lord.
Now that this was finished, he did not propose to neglect them. To
prevent any suspicion of neglect in the meantime, he declares that for
a long time now there had been no want of desire on his part. There
were good reasons why the earlier fulfilment of his hope had been
prevented. Now he bids them look for his arrival as soon as his calling
permits. Those who argue from this passage that Paul went to Spain
are on unsure ground. It does not follow that he made this journey
which he had proposed. He simply expresses a hope that he may do
so. But like other believers, it was possible that hope should sometimes be disappointed.

24. *For I hope to see you in my journey.* The reason for his long-
continued wish and present plan to come to them, he says, is to see
them—to enjoy the opportunity of seeing and talking to them, and
also make himself known to them in his official character, for the
arrival of any of the apostles also meant the coming of the Gospel.
When he says *to be brought on my way thitherward by you,* he means that
he has cause to expect great kindness from them. This, as we have
already stated, was the best method of securing their favour. The more
we learn that others put their trust in us, the stronger is the obligation
we feel we owe them. It is, we feel, dishonourable and lacking in
courtesy to prove false to the opinion which has been formed of us.
When he adds *if first in some measure I shall have been satisfied with your
company,* he is speaking of the attitude of kindness which he felt
towards them. It was of great importance for the Gospel to convince
them of this.

But now, I say, I go unto Jerusalem, ministering[1] unto the saints. For it hath been the good pleasure of Macedonia and Achaia to make a certain contribution for the poor among the saints that are at Jerusalem. Yea, it hath been their good pleasure; and their debtors they are. For if the Gentiles have been made partakers of their spiritual things, they owe it to them also to minister unto them in carnal things. When therefore I have accomplished this, and have sealed to them this fruit, I will go on by you unto Spain. And I know that, when I come unto you, I shall come in the fulness of the blessing of Christ. (23-29)

25. *But now, I say, I go unto Jerusalem.* To prevent them from looking for his immediate arrival, and imagining that they had been misled if his coming were delayed longer than they expected, he tells them of the business in which he is at present engaged, and which prevents him from beginning the journey to Rome at once. He is travelling to Jerusalem with the alms which had been collected in Achaia and Macedonia. At the same time, however, he takes this opportunity of commending this contribution, in order to suggest that they should seek to emulate it. Although he does not make an open request that they should do so, yet by saying that Achaia and Macedonia had done what was required of them, he indicates what the responsibility of the Romans was, since their circumstances were the same. In his letter to the Corinthians he states quite openly that this was his object: 'I glory on your behalf to them of Macedonia, that Achaia hath been prepared for a year past; and your zeal hath stirred up very many of them' (II Cor. 9.2).

It was a mark of unusual godliness that when the Greeks learned of the extreme poverty of their brethren at Jerusalem, they gave no thought to the great distance which separated them, but held that those to whom they were united by the bond of faith were not too far removed from them, and relieved their distress out of their own abundance. The word *communicatio* here used is to be noted as expressing in the very best way the feelings with which we ought to assist the wants of our brethren, for the unity of the body creates a mutual concern for others. I have not translated the pronoun τινά, because it is often redundant in Greek, and seems to lessen the emphasis of the present passage. I have rendered the Greek participle *ministering* by *to minister*, but the latter seems to express Paul's meaning better, for he is making the excuse that legitimate business was preventing his immediate departure for Rome.

27. *And their debtors they are.* It is quite obvious that the obligation referred to here is mentioned not so much for the sake of the Corinth-

[1] Calvin's version reads 'to minister', *ad ministrandum.*

ians as of the Romans themselves, for the Corinthians and Macedonians had no greater obligation to the Jews than the Romans. Paul also provides the reason for the obligation, which was that they had received the Gospel from the Jews. He derives his argument from a comparison of the less with the greater. He uses this argument also in I Cor. 9.11 when he says that it should not appear unjust or hard for them to exchange carnal things, which are of far less worth, for spiritual things. Paul shows us the value of the Gospel by declaring that they were indebted not only to its ministers, but to the whole Jewish nation, from which these ministers had come.

We should note the verb λειτουργῆσαι, to minister. It means to perform the duty appointed by the state, and undertake the burdens of one's calling. It sometimes refers also to the performance of sacred rites. Paul, I am quite sure, is referring to some kind of sacrifice made by believers when they give of their own substance for the relief of the poverty of their brethren. In so paying the duty of love which they owe, they offer to God at the same time a sacrifice of sweet-smelling savour. In this passage, however, Paul was referring strictly to the mutual right of compensation which we have noted above.

28. *And have sealed to them this fruit.* I am prepared to accept that this is an allusion to the ancient custom of securing by seals what was desired to be kept in safe keeping. Paul thus commends his own fidelity and integrity. He would honestly guard the money entrusted to him as if he carried it under a seal. By *fruit* Paul seems to denote the increase which, as he has just said, accrued to the Jews after they had sown the Gospel, just as fields support the farmer by the fruit which they yield.

29. *And I know that when I come.* These words may be explained in one of two ways. The first meaning is that he would find that the Gospel would have abundant fruit at Rome, for the blessing of the Gospel consists in producing the fruits of good works. I do not agree with those who restrict this expression to almsgiving. The second explanation is that for the purpose of whetting their appetite for his arrival, Paul expresses the hope that it would not be unfruitful, since it would greatly increase the Gospel by what he calls *the fulness of the blessing of Christ,* i.e. the full blessing of Christ. By this he means great success and growth. But this blessing depended partly on Paul's ministry, and partly on their faith. He promises, therefore, that his coming to them would not be in vain, since he would not fritter away among them the grace which he had been given, but employ it to good purpose with as much enthusiasm as they displayed in receiving the Gospel.

The former explanation is more generally accepted, and also seems to me the better of the two. Paul hopes that on his arrival he will find his dearest wish fulfilled—the Gospel flourishing and prospering among them with notable success, because they excelled in holiness and every kind of virtue. The reason which he gives for his desire is that he looks for particular joy in seeing them abounding in the spiritual riches of the Gospel.

Now I beseech you, brethren, by our Lord Jesus Christ, and by the love of the Spirit, that ye strive together with me in your prayers to God for me; that I may be delivered from them that are disobedient in Judaea, and that my ministration which I have for Jerusalem may be acceptable to the saints; that I may come unto you in joy through the will of God, and together with you find rest. Now the God of Peace be with you all. Amen. (30-33)

30. *Now I beseech you.* We know from very many passages how greatly Paul was hated among his own nation, because of the false accusations levelled against him that he taught the Jews to forsake Moses. Paul knew how greatly misrepresentations could affect the innocent, particularly among those who get carried away by blind enthusiasm. There was also, he knew, the testimony of the Spirit, mentioned in Acts 20.23, which frequently forewarned him that pain and imprisonment awaited him at Jerusalem. The more danger he saw, therefore, the more he was roused. This explains his great anxiety to commend his safety to the Churches. We need not be surprised that he was anxious about his life, the loss of which he knew involved so much danger to the Church.

He therefore demonstrates the extent of his distress and the vehemence of it by connecting *the love of the Spirit* (by which the saints ought to embrace one another) with *the Lord.* Even in the midst of such fears, however, he does not cease to continue on his way, nor shrink from danger, but is ready and willing to undergo it. He takes for his assistance, however, the remedies provided by God, and calls for the aid of the Church, so that, helped by her prayers, he may receive some comfort, according to the promise of the Lord, 'Where two or three are gathered together in my name, there am I in the midst of them' (Matt. 18.20); and, 'If two of you shall agree on earth as touching anything that they shall ask, it shall be done for them of my Father which is in heaven' (Matt. 18.19). Lest anyone should think that the object of his commendation was slight, he beseeches them both by Christ and by the love of the Spirit. The love of the Spirit means the love by which Christ joins us together, because it is not of the flesh, nor of the world, but proceeds from His Spirit who is the bond of our unity.

Since therefore to be assisted by the prayers of believers is so great a blessing of God that even Paul, the chosen instrument of God, did not think of neglecting it, we shall be greatly remiss if worthless and wretched creatures like ourselves despise it. It is quite shameless to use passages like these in support of intercession for the saints departed.

That ye strive together with me. The version of Erasmus, 'to assist me in my labours', is on the whole quite good, but I prefer a literal translation, since the Greek word used by Paul is more emphatic. By the word *strive* he indicates the difficulties in which he is placed, and by requesting their help in this struggle he shows us the feelings which should inspire the prayers made by believers for their brethren. They should, he states, actually take the part of their afflicted brethren, as though they were placed in the same difficult circumstances. He also shows the effect which such prayers ought to have. A believer who commends a brother to the Lord affords him so much support by taking part of his distress upon himself. If indeed our strength is dependent upon prayer to God, the best way by which we can strengthen our brethren is to pray to God for them.

31. *That my ministration which I have for Jerusalem may be acceptable.* Paul's detractors had been so successful in laying accusations against him, that he was afraid that the present which he was bringing might not be too welcome, although it was offered to them at the most appropriate time to relieve their great distress. Paul's remarkable forbearance is seen clearly in the fact that he did not cease to work for those who might not, he felt, be prepared to welcome him. We must imitate this attitude, so that we do not cease to do good to those from whom we are quite uncertain whether we shall receive thanks. We are to note that Paul honours the Jerusalem Christians with the title of *saints*, in spite of his fear that he would be suspected and unwelcome. He was aware that even the saints may on some occasions be led astray by false accusations to entertain unfavourable opinions of others, and although he knows that they were doing him an injustice, yet he continues to speak honourably of them.

By adding *that I may come unto you*, he indicates that this prayer would also be to their advantage, and that it was important to them that he should not be killed in Judaea. The phrase *with joy* has the same reference. It would also be of advantage to the Romans that he should come to them in good spirits and free from any worries, in order to give his time and efforts to them with greater enthusiasm and vigour. By the verb *find rest* or *rest content*, he again shows how fully convinced he was of their brotherly love. The phrase *through the will of God* reminds us of the necessity of devoting ourselves to prayer, since God alone directs all our paths by His providence.

Now the God of peace. In using the universal expression *you all*, Paul is expressing the wish, I gather, not simply that God would be present with the Romans and give them His blessing, but that He would also direct each one of them. The words *of peace* refer, I think, to their circumstances at the time, and is a prayer that God, who is the author of peace, may hold them all together.

CHAPTER SIXTEEN

I commend unto you Phoebe our sister, who is a servant of the church that is at Cenchreae: that ye receive her in the Lord, worthily of the saints, and that ye assist her in whatsoever matter she may have need of you: for she herself also hath been a succourer of many, and of mine own self. Salute Prisca and Aquila my fellow-workers in Christ Jesus, who for my life laid down their own necks; unto whom not only I give thanks, but also all the churches of the Gentiles: and salute the church that is in their house. Salute Epaenetus my beloved, who is the firstfruits of Asia unto Christ. Salute Mary, who bestowed much labour on you. Salute Andronicus and Junias, my kinsmen, and my fellow-prisoners who are of note among the apostles, who also have been in Christ before me. Salute Ampliatus my beloved in the Lord. Salute Urbanus our fellow-worker in Christ, and Stachys my beloved. Salute Apelles the approved in Christ. Salute them which are of the household of Aristobulus. Salute Herodion my kinsman. Salute them of the household of Narcissus, which are in the Lord. Salute Tryphaena and Tryphosa, who labour in the Lord. Salute Persis the beloved, which laboured much in the Lord. Salute Rufus the chosen in the Lord, and his mother and mine. Salute Asyncritus, Phlegon, Hermes, Patrobus, Hermas, and the brethren that are with them. Salute Philologus and Julia, Nereus and his sister, and Olympas, and all the saints that are with them. Salute one another with a holy kiss. All the churches of Christ salute you. (1-16)

1. *I commend unto you Phoebe our sister.* A considerable part of this chapter is taken up with greetings, but since they present no difficulty, it would be wasted effort to spend much time on them. I shall touch only on those points which call for some elucidation.

He begins by commending Phoebe, the bearer of the epistle, first on account of her office, because she exercised a very honourable and holy ministry in the Church. The second reason, he suggests, which should make it their duty to welcome her and show her every kindness, is that she has always devoted herself to all the godly. Paul therefore requests that she should be received in the Lord, because she is a servant (*ministra*) of the Church at Cenchreae. By adding *worthily of the saints*, he hints that it would be unworthy of the servants of Christ to show her no honour or kindness. It is fitting that we should not only embrace with affection all members of Christ, but also respect and bestow particular

320

love and honour upon those who exercise any public office in the
Church. But also, as she has invariably shown kindness to all the
brethren, Paul now bids them in return provide her with help and
assistance in the matters that concerned her. It is an act of simple
courtesy not to forsake one whose disposition is naturally benevolent,
if ever he requires the assistance of others. To encourage this attitude
in them, Paul includes himself among those who had received kindness
from her. The character of the ministry which he is discussing is also
described in I Tim. 5.10. The poor were supported out of the public
funds of the Church, and were looked after by persons charged with
that duty. For this last widows were chosen who, since they were free
from domestic duties and not hindered by children, desired to dedicate
themselves wholly to God for religious service. They were therefore
received into this office to which they were bound and under obligation, just as one who hires his services ceases to be free and to be his
own master. The apostle therefore accuses them of breach of faith if,
having taken on an office, they later renounce it (I Tim. 5.11). Since
they were to live a single life, he forbids them to be chosen if they are
less than sixty years of age, because he foresaw that a vow of perpetual
celibacy was dangerous and indeed harmful below that age. At a time
of increasing degeneracy in the Church this most holy office, which
was of very great use to the Church, became corrupted into the idle
order of nuns. Although this order was corrupt from its beginnings
and contrary to the Word of God, it has so far fallen from its original
purpose that there is no difference now between some sanctuaries of
'chastity' and a brothel.

3. *Salute Prisca and Aquila.* The testimonies offered in favour of
several individuals are designed partly to do honour to rectitude, by
honouring those who are upright and deserving of respect, and to give
authority to those who have the ability and desire to do more good
than others. They are also designed to encourage them to act in a
manner corresponding to their past life, and not to fail in their spiritual
life, or even to let their religious devotion flag.

It is a singular honour which Paul here confers on Prisca and Aquila,
and particularly on Prisca, because she was a woman. This reveals all
the more the unassuming nature of the holy apostle, since he does not
refuse to have, and is not ashamed to admit that he has, a woman as his
associate in the work of the Lord. Prisca was the wife of Aquila, and
Luke calls her Priscilla (Acts 18.2).

4. *Unto whom not only I give thanks, but also all the churches.* Paul
states that he has a particular reason of his own to be grateful to Prisca
and Aquila, for they had not spared their own lives in safeguarding his
own. He adds, however, that all the churches of Christ are grateful

to them, so that their example may also influence the Romans. Paul was deservedly valued and held in affection by all the Gentiles, since his life was an incomparable treasure. It is not strange, therefore, that all the churches of the Gentiles felt an obligation to those who had kept him safe.

It is worth noting the remark which he adds concerning the Church in their own home. He could not have conferred a greater honour on their family than by referring to it as a *Church*. I disagree with Erasmus' translation of *congregation*, for it is quite clear that Paul had made use of the sacred name *Church* as a mark of respect.

5. *Who is the firstfruits of Asia unto Christ.* Paul is alluding here to the ceremonies of the law. Since men are sanctified to God by faith, those who offer themselves first are appropriately called the firstfruits. Paul gives the first place of honour to those who were first to be called to the faith, but they retain this position only as long as they continue faithfully to the end. It is no small honour when God chooses some to be the firstfruits. Faith is more fully and adequately proved by the period of time during which it continues, when those who were the first to begin in the faith do not grow weary in following their true course.

6. He again declares his gratitude, in recording the kindnesses which Mary had shown towards him. His purpose in thus commending these persons is, no doubt, to commend them more favourably to the Romans.

7. *Salute Andronicus.* Although Paul does not normally set much store by kinship or other physical privileges, yet because his relationship to Junias and Andronicus might have helped in some way to make them better known to the Romans, he does not omit to make even this recommendation on their behalf. The second tribute which he pays them, that they were his *fellow-prisoners*, is of greater importance, for in Christ's service bonds are worthy honours indeed. In the third place, Paul calls them *apostles*. He does not, however, use this word in its proper and generally accepted sense, but extends it to include all those who do not just establish one church, but give their whole efforts to spreading the Gospel everywhere. In this passage, therefore, Paul is referring in a general way to those who planted churches, by bringing the doctrine of salvation to various places, as apostles. He restricts the word elsewhere to the principal order (*ad primarium illum ordinem*) which Christ established at the beginning when He chose the twelve disciples. It would have been ridiculous otherwise to ascribe so great an honour as this to the few whom he has mentioned. But since they had embraced the Gospel by faith before he had, he does not hesitate to put them before himself.

11. *Of the household of Narcissus.* It would have been a great insult to have made no mention of Peter in this long catalogue if he was then at Rome. If the Roman Catholics are to be believed, he must have been. But if our best procedure in matters of doubt is to employ a likely guess, no moderate critic will be induced to believe the truth of their statement, for Paul would never have omitted to mention him. It is also worthy of note that none of these magnificent and high-sounding titles are here mentioned, which might allow us to conclude that the Christians were men of high rank. All those whom Paul mentions at Rome were obscure and of humble origin. Narcissus, who is here mentioned, was, I think, the freeman of Claudius, and was notorious for his many criminal offences and profligate conduct. So much the more wonderful is the grace of God that it penetrated right into that impure house which teemed with every kind of wickedness. Narcissus himself was not converted to Christ, but it was a momentous thing that a house which resembled hell itself should be visited by the grace of Christ. But since those who lived with a debased pimp, a thief of voracious greed, and a creature who was quite corrupt, nevertheless worshipped Christ in purity, servants have no reason to wait for their masters, but each may follow Christ for himself. Indeed, the exception mentioned by Paul shows that the family was divided, so that there were only a few believers.

16. *Salute one another with a holy kiss.* A kiss, as we see from many passages of Scripture, was a frequent and quite customary symbol of friendship among the Jews. This custom was, perhaps, less frequent among the Romans. It was not, however, unusual, although only relatives were allowed to kiss women. It became customary, however, in an early period for Christians to kiss one another before receiving the Lord's Supper, as a seal to their friendship. After this they offered their alms to prove in deed and effect what they had represented by the kiss, as we see in one of the homilies of Chrysostom. From this has sprung the ceremony now adopted by the Papists of kissing the cup and offering the oblation. The former of these is nothing but superstition, and has no benefit at all. The other serves no purpose but that of satisfying, if that is possible, the avarice of the priests. Paul, however, does not appear to be specifically enjoining a ceremony of any kind at this point, but is simply exhorting them to cherish brotherly love, which he distinguishes from the unholy friendships of the world. These for the most part are artificial, or are achieved by misdeeds, or are kept together by evil means, but never tend to any good object. By sending greetings from the Churches, he was doing all that he could to bind together all the members of Christ by the bond of love.

Now I beseech you, brethren, mark them which are causing the divisions and occasions of stumbling, contrary to the doctrine which ye learned: and turn away from them. For they that are such serve not our Lord Christ, but their own belly; and by their smooth and fair speech they beguile the hearts of the innocent. For your obedience is come abroad unto all men. I rejoice therefore over you: but I would have you wise unto that which is good, and simple unto that which is evil. And the God of peace shall bruise Satan under your feet shortly. The grace of our Lord Jesus Christ be with you. (17-20)

17. *Now I beseech you.* He now gives an exhortation which is necessary on occasions for the purpose of stirring up every Church, since the ministers of Satan constantly watch every opportunity for disturbing the kingdom of Christ. They attempt to achieve this disturbance in one of two ways, either by sowing dissensions by which men's minds are led away from the unity of the truth, or by creating offences, by which they are alienated from the love of the Gospel. Men are distracted from the unity of the truth when the truth of God is destroyed by doctrines of human invention. They are alienated from the love of the Gospel when it is made the object of hatred or contempt by various means. He therefore orders us to watch all who are responsible for either of these things, to prevent them from deceiving believers, or catching them unawares. We are also to avoid them, he says, because they cause harm. He has good reasons for demanding this precaution from believers, for often our neglect or want of care allows vicious scoundrels to do great harm to the Church, before they are opposed. Unless carefully watched, they often work their way in to do their damage with astonishing cunning.

Note, too, that Paul is speaking to those who had been taught the pure truth of God. It is a blasphemy and sacrilege to divide those who agree in the truth of Christ. But it is a shameless piece of trickery to defend a conspiracy of lying and godless doctrines under the pretext of peace and unity. The Papists, therefore, have no grounds for using this passage to stir up ill-will against us, for we do not attack or destroy the Gospel of Christ, but the falsehoods of the devil by which it has hitherto been obscured. Indeed, Paul clearly demonstrates that he does not condemn every kind of disagreement without exception, but only those which destroy agreement in the orthodox faith. The force of the passage lies in the words, *which ye learned,* for the Romans had to forsake the customs of their forefathers and the institutions of their ancestors before they were properly instructed in the Gospel.

18. *For they that are such serve not our Lord.* He adds that false prophets are to be perpetually distinguished from the servants of Christ

by the fact that they have very little respect for the glory of Christ, and care only for their bellies. At the same time, however, to prevent anyone from being deceived, since they work their way in by deceit and conceal their wickedness by assuming a different character, Paul points out their trick of gaining favour by using flattering language. The preachers of the Gospel are also characterized by friendliness and a pleasant manner, but this is combined with a freedom of expression, which prevents them from wheedling men with empty praise or being complaisant to their faults. These impostors, however, not only win men's hearts by their flattery, but shut their eyes to their faults, and are indulgent to them, so as not to lose hold of their followers. By *innocent* Paul means those who do not exercise sufficient care to avoid deception.

19. *For your obedience is come abroad.* These words are intended to answer a possible objection, and by them Paul shows that he was not admonishing those at Rome as though he thought little of them, but because they could easily fall. 'Your obedience', he says, 'is indeed universally praised. I have therefore cause for rejoicing on your account. But since people often fall in this matter through sheer guilelessness, I want you to be inexperienced and guileless in doing evil, but to display the greater maturity in doing good, whenever it is required, so that you may preserve your integrity.'

We see here the character of the simplicity which Paul extols in Christians, and those who regard their stupid ignorance of the Word of God as the highest virtue are not to lay claim to this title. Although he commends the Romans for being submissive and receptive, yet he desires them to exercise wisdom and discernment, lest their credulity should be exposed to any kind of imposture. He congratulates them, therefore, on their absence of malice, but he does so in such a way as to show that he desires them to act with prudence and care.

20. The expression which follows, *the God of peace shall bruise Satan*, is a promise to strengthen them, rather than a prayer. He exhorts them to fight against Satan without fear, and promises them a speedy victory. Christ has once defeated Satan, but Satan is ever ready to renew the battle. Paul therefore, promises the ultimate defeat of Satan, though this is not evident while the contest is still being fought. He not only speaks of the last day when Satan will be openly trodden under foot, but since Satan will then break off and fling loose his reins, and in his arrogance throw everything into confusion, he promises that the Lord will subdue him and make him to be trodden under foot. A prayer soon follows that the grace of Christ may be with them, i.e. that they may enjoy all the blessings which have been procured for us by Christ.

*Timothy my fellow-worker saluteth you; and Lucius and Jason and
Sosipater, my kinsmen. I Tertius, who write this epistle, salute you in
the Lord. Gaius my host, and of the whole church, saluteth you. Erastus
the treasurer of the city saluteth you, and Quartus the brother. Now to
him that is able to stablish you according to my gospel and the preaching
of Jesus Christ, according to the revelation of the mystery which hath
been kept in silence through times eternal, but now is manifested, and by
the scriptures of the prophets, according to the commandment of the eternal
God, is made known unto all the nations unto obedience of faith; to the
only wise God, through Jesus Christ, to whom be the glory for ever.
Amen.* (21-27)

21. *Timothy saluteth you.* The greetings which he addresses to them
are intended partly to promote the unity of those who are far separated
from one another, and partly to let the Romans know that their
brethren subscribed to the epistle. He addresses them in this way not
because he required the testimony of others, but because the agreement
of believers is of very great profit.

The epistle closes, as we may see, with praise and thanksgiving to
God. Paul makes mention of the singular benefit of God in granting
the Gentiles the light of the Gospel, in which His boundless goodness
which surpasses all telling has been revealed. His words of praise are
sufficient to raise and confirm the confidence of the godly, so that with
hearts lifted up to God, they may look with assurance for all those
things which are here ascribed to Him, and may also confirm their hope
for the future by considering His former benefits. Since, however,
Paul has made a long period by introducing many ideas into a single
sentence, and has complicated this period by a grammatical rearrange-
ment, we must separate the different clauses.

Paul first ascribes all the glory to God alone. Then, in order to show
that this is rightly due to Him, he mentions incidentally some of His
attributes in order to make it evident that God alone is worthy of all
praise. Paul says that *He is the only wise God.* In ascribing this praise
to Him, he deprives all other creatures of such merit. Having mentioned the secret counsel of God, Paul seems to have added this tribute
of praise deliberately for the purpose of drawing all men to revere and
admire the wisdom of God. For we know how ready men are to voice
their disapproval when they fail to discover the reason for the works
of God.

By adding that God was *able to stablish* the Romans, he makes them
more certain of their final perseverance. And to make them acquiesce
with greater certainty in this power, he adds that it is witnessed to in
the Gospel which not only gives us a promise of present peace, but also

brings us the assurance that this grace is to last for ever. God does not declare in the Gospel that He is our Father only for the present, but that He will continue to be such to the end. Indeed, His adoption extends beyond death, for He is bringing us to an eternal inheritance.

Paul's remaining statements are made for the purpose of commending the power and dignity of the Gospel. He calls the Gospel *the preaching of Jesus Christ*, since the whole sum of it is contained in our knowledge of Christ. He refers to the doctrine of the Gospel as *the revelation of the mystery*. This ought not only to make us more attentive to listen to it, but also to impress on our minds the highest respect for it. Paul denotes how sublime a secret this is by adding that it was hidden for many ages from the beginning of the world. It does not have the inflated and proud wisdom which is sought for by the children of this world, who despise it on this account, but it unfolds the unspeakable treasures of heavenly wisdom, which are much higher than all human learning. If the angels themselves regard them with wonder, no human being can surely admire them enough. This wisdom ought not to be less esteemed because it is concealed beneath a humble, ordinary, and simple style, for it has pleased God thus to subdue the pride of the flesh.

Since there might have been some doubt how this mystery, concealed for so many ages, could have emerged so suddenly, Paul tells us that this has not happened through any heedless human act or accident, but through the eternal ordination of God. Here too he closes the door against the prying questions which the impudence of the human mind is accustomed to raise. Any event which takes place suddenly and unexpectedly men consider to have happened without purpose. From this they often wrongly deduce that the works of God are lacking in any reason, or at least they get involved in many perplexing doubts. Paul, therefore, reminds us that that which has now appeared unexpectedly has been decreed by God before the foundation of the world. But to prevent anyone from entering into controversy for the purpose of discrediting the Gospel by its novelty, he quotes the writings of the prophets, whose predictions we now see to have been fulfilled. All the prophets bore so clear a testimony to the Gospel, that it cannot receive better confirmation from any other source. God has thus duly prepared the minds of His people from being struck with perplexity by the novelty of something to which they were unaccustomed.

If it is objected that Paul contradicts himself in saying that the mystery, to which God bore testimony by His prophets, had been concealed throughout all the ages, Peter gives an easy solution to this difficulty. In their careful inquiries into the salvation which was offered to us, he says, the prophets ministered not to themselves but to us

(I Pet. 1.12). God, therefore, was silent at that time, because He held in suspense the revelation of these things concerning which He desired His servants to prophesy.

Although it is not agreed even among scholars in what sense Paul calls the Gospel a hidden mystery in the present passage, as well as in Eph. 3.9 and Col. 1.26, the most likely view is that of those who apply it to the calling of the Gentiles. Paul himself explicitly alludes to this in his epistle to the Colossians (Col. 1.27). I grant that this may be one reason, but I cannot be persuaded to believe that it is the only one. It seems to me more probable that Paul was also thinking of other differences between the Old Testament and the New. Although the prophets had formerly taught all that Christ and the apostles have explained, yet they taught with so much obscurity, when compared with the shining clarity of the light of the Gospel, that we need not be surprised if those things which are now revealed are said to have been hidden. Malachi does not prophesy in vain that the Sun of righteousness would arise (4.2), nor had Isaiah extolled the embassy of the Messiah in vain. Finally, it is not without reason that the Gospel is called the kingdom of God. We may, however, more properly conclude from the subject itself that only when God appeared to His ancient people face to face through His only begotten Son, were the shadows dispersed and the treasures of heavenly wisdom finally opened. He again refers to the purpose in preaching the Gospel which he mentioned at the beginning of the first chapter, viz. that God may lead all nations to the obedience of faith.

COMMENTARY ON THE
FIRST EPISTLE TO THE THESSALONIANS

To
MATURINUS CORDERIUS

A Man of outstanding Godliness and Learning, Principal of the College of Lausanne

It is fitting that you also should have a part in my labours, for it was under your guidance that I entered on a course of studies, and made progress at least to the extent of being of some benefit to the Church of God. When my father sent me as a boy to Paris I had done only the rudiments of Latin. For a short time, however, you were an instructor sent to me by God to teach me the true method of learning, so that I might afterwards be a little more proficient. You presided over the first class in the most estimable way. You saw, however, that pupils who had been trained ambitiously by other teachers produced mere show and nothing of worth, which meant that you had to train them all over again. In that year, therefore, you came down to the fourth class, since you were tired of having this trouble. This, at any rate, was your intention, but for me it was a singular kindness of God that I happened to have a propitious beginning to my studies. Although I was permitted to enjoy this for only a brief period, because we were soon advanced in our studies by an unenlightened individual, who regulated our course as his own choice or rather fancy led him, yet I received such help afterwards from your instruction that it is with good reason that I acknowledge such progress as I have made to be due to you. It was my desire to testify to posterity that, if they derive any profit from my writings, they should know that to some extent you are responsible for them.

GENEVA, 17th February 1550

THE THEME OF THE FIRST
EPISTLE OF PAUL TO THE THESSALONIANS

THE greater part of this Epistle consists of exhortations. Paul had instructed the Thessalonians in the true faith. On learning, however, that persecutions were flaring up there, he had sent Timothy to arouse them for the struggle, lest they should grow weary from fear, as human weakness tends to do. Being advised later by Timothy of their condition as a whole, he uses various arguments to strengthen them both in the constancy of their faith and in patience, in case they should be called to endure any suffering for the testimony of the Gospel. This forms the subject of chapters 1-3.

At the beginning of chapter 4 he encourages them in general terms to pursue a life of holiness, and then commends to them a mutual desire for the well-being of one another, with all the duties that flow from this. Towards the end, however, he touches on the question of the resurrection, and explains in what manner we are all to be raised from death. From this we learn that there were some wicked or thoughtless persons who were trying to unsettle their faith by introducing at an inopportune moment much that was trivial. With the purpose, therefore, of cutting off any excuse for stupid and unnecessary arguments, he instructs them briefly in the views which they ought to hold.

In chapter 5 he prohibits them with even greater strictness from inquiring as to *times*, but warns them to exercise continual vigilance, lest they should be taken unawares by the sudden and unexpected coming of Christ. From this he passes to various exhortations, and so concludes the Epistle.

CHAPTER ONE

Paul, and Silvanus, and Timothy, unto the church of the Thessalonians in God the Father and the Lord Jesus Christ: Grace to you and peace. (1)

The brevity of the inscription indicates that the Thessalonians had received Paul's teaching with respect, and had unanimously and without any disagreement accorded him the honour which was his due. Paul's reference to himself in other epistles as an apostle is intended to secure authority for himself. Hence the simple use of his own name here without any honorary title is a proof that those to whom he is writing had had no reluctance in recognizing him for what he was. The ministers of Satan, it is true, had tried to create a disturbance in this church as well, but it is clear that their manoeuvres had failed. Two others are mentioned in addition to Paul as sharing with him the authorship of the epistle. He makes no additional comment here which has not been explained elsewhere, except that he says, *the church . . . in God the Father and the Lord Jesus Christ.* By these words, unless I am mistaken, he affirms that the Church of God truly exists among the Thessalonians. This mark, therefore, is a proof of a true and lawful church. At the same time, however, these words inform us that we are to seek the Church only where God is Head and where Christ reigns. In short, there is no other Church than that which is founded upon God, gathered together by the protection of Christ, and united in His name.

We give thanks to God always for you all, making mention of you in our prayers; remembering without ceasing your work of faith[1] and labour of love and patience of hope in our Lord Jesus Christ, before our God and Father; knowing, brethren beloved of God, your election, how that our gospel came not unto you in word only, but also in power, and in the Holy Ghost, and in much assurance; even as ye know what manner of men we shewed ourselves toward you for your sake. (2-5)

2. *We give thanks to God always for you all.* Paul follows his custom of commending their faith and other virtues. He does so, however, not so much to commend them as to encourage them to perseverance. It is a powerful stimulus to the pursuit of progress to consider that God has bestowed superlative gifts upon us for the purpose of perfecting

[1] Calvin's version reads, *Indesinenter memores vestri, propter opus fidei,* etc., 'Remembering you without ceasing, on account of your work of faith,' etc.

what He has begun, and that we have moved in the right direction towards achieving our goal under His guidance and direction. Just as a groundless confidence in the virtues which men claim in their folly to possess fills them with pride, and for the future makes them careless and lazy, so the recognition of the gifts of God humbles godly minds and stirs them to apprehensive concern. Hence, instead of congratulating them, Paul says that he gives thanks, in order to remind them that every commendable gift which he says they possess is a benefit which God has given. In mentioning *prayers* he immediately turns to the future. We see thus his purpose in commending their previous life.

3. *Remembering you without ceasing.* The adverb *without ceasing* may be taken in conjunction with the previous words, but it makes more sense as it stands. The words which follow may also be rendered in this way: *Remembering your work of faith and labour of love*, etc. It is no objection that the article is put between the pronoun ὑμῶν and the noun ἔργου. We frequently find this in Paul. I make this point to prevent the accusation of ignorance from being directed at the Vulgate for having given this translation. It is, however, of little importance in regard to the main point which version we choose, and therefore I have retained the rendering of Erasmus.

Paul explains why he has so great a concern for them and prays assiduously on their behalf. It is because he has grown aware of their possession of gifts of God which ought to arouse him to treat them with affection and regard. The more a person excels in godliness and other virtues, the more we ought to show him care and consideration. Is there anything more worthy of our love than God? There is nothing, therefore, which ought to make us seek the friendship of men more than God's manifestation of Himself among them through the gifts of His Spirit. This is the highest of all commendations among the godly. It is the most sacred bond of relationship which more than any other binds men together. This is my reason for saying that it makes little difference whether we render the words by *remembering your faith* or *remembering you on account of your faith*.

By *your work of faith* I understand the *effect* of your faith. This effect may be explained in two ways, either passively or actively. It may mean that faith was in itself a notable example of the power and efficacy of the Holy Spirit, because it worked powerfully in arousing faith, or because it later produced its fruit outwardly. I am of the opinion that the effect is in the root of faith rather than in its fruits. An unusual degree of faith, Paul is saying, has shown itself powerfully in you.

He adds *labour of love*, meaning that in the exercise of their love they had avoided no trouble or pains. We know, of course, from experience how burdensome love is. But that age in particular gave believers many opportunities of *labouring*, if they wanted to discharge the responsibilities of love. The Church was burdened fearfully by many an affliction. Many were stripped of their wealth, many were exiled from their homes, many were left not knowing what to do, and many were weak and defenceless. Almost all were in a state of confusion. So much distress did not permit love to remain inactive.

He refers *patience* to hope, as being always connected with it. We hope for what we wait for with patience (Rom. 8.24). The statement should be interpreted to mean that Paul remembers their patience in hoping for the coming of Christ. From this we may gain a brief definition of true Christianity. It is an earnest faith, full of power, so that it shirks no task when our neighbours are in need of help. On the contrary, the godly are all to be strenuously occupied in the duties of love, and on these to spend their energies. Intent on the hope of the manifestation of Christ they are to despise all other things, and armed with patience are to rise superior both to wearisome delay and all the temptations of the world.

The phrase *before our God and Father* may refer either to what Paul recollects, or to the three things of which he has just spoken. This latter is my own explanation. Since he had spoken of his prayers, he now states that as often as he lifts his thoughts to the kingdom of God, he recalls at the same time their faith, hope, and patience. Since, however, all pretence is to be done away with when we come into the presence of God, he adds this point in order that his affirmation may have more weight. By this declaration of his good-will he also desired to make them more ready for his teaching and eager to listen.

4. *Knowing, brethren beloved of God.* The participle *knowing* may apply to Paul as well as to the Thessalonians. Erasmus refers it to the Thessalonians. I prefer, however, to follow Chrysostom, who understands it of Paul and his colleagues, for in my view it is a stronger confirmation of his previous statement. It was much to their praise that God Himself had proved by many signs that He loved and found favour with them.

Your election. I am quite happy with the interpretation of Chrysostom, which is that God has exalted the Thessalonians, and proved their worth. Paul, however, intended to express something more. He mentions their calling, and since it had displayed exceptional marks of God's power, he infers from it that they had been particularly called with evidence of certain election. The reason is given immediately afterwards. It was no bare preaching that had been brought to them, but preaching conjoined to the power of the Holy Spirit, so that it might obtain full credit among them.

When he says *in power, and in the Holy Ghost*, he means, in my opinion, *in the power of the Holy Ghost*, so that the latter term is added in explanation of the former. *Assurance*, which he puts third, was either in the object of their assurance, or in the attitude of the Thessalonians. I am inclined to think that the meaning is rather that Paul's Gospel has been confirmed by substantial proofs, as if God had shown from heaven that He had ratified their calling. When, however, Paul brings forward the proofs by which he had been informed that the calling of the Thessalonians was wholly of God, he takes occasion at the same time to commend his ministry so that they themselves may also recognize him and his colleagues as having been raised up by God.

Some take the word *power* to mean miracles. I extend the word to apply to the spiritual power of doctrine. As in the First Epistle to the Corinthians, Paul contrasts it with *speech*. It is the living voice of God, inseparable from its effect, as compared with the empty and lifeless eloquence of men. It is to be noted, however, that the election of God, which by itself is hidden, is made known by its marks, when God gathers to Himself the lost sheep, and joins them to His flock, and stretches out His hand to those who are wandering and estranged from Him. The knowledge of our election, therefore, must be sought from this source. But just as the secret counsel of God is a labyrinth to those who disregard His calling, those who under the pretext of faith and calling obscure this first grace, from which faith itself flows, are obstinate in their error. 'By faith,' they say, 'we obtain salvation. There is, therefore, no eternal predestination of God that distinguishes us from the reprobate.' It is as though they said, 'Salvation is of faith. There is, therefore, no grace of God which lightens us to faith.' It is not so, but as free elections must be connected with calling, as though with its effect, so in the meantime it must retain its primacy. It makes little difference in regard to the sense whether we connect ὑπό with the participle *beloved* or with the noun *election*.

5. *Even as ye know.* Paul's present intention, as I have stated above, is that the Thessalonians should allow the same arguments to convince them that they have been chosen by God. God's purpose in honouring Paul's ministry had been to disclose to them their adoption. Accordingly, having said that they knew what manner of men Paul and the others had been, he adds at once after this that he had been what he was for their sakes. By this he means that all this provision had been made for them in order that they might be fully convinced of God's love and the certainty of their election.

And ye became imitators of us, and of the Lord, having received the word in much affliction, with joy of the Holy Ghost; so that ye became an ensample to all that believe in Macedonia and in Achaia. For from you hath sounded forth the word of the Lord, not only in Macedonia and Achaia, but in every place your faith to God-ward is gone forth; so that we need not to speak anything. (6-8)

6. *And ye became imitators of us.* To render them more enthusiastic Paul declares that there is a concurrence and harmony between his preaching and their faith. If men do not answer to God, the grace which is offered to them will accomplish nothing, not because they could do so by themselves, but because God, as He begins our salvation by calling us, accomplishes it by forming our hearts to obey Him. The conclusion, therefore, is that a proof of divine election was seen not only in Paul's ministry to the extent that it was endowed with the power of the Holy Spirit, but also in the faith of the Thessalonians, so that this obedience of theirs is a strong confirmation of faith. He says, however, *Ye became imitators of us, and of the Lord,* in the same sense in which it is said that the people believed in the Lord, and in His servant Moses (Exod. 14.31). It was not that Paul and Moses differed in any regard from God, but that He worked powerfully through them as His servants and instruments. *Having received the word.* Paul calls their readiness to receive the Gospel the *imitation* of God, because as God had displayed His generosity to the Thessalonians, so they had freely chosen to present themselves to Him.

He says *with joy of the Holy Ghost* so that we may know that it is not the impelling force of the flesh or the promptings of their own nature that will make men ready and willing to obey God. Rather, this is the work of the Spirit of God. The fact that even though they were *in much affliction* they still embraced the Gospel serves to illustrate this. There are very many, we observe, not otherwise hostile to the Gospel, who still evade it because of their fear of the Cross. Those, therefore, who do not hesitate to embrace the afflictions which threaten them along with the Gospel display a loftiness of purpose in doing so which affords a magnificent example. We see more clearly from this how much we need the aid of the Spirit in this regard. The Gospel cannot be truly or genuinely received without a glad heart. Nothing, however, is more at variance with our character than to rejoice in affliction.

7. *So that ye became an ensample.* Paul offers a further illustration—they have moved believers as well by their example. It is an achievement to put such a distance between ourselves and those who had started before us that we may be of help to them in finishing their course. The word which Paul uses is τύπος in Greek, *exemplar* in Latin, and *patron* in French. He is saying, therefore, that the courage of the Thessalonians in accepting affliction was so conspicuous that the

other believers borrowed from them their rule of constancy. My preference, however, was to render the word literally as *examples*. This prevented making any unnecessary change in the Greek wording used by Paul. Furthermore, the plural number in my opinion expresses somewhat more than if he had said that that Church as a whole had been set forth as an object of imitation, for the meaning is that there were as many examples as there were individuals.

8. *For from you hath sounded forth the word of the Lord.* The metaphor is a felicitous one. Paul means by it that their faith was so alive that it aroused other nations by its sound. He says that the Word of God *sounded forth* from them, for their faith shouted aloud, calling men to put their trust in the Gospel. This sound, he says, had not only been heard in the places nearby, but had also gone far and wide and had been clearly heard, so that he did not require to publish the matter abroad.

For they themselves report concerning us what manner of entering in we had unto you; and how ye turned unto God from idols, to serve a living and true God, and to wait for His Son from heaven, whom He raised from the dead, even Jesus, which delivereth us from the wrath to come.

(9-10)

He states that the report of their conversion was in everyone's mouth. His mention of his entering in to them refers to that power of the Spirit by which God had adorned His Gospel. He says, however, that the details of both are freely discussed among other nations as being worthy of mention. In the account which follows he first shows us what the condition of mankind is before the Lord enlightens them by the teaching of His Gospel. He then shows the purpose for which the Lord would have us taught, and explains the fruit of the Gospel. Though all men do not worship the same idols, they are all nevertheless in bondage to idolatry, and immersed in blindness and insanity. It is, therefore, of the kindness of God that we are free from the deceptions of the devil and of all kinds of superstition. The conversion of some comes early while that of others comes later, but since all men are estranged from God, it is necessary that we be converted to Him before we may serve Him. From this we also learn the meaning and nature of true faith, for only those who renounce the worthlessness of their own instincts and embrace and receive the pure worship of God truly believe in Him.

9. *How ye turned unto God.* This is the aim of true conversion. We see many abandoning their superstitions, only to fall into a worse condition when they have taken this step, because they fail to advance in godliness. Laying aside all sense of God they give themselves up to

cruel and irreverent scorn. Thus in ancient times the superstitions of the common people were made objects of derision by Epicurus, Diogenes the Cynic, and others like them, but in such a way that they corrupted the worship of God with their debased absurdities. We must therefore see to it that the pulling down of error is followed by the building up of faith. In ascribing the epithets *living* and *true* to God the apostle is making an indirect reference also to idols, for these are lifeless, worthless fabrications, and are erroneously called gods. Paul states that the purpose of conversion is, as I have mentioned, that they might serve God. Hence the purpose of the doctrine of the Gospel is to lead us to worship and obey God. As long as we are the *servants of sin*, we are *free in regard of righteousness* (Rom. 6.20), for we go as our passions lead us, free from any constraining yoke. Only the man who has learned to put himself wholly in subjection to God is truly converted to Him.

Because, however, of the excessive difficulty of doing this in our greatly corrupted nature, he shows at the same time how we are kept and confirmed in the fear of God and in obedience to Him by waiting for Christ. The world will quickly draw us to itself unless we are aroused to the hope of eternal life. As trust alone in the divine goodness induces us to serve God, so also it is the expectation of final redemption alone that keeps us from growing weary. So let all who would persevere in a life of holiness give their whole minds to the hope of Christ's coming. It is worth noting that Paul speaks of waiting for Christ rather than of hope of eternal salvation. Without Christ we are assuredly lost and without hope, but when Christ appears life and good fortune shine upon us. Let us, however, remember that these words are addressed exclusively to believers. As for the wicked, He will come to be their Judge, and they can do no more than tremble as they await Him.

After this he adds that Christ *delivereth us from wrath*. Only those who have been reconciled to God through faith and whose consciences are pacified are aware of this deliverance. Otherwise His name is to be feared. Christ by His death has delivered us from the wrath of God, but the meaning of that deliverance will be made plain on the last day. This statement consists of two parts. The first is that the wrath of God and eternal destruction are hanging over the human race, because *all have sinned, and fall short of the glory of God* (Rom. 3.23). The second is that there is no way of escape except through the grace of Christ. Paul does well to ascribe this office to Christ. It is a gift beyond value that whenever the judgment is mentioned the godly know that Christ will come to them as Redeemer.

Paul speaks explicitly of the wrath *to come*. He does so for the purpose of arousing godly minds, and keeping them from sinking when they consider the present life. Since faith is the vision of things not seen (cf. Heb. 11.1), there is nothing more incongruous than that we should measure the wrath of God by the suffering which we see in the world, just as there is nothing more absurd than to take the passing blessings which we enjoy as a means of estimating the grace of God. So while the wicked take their ease and we labour under afflictions let us learn to fear the vengenace of God which is hidden to the eye of flesh, and take our rest in the secret delights of the spiritual life.

10. *Whom he raised from the dead.* Paul mentions here the resurrection of Christ, on which the hope of our own resurrection is based, for death attacks us on every side. Unless, therefore, we learn to look to Christ, our hearts will fail us at every moment. For the same reason he warns us that Christ is to be awaited from heaven, for we shall find nothing in the world to bear us up, while there are innumerable trials to make us despair. There is another fact also to be noted. Since Christ rose for the purpose of making us all at length partakers of the same glory with Himself, because we are His members, Paul intimates that His resurrection would be of no effect, unless He appears a second time as their Redeemer, and extends to the whole body of the Church the fruit and effect of that power which He displayed in Himself.

CHAPTER TWO

For yourselves, brethren, know our entering in unto you, that it hath not been found vain: but having suffered before, and been shamefully entreated, as ye know, at Philippi, we waxed bold in our God to speak unto you the gospel of God in much conflict. For our exhortation is not of error, nor of uncleanness, nor in guile: but even as we have been approved of God to be intrusted with the gospel, so we speak; not as pleasing men, but God which proveth our hearts. (1-4)

1. *For yourselves, brethren.* Dropping the evidence of other churches Paul now reminds the Thessalonians of what they themselves had experienced. In fuller detail he explains his conduct among them, and similarly that of his two other colleagues. This was of the greatest importance for confirming their faith. His purpose in declaring his integrity is to let the Thessalonians see that they had been called to the faith not so much by a mere mortal as by God. He says, therefore, that his *entering in* to them *hath not been found in vain*, as in the case of ambitious men who make much show when they have nothing of substance to display. He uses the word *vain* in contrast to efficacious.

He proves this by two arguments. The first is that he had suffered persecution and indignity at Philippi. The second is that a conflict of considerable proportions had developed at Thessalonica. We know that indignity and persecution weaken and indeed completely break men's minds. It was, therefore, a work of God that, although Paul had suffered various misfortunes and indignity, he appeared unaffected, and did not hesitate to launch an assault on a large and wealthy city for the purpose of leading its people captive to Christ. In this entering in we see nothing that savours of empty show. In the second clause the same divine power is to be seen, for Paul does not discharge his duty to the accompaniment of applause or favour, but had to wage a fierce conflict. In the meantime he stood firm and undaunted, which proves that he was borne up by the hand of God. This is what he means when he says that he *waxed bold*. Certainly if all these circumstances are carefully weighed, it cannot be denied that God made there a magnificent display of His power. The record of this is to be found in Acts 16.17.

3. *For our exhortation is not of error.* He employs another argument to confirm the Thessalonians in the faith which they had embraced. They have, he says, received pure and faithful instruction in the Word

341

of the Lord, for he maintains that his doctrine had been free from all taint or deception. In order to remove all doubts in this matter he calls their conscience to witness. He uses three terms which, it appears, may be distinguished in the following way: *error* (*impostura*) refers to the content of his doctrine, *uncleanness* to the affections of the heart, and *guile* to the manner of his conduct. In the first place, therefore, he denies that they had been deluded or cheated by any fallacies when they embraced the kind of doctrine that he delivered to them. In the second place he declares his integrity, for it was no squalid ambition but sincere affection alone which moved him to come to them. In the third place he states that there was no deception or malice in what he did, but he had rather displayed the simplicity which befits a minister of Christ. Since these facts were well known to the Thessalonians, they had a sufficiently firm foundation for their faith.

4. *But even as we have been approved of God.* Paul goes even higher and calls God to witness as the Author of his apostleship. His argument goes as follows: 'When God laid this office upon me, He bore witness that I was His faithful servant. There is no reason, therefore, for men to doubt my trustworthiness, which they know has been *approved of God*.' Paul's boast, however, is not that he has been approved of, as though he were such of himself. He does not argue here about his natural endowments, nor does he set his own power in conflict with the grace of God. He simply says that the Gospel had been committed to him as a loyal and approved servant. God approves of those whom He has formed for Himself according to His own good pleasure.

Not as pleasing man. The meaning of *pleasing men* has been explained in the Epistle to the Galatians (Gal. 1.10). The present passage too makes it very clear. Paul compares pleasing God and pleasing men as opposites. When afterwards he says, *God which proveth our hearts*, he means that those who seek men's favour are not guided by an upright conscience and do not act with sincerity. Let us, therefore, know that true ministers of the Gospel should make it their purpose to do their utmost for God, and to do it from the heart, not with any outward regard for the world, but because their conscience tells them it is right and proper. Thus they will refrain from seeking to please men, that is, from having any ambition to curry men's favour.

For neither at any time were we found using words of flattery, as ye know, nor a cloke of covetousness, God is witness; nor seeking glory of men, neither from you, nor from others, when we might have been burdensome, as apostles of Christ. But we were gentle in the midst of you, as when a nurse cherisheth her own children: even so, being affectionately desirous of you, we were well pleased to impart unto you, not the gospel of God only, but also our own souls, because ye were become very dear to us. (5-8)

5. *For neither at any time.* Paul has good reason for repeating so frequently that the Thessalonians know that all he is saying is true. Our surest proof is the experience of those with whom we are speaking. This was of the greatest importance to them, for Paul's only object in referring to the integrity of his behaviour is to gain greater respect for his teaching with a view to establishing their faith. This is a confirmation of the previous sentence, for those who want to please men must take the shameful course of stooping to flattery. Those on the other hand who are truly and earnestly intent upon their duty will keep a good distance from all appearance of flattery.

When he adds *nor a cloke* (lit.: *occasion) of covetousness*, he means that in teaching them he had not sought any personal gain. Πρόφασις is used in Greek to mean both *occasion* and *pretext*, but the former sense suits this passage better, so that 'occasion of covetousness' means a snare to trap them. 'I have not abused the Gospel,' he is saying, 'for the purpose of gaining any advantage.' Human cunning, however, has so many labyrinthine recesses that greed and ambition are often concealed in it. He therefore calls God as his witness. Paul mentions two faults here. In stating that he was free from them, he warns us that the servants of Christ should have nothing to do with them. Thus, if we would distinguish between the true servants of Christ and those who are false and servants so-called, they must be examined by this rule, and all who would serve Christ aright must also regulate their endeavours and actions according to the same rule. Where greed and ambition hold sway, innumerable corruptions follow, and the whole man turns to vanity. These are the two sources from which stems the corruption of the whole of the ministry.

7. *When we might have been burdensome.* Some interpret this to mean, *when we might have been a burden*, i.e. might have caused you expense. The context, however, requires that τὸ βαρύ should be taken to mean *authority*. Paul says that he was so far removed from empty show, boasting, or arrogance, that he waived even his just rights as far as his claim to authority was concerned. Since he was an apostle of Christ he deserved to be received with a greater degree of respect, but he had held back from any show of dignity, as though he had been some undistinguished minister. From this it is seen how far he was from arrogance.

Where we have *gentle*, the Vulgate has *little*. The reading which I have used is more widely followed in the Greek texts. Whichever version is preferred, however, there can be no doubt that Paul is describing his voluntary submission to them.

As when a nurse. In this metaphor he expresses two points which he had touched upon, viz. that he has sought neither glory nor gain among the Thessalonians. A mother in nursing her child makes no show of authority and does not stand on any dignity. This, says Paul, was his attitude, since he willingly refrained from claiming the honour that was due to him, and undertook any kind of duty without being ruffled or making any show. In the second place, a mother in rearing her children reveals a wonderful and extraordinary love, because she spares no trouble or effort, avoids no care, is not wearied by their coming and going, and gladly even gives her own life blood to be drained. In the same way Paul declares that his feelings towards the Thessalonians were such that he was prepared to lay down his own life for their good. This was certainly not the mark of a shabby or ungenerous man, but of one who entertained an impartial affection. He expresses this in the phrase *because ye were become very dear to us.*

In the meantime we must remember that those who want to be counted true pastors must entertain the same feelings as Paul—to have a higher regard for the well-being of the Church than for their own life. They are to do their duty with no regard to their own advantage, but with a sincere love for those to whom they know that they are bound and connected.

> *For ye remember, brethren, our labour and travail: working night and day, that we might not burden any of you, we preached unto you the gospel of God. Ye are witnesses, and God also, how holily and righteously and unblameably we behaved ourselves toward you that believe: as ye know how we dealt with each of you, as a father with his own children, exhorting you, and encouraging you, and testifying, to the end that ye should walk worthily of God, who calleth you into his own kingdom and glory. (9-12)*

9. *For ye remember, brethren.* The object of these remarks is to prove his previous statement that he did not spare himself in order to spare them. He must certainly have burned with an amazing and super-human enthusiasm in doing even manual labour along with the task of preaching in order to earn his livelihood. In this respect too he refrained from claiming his rights, for it is the law of Christ, as he also teaches elsewhere (I Cor. 9.14), that every church furnish its ministers with food and other necessities. In refraining from laying a burden on the Thessalonians, therefore, Paul does more than the responsibility of his office could require him to do. In addition, he does not merely decline to cause public expense, but avoids burdening any one individual. There can be no doubt that there was some worthy and particular motive which induced him to refrain from claiming his rights, for in

other churches he exercised the privilege accorded to him as the others had done. He took nothing from the Corinthians, so that the false apostles should have no handle for gloating in this regard. In the meantime he did not hesitate to ask for what was necessary from other churches, for he writes that while he expended his efforts upon the Corinthians without cost to them, he *robbed* the churches which he did not serve (II Cor. 11.8). Although, therefore, he does not give his reason here, we may nevertheless conjecture that Paul was unwilling to have the Thessalonians minister to his needs, lest such an act should put any hindrance in the way of the Gospel. This too should always be a matter of concern to good pastors, not only that they should run with vigour in their ministry, but also that they should remove all obstacles in their course as far as they are able.

10. *Ye are witnesses.* In order to affirm his integrity, he again calls God and the Thessalonians to witness, and cites God as the witness of his conscience, and the Thessalonians as the witnesses of an acknowledged fact. We behaved, Paul says, *holily* and *righteously*, i.e. with a genuine fear of God and faithfulness and lack of offence towards men. We behaved, in the third place, *unblameably*, by which he means that he had given no occasion for complaint or contradiction. The servants of Christ cannot avoid slanders or misrepresentations, for since they are hated by the world, they must have a bad reputation among the wicked. Paul, therefore, confines this remark to believers, who judge with integrity and uprightness, and do not wilfully or groundlessly detract from the reputation of others.

11. *We dealt with each one of you, as a father.* Paul now dwells particularly on those matters which belonged to his office. He has compared himself to a *nurse*; he now compares himself to a *father*. What he means is that he was concerned for them as a father is generally concerned for his children, and that he had taken pains, like a true father, to instruct and admonish them. No man will ever be a good pastor, unless he shows himself to be a *father* to the church entrusted to him. Paul does not state that he had been a father merely to the whole body, but also to the individual members. It is not enough that a pastor in the pulpit should teach all the people together, if he does not also add particular instruction as necessity requires or occasion offers. Hence in Acts 20.26 Paul declares that he is *pure from the blood of all men*, because he did not cease to give public admonition to all and private instruction to individuals in their own homes. Instruction given to all is sometimes of little service, and some cannot be cured or corrected without particular medicine.

12. *Exhorting you.* He shows how genuinely he was concerned about their well-being, and says that when he preached about reverence

to God and the duties of the Christian life, it was in no half-hearted manner, but he employed exhortations and earnest requests. The preaching of the Gospel has life when men are not merely told what is right, but are pricked by exhortation and summoned to the judgment-seat of God, so that they may not sleep in their errors. This is what is properly meant by *encouraging*, but if the godly souls whose readiness Paul so highly commends needed to be aroused by exhortation and indeed encouragement, what is to be done with us in whom the indolence of the flesh dominates more powerfully? In the meantime as regards the wicked, whose obstinacy is beyond correction, we must give them warning of the dire vengeance of God, not so much with hope of success, as to leave them without excuse.

Some render the participle παραμυθούμενοι as *consoling*. If we accept this rendering he means that he brought comfort to the afflicted who need to be sustained by the grace of God and refreshed with the taste of heavenly blessings, that they may not lose heart or become impatient. The other meaning, however, suits the context better, viz. that he *admonished* them. The three words clearly refer to the same thing.

That ye should walk. He touches briefly on the main point of his exhortation, viz. the warning which he gives while extolling the mercy of God that they should not neglect their calling. His tribute to the grace of God is contained in the phrase, *who calleth* (Calvin: *called*) *you into his own kingdom.* Since our salvation is based on God's free adoption of us, every blessing that Christ has brought us is included in this single phrase. It now remains for us to respond to God's call, i.e. to show ourselves to be such children to Him as He is a Father to us. He who lives otherwise than as befits a child of God deserves to be expelled from the household of God.

And for this cause we also thank God without ceasing, that, when ye received from us the word of the message, even the word of God, ye accepted it not as the word of men, but as it is in truth, the word of God, which also worketh in you that believe. For ye, brethren, became imitators of the churches of God which are in Judaea in Christ Jesus: for ye also suffered the same things of your own countrymen, even as they did of the Jews; who both killed the Lord Jesus and the prophets, and drave out us, and pleased not God, and are contrary to all men; forbidding us to speak to the Gentiles that they may be saved; who fill up their sins alway: but the wrath is come upon them to the uttermost.
(13-16)

13. *For this cause we also thank God.* Having spoken of his ministry, he addresses the Thessalonians again in order that he may always commend the mutual harmony which he has previously mentioned.

He says, therefore, that he gives thanks to God that when they received from him *the word of the message, even the word of God,* they accepted it *not as the word of men, but, as it is in truth, the word of God.* By these words he means that they had received it with reverence and proper obedience. As soon as this conviction has gained strength, inevitably our minds are filled with a conscientious desire to render obedience. Who would not tremble to strive against God? Who would not also regard contempt of God with repugnance? If, therefore, very many people hold the Word of God in such contempt that it has scarcely any value, and if many are unmoved by any fear, this circumstance arises from the fact that they do not consider that they have anything to do with God. Hence we learn from this passage what manner of trust we are to have in the Gospel. It is a trust which does not depend on human authority, but rests on the known and certain truth of God, and is lifted above the world. In a word it is as far removed from conjecture as heaven is from the earth. In the second place, it begets reverence, fear, and obedience, for when men have been affected by a consciousness of the divine majesty they will never allow themselves to treat it lightly. Teachers, on the other hand, are warned against venturing to introduce anything but the pure Word of God. If Paul was not allowed to do this, no one today will be allowed. He proves, however, from its effect that it was the word of God which he had delivered to them, since it had produced the fruit of heavenly doctrine, commended by the prophets, in the renewing of their life. Human doctrine could not achieve any such thing. The relative pronoun may be taken as applying either to God or to His word. However we choose, the meaning will be the same, for since the Thessalonians felt within themselves a divine power which came from faith, they could rest assured that what they had heard was not the passing sound of the human voice, but the living and efficacious doctrine of God.

The expression *the word of the message of God* means simply, as I have rendered it, the word of God preached by man. Paul meant to state explicitly that they had not regarded his doctrine with contempt, even though it came from the lips of a human being, because they recognized that God was the Author of it. He therefore praises the Thessalonians because they looked beyond the minister, and lifted up their eyes to God in order to receive His Word. I have, therefore, had no hesitation in inserting the particle *ut,* which helped to make the meaning more clear. Erasmus has misinterpreted the phrase to mean *the word of the hearing of God,* as if Paul meant that God had been disclosed. He afterwards changed this to *the word by which you learned God,* for he did not notice that it was a Hebrew idiom.

14. *For ye, brethren, became imitators.* If we choose to restrict this

phrase to the following clause, the meaning will be that the power of God or of His Word is displayed in their patience, while they endure persecution with courage and optimism. For myself, however, I prefer to extend the reference to the whole of the previous sentence. Paul is confirming his statement that the Thessalonians had embraced the Gospel in earnest as having been offered to them by God, for they courageously endure the assaults which Satan makes against them, and do not shrink from facing any suffering rather than cease to obey the Gospel. It is assuredly a great test of our faith when with all his devisings Satan fails to part us from our fear of God.

In the meantime Paul wisely counteracts a dangerous temptation which might have daunted or upset them, for they were being severely afflicted by that nation which alone in the world gloried in the name of God. The thought might have entered their minds, 'If this is the true religion, why do the Jews, who are the holy people of God, oppose it with such hostility?' To remove this possibility of offence, he first reminds the Thessalonians that they have this in common with the first churches which were in Judaea. He then says that the Jews are the determined enemies of God and of all sound doctrine. His statement that they suffered at the hands of their own countrymen may be explained as referring to others rather than to the Jews, or at least should not be restricted to the Jews alone. But since he presses the point in describing their obstinacy and ungodliness, it is clear that it is to these he is referring from the very beginning. It is likely that some of the Thessalonians had been converted to Christ. Yet from the account in Acts it is evident that there, no less than in Judaea, the Jews were persecutors of the Gospel. I therefore take this statement to apply both to the Jews and to the Gentiles, because both endured much opposition and bitter attacks from their own countrymen.

15. *Who killed the Lord Jesus.* Since that nation had been honoured with so many of God's favours, their very name had great authority among many people on account of the renown of their ancient fathers. Lest therefore any should be dazzled by this outward show, he strips the Jews of all honour, so as to leave them nothing but hatred and ill repute. 'There are the virtues,' he says, 'for which they merit praise among the good and the godly. They have killed their own prophets and finally the Son of God. They have persecuted me His servant. They wage war against God. They are universally hated by the world. They are opposed to the salvation of the Gentiles. In short, they are destined for eternal destruction.' The question is asked why he says that these same people had killed Christ and the prophets. My answer is that the reference is to the whole body. Paul means that there is nothing strange or unusual in their opposition to God, but that in so

opposing Him they are filling up the measure of their fathers, as Christ says (Matt. 23.32).

16. *Forbidding us to speak to the Gentiles.* Paul, as we have stated, has good reason for spending such time in attacking the wickedness of the Jews. Their impassioned opposition to the Gospel in every part of the world was producing a stumbling-block of vast proportions, especially since they claimed that Paul was profaning the Gospel by spreading it among the Gentiles. By this misrepresentation they were dividing the churches, depriving the Gentiles of the hope of salvation, and blocking the course of the Gospel. Paul therefore charges them with being jealous of the salvation of the Gentiles, but adds, in order to deprive them of all their reputation for godliness, that the purpose of this was that their sins should be *filled up.* So when he said just before this that they *please not God,* he meant that they were unworthy to be numbered among the worshippers of God. His expression, however, is to be noted as implying that those who continue to do wrong fill up in this way the measure of their judgment, until they reach a climax. This is why the punishment of the ungodly is often postponed—it is because their acts of ungodliness are so to speak not yet ripe. This provides us with a warning. If we are continually adding sin to sin, we must take great care that our accumulation of sins may not finally reach to heaven itself, as usually happens.

But the wrath is come. He means that they have absolutely no hope, because they are the vessels of the wrath of the Lord. What he is saying is that the just vengeance of God besets and harries them, and will not leave them until they perish. This fate applies to all the reprobate who plunge headlong into their appointed death. The apostle, however, makes this statement about the entire body of the people, but in such a way as not to deprive the elect of hope. Since the greater part of them were opposed to Christ, he speaks in general terms of the whole nation. We must remember, however, the exception which he himself makes in Rom. 11.5, that the Lord will always have some seed remaining. We must always bear in mind Paul's purpose, which is that believers must carefully avoid associating with those who are being punished by the just vengeance of God, until they perish in their blind obstinacy. *Wrath,* when it is used by itself, means the judgment of God, as in Rom. 4.15, *the law worketh wrath,* and also in Rom. 12.19, *give place unto wrath.*

But we, brethren, being bereaved of you for a short season, in presence, not in heart, endeavoured the more exceedingly to see your face with great desire: because we would fain have come unto you, I Paul once and again; and Satan hindered us. For what is our hope, or joy, or crown

*of glorying? Are not even ye, before our Lord Jesus at his coming?
For ye are our glory and our joy.* (17-20)

17. *But we, brethren, being bereaved of you.* The addition of this
excuse is appropriate, lest the Thessalonians should imagine that Paul
had deserted them when such an emergency demanded his presence.
He has spoken of the persecutions which they were enduring from their
own people. He himself in the meantime was absent, though it was
his duty above all others to come to their assistance. He has previously
referred to himself as a *father*. But it is not the mark of a father to
desert his children in the midst of such distress. He therefore anticipates
any suspicion of contempt or negligence by saying that he did not
lack the inclination, but had been denied the opportunity. He does not
say simply, 'I wanted to come to you, but my way was blocked,' but
by the particular expression that he uses declares the intensity of his
affection: 'When,' he says, 'I was *bereaved* of you.' By the word
bereaved he expresses how grieved and distressed he was to be absent
from them. There follows a fuller expression of his longing for them
—he was dissatisfied with being absent from them even for a short
period. It is not strange that a long period should cause weariness or
sorrow, but our affection must be strong when we are not able to bear
separation for a single hour. By *a short season* (R.V. marg.: *a season of
an hour*) he means a small space of time.

Paul then corrects himself by saying that he has been separated from
them *in presence, not in heart*, so that they may know that distance does
not weaken his affection for them in any way. At the same time this
could apply no less appropriately to the Thessalonians, meaning that
they on their side were united in their affection for Paul while absent
in the body. It was of great importance to him that the extent of his
confidence in their affection for him should be expressed. He reveals
his feelings more fully, however, when he says that he *endeavoured the
more exceedingly*. He means that his affection was so far from being
diminished by his departure from them, that it was the more inflamed.
When he says, *We would fain have come unto you, I Paul once and again*,
he declares that his passion was not a sudden one, which at once cooled
down (as sometimes we see happening), but that he had been resolute
in this purpose, since he sought various opportunities.

18. *And Satan hindered us.* Luke relates that on one occasion Paul
was hindered (Acts 20.3), because the Jews laid an ambush for him on
his journey. The same thing or something like it may frequently have
taken place. Paul, however, is quite right to ascribe all of this to Satan,
for, as he teaches us elsewhere (Eph. 6.12), we have to wrestle *not
against flesh and blood, but against the principalities, against the powers,*

against the world-rulers. Whenever the ungodly cause us trouble, they are fighting under the banner of Satan, and are his instruments for harassing us. More particularly, when our efforts are given to the work of the Lord, any hindrance there is undoubtedly comes from Satan. Would that this truth were deeply impressed upon the minds of all the godly, that Satan is continually striving by every means to hinder or obstruct the upbuilding of the Church. We should be more intent on resisting him. We should take more care to maintain sound doctrine, of which that foe so eagerly strives to deprive us. We should also know the source of the hindrance whenever the course of the Gospel is delayed. He says elsewhere (Rom. 1.13) that *God* had not permitted him, but both statements are true. Although Satan does his part, God still retains supreme authority to open up a way for us as often as He pleases against the will of Satan and despite his opposition. Paul, therefore, rightly says that God does not permit him, although the hindrance comes from Satan.

19. *For what is our hope?* He confirms the warmth of his yearning for them which he has mentioned, because his happiness in a way is laid up in them. 'If I do not forget myself,' he is saying, 'I must long for you, for you are my *glory* and *joy.*' When he calls them his *hope* and *crown of glorying*, we should not take this to mean that he glories in any other than God, but that we are allowed to glory in all of God's favours in their proper place in such a way that He Himself is always our point of aim. I have explained this at greater length in my Commentary on I Corinthians. We are to learn from this that the ministers of Christ will share His glory and triumph on the last day, according as each of them has extended His kingdom. Let them now therefore learn to rejoice and glory in the success of their labours alone, while they see that the glory of Christ is increased by their efforts. In this way they will come to have a proper feeling of love for the Church. The particle *even* denotes that the Thessalonians are not the only ones in whom Paul triumphs, but there are many others. The causal particle γάρ, which follows shortly after, is used as an affirmative, 'Surely ye are,' and not in its proper sense.

CHAPTER THREE

Wherefore when we could no longer forbear, we thought it good to be left behind at Athens alone; and sent Timothy, our brother and God's minister in the gospel of Christ, to establish you, and to comfort you concerning your faith; that no man be moved by these afflictions; for yourselves know that hereunto we are appointed. For verily, when we were with you, we told you beforehand that we are to suffer affliction; even as it came to pass, and ye know. For this cause I also, when I could no longer forbear, sent that I might know your faith, lest by any means the tempter had tempted you, and our labour should be in vain. (1-5)

1. *Wherefore when we could no longer forbear.* Paul assures the Thessalonians of his desire for them in the account which follows. Had he sent no one else to Thessalonica in his place when he was detained elsewhere, it might have seemed that he had no great consideration for them, but by putting Timothy in his place he removes that suspicion, and more especially when he gives them preference before himself. He shows that he had greater consideration for them than for himself by choosing to be left alone rather than that they should be deserted. The words *we thought it good to be left behind* are emphatic. Timothy was a most faithful companion to him. At that time he had no others with him. Hence it was a trouble and an inconvenience for him to be without Timothy. It is, therefore, a sign of unusual affection and anxious desire that he is willing to deprive himself of all consolation for the purpose of succouring the Thessalonians. The word εὐδοκήσαμεν, which denotes an eager disposition of mind, means the same thing.

2. *Timothy, our brother.* He commends Timothy in this way for the purpose of showing more clearly how he wanted to consult their interests. If his emissary had been undistinguished, he could not have afforded them much help, and since Paul would have taken this action without inconvenience to himself, he would have offered no distinctive proof of his fatherly concern for them. The important thing, however, is that he is depriving himself of a *brother* and *fellow-worker*, and one whose equal, as he states in Phil. 2.20, he failed to find, since all men were concerned with their own advantage. In the meantime he secures authority for the doctrine which they had received from Timothy, so that it may remain more deeply fixed in their memory.

He is right, however, in saying that he had sent Timothy in order that they might receive confirmation of their faith from his example.

352

Unpleasant reports of persecution might have made them afraid, but Paul's undaunted constancy was bound to revive them and keep them from growing faint-hearted. The fellowship which ought to exist among the saints and members of Christ surely extends also to this point, that the faith of one proves the consolation of others. Thus, when the Thessalonians learned that Paul was carrying on with unwearied zeal, and by his steadfastness of faith was overcoming every danger and difficulty, and that his faith was everywhere victorious against Satan and the world, this brought them no little consolation. In particular we are, or at least ought to be, moved by the examples of those by whom we have been instructed in the faith, as we read at the end of the Epistle to the Hebrews (Heb. 13.7). Paul means, therefore, that his example ought to have buoyed them up, and kept them from losing heart in affliction. Since, however, they might have been offended if Paul had had qualms that they might all give way under persecution (for this would have been a mark of an extraordinary lack of trust), he modifies his harsh expression by saying *lest anyone*, or *that no one*. There was, however, good reason to fear this, since there are always some timorous souls in any society.

3. *For yourselves know.* Since all men would willingly except themselves from the necessity of bearing the Cross, Paul warns us that there is no reason for believers to entertain excessive fears in times of persecution, as though this were something strange or unprecedented. This is our condition, which the Lord has laid upon us. The expression *hereunto we are appointed* means that these are the terms on which we are Christians. He says, however, that they *know* this, because it was fitting for them to fight with greater courage, since they had been forewarned in time. There is the additional fact that unceasing affliction made Paul an object of contempt among the ignorant and uneducated. On this account he states that nothing had befallen him but what prophetically he had long before predicted.

5. *Lest by any means the tempter had temped you.* By this expression he teaches us that temptations are always to inspire us with fear, because it is the proper office of Satan to tempt. As Satan does not cease to lay ambushes for us on all sides and to set snares all around us, so we must keep watch and take vigorous precautions. Now he states openly what he had avoided at the beginning as being too harsh. He had been concerned lest his labour should be in vain, if perchance Satan should prevail. His purpose in this is that they should be earnest in their vigilance and bestir themselves more energetically to resist.

But when Timothy came even now unto us from you, and brought us glad tidings of your faith and love, and that ye have good remembrance of us always, longing to see us, even as we also to see you; for this cause, brethren, we were comforted over you in all our distress and affliction through your faith: for now we live, if ye stand fast in the Lord. For what thanksgiving can we render again unto God for you, for all the joy wherewith we joy for your sakes before our God; night and day praying exceedingly that we may see your face, and may perfect that which is lacking in your faith? (6-10)

He uses another argument here to show how remarkable was the affection which he bore towards them, for he was enraptured by the good news of their fortunate position. We must take note of the circumstances which he describes. He was in *distress and affliction*. Any cheerfulness, therefore, was evidently out of place. But when he hears from the Thessalonians what he wanted to hear, any consciousness of distress is quenched, and he is beside himself with joy and self-congratulation. Nevertheless, he proceeds to express the extent of his joy step by step. He says, first, *we were comforted*. He afterwards speaks of a joy that was poured forth in profusion. His self-congratulation, however, is exhortatory in nature. Paul's intention was to summon the Thessalonians to undertake some task. It must certainly have been a most powerful stimulus to them to learn that the holy apostle got such comfort and joy from their progress in godliness.

6. *Faith and love*. Whenever we find this form of expression occurring in Paul, we should note it with corresponding care. In these two words he states concisely the sum total of godliness. All who aim at this double mark are beyond the danger of error for the whole of their life. All others, however, to whatever extent they may punish themselves, wander about in misery. The third point which he adds about their *good remembrance* of him refers to their regard for the Gospel. It was for no other reason that they held Paul in such affection and esteem.

8. *For now we live*. Here it is still clearer that Paul almost forgot himself on account of the Thessalonians, or at least paid less regard to himself and considered them first and foremost. He did this, however, not so much from partiality towards men as from devotion to the glory of the Lord. A zeal for God and Christ glowed so hotly in his sacred breast that in a measure it consumed all his other cares. *We live*, he says, i.e. we are in good health, *if ye stand fast in the Lord*. By the adverb *now* he repeats his previous statement that he had borne the heavy burden of *distress* and *affliction*. Any personal misfortune, however, which he endures does not, he affirms, stand in the way of his joy. 'Although I am dead in myself,' he says, 'yet I *live* in your well-being.' All pastors are reminded by this of the kind of relationship which ought to exist between them and the church. When things go well with the

Church, they are to count themselves happy, even though in other respects they are surrounded by much distress. On the other hand, however, if they see the building which they have constructed falling down, they are to die of grief and sorrow, even though in other respects there is good success and prosperity.

9. *For what thanksgiving can we render?* Not being content with a simple affirmation, he tells them how great his joy is by asking himself what thanksgiving he can render to God. By speaking in this way he declares that he has no expression of gratitude that can come up to the measure of his joy. He says that he rejoices *before our God,* i.e. truly and without pretence.

10. *Praying exceedingly.* He again expresses his yearning for them. We are never allowed to congratulate men as long as they live in this world in such unqualified terms that we do not always want something better for them. They are still on their way. They may fall, or go astray, or even go back. Paul therefore desires to be given the opportunity of restoring what is lacking in the faith of the Thessalonians, or, which is the same thing, of completing their faith which is still imperfect in all its parts. Yet this is the faith on which he has previously bestowed extraordinary praise. We learn from this, however, that those who far outdistance others are still a long way from their goal. Whatever progress we may therefore have made, let us always remember our deficiencies, so that we may have no reluctance in undertaking a further task.

From this too we see how necessary it is to give constant attention to doctrine, for teachers were not appointed merely to lead men to faith in Christ in one day or in one month, but to perfect the faith which has been begun in them. When Paul ascribes to himself what elsewhere he declares to belong peculiarly to the Holy Spirit (I Cor. 14.16), this must be restricted to the ministry. Since further the ministry of an individual is inferior to the power of the Spirit, and is subordinate to it, the power of the Spirit is in no way lessened. When he says that he prayed *night and day* beyond all ordinary measure, we may learn from these words how continuously he was engaged in prayer to God, and how eagerly and earnestly he performed that task.

Now may our God and Father himself, and our Lord Jesus, direct our way unto you: and the Lord make you to increase and abound in love one toward another, and toward all men, even as we also do toward you; to the end he may stablish your hearts unblameable in holiness before our God and Father, at the coming of our Lord Jesus with all his saints.

(11-13)

11. *Now may our God and Father.* He now prays that the Lord,

having removed the obstacles of Satan, may clear the way for him, and on his journey to the Thessalonians may be, as it were, his Guide and Conductor. By this he means that we can never take a successful step except under the guidance of God; but when God stretches out His hand, every attempt of Satan to turn us from our course is in vain. We must notice that Paul assigns the same office to God and to Christ, inasmuch as the Father, it is certain, confers no blessing upon us except through the hand of Christ. When, however, he speaks of both in the same terms, he teaches us that Christ possesses divinity and power in common with the Father.

12. *And the Lord make you to increase.* His second prayer is that in the meantime, while his way is blocked, the Lord may nonetheless in his absence confirm the Thessalonians in holiness, and fill them with love. From this again we learn in what the perfection of the Christian life consists, viz. in love and the pure holiness of heart which flows from faith. He commends to them first love *one toward another*, and then *toward all men*, for though it is fitting that we should begin with those who are of the household of faith, our love ought to extend to the whole human race. Then too, though our closer relationships are to be the object of our care, we are not to neglect those who are scattered far from us, and keep them from taking their proper place.

He desires the Thessalonians to abound and increase in love, because to the extent that we progress in the knowledge of God, the love of our brethren must at the same time increase in us, until it overcomes our corrupt love of self and takes possession of our whole heart. He prays that the love of the Thessalonians may be perfected by God, and means that its increase as well as its beginning was from God alone. This clearly reveals the absurdity of those who measure our strength by the precepts of divine law. The end of the Law is love, Paul says (I Tim. 1.5), and yet he declares that it is also a work of God. When, therefore, God frames our life, He does not consider what we can do, but demands of us what is beyond our capacity, so that we may learn to ask Him for the power to accomplish it. By saying *even as we also do toward you*, he stimulates them by his own example.

13. *To the end he may stablish your hearts. Hearts* here is used to mean conscience, or the innermost part of the soul. He means that a man is acceptable to God only if he brings Him holiness of heart. This means not merely outward holiness, but also inward. The question, however, is asked whether it is by our holiness that we stand at the judgment-seat of God. If so, to what purpose is the remission of sins? Yet Paul's words appear to suggest that their consciences are *unblameable in holiness.* My answer is that Paul does not exclude remission of sins for this is the means by which our holiness, which otherwise is

marked by many defilements, can stand in the sight of God. Faith, by which God is reconciled to us so as to pardon our faults, always comes before anything else, just as the foundation precedes the building. Paul, however, does not explain the nature or the extent of the holiness of believers in this world, but desires that it may be increased until it reaches its perfection. For this reason he says *at the coming of our Lord*, meaning that the completion of what our Lord is now beginning in us is being delayed until that time.

With all his saints. This phrase may be explained in two ways, either that the Thessalonians together with all the saints are to have pure hearts at the coming of Christ, or that Christ is to come *with all His saints*. Although as far as syntax is concerned I accept the second sense, I am quite sure that Paul used the term *saints* to remind us that we are called by Christ for the purpose of being gathered together with all His saints. This thought ought to arouse in us a desire for holiness.

CHAPTER FOUR

Finally then, brethren, we beseech and exhort you in the Lord Jesus, that, as ye received of us how ye ought to walk and to please God, even as ye do walk,—that ye abound more and more. For ye know what charge we gave you through the Lord Jesus. For this is the will of God, even your sanctification, that ye abstain from fornication; that each one of you know how to possess himself of his own vessel in sanctification and honour, not in the passion of lust, even as the Gentiles which know not God. (1-5)

1. *Finally then, brethren.* This chapter contains various precepts by which he instructs the Thessalonians in a holy life, or confirms them in their devotion to it. They had previously learned what was the rule and method of godly living, and he reminds them of this. *As*, he says, *ye received of us.* In order, however, that he should not appear to be depriving them of what he had given them, he does not simply exhort them to *walk* in such a way, but to *abound more and more.* When, therefore, he urges them to make progress, he suggests that they are already on the way. The main point is that they are to be particularly careful to make progress in the doctrine which they have received. Paul appears to be contrasting this with the petty and superficial pursuits in which we see a good part of the world so greatly occupied that there is hardly any room left for holy and profitable meditation on the proper regulation of life. Paul therefore reminds them of the manner of their instruction, and bids them devote their whole efforts to this task. He here prescribes a law for us—*forgetting the things which are behind* we are always to stretch forward to further progress (Phil. 3.13). Pastors are at the same time to make this their aim. His *beseeching* them, when he might rightfully enjoin them, is a mark of the courtesy and restraint which pastors should imitate, in order to win their people, if possible, with kindliness, rather than to coerce them with force.

3. *For this is the will of God.* This is a general doctrine from which at once he draws, as from a well, particular admonitions. In saying that *this is the will of God*, he means that we have been called by God for this purpose. 'This,' he says, 'is the purpose for which you are Christians, and this is the aim of the Gospel, that you may sanctify yourselves to God.' The meaning of the term sanctification has been quite frequently explained elsewhere. It means that we are to renounce the world, put off the defilement of the flesh, and offer ourselves to

God in sacrifice, for only a pure and holy offering is fit to be given to Him.

That ye abstain. This is one precept which he derives from the well which he has just mentioned. There is nothing more opposed to holiness than the impurity of fornication, which corrupts the whole man. For this reason he relegates the *passion of lust* to the Gentiles, who are ignorant of God. 'Where the knowledge of God holds sway,' he says, 'lust must be subdued.'

By *the passion of lust* he means all base desires of the flesh. In this way, however, he discredits all desires that arouse us to sensual gratification and pleasure, as in Rom. 13.14 he bids us to *make not provision for the flesh, to fulfil the lusts thereof.* When men allow themselves to whet their desires, there are no bounds to their lustful emotions. The only means of self-control is therefore to bridle all our passions.

The expression *that each one of you know how to possess himself of his own vessel* is interpreted by some to refer to one's *wife*, as though Paul had said, 'Let husbands dwell with their wives in continence.' Since, however, he addresses husbands and wives without distinction, there can be no doubt that he uses the term *vessel* to mean *body*. Each man's body is, as it were, the house in which he dwells. Paul, therefore, would have us keep our body pure from any defilement. *In honour* means honourably, for the man who prostitutes his body to fornication covers it with shame and defilement.

That no man transgress, and wrong his brother in the matter: because the Lord is an avenger in all these things, as also we forewarned you and testified. For God called us not for uncleanness, but in sanctification. Therefore he that rejecteth, rejecteth not man, but God, who giveth his Holy Spirit unto you.[1] *(6-8)*

6. *That no man transgress.* Here is another exhortation which flows like a stream from the doctrine of sanctification. 'God,' he says, 'desires to sanctify us, *that no man* may *wrong his brother.*' Chrysostom connects this statement with the preceding one, and explains ὑπερβαίνειν καὶ πλεονεκτεῖν to mean 'to desire and lust after other men's wives', but this is too forced. Having, therefore, given a brief look at one example of impurity in the case of lustful passion and debauchery, Paul teaches us that it is also a part of holiness to act fairly and without offence toward our neighbours. The former verb refers to violent oppression, where the stronger has the effrontery to inflict injury. The latter includes every excessive or unlawful desire. Since, however, there is a general tendency for men to indulge themselves in greed and wanton desire, he reminds them of what he had previously taught

[1] Calvin's version reads *nos*, 'us'.

them, that God would be the *avenger* of such. We should, however, note that Paul says *we testified*. Men's dullness is such that unless they are struck forcefully they have no sense of the divine judgment.

7. *For God called us not for uncleanness.* The meaning here seems to be the same as above, viz. that the will of God is our sanctification. There is, however, a slight difference. Having made some remarks about correcting the faults of the flesh, he proves that this is the will of God from the purpose of our calling, for God sets us apart to Himself as His peculiar possession. Again, he proves by contrary statements that God calls us to holiness, because He rescues and calls us back from uncleanness. From this he concludes that all who reject this doctrine reject not man but God, the Author of our calling. This calling completely disappears when the principle of newness of life has been destroyed. Paul is aroused to such violent emotion because there are always shameless creatures who show a heedless contempt for God, mock every warning of His judgment, and at the same time treat all rules for a holy and godly life with derision. Such persons as these are not to be taught, but need to have a severe reproof administered to them as with a hammer blow.

8. *Who giveth his Holy Spirit.* In order the more effectively to turn the Thessalonians away from such contempt and obstinacy, he reminds them that they have been endowed with the Spirit of God. His purpose in this is first, that they may discern what is of God, second, that they may make such distinction as is necessary between holiness and uncleanness, and third, that they may with divine authority pass judgment upon every kind of defilement. This will fall upon their own heads unless they are free from infection. To whatever extent, therefore, the ungodly mock every teaching about a holy life and the fear of God, those who are endowed with the Spirit of God have quite a different testimony sealed on their hearts. We must be on our guard, therefore, not to extinguish or obliterate it. This phrase, however, may refer to Paul and the other teachers. They are not, he is saying, condemning uncleanness out of human understanding, but are pronouncing the repeated verdict of the Spirit on the authority of God. I am willing, however, to accept both interpretations. Some manuscripts have the second person *you*,[1] which restricts the gift of the Spirit to the Thessalonians.

But concerning love of the brethren ye have no need that one write unto you: for ye yourselves are taught of God to love one another; for indeed ye do it toward all the brethren which are in all Macedonia. But we exhort you, brethren, that ye abound more and more; and that ye study

---

[1] Calvin's version reads 'us', *nos*.

to be quiet, and to do your own business, and to work with your hands,
even as we charged you; that ye may walk honestly toward them that are
without, and may have need of nothing. (9-12)

9. *Concerning love of the brethren.* Since he has previously commended
their love in exalted terms, he now anticipates any objection by saying,
ye have no need that one write unto you. He gives the reason for this, *for*
ye yourselves are taught of God. By this he means that love was engraved
on their hearts, so that there was no need of letters written on paper.
His meaning is not simply, as John says in his Canonical Epistle, that
his anointing teacheth you (I John 2.27), but that their hearts were
fashioned for love, so that it appears that the Holy Spirit inwardly and
effectively dictates their duty to them. There is thus no need to give
instructions in writing. He adds an argument from the greater to the
less. Since their love extends throughout the whole of Macedonia, he
concludes that there can be no doubt that they *love one another.* The
particle *for indeed,* therefore, means *nay even,* or *nay rather.* Paul, as I
have stated, has added this for the sake of emphasis.

10. *But we exhort you.* Although he affirms that they were willing
enough to undertake all the duties of love, he does not, however, cease
to exhort them to make progress, for there is no perfection among
men. Certainly, we are to wish for improvement even in what seems
best in us. Some connect the verb φιλοτιμεῖσθαι with what follows, as
if he bade them strive to be quiet, but it goes better with the former
expression. Having admonished them to increase in love, he commends
to them a holy rivalry, so that they may vie with one another in
mutual affection, or at least charges each one of them to strive for self-
mastery. I prefer to adopt this latter interpretation. In order, therefore, that their love may be perfect, he expects of them the competition
which is usually found among those who eagerly aspire to victory.
The best rivalry is when each attempts to surpass himself in doing
good. There is, in my view, one sufficiently valid reason for not sub-
scribing to the view of those who interpret the words as *strive to*
maintain peace. Paul would not have required so hard a struggle in an
undertaking of less difficulty. This accords very well with progress in
love, where so many obstacles present themselves. I also accept the
other meaning of the word, that they should give freely for the
common good.

11. *That ye study to be quiet.* I have already stated that this clause is
to be separated from the previous words, for this is a new sentence.
To be at peace in this passage means to act peacefully and with com-
posure, as we also say in French *sans bruit.* In short, he bids them to be
free from disturbance and at peace. Connected with this is the phrase

which he adds immediately afterwards, *and to do your own business.* It can be seen that those who rudely interfere in the business of others cause great disturbance, and are a trouble to themselves and to others. The best way, therefore, to maintain a peaceful life is when each one is intent upon the duties of his own calling, carries out the commands which the Lord has given, and devotes himself to these tasks; when the farmer is busy with the work of cultivation, the workman carries on his trade, and in this way each keeps within his proper limits. As soon as men turn aside from this, everything is thrown into confusion and disorder. Paul, however, does not mean that every individual is to mind his own business in such a way that all are to live apart from one another and have no concern for others, but simply wants to correct the idle triviality which makes men open disturbers of peace, when they ought to lead a quiet life at home.

To work with your hands. He commends manual labour for two reasons, so that they may have enough to support life, and that they may act honourably even before unbelievers. There is nothing more disgraceful than an idle good-for-nothing who is of no use either to himself or to others, and seems to have been born merely to eat and drink. Further, this task or way of working has a wide reference, for when Paul speaks about *hands,* he is using the part for the whole. It is quite certain that he includes every useful occupation of human life.

But we would not have you ignorant, brethren, concerning them that fall asleep; that ye sorrow not, even as the rest, which have no hope. For if we believe that Jesus died and rose again, even so them also that are fallen asleep in Jesus will God bring with him. (13-14)

13. *But we would not have you ignorant.* It is unlikely that blasphemers had destroyed the hope of the resurrection among the Thessalonians, as had happened at Corinth. We note how he severely reprimands the Corinthians, but here he speaks of the hope of the resurrection as though it were undisputed. It is possible, however, that this conviction was insufficiently firm in their minds, and that accordingly they retained something of their old superstition in mourning the dead. The main thing is that we must not grieve inordinately for the dead, because we are all to be raised again. If the sorrow of unbelievers has no limit or bound, is this not simply because they have no hope of resurrection? It is, therefore, unfitting that we, who have been fully grounded in the resurrection, should express our grief unduly. Paul will subsequently discuss the manner of the resurrection, and therefore will say something about the *times.* In this passage, however, he simply intended to check immoderate grief. This would never have had such sway over them if they had seriously reflected on the resurrection and

borne it in mind. He does not, however, forbid us to express any grief at all, but calls for restraint in our sorrow, for he says that *ye sorrow not, even as the rest, which have no hope*. He forbids them to mourn after the fashion of unbelievers who give free rein to grief, because they look on death as the final destruction, and hold that anything that is taken out of the world is lost. But since believers know that they depart from the world in order finally to be gathered into the kingdom of God, they do not have a similar reason for sorrow. Hence the knowledge of the resurrection should be a means of alleviating grief. He speaks of the dead as being *asleep* in the common usage of Scripture, a term by which the pain of death is lessened, for there is a great difference between sleep and destruction. The reference, however, is not to the soul but to the body, for the dead body rests in the tomb as on a bed, until God raises the person up. Those, therefore, who conclude from this that it is souls which sleep, lack understanding.

We now see what Paul's intention is. He is lifting the minds of believers to consider the resurrection, lest they should indulge in excessive grief on the death of their dear ones. It is absurd that there should be no difference between them and unbelievers who, because they see in death nothing but destruction, put no limit or bound to their sorrow. Those who misuse this statement for the purpose of establishing among Christians a Stoic indifference, i.e. a hardness of iron, will find nothing of this nature in the words of Paul. Their objection that we are not to grieve at the death of our dear ones, lest we withstand God, would apply in all occasions of adversity. But it is one thing to restrain our grief, so that it should be subject to God, and another thing to set aside human feelings and become as hard as stone. Let the sorrow of the godly be mingled with comfort, which may instruct them in patience. The hope of blessed immortality, which is the mother of patience, will accomplish this.

14. *For if we believe*. He assumes it as an axiom of our faith that Christ was raised from the dead in order that we should be partakers of the same resurrection. He infers from this that we shall live with Him for ever. As, however, Paul has stated in I Cor. 15.13, this doctrine depends on another principle, that it was not for Himself but for us that Christ died and rose again. Those, therefore, who entertain doubts concerning the resurrection do great injury to Christ, and indeed, as Paul says in Rom. 10.6, take Christ down from heaven.

To *sleep in Jesus* means to retain in death the union which we have with Christ, for those who are ingrafted into Christ by faith share death in common with Him, in order that they may share with Him in life. The question is asked whether unbelievers will not also rise again, for Paul states that there will be a resurrection only for those who are members of Christ. My answer is that in the present passage Paul is mentioning only what suited his present purpose. His intention here was not to strike fear into the ungodly, but to correct the excessive anguish of the godly, and to cure it, as he does, with the medicine of consolation.

For this we say unto you by the word of the Lord, that we that are alive, that are left unto the coming of the Lord, shall in no wise precede them that are fallen asleep. For the Lord himself shall descend from heaven, with a shout, with the voice of the archangel, and with the trump of God: and the dead in Christ shall rise first: then we that are alive, that are left, shall together with them be caught up in the clouds, to meet the Lord in the air: and so shall we ever be with the Lord. Wherefore comfort one another with these words. (15-18)

15. *For this we say.* He now gives a brief description of the manner in which believers are to be raised from the dead. Since he is speaking of something that is of the very greatest importance, and incredible to the human mind, and at the same time promises something that is beyond human power or choosing, he states in advance that he is not introducing any personal or human opinion, but that the Lord is the Author of what he says. It is probable, however, that the *word of the Lord* to which he refers means a statement taken from his own discourses. Although Paul had learned by revelation all the secrets of the kingdom of heaven, he could, however, more suitably establish the belief in the resurrection among believers by relating what Christ's own mouth had uttered. 'It is not we,' he is saying, 'who are the first witnesses of the resurrection, but the Master Himself has declared it.'

We that are alive. Paul has made this statement in order that they might not think that only those who remained alive until the coming of Christ would share in the resurrection, and that those who had previously died would have no part in it. 'The order of the resurrection,' he says, 'will begin with them. We therefore shall not rise without them.' It appears from this that in the minds of some, the belief in a final resurrection had been tenuous, unintelligible, and confused by many errors, since they imagined that the dead would be deprived of it. Eternal life, they supposed, belonged only to those whom Christ would find still alive on earth at His final coming. In order to amend these errors, Paul gives first place to the dead, and then teaches us that those who at that time will still be alive will follow them.

By speaking in the first person he numbers himself among those who will live until the last day. His purpose in doing this is to arouse the Thessalonians to wait for it, and to keep all the godly in suspense, so that they may not promise themselves some particular time. Granting that he knew by a special revelation that Christ would come at a somewhat later date, it was still necessary that this common doctrine should be delivered to the Church, in order that believers might be ready at all times. In the meantime it was necessary to curtail the opportunity taken by many of indulging their curiosity, as he will afterwards do at greater length. When he says *we that are alive* he is using the present tense in place of the future in accordance with Hebrew usage.

16. *For the Lord himself.* He uses the term κελεύσματος (*shout*), and then adds *the voice of the archangel* by way of explanation to denote what is to be the nature of that shout of encouragement. The archangel will perform the duty of a herald in summoning the living and the dead to the judgment-seat of Christ. Though this task will be common to all the angels, yet in accordance with customary practice among different ranks, he gives foremost place to the one whose voice sounds forth first. I leave it to others to debate in finer detail the meaning of the word *trump*. I have nothing to add to my brief remarks in I Corinthians. It is quite certain that the sole purpose of the apostle in the present passage was to give a brief glimpse of the magnificent and venerable appearance of the Judge, until we behold it in full. In the meantime we are to be content with this glimpse.

The dead in Christ. He again states that *the dead in Christ*, i.e. those who are kept in the body of Christ, *shall rise first*, in order that we may know that the hope of life is laid up in heaven for them no less than for the living. He says nothing of the reprobate, because this has nothing to do with the consolation of the godly with which he is now dealing.

He says that those who are left will be *caught up* together with them. In their case he makes no mention of death. He appears, therefore, to be suggesting that they will be exempt from death. Augustine, both in his *City of God*, XX, and his *Answer to Dulcitius*, has great difficulty on this point, because Paul appears to contradict himself. He states elsewhere that the seed cannot grow again *except it die* (I Cor. 15.36). The solution, however, is easy, since a sudden change will be like death. Death, it is true, ordinarily is the separation of the soul from the body, but this does not prevent the Lord from destroying this corruptible nature in a moment in order to create it anew by His power, for in this way is accomplished what Paul tells us must take place, viz. that *what is mortal may be swallowed up of life* (II Cor. 5.4). The phrase which occurs in our Confession that Christ will be 'Judge of the dead and of the living', is recognized by Augustine to be literally true. His only hesitation is how those who have not died are to rise again. As I have said, however, it is a kind of death when this flesh is destroyed, even as it is now subject to corruption. The only difference is that those who sleep put off the substance of the body for a space of time, while those who will be suddenly renewed will put off nothing but the quality.

17. *So shall we ever be with the Lord.* To those who have once been united with Christ he gives the promise of eternal life with Him. These words more than sufficiently disprove the aberrations of Origen and of the Chiliasts. When believers have once been gathered together into one kingdom, their life will have no end any more than Christ's. To allot Christ a thousand years, so that afterwards He would cease to reign, is too horrible to speak of. Those, however, who limit the life of believers to a thousand years commit this absurdity, for believers must live with Christ for as long as He Himself will exist. We must also note the words *we shall be*, for he means that our hope of eternal life is profitable only when we hope that it has been appointed for us personally.

18. *Comfort one another.* He now expresses more openly what I have stated previously, that in the belief in the resurrection we have good grounds for comfort, provided that we are members of Christ and are truly united to Him as our Head. The apostle, however, bids each individual not only to seek consolation for his own sorrow, but also to pass it on to others.

CHAPTER FIVE

But concerning the times and seasons, brethren, ye have no need that aught be written unto you. For yourselves know perfectly that the day of the Lord so cometh as a thief in the night. When they are saying, Peace and safety, then sudden destruction cometh upon them, as travail upon a woman with child; and they shall in no wise escape. But ye, brethren, are not in darkness, that that day should overtake you as a thief: for ye are all sons of light, and sons of the day: we are not of the night, nor of darkness. (1-5)

1. *But concerning the times.* In the third place he now calls them back from a curious and unprofitable inquiry concerning *times*, but in the meantime he admonishes them to be in constant readiness to receive Christ. He anticipates any objection, however, by saying that they have no need that he should write about those things which the curious desire to know. It is a sign of excessive incredulity to disbelieve what the Lord foretells, unless He marks out the day by incontrovertible circumstances and points it out with His finger. Those who insist that divisions of time should be marked out for them, as if they would speculate on the basis of a likely indication, move from one uncertain position to another. Paul states, therefore, that discussions of this nature are not necessary for the godly. There is also another reason. Believers do not seek to know more than they are permitted to learn in the school of God. Christ, however, desired that the day of His coming should be hidden from us, so that we should keep watch in eager expectation.

2. *For yourselves know perfectly.* He contrasts precise knowledge with an anxious desire to make inquiry. But what is it that he says the Thessalonians know well? It is that the day of Christ will come suddenly and unexpectedly, so as to take unbelievers by surprise, as a thief does those who are asleep. This, however, is opposed to visible signs which make known from afar His coming to the world. It would, therefore, be foolish to want to determine the time from presages and portents.

3. *When they are saying, Peace and safety.* This is an explanation of the metaphor, *The day of the Lord* will be like *a thief in the night*. Why is this? Because it will come suddenly to unbelievers when it is least expected, to take them by surprise as though they were asleep. What is the source of this 'sleep'? Surely a profound contempt of God. This

heedless indifference is frequently laid by the prophets to the charge of the ungodly, who await not merely the last judgment but also our daily judgments without any apprehension. Even though the Lord threatens them with destruction, they have no hesitation in promising themselves peace and every good fortune. And so they fall into this deadly apathy, because they do not see the immediate fulfilment of what the Lord declares will take place. Anything that is not immediately visible to their eyes they consider to be mythical. This is why the Lord, to punish this carelessness which is full of obstinacy, comes upon them suddenly and, contrary to the expectation of all, casts down the ungodly from the height of their happiness. He sometimes gives evidence such as this about His sudden arrival, but the outstanding proof will be when Christ will come down to judge the world, as He Himself testifies (Matt. 24.37), when He compares that time with the age of Noah, since men will all abandon themselves to dissipation in complete freedom from disturbance.

As travail upon a woman with child. The metaphor is very appropriate, since there is no evil which seizes with more suddenness and presses with greater severity or danger at its very first onset. Besides this a *woman with child* carries about in her womb that which occasions bodily pain without being aware of it, until she is seized amidst feasting and laughter, or in the midst of sleep.

4. *But ye, brethren.* He now calls to their attention the nature of the duty of believers, which is that they look to that day in hope, even though it be remote. This is the purpose of the metaphor *day* and *light*. The coming of Christ will take by surprise the ungodly who are heedlessly abandoning themselves to pleasure, because being covered in darkness they can see nothing. There is no darkness greater than ignorance of God. There is, however, a great difference between us, on whom Christ has begun to shine by the faith of His Gospel, and them, for the prophecy of Isaiah is fulfilled in us, that while darkness covers the earth, the Lord arises upon us, and His glory is seen in us (Isa. 60.2). He warns us, therefore, that it would be unseemly for us to be caught by Christ asleep, or seeing nothing when the light is shining full on us. He calls them *sons of light* according to Hebrew usage, meaning furnished with light, as he also calls them *sons of the day,* meaning those who derive advantage from the day. He confirms this again when he says that we are *not of the night, nor of darkness,* because the Lord has rescued us from this. It is as though he said that we have not been elightenend by the Lord for the purpose of walking in darkness.

So then let us not sleep, as do the rest, but let us watch and be sober.

For they that sleep sleep in the night; and they that be drunken are drunken in the night. But let us, since we are of the day, be sober, putting on the breastplate of faith and love; and for a helmet, the hope of salvation. For God appointed us not unto wrath, but unto the obtaining of salvation through our Lord Jesus Christ, who died for us, that whether we wake or sleep, we should live together with him. (6-10)

6. *So then let us not sleep.* He adds other metaphors connected with the previous one. As he has just shown that it is quite improper for them to be blind in the light of day so now he warns them that it is unbecoming and discreditable to sleep or to be drunk in the middle of the day. Just as he refers to the teaching of the Gospel by which Christ the sun of righteousness is revealed to us as the *day*, so when he speaks of sleep and drunkenness he does not mean natural sleep or drunkenness caused by wine, but the insensibility of the mind when we forget God and ourselves, and indulge our wicked conduct without a care. He says, *let us not sleep*, i.e. let us not sink into apathy and grow unfeeling in the world, *as do the rest*, i.e. unbelievers, whose ignorance of God deprives them like a dark night of sense and reason. *But let us watch*, i.e. let us look steadfastly to the Lord, *and be sober*, i.e. let us cast away the cares of this world which burden us with their weight and let us obliterate our perverted desires, and mount swiftly and without entanglement to heaven. This is spiritual sobriety when we use this world with such moderation and restraint that we are not entangled with its charms.

8. *Putting on the breastplate of faith.* He adds this for the purpose of shaking us more thoroughly out of our inertia, for he calls us to arms to show us that it is not time to sleep. He does not, it is true, make use of the term *war*, but when he arms us with a *breastplate* and *helmet*, he reminds us that we have a battle to fight. Any, therefore, who are afraid of being seized by the enemy, must keep awake so that they may be constantly on watch. As, therefore, he has encouraged us to be watchful on the grounds that the doctrine of the Gospel is like the light of day, so now he arouses us by another argument, that we are to wage war with our enemy. It follows that dilatoriness is too fraught with danger. We note that, though otherwise given to indulgence, yet when the enemy is close, soldiers refrain from drunken sprees and all physical pleasures and keep careful watch. Since, therefore, Satan is ever pressing upon us, and threatening us with a thousand dangers, we ought at least to be no less diligent and watchful.

It is pointless to look for a more subtle explanation of the names of the pieces of armour, as certain scholars do, for Paul's language here is different from that in Eph. 6.14. There he makes righteousness the breastplate. It will be sufficient, therefore, to understand his meaning that he desires to teach us that the life of Christians is like a perpetual warfare, because Satan does not cease to cause us trouble or to be filled with hatred towards us. He would, therefore, have us in constant readiness and on the alert to resist. He then reminds us that we have need of arms, because we cannot withstand so powerful a foe unless we are well armed. He does not, however, here enumerate *the whole armour* (πανοπλίαν), but simply mentions two parts of our equipment, the *breastplate* and the *helmet*. In the meantime he omits nothing that relates to spiritual defence, for those who are furnished with faith, love, and hope, will not be caught unarmed in any respect.

9. *For God appointed us.* Since he had spoken of the hope of salvation, he develops this argument and says that God has ordained that we should obtain salvation through Christ. We could, however, explain the passage simply to mean that we must put on the helmet of salvation, because God does not will that we should perish but rather that we should be saved. This indeed is Paul's meaning, but in my judgment his reference is wider. Since we regard the day of Christ for the most part with alarm, he says that we have been *appointed* to salvation, since his purpose is to close by making mention of this.

The Greek term περιποίησις means *enjoyment* as well as *acquisition.* Paul unquestionably does not mean that we have been called by God in order to get salvation for ourselves, but that we may keep hold of it, since in fact it has been acquired for us by Christ. Paul encourages believers to fight with all their might, setting before them the assurance of victory. The man who fights in fear and uncertainty is half defeated. His purpose, therefore, in these words was to remove the disquiet which arises from lack of confidence. There is no better assurance of salvation to be found anywhere than can be gained from the decree of God. The word *wrath* in this passage, as elsewhere, means the judgment or vengeance of God against the reprobate.   -

10. *Who died for us.* He confirms his statement from the purpose of Christ's death. For if he died in order to let us share His life, we have no reason for entertaining doubts concerning our salvation. It is uncertain, however, what he now means by sleeping or waking, and it might seem that he meant life and death. This meaning would be more comprehensive. At the same time, however, we may also explain it not inappropriately to mean ordinary sleep. The essential point is that Christ died in order that He might bestow upon us His life, which is eternal and unending. Again, there is nothing strange in the fact that he now declares that we live with Christ, since having entered by faith into the kingdom of Christ, we are passing from death into life. Christ Himself, into whose body we have been ingrafted,

revives us by His power, and the Spirit who dwells in us is life *because of righteousness* (Rom. 8.10).

Wherefore exhort one another, and build each other up, even as also ye do. But we beseech you, brethren, to know them that labour among you, and are over you in the Lord, and admonish you; and to esteem them exceedingly highly in love for their work's sake. Be at peace among yourselves. And we exhort you, brethren, admonish the disorderly, encourage the fainthearted, support the weak, be longsuffering toward all. (11-14)

11. *Exhort.* This is the same word which we found at the end of the previous·chapter, and which we translated *comfort*, because the context required it. The same meaning would also suit the present passage quite well. The subjects which he has discussed previously afford material for both, comfort as well as exhortation. He bids them, therefore, impart to one another what the Lord bestows upon them. He adds that they are to *build each other up*, i.e. that they confirm each other in that doctrine. In order, therefore, to avoid the appearance of reproaching them for carelessness, he says at the same time that they were doing what he charges them to do of their own free will. But so dilatory are we in doing good, that even those who are best disposed of all always require an incentive.

12. *But we beseech you.* The admonition is very necessary. Since the kingdom of God is held in little regard, or at least is not esteemed in proportion to its dignity, this also gives rise to contempt for its godly teachers. The majority of these, being offended by this ingratitude, not so much because they see themselves scorned as because they conclude from this that their Lord is being dishonoured, become less enthusiastic. God also rightly punishes the world, because He withdraws from it good ministers to whom it is ungrateful. It is, therefore, not so much in the interests of His ministers as of the whole Church that those who govern it faithfully should be held in esteem. It is for this reason that Paul is so careful to compliment them. To *know* means to have regard or respect for; but Paul suggests that less respect is shown to teachers than is fitting, because their efforts are not generally taken into consideration. We must, however, note the titles of honour by which he designates pastors. In the first place he states that they *labour*. It follows from this that all idle bellies are excluded from the number of pastors. He further describes the kind of labour by adding, who *admonish* or instruct you. Those, therefore, who do not undertake the duty of instruction boast in vain in the name of pastors. The Pope, it is true, readily admits such persons into his catalogue, but the Spirit of God strikes them out of His. But since, as we have stated, these

teachers are held in contempt in the world, Paul honours them at the same time with the distinction of having authority over others.

He bids his readers pay more than ordinary respect to such as are engaged in teaching and govern only for the purpose of serving the Church. He says literally that they are to be honoured *more than abundantly*, and rightly so, for we are to note the reason which he then adds. We are to do this *for their work's sake*. Now this *work* is the edification of the Church, the eternal salvation of souls, the restoration of the world, and in short the kingdom of God and Christ. The excellence and splendour of this work are beyond value. We are, therefore, to think highly of those whom God makes ministers of so great a task. It may, however, be inferred from Paul's words that judgment is entrusted to the Church so that it may distinguish true pastors. It would have been to no purpose to attribute these distinctions to pastors had Paul not wanted believers to take notice of them. When he bids honour to be bestowed upon those who labour and those who duly and faithfully govern by teaching, he certainly does not honour the lazy and the wicked, nor does he point to them as being worthy of it.

And are over you in the Lord. This appears to have been added to denote spiritual rule. Although kings and magistrates also hold office by the appointment of God, yet because the Lord would have the government of the Church to be especially acknowledged as His own, those who govern the Church in the name and by the commandment of Christ are for this reason expressly described as being over in the Lord. The conclusion, however, which may be drawn from this is that those who exercise an absolute power that is completely opposed to Christ are far from the order of pastors and overseers (*praesulum*). In order to be counted among lawful pastors, it is necessary that one should prove that he governs in the Lord, and has nothing different from Him. What else does this mean but to put Christ in His own place by pure doctrine, so that He alone may be Lord and Master?

13. *In love (cum caritate)*. Others render *by love (per caritatem)*. Paul says *in love*, which in Hebrew is equivalent to *by* or *with*. For myself, however, I prefer to explain it to mean that he bids them not just to respect those who are over them, but also to regard them with affection. For as the doctrine of the Gospel is to be held dear, so also it is fitting that we should regard its ministers with affection. The expression to *esteem by love* would be a little awkward, when it is quite suitable to connect love with honour.

Be at peace. Although this passage has various readings even in the Greek manuscripts, I prefer the rendering which the Vulgate has given, and which Erasmus has followed, viz. *have, or cultivate, peace with them.*

In my view Paul's intention was to counter the wiles of Satan, who does not cease to make every attempt to stir up quarrels or disagreements or feuds between people and pastor. So we see daily how pastors are treated with hostility by their churches for some trivial reason, or for no reason at all, because the desire to foster peace which Paul so strongly commends is not found as widely as it ought to be.

14. *Admonish the disorderly.* It is a common doctrine that the welfare of our brethren should be a matter of concern to us. We show this concern by teaching, admonishing, correcting, and arousing. But since men's characters are different, the apostle with good reason enjoins believers to adjust themselves to this variation. He therefore commands the disorderly, i.e. those who live in an undisciplined way, to be admonished. Admonition is used to mean the reproof by which they are restored to order, for they deserve greater strictness, and cannot be brought to repentance by any other remedy.

Toward the *fainthearted* other measures are to be applied, for they have need of consolation. The *weak* are also to be supported. By fainthearted he means those who are of a broken and despondent spirit. His care of the weak is therefore such that he desires the disorderly to be restrained with some degree of severity. On the other hand he commands them to be admonished sharply, in order that the weak may be treated with civility and courtesy, and the fainthearted receive comfort. Those, therefore, who are stern and truculent demand in vain to be coaxed and flattered, since the remedy must be adapted to the disease.

He commends *longsuffering toward all*, however, for severity must be tempered with some degree of gentleness, even in dealing with the disorderly. This longsuffering is properly speaking contrasted with that which repels us, for we are especially liable to be wearied in healing the diseases of our brethren. If a man has comforted a person who is fainthearted more than once, and has to do the same thing a third time, he will experience a certain disgust and indeed indignation, which prevents him from doing his duty. Thus if by admonishing or ascribing blame we do not immediately make the desired progress, we abandon hope of further success. Paul's purpose was to hold this kind of impatience in check by commending to us forbearance toward all.

See that none render unto any one evil for evil; but alway follow after that which is good, one toward another, and toward all. Rejoice alway; pray without ceasing; in everything give thanks; for this is the will of God in Christ Jesus to you-ward. Quench not the Spirit; despise not prophesyings; prove all things; hold fast that which is good; abstain from every form of evil. (15-22)

15. *See that none render unto any one evil for evil.* Since it is difficult to observe this precept because of our strong natural tendency to seek revenge, he consequently bids us take good care to be on guard. The word *see* connotes eager application. Although he directly forbids vying with one another in inflicting injury, it is, however, plain that he intended to condemn at the same time every tendency to do harm. For if it is forbidden to *render evil for evil,* every desire to do injury is wrong. This doctrine is peculiar to Christians, not to return wrong for wrong but to endure it with patience. Lest the Thessalonians should think that revenge was forbidden only in regard to their brethren, he explicitly states that they are to do evil to no one. At times plausible excuses are frequently made. 'What? Why should I not be allowed to take vengeance on one who is such a good-for-nothing, scoundrel, or brute?' But since vengeance is forbidden to us without exception, we must keep from doing harm, whoever may have hurt us.

Alway follow after that which is good. By this last clause he teaches us that we must not simply refrain from taking vengeance if anyone has injured us, but must also show kindness towards all men. Though his desire in the first place is that kindness should be reciprocated among believers, yet he afterwards extends it to all, however undeserving, so that we may seek to overcome evil with good, as he also teaches elsewhere (Rom. 12.21). The first stage, therefore, in patience, is not to avenge wrong, while the second is to treat even our enemies with kindness.

16. *Rejoice alway.* I refer this to the moderation of spirit, when the spirit keeps calm in adversity and does not give rein to grief. For this reason I connect these three phrases, *rejoice alway, pray without ceasing,* and *in everything give thanks.* When Paul commends unceasing prayer, he shows us the way of lasting joy, because it is thus that we seek from God relief in all our affliction. So in Phil. 4.4, having said, *rejoice in the Lord alway; again I will say, Rejoice. Let your forbearance be known unto all men. The Lord is at hand. In nothing be anxious,* he afterwards shows how this may be done, *in everything by prayer and supplication with thanksgiving let your requests be made known unto God.* In this passage, as we see, he argues that the reason for joy is a quiet and tranquil spirit that is not unduly disturbed by injury or adversity. Lest, however, we should be weighed down by pain, sorrow, anxiety, or fear, he bids us rest in the providence of God. Further, since doubts concerning whether God cares for us frequently come upon us unawares, he also prescribes the cure, which is that we unload our anxieties on to His bosom in prayer, as David commands us in Ps. 37.5, 55.22, and also Peter, following his example (I Pet. 5.7). Since, however, we are far

too impetuous in our prayers, he appoints a middle way, so that even though we long for what we do not have, we should not, however, cease to give thanks.

He has followed here almost the same classification, though in fewer words. In the first place he desires to have us think so highly of the benefits of God, that our recognition of them and consideration of them may overcome all our sorrow. And certainly, if we consider what Christ has bestowed upon us, there will be no bitterness of grief so intense that it may not be relieved and give place to spiritual joy. If this joy does not rule in us, the kingdom of God at once departs from us or we from it. The man who does not think so highly of the righteousness of Christ and the hope of eternal life that he rejoices in the midst of sorrow is exceedingly ungrateful to God. But since our hearts are easily depressed, until they give way to impatience, we are to note the remedy which he presently adds. When we are cast down and laid low, we are raised up again by prayer, because we lay the burden which oppressed us upon God. But since every day, and indeed every moment, there are many things which can disturb our peace and drive away our joy, he bids us pray without ceasing. We have spoken elsewhere of this constancy in prayer. As I have said, Paul adds *thanksgiving* in qualification. Many pray in such a way that they still murmur against God, and grumble if He does not immediately comply with their wishes. It is fitting, however, that our desires should be restrained, so that we may be contented with what we are given, and always blend thanksgiving with our petitions. We may, it is true, entreat, and indeed groan and complain, but in such a way that the will of God becomes more acceptable to us than our own.

18. *For this is the will of God.* I.e., according to the view of Chrysostom, that we *give thanks*. For myself, however, I am of the opinion that these words have a fuller meaning—God is so disposed toward us in Christ that even in our afflictions we have abundant cause for thanksgiving. What is more appropriate or suitable to pacify us than when we learn that God embraces us so lovingly in Christ that He turns to our advantage and welfare everything that befalls us? Let us, therefore, bear in mind that it is a singular remedy for correcting our impatience to turn our eyes from looking at the present misfortunes which torment us, and consider rather how God is disposed toward us in Christ.

19. *Quench not the Spirit.* This metaphor is taken from the power and nature of the Spirit. Since it is the proper office of the Spirit to illuminate the mind, and on this account He is called our light, we are said to quench Him in the proper sense when we make void His grace. Some interpreters are of the opinion that the present and the preceding

clause express the same thing. In their view to *quench the Spirit* is exactly the same as to *despise prophesyings*. But since the Spirit is quenched in different ways, the distinction which I make between these two phrases is that one is general, the other particular. Although contempt of prophecy is a quenching of the Spirit, yet those also quench the Spirit whose laziness renders void the gift of God, when they should fan more vigorously the sparks which God has kindled in them by daily progress. This admonition, therefore, about not quenching the Spirit has a wider reference than that which follows about not despising prophesyings. The meaning of the former is, 'You have been enlightened by the Spirit of God. See that you do not lose that light through your ingratitude.' The admonition is of very great profit, for when those who have been once enlightened brush aside so precious a gift of God, or close their eyes and allow themselves to be dragged into the vainglory of the world, we see that they are struck with a fearful blindness so as to be an example to others. We must, therefore, be on our guard against apathy, by which the light of God is smothered in us.

Those, however, who conclude from this that it is in man's power to choose either to quench or to cherish the light which is offered to him, with the result that they detract from the efficacy of grace and extol the powers of free will, are arguing on false grounds. Although God works efficaciously in His elect, and does not simply bring the light near to them, but makes them see, and opens the eyes of their heart and keeps them open, yet since the flesh is always inclined to be lazy, it needs to be spurred on by encouragement. The command which God gives by the voice of Paul He Himself accomplishes inwardly. In the meantime it is our duty to request the Lord to furnish oil for the lamp which He has lit, keep its wick clean, and even enhance it.

20. *Despise not prophesyings.* This sentence is appropriately added to the other, for since the Spirit of God enlightens us most of all by means of doctrine, those who do their utmost to deny doctrine its proper place *quench the spirit*. We must always consider in what way or by what means God wills to communicate Himself to us. Let all those, therefore, who desire to make progress under the direction of the Holy Spirit allow themselves to be taught by the ministry of the prophets.

By the term prophesying, however, I do not mean the gift of foretelling the future, but as in I Cor. 14.3, the science of the interpretation of Scripture, so that a prophet is the interpreter of the divine will. In the passage which I have quoted Paul ascribes to prophets teaching for edification, encouragement, and comfort, and enumerates these functions. In the present passage, therefore, let us understand prophesying to mean the interpretation of Scripture applied to present need. Paul forbids us to despise it, unless we would freely choose to wander in darkness.

The statement is remarkable for its commendation of outward preaching. It is an illusory belief of the Enthusiasts that those who keep reading Scripture or hearing the Word are children, as if no one were spiritual unless he scorned doctrine. In their pride, therefore, they despise the ministry of men, and even Scripture itself, in order to attain the Spirit. They then proudly try to peddle all the delusions that Satan suggests to them as secret revelations of the Spirit. Such are the Libertines and frenzied individuals like them. The more ignorant a man is, the greater the pride with which he is bloated and puffed up. Let Paul's example instruct us to connect the Spirit with the voice of men, which is nothing else but His instrument.

21. *Prove all things.* Since misguided individuals and impostors frequently pass off their nonsense under the name of *prophesying*, prophecy in this way might be rendered suspect or even repulsive. So at the present day there are many who are well-nigh sickened by the very name of preaching, because there are so many stupid, ignorant men who blurt out their worthless brainwaves from the pulpit, while there are other ungodly and irreverent individuals who babble on with their detestable blasphemies. Since, therefore, it was possible that such persons as these were responsible for prophecy being accepted with contempt, and indeed scarcely being given a place, Paul bids the Thessalonians to *prove all things.* He means that although men do not all speak exactly in accordance with an absolute rule, we must form a judgment before we condemn or reject any doctrine.

In this regard there are two errors which are customarily made. There are some who reject every doctrine without distinction, either because they have been deceived under the cover of the name of God, or because they know that very many are commonly deceived. There are others, on the other hand, who with absurd credulity embrace everything that is presented to them in the name of God without distinction. Both of these ways are in error. The former, who are filled with arrogant prejudice, deprive themselves of the opportunity of making progress, while the latter heedlessly expose themselves to every wind of error. Paul calls the Thessalonians back from these two extremes to a middle way by forbidding them to condemn anything without having first examined it. On the other hand he admonishes them to use their judgment before accepting as true what is brought before them. This respect at least should certainly be given to the name of God, that we do not despise prophecy of which He is stated to be the Author. Just as examination or discrimination should precede the rejection of doctrine, so it should also precede the reception of true and sound doctrine. It ill becomes the godly to have such indeterminate views that they grasp equally at what is true as at what is false. We conclude from this passage that the Spirit of judgment is being given by God to the Thessalonians, so that they may have the discernment not to be cheated by the deceptions of men. Had they not had this discernment, it would have been to no purpose that Paul had said *prove all things* and *hold fast that which is good*. If we feel that we are losing the power to prove aright, we must seek it from the same Spirit who speaks by His prophets. But the Lord declares in this passage by the mouth of Paul that the course of doctrine should not be prevented by any human error, any unconsidered view, ignorance, or indeed by any abuse, from having continual prosperity in the Church. Since the abolition of prophecy means the destruction of the Church, let us allow heaven and earth to fall into disorder rather than that prophecy should cease.

It may, however, seem that Paul is here granting too wide a liberty in teaching when he would have all things proved, for if all things are to be proved, they must be heard. This, however, would open a door to impostors for disseminating their untruths. My answer is that in the present case he does not by any means demand that we should pay attention to false teachers, whose *mouths*, as he teaches elsewhere (Titus 1.11), *must be stopped*, and whom he excludes so rigidly. No more does he set aside the order to be followed in selecting teachers which he elsewhere (I Tim. 3.2) so highly recommends. Since, however, we can never take such great care that there may not be prophesying some persons who have less instruction than they ought to have, while at other times good and godly teachers miss the mark, he requires believers to display such forbearance that they do not refuse to listen to them. There is nothing of greater danger than the pedantry which makes every doctrine become stale, while we do not have the inclination to prove what is right.

22. *Abstain from every form of evil*. Some consider that this is a general statement, as though Paul commanded them to abstain from everything that has the appearance of evil. In this case the meaning would be that it is not enough to have the inward testimony of the conscience, unless we also have regard for our brethren, so that we set ourselves against giving occasion for offence by avoiding anything that may appear to be evil.

Those who explain *form* in terms of logic to mean 'species' as opposed to 'genus' are suffering from a gross misapprehension. He has used the term to mean what is commonly called *appearance*. It may be rendered either *evil appearance* or *appearance of evil*, with *mali* in the genitive. The meaning, however, is the same. I prefer to follow Chrysostom and Ambrose who connect this sentence with the previous one. Neither of them, however, explains Paul's way of thinking, and perhaps neither has wholly grasped his meaning. I shall state briefly my own view.

In the first place, I interpret the phrase *form of evil* or *evil appearance* to refer to the situation when error of doctrine has not yet been discovered, so that it can rightly be rejected, but nonetheless an uneasy suspicion remains, and there is a fear that some poison may be concealed. He therefore orders us to abstain from that kind of doctrine which has the appearance of evil, even though it is not such. He does this, however, not because he allows us to reject it altogether, but because it should not be admitted or gain credence. Why has he previously required them to *hold fast that which is good*, while he now desires that they should *abstain* not simply from evil, but *from all appearance of evil?* The reason is that when truth has been brought to light by carefully distinguishing it, it is fitting that we should then give it credence. When, on the other hand, there exists any fear of falsehood, or when the mind is confused with doubt, it is proper that we should withdraw or walk on tiptoe, lest we should adopt any doctrine with an uneasy and disturbed conscience. In short, he teaches us how prophecy will be of use to us without there being any danger, i.e. if we are careful to *prove all things*, and if we are not inconsistent and impulsive.

And the God of peace himself sanctify you wholly; and may your spirit and soul and body be preserved entire, without blame at the coming of our Lord Jesus Christ. Faithful is he that calleth you, who will also do it. Brethren, pray for us. Salute all the brethren with a holy kiss. I adjure you by the Lord that this epistle be read unto all the brethren. The grace of our Lord Jesus Christ be with you. (23-28)

23. *And the God of peace.* Having given various precepts, he at length passes to prayer. There is certainly no purpose in promulgating doctrine, if God does not put it into our hearts. We see from this the absurdity of those who measure the strength of men by the precepts of God. Knowing, therefore, that any doctrine is useless until God engraves it with His finger on our hearts, Paul prays that God would *sanctify* the Thessalonians. I am not quite clear why he calls God here the *God of peace*, unless we choose to refer it to his previous remarks, where he mentions brotherly agreement, patience, and justice.

We know, however, that the word *sanctification* includes the whole renewal of man. Now the Thessalonians, it is true, had been renewed in part, but Paul desires that God would complete what was left. We learn from this that throughout our life we must make progress in the pursuit of holiness. If, however, it is God's part to refashion the whole man, there is nothing left for free will. If it had been our responsibility to co-operate with God, Paul would have said, 'May God assist or advance your sanctification.' But when he says, *sanctify you wholly*, he makes Him the sole author of the whole work.

And may your spirit and soul and body. This is added by way of explanation, so that we may know what is the meaning of the sanctification of the whole man. It is when he is kept *entire*, or pure and undefiled, in spirit, soul, and body, until the day of Christ. Since, however, such wholeness is never found in this life, it is fitting that each day our purity should be in some measure increased, and our corruption in some measure cleansed, as long as we live in the world. We should note this division of man into his constituent parts. In some instances a man is said to consist simply of *body* and *soul*, and in this case soul denotes the immortal spirit which dwells in his body. But since the soul has two particular faculties, the understanding and the will, Scripture quite frequently represents these two parts separately when it wants to express the power and nature of the soul. In that case *soul* is used to mean the seat of the affections, so that it is the part which is opposed to the spirit. When, therefore, we hear the term *spirit*, we are to understand it to denote reason or intelligence, as on the other hand by the term *soul* is meant the will and all the affections.

I am aware that many interpret Paul's words in a different sense. Their view is that by *soul* he means man's vital impulse, and by *spirit* the part of man which has been renewed. But in that case Paul's prayer would be absurd. Then, too, as I have stated, the usage of Scripture is different. When Isaiah says, *With my soul have I desired thee in the light; yea, with my spirit within me will I seek thee early* (Isa. 26.9), no one has any doubt that he is speaking of understanding and affection, and is thus enumerating the two parts of the soul. These two terms are joined together in the Psalms with the same meaning. This also corresponds better with Paul's statement. For how is the whole man *entire*, except when his thoughts are pure and holy, his affections all honourable and well-arranged, and when too his body itself devotes its energies and service to good works alone? The philosophers hold that the faculty of understanding is like a mistress, while the affections are the means of exercising command, and the body renders obedience. We now see how well everything corresponds. Only if a man harbours no fancy in his mind, has no ambition in his heart, and does nothing with his body that is not approved by God, is he pure and entire. Because Paul in this way commits to God the keeping of the whole man with all its parts, we are to infer from this that unless we are guarded by His protection, we are exposed to countless dangers.

24. *Faithful is he that calleth you.* As he has declared in his prayer the extent of his regard for the well-being of the Thessalonians, so now he confirms them in their assurance of the divine grace. Note, however, his argument in promising them the continuing help of God—it is because He has called them. By these words he means that when the Lord has once adopted us as His children, we are to hope that His grace will be continued to us. He does not promise that He will be our Father for one day only, but adopts us on condition that He is to cherish us ever afterwards. Our calling should therefore be to us evidence of eternal grace, for He will not leave the work of His hands incomplete. Further, Paul is addressing believers who had not been called by outward preaching alone, but had been brought effectually by Christ to the Father, so that they might be numbered among His children.

26. *Salute all the brethren.* The *kiss* was a customary token of greeting, as we have stated elsewhere. In these words he declares his affection for all the saints.

27. *I adjure you.* It is not certain whether he was afraid that malicious and envious persons would suppress his epistle, as often happened, or whether he wanted to avert the other danger, that by misplaced prudence and precaution on the part of some, it might be confined to a few. There are always those who say that it is of no advantage to publish what they otherwise acknowledge to be of the greatest merit. At least, whatever stratagem or pretext Satan may at that time have devised to prevent the epistle from coming to the attention of the world, we may gather from Paul's words how earnestly and vigorously he opposed it. It is no trifling or trivial matter to *adjure* by the name of the Lord. We maintain, accordingly, that it was the will of the Spirit of God to spread through all the Church the teachings which He has given in this epistle by the ministry of Paul. We see from this that those who at the present day prevent the people of God from reading the writings of Paul are more hardened than even the devils themselves, since they are unmoved by so strong an adjuration.

COMMENTARY ON THE
SECOND EPISTLE TO THE THESSALONIANS

To the distinguished
BENEDICT TEXTOR,
Physician

WHILE the judgment of those who are qualified witnesses in the matter is that you excel in the knowledge of your profession, for my own part I have always regarded the scrupulous fidelity and care which you are in the habit of exercising both in attending to the sick and in offering your opinions as being of the greatest merit. In particular, however, I have noticed that in restoring or maintaining my own health you have displayed such painstaking attention that it was easily seen that you were not so much regarding one individual as exhibiting devotion to and concern for the common good of the Church. Someone else might perhaps think that your attention was less because it was not given to himself as an individual. For myself, however, I feel rather that I am under a double obligation to you, for though you omitted nothing whatever in fulfilling the duties of friendship, you were no less concerned about my ministry too, which ought to be dearer to me than my own life. The memory, besides, of my departed wife reminds me each day of how much I owe you, not only because she was repeatedly brought to health by your help, and on one occasion was restored from a serious and dangerous illness, but also because even in the last affliction which took her from us, you did everything that you could to help her as far as diligence, effort, and application were concerned. Since, further, you do not allow me to make you any other payment, I have wanted to inscribe your name on this Commentary, so that there may be some proof on my part of the good wishes which I bear towards you.

GENEVA, 1st July 1550

THE THEME OF THE SECOND
EPISTLE OF PAUL TO THE THESSALONIANS

It seems to me unlikely that this Epistle was sent from Rome, as the Greek manuscripts generally state, for Paul would have made some mention of his imprisonment, as he usually does in other epistles. Then too, he suggests near the beginning of chapter 3 that he is in danger from troublemakers. We may conjecture from this that he wrote the Epistle in the course of his journey when he was going to Jerusalem. From an early date it was widely held by Latin writers that it was written at Athens. The occasion, however, of his writing was to prevent the Thessalonians from thinking that they were neglected because he had not visited them on the hurried journey which he was making elsewhere. In chapter 1 he exhorts them to patience. In chapter 2 he disproves a profitless and fanciful belief about the imminent return of Christ which had gained wide currency. He does so by arguing that first there must come apostasy in the Church, and a great part of the world turn from God in faithlessness; indeed, Antichrist must reign in the temple of God. In chapter 3, having commended himself to their prayers and having briefly encouraged them to perseverance, he orders them to deal severely with those who lead an idle life at the expense of others. If they do not obey these warnings they are, he states, to be excommunicated.

CHAPTER ONE

Paul, and Silvanus, and Timothy, unto the church of the Thessalonians in God our Father and the Lord Jesus Christ; grace to you and peace from God the Father and the Lord Jesus Christ. We are bound to give thanks to God alway for you, brethren, even as it is meet, for that your faith groweth exceedingly, and the love of each one of you all toward one another aboundeth; so that we ourselves glory in you in the churches of God for your patience and faith in all your persecutions and in the afflictions which ye endure; which is a manifest token of the righteous judgment of God; to the end that ye may be counted worthy of the kingdom of God, for which ye also suffer: if so be that it is a righteous thing with God to recompense affliction to them that afflict you, and to you that are afflicted rest with us. (1-7)

1. *Unto the church.* It would be unnecessary to say anything about the form of the greeting. The only point worth noting is that *the church in God and Christ* means one that has not simply been gathered together under the banner of faith, for the purpose of worshipping one God and Father and of trusting in Christ, but is also the work and building both of the Father and of Christ, because we begin to be *of Him in Christ* when God adopts us to Himself and regenerates us (I Cor. 1.30).

3. *To give thanks.* He begins by praising them, so that he may allow himself to proceed to exhorting them. In this way we have more success among those who are already on their way, when without remaining silent about their progress, we remind them how far distant they still are from their goal, and urge them to continue. Since he had commended their faith and love in his former Epistle, he now affirms that both have increased. Indeed, the godly should all hold to the principle of examining themselves each day and seeing the extent of their progress. It is, therefore, a true commendation of believers if they grow in faith and love each day. When he says *alway,* he means that he is constantly provided with a new opportunity. He had previously given thanks to God for them. He now says that he has occasion to do so again, because of their daily progress. In giving thanks to God for this reason, however, he affirms that the increase no less than the beginning of their faith and love is due to him. If these had their source in human goodness, his thanksgiving would be a sham or at least without any basis. He shows, moreover, that their achieve-

ments were not insignificant or even just passable, but very considerable. Our own leisureliness is all the more disgraceful when we hardly move a single foot over a protracted period.

As it is meet. By these words Paul shows us that we are under an obligation to give thanks to God not only when He does us a kindness, but also when we consider the kindness which He has shown towards our brethren. Whenever the goodness of God shines forth, it is fitting that we should show appreciation of it. Then too, the well-being of our brethren ought to be of such concern to us that we reckon among our own blessings any blessing that has been bestowed on them. Indeed, if we consider the nature and holiness of the unity of Christ's body, there will be such a sharing in common amongst us that we shall consider the benefits enjoyed by every member to be to the advantage of the whole Church. Consequently, in extolling the kindnesses of God we must always have regard to the whole of the Church.

4. *We ourselves glory in you.* He could not have bestowed any higher commendation on them than when he says that he sets them before other churches as an example. This is the meaning of the words, 'We glory in you among other churches.' Paul did not boast of the faith of the Thessalonians with a view to his own interest, but because his commendation of them might stimulate a desire to imitate them. He does not say, however, that he glories in their faith and love, but in their *patience* and *faith*. It follows from this that patience is the fruit and proof of faith. These words, therefore, should be explained in the following way: 'We glory in your patience which arises from faith, and we bear witness that it is prominent in you,' otherwise the context will not correspond. There is nothing, it is true, that sustains us in tribulation as faith does, and this truth is sufficiently clear from the fact that as soon as we cease to be aware of the promises of God, we completely fail. The more, therefore, a man has advanced in faith, the more he will be equipped with patience to bear every burden with courage. So on the other hand weakness and impatience in adversity betray our lack of faith. But when in particular we are to bear persecution for the sake of the Gospel, there the strength of our faith reveals itself.

5. *A manifest token of the righteous judgment of God.* I omit any reference to the interpretations of other commentators. The real meaning, I believe, is that the wrongs and persecutions which the innocent and the godly suffer at the hands of rogues and criminals clearly show that one day God will be judge of the world. This statement is quite the reverse of the blasphemous opinion which we are in the habit of expressing whenever things go well with the good and ill with the wicked. We suppose that the world goes round by mere chance, and

we leave no control remaining to God. The result of this is that ungodliness and contempt take hold of men's hearts, as Solomon says (Eccles. 9.3), for those who endure any undeserved suffering either blame God or do not think that He is concerned with human affairs. We hear what Ovid says: 'I am led to the belief that there are no gods' (Ovid, *Amores*, Book III.ix.36). David, indeed, confesses that because he saw such confusion in the world he had almost lost his footing and slipped (Ps. 73.1-12). The ungodly, on the other hand, become more insolent in success, as though there were no punishment for their crimes awaiting them, just as Dionysius, when he made a favourable voyage, boasted that the gods befriended the blasphemous. In short, when we see that the cruelty of the ungodly is directed against the innocent without their being punished, men's unredeemed instincts conclude that there is no judgment of God, no punishment for men's crimes, and no reward for righteousness.

On the other hand, however, Paul declares that when God in this way spares the ungodly and shuts His eyes at the wrongs inflicted on His people, His judgment to come is clearly shown to us. Paul takes it for granted that since God is a righteous judge, it cannot but happen that at some time He will give peace again to the poor souls who are provoked unjustly, and will repay to those who oppress the godly the reward that they have earned. If, therefore, we hold as a principle of faith that God is the righteous Judge of the world, and that it is His office to reward every man according to his works, this second principle will incontrovertibly follow—our present confusion, ἀταξία, is a proof of the judgment which does not yet appear. For if God is the righteous judge of the world, the present confusion must of necessity be restored to order. Now there is nothing more anomalous than that the ungodly should trouble the good and go on their way with unrestrained violence, while the good are viciously assailed through no fault of their own. The obvious conclusion of this is that God will one day mount His judgment-seat in order to remedy the condition of this world.

The statement which he adds that it is a *righteous thing with God to recompense affliction* is the basis of the doctrine that God affords signs of His judgment to come when for the present He refrains from exercising His office as Judge. Indeed, if our present position were reduced to a tolerable order revealing the ultimate judgment behind it, such a state of affairs would hold us down to life on earth. In order, therefore, to arouse us to the hope of the judgment to come, for the present God judges the world only in part. He gives us, it is true, many proofs of His judgment, but in such a way as to compel us to enlarge our hope. The passage is a notable one, for it teaches us how our minds are to be raised up from all the obstacles of the world whenever we suffer any adversity—we are to remember the righteous judgment of God, which will raise us above this world. Death will thus be for us the image of life.

That ye may be counted worthy. No persecution is of such profit to us that it may make us *worthy of the kingdom of God*, nor is Paul arguing here about the cause of worthiness. He is simply taking the common doctrine of Scripture that God destroys in us what is of the world, in order to restore a better life within us. He also shows us by means of affliction the value of eternal life. In short, He simply shows us the manner in which believers are prepared and as it were polished beneath the anvil of God, because they are taught by means of affliction to renounce the world and aim at God's heavenly kingdom. Further, they are confirmed in the hope of eternal life even while they fight for it. This is the entering in of which Christ spoke to His disciples (Luke 13.24).

6. *To recompense affliction.* We have already stated why he mentions the punishment which God inflicts upon the reprobate—it is that we may learn to rest in expectation of the judgment to come, because God does not yet punish the wicked, though it is necessary that they should pay the penalty for their wrong-doing. At the same time, however, believers understand that there is no reason why they should envy the temporary and precarious happiness of the ungodly, which before long is to be changed into terrifying destruction. His additional remark about the *rest* of the godly coincides with the statement of Peter when he calls the day of the last judgment the day of *refreshing* (Acts 3.19).

In his remarks concerning the good and the evil, however, Paul desired to show more clearly how unjust and perverse the government of the world would be if God did not postpone rewards and punishments to another judgment. If this were so, the name of God would have ceased to exist. Those, therefore, who are not intent on the righteousness of which Paul is speaking rob Him of His office and power.

He adds *with us* in order to use their awareness of his own faith to secure credit for his doctrine. He proves that he is not arguing about something of which he is ignorant by putting himself into the same situation and class as they are in. We know how much more authority is due to those who have had long experience in the subject which they teach, and who demand of others only what they themselves are prepared to do. Paul, therefore, does not tell the Thessalonians how they are to fight in the heat of the day while he himself is in the shade, but, even while engaged in the strenuous conflict himself, spurs them on to the same warfare.

At the revelation of the Lord Jesus from heaven with the angels of his power in flaming fire, rendering vengeance to them that know not God, and to them that obey not the gospel of our Lord Jesus: who shall suffer punishment, even eternal destruction from the face of the Lord and from the glory of his might, when he shall come to be glorified in his saints, and to be marvelled at in all them that believe (because our testimony unto you was believed) in that day. (7-10)

7. *At the revelation of the Lord.* This is a confirmation of his previous statement. It is one of the articles of our faith that Christ will come from heaven, and will not come in vain. Faith, therefore, must examine the purpose of His coming. Now this is that He is to come to His own as Redeemer, and indeed is to judge the whole world. The description which follows has reference to this, so that the godly may understand that God's concern with their afflictions is in proportion to the fearful nature of the judgment which awaits His enemies. The main reason for our distress and chagrin is that we think that God is affected by our misfortunes only to a small extent. We note the complaints into which David bursts from time to time, while he is consumed by the pride and insolence of his enemies. He has therefore mentioned all this for the consolation of believers, for he depicts the judgment-seat of Christ as being filled with terror, so that they may not be discouraged by their own lowly position at present, while they see that they are being trodden underfoot by the ungodly in their pride and insolence.

I leave to men's idle curiosity the discussion of what is to be the nature of that fire, and of what materials it is to consist. It is sufficient for me to hold fast to what Paul proposed to teach, viz. that Christ will avenge with the strictest severity the wrongs which the wicked inflict upon us. The metaphor of flame and fire is very frequent in Scripture where the writer is dealing with the wrath of God. When Paul refers to the *angels of his power*, he means those in whom He will manifest His power. He will bring His angels with Him, in order to set forth the glory of His kingdom. Hence, too, they are elsewhere called *the angels of his majesty*.

8. *Rendering vengeance.* In order to persuade believers more surely that the persecution which they endure will not go unpunished, he teaches them that this too is a matter of concern to God Himself, because the same individuals who oppress the ungodly are also in rebellion against God. God must therefore take vengeance upon them not only for the sake of our salvation but also for the sake of His own glory. Further, the expression, *who shall suffer punishment*, refers to Christ, for Paul suggests that this office has been laid upon Him by God.

It may be asked whether it is lawful for us to seek revenge, because Paul promises revenge as something that may rightfully be sought. My answer is that it is wrong to seek for revenge from any man, because we are bidden to wish all men well. Then too, though we in a general way long to take vengeance on the wicked, yet since we do not as yet know who they are, we should desire the welfare of all. In the meantime it is legitimate for us to look eagerly forward to the destruction of the ungodly, provided that a pure and properly regulated zeal for God holds sway in our hearts, and that there are no feelings of inordinate desire.

Them that know not God. He distinguishes unbelievers by these two marks, that they *know not God* and *obey not the gospel* of Christ. If, as he teaches us in the first and last chapters of the Epistle to the Romans, obedience is rendered to the Gospel by means of faith, then unbelief is the reason for resistance to it. He also accuses them of being ignorant of God, for a true knowledge of God begets reverence of itself. Unbelief is therefore always blind, not because unbelievers are wholly devoid of light and understanding, but because their minds are so involved in darkness that *seeing they see not* (Matt. 13.13). It is with good reason that Christ declares that *this is life eternal, that they should know Thee, the only true God* (John 17.3). Accordingly, the lack of this salutary knowledge gives rise to a contempt for God and finally death. I have discussed this point in fuller detail in my Commentary on I Corinthians 1.

9. *Eternal destruction from the face of the Lord.* The phrase which he adds in apposition explains the nature of the punishment which he had mentioned—it is eternal punishment and death which has no end. The perpetual duration of this death is proved from the fact that its opposite is the glory of Christ. This is eternal and has no end. Hence the violent nature of that death will never cease. From this too we may deduce the terrifying ferocity of the punishment, because it will correspond in extent to the glory and majesty of Christ.

10. *When he shall come to be glorified.* Because the punishment of the wicked has formed the theme of his discourse up to this point, he now returns to the godly and says that Christ will come to be glorified in them, i.e. that He may shine upon them with His glory and that they may partake of it. 'Christ,' he says, 'will not possess this glory for Himself alone, but it will be shared among all the saints.' It is the chief and unique consolation of the godly that when the Son of God will be manifested in the glory of His kingdom, He will gather them together into the same fellowship with Himself. There is, however, an implied contrast between the present condition in which believers suffer and complain and that final restoration. Now they are exposed to the

world's abuse and are regarded as contemptible and of no significance. Then they will be highly esteemed and full of honour, when Christ will pour His glory upon them. The aim is that the godly should pass over this brief course of their earthly life with eyes closed and their minds ever intent on the future manifestation of Christ's kingdom. For to what purpose does he mention His coming in power if not that they may leap forward in hope to that blessed resurrection which is still hidden from sight?

We should also note that having used the term *saints*, he adds in explanation *who believe*. By this he means that men have no holiness apart from faith, but that all are unsanctified (*profanos*). He concludes by repeating the phrase *in that day*, for that expression is connected with this sentence. He repeats it for the purpose of holding the desires of believers in check, and keeping them from pressing beyond the bounds.

Because our testimony was believed. He now applies to the Thessalonians the general observations which he has made concerning saints, so that they may not have any doubt that they are counted among them. 'Because,' he says, 'my preaching was believed among you, Christ has now numbered you among His own, and He will make you partakers of His glory.'

He calls his doctrine a *testimony*, because the apostles are Christ's *witnesses* (Acts 1.8). Let us therefore learn that the promises of God are confirmed in us when we put our faith in them.

> *To which end we also pray always for you, that our God may count you worthy of your calling, and fulfil every desire of goodness and every work of faith, with power; that the name of our Lord Jesus may be glorified in you, and ye in him, according to the grace of our God and the Lord Jesus Christ.* (11-12)

11. *To which end we also pray always.* So that they may know that they are in continual need of God's help, he affirms that he prays on their behalf. When he says, *to which end*, he means in order that they may reach the last lap of their journey, as we see clearly from the rest of the context, *that our God may fulfil every desire of goodness*, etc. It appears, however, that his first statement is unnecessary, for God had already accounted them worthy of His calling. But Paul is speaking of the end or completion which depends on our perseverance. As far as we are concerned, since we are liable to lose heart, our calling would inevitably come to naught unless God established it. He is therefore said to *count us worthy* when He brings us to our goal.

And fulfil every desire. Paul pays a high tribute to the grace of God. Not content with the phrase *good pleasure*, he states that it flows from the goodness of God. It may, however, be preferred to regard His kindness as flowing from His good pleasure, but this means the same thing. When we learn that the gracious will of God is the cause of our salvation, and that this is grounded in the goodness of the same God, are we not more than crazy if we dare to attribute even the least accomplishment to our own good works? These words are very emphatic. He might have used a single word, *that your faith may be fulfilled*, but he says *good pleasure*. He then states his point with still greater clarity by saying that God was persuaded by nothing other than His own goodness, for there is nothing that He finds in us but our miserable condition.

Paul does not ascribe merely the beginning of our salvation to the grace of God, but every part of it. This refutes the misrepresentation of the Sophists that the grace of God, it is true, precedes our own action, but that this grace is assisted by our subsequent good works. In the whole course of our salvation, however, Paul sees nothing but the pure grace of God. But because the good pleasure of God has already been perfected in him, he refers in the following phrase to the effect which is seen in us, and explains his meaning by adding *every work of faith*. He calls it a work with reference to God, who forms or produces faith in us, as though he said, 'that He may complete the structure of faith which He has begun'.

He says *with power* advisedly, for he suggests that the perfecting of faith is a hard and extremely difficult task. We are quite well aware of this from experience. The reason, too, is not hard to find if we consider the extent of our weakness, the variety of the obstructions which are heaped upon us on every side, and the severity of the attacks of Satan. Unless, therefore, the power of God gives us more than ordinary support, our faith will never rise to its full height. It is as easy to bring faith to perfection in a person as it is to build a tower in the water to withstand every gale and the battering of the storms, and to over-top the clouds. For we are as fluid as water is, and faith must extend into heaven.

12. *That the name of our Lord Jesus may be glorified.* He recalls us to the main purpose of our whole life, that we devote ourselves to the glory of the Lord. Particularly worthy of notice is the remark which he adds that those who have extolled the glory of Christ are to be glorified in their turn in Him. The amazing goodness of God is especially seen in the fact that He desires His glory to be conspicuously displayed in us who are entirely covered with dishonour. It is, however, a double miracle, that He afterwards shines upon us with His glory, as though He would do the same for us in return. For this reason he adds *according to the grace of our God and the Lord Jesus Christ*. There is nothing here that is ours, either in the action itself or in its effect or fruit. It is

by the guidance of the Holy Spirit alone that our life is ordered to the glory of God. The fact that so much fruit comes from this should be attributed to the great mercy of God. In the meantime, unless we are more than unwise, we must aim with all our might at the advancement of the glory of Christ, which is connected with ours. I refrain from explaining at present in what sense he represents the glory of God and of Christ as belonging together, because I have done so elsewhere.

CHAPTER TWO

Now we beseech you, brethren, touching the coming of our Lord Jesus Christ,[1] *and our gathering together unto him; to the end that ye be not quickly shaken from your mind, nor yet troubled, either by spirit, or by word or by epistle as from us, as that the day of the Lord is now present.*
(1-2)

1. *Now we beseech you, brethren.* As I have noted in the margin, *in regard to the coming* is a possible reading, but the earnest request derived from the subject with which he is dealing is more appropriate. So, in I Cor. 15.31, in discussing the hope of the resurrection, he takes an oath by that *glorying* which believers are to look for. It is much more effective when he adjures believers not to entertain the unreasonable belief that His day is at hand, for at the same time he warns us to think of it only with reverence and restraint. An earnest entreaty is customarily made in reference to those things which we hold in respect. The meaning, therefore, is, 'By His coming Christ will gather us to Himself and will indeed accomplish the unity of the body which at present we esteem only in part by means of faith. As this coming is a thing of great value to you, I earnestly beseech you by it not to be overcredulous if anyone should affirm on whatever pretext that His day is at hand.'

Since he had made some reference in his previous Epistle to the resurrection, it is possible that some discredited individuals or fanatics used this as an occasion to fix upon a definite day which was close at hand. It is unlikely that this misrepresentation had arisen among the Thessalonians before that. When Timothy, for instance, had returned there, he had informed Paul of their state of affairs as a whole and as a man of wisdom and experience had omitted nothing of importance. Now if Paul had been informed of it, he could not have been silent about a matter of such gravity. I am thus of the opinion that when Paul's epistle, which contains a vivid description of the resurrection, had been read, some overcurious individuals seized this inappropriate moment to begin a discussion concerning the time of this day. This fantastic idea, however, was utterly destructive, as were also other ideas of this kind which were later circulated by the cunning of Satan. If, when we say that a day is near, it does not come at once, men become dispirited, since by nature they are unable to endure a longer delay, and their lack of spirit is followed shortly afterwards by despair.

[1] Calvin's version has *per adventum* (*vel, de adventu*) *Domini*, 'by (or, in regard to) the coming of our Lord'.

This, then, was Satan's cunning. Since he could not openly destroy the hope of the resurrection, he promised that the day was close and would soon be at hand, in order to undermine it by stealth. After this he did not cease to try various stratagems by which he might gradually wipe out from men's minds the belief in the resurrection, because he could not openly erase it. It sounds well, of course, to say that the day of our redemption is already fixed, and for this reason it meets with popular approval, just as we see that the ravings of Lactantius and the Chiliasts were highly acceptable in a former period. Their only purpose, however, was to destroy the hope of the resurrection. This was not the intention of Lactantius, but Satan in his artfulness misdirected the curiosity of this man and those like him, so as to leave nothing left in religion that was precise or definite. Even at the present day he continually makes use of the same means of attack. We now see how necessary Paul's warning was, since but for this a specious pretext would have destroyed all religion among the Thessalonians.

2. *That ye be not quickly shaken from your mind.* He uses the term *mind* to mean a settled faith which rests on sound doctrine. The fabrication which he rejects would have transported them into raptures. He notes three kinds of deception against which they are to be on their guard— spirit, word, and false epistle.

By the word *spirit* he means false prophecies. It appears that this manner of speaking was customary among the ungodly, so that they used the term spirit in reference to prophetic statements in commendation of them. If prophecy is to have its due authority, we must have regard to the Spirit of God rather than to men. The devil, however, is wont to fashion himself into an angel of light (II Cor. 11.14), and so also impostors have stolen this title for the purpose of deceiving the simple-minded. Although Paul could have stripped this mask from them, he chose to speak in these terms by way of concession, as if to say, 'Whatever pretence they may make at possessing the spirit of revelation, do not believe them.' So also John says, *Prove the spirits, whether they are of God* (I John 4.1).

Word, in my view, includes every kind of doctrine, while false teachers eagerly put forward reasons or conjectures or other clever devices in order to gain credence for their falsehoods. His additional remark about *epistle* is proof that the effrontery of forging other people's names is of long standing. The mercy of God towards us is the more wonderful, in that even though Paul's name was used falsely in spurious writings while he was still alive and able to see, his writings have been kept safe to our own day. This certainly could not have taken place by chance or human effort, if God Himself had not held Satan and all his ministers in check by His power.

As that the day of the Lord is now present. This appears to contradict
many passages of Scripture in which the Spirit declares that that day
is at hand. But the solution is easy. It is at hand in regard to God, with
whom *one day is as a thousand years* (II Pet. 3.8). In the meantime the
Lord would have us keep in constant watch for Him in such a way as
not to limit Him in any way to a particular time. *Watch*, He says, *for
ye know not the day nor the hour* (Matt. 25.13). The false prophets on
the other hand, who are refuted by Paul, were bidding men feel assured
of His speedy advent, so that they might not be wearied by a burdensome delay, when they ought to have kept men's minds in suspense.

*Let no man beguile you in any wise: for it will not be, except the falling
away come first, and the man of sin be revealed, the son of perdition, he
that opposeth and exalteth himself against all that is called God or that
is worshipped; so that he sitteth in the temple of God, setting himself
forth as God.* (3-4)

3. *Let no man beguile you.* In order to keep from vainly promising
themselves the glad day of redemption within so short a period, he
gives them a gloomy prediction concerning the future dispersion of
the Church. This discourse corresponds in every respect to that which
was addressed by Christ to His disciples when they had asked Him
about the end of the world. He urges them to prepare themselves for
hard struggles (Matt. 24.6), and having spoken of the extreme and
unprecedented catastrophes by which the earth was to be turned almost
into a desert, he adds that *the end is not yet, but these things are the
beginning of travail.* In this way Paul affirms that believers are to wage
a protracted conflict before they gain the victory.

This is a remarkable passage and particularly worth noting. To see
the Church, which had been built up gradually into a position of some
importance by such great effort and with difficulty, suddenly falling
down as if wrecked by a storm was a critical and pressing temptation
which could alarm and unsettle even the most level-headed. Paul,
therefore, buttresses the minds not simply of the Thessalonians but of
all the godly, so that when it should come about that the Church was
dispersed, they should not be frightened as if it were unexpected or
unforeseen. Since, however, commentators have misinterpreted this
passage in various ways, we must first attempt to understand Paul's
real meaning.

The day of Christ, he says, will not come until the world has fallen
into apostasy, and the rule of Antichrist has held sway in the Church.
The interpretation which some have given that this passage refers to
the end of the Roman Empire is too stupid to need lengthy refutation.
I am also surprised that so many writers, who are intelligent and good

scholars in other respects, have been led into error in such an elementary matter, except that when one has gone astray, others, lacking judgment, followed in droves. Paul, therefore, uses the term *apostasy* to mean a treacherous rebellion from God. This would not be confined to a single individual or even a few, but would spread far and wide among a considerably large number of persons. When the word apostasy is used without any addition it cannot be confined to a few individuals. Now the word apostates can be understood only of those who have previously enlisted in the service of Christ and His Gospel. Paul, then, is predicting a general defection on the part of the visible Church, as if he were saying, 'The Church must be reduced to a ghastly and horrifying state of ruin, before its full restoration is achieved.'

From this we may at once conclude how useful this prediction of Paul's is. For it might have seemed that a building which was suddenly destroyed, and which lay for so long in ruins, could not have been the work of God, had Paul not warned them long before that this would take place. In our own day, indeed, very many people begin to waver when they consider the long continued dispersion of the Church, as if this had not been regulated by the purpose of God. The pretext of the Romanists which they make in extenuation of the tyranny of their idol is that it was not possible for Christ to forsake His bride. But here the weak have an assurance on which to rest, when they learn that the disfigurement which they see in the Church has long since been foretold. The impudence of the Romanists, on the other hand, is clearly exposed, because Paul declares that when the world has been brought under the rule of Christ, a defection will take place. We shall soon see why the Lord has allowed the Church, or at least what seemed to be the Church, to fall down in such an unsightly manner.

And the man of sin be revealed. It was said of Nero that he was taken up from the world and would return again to persecute the Church by his tyranny. This was nothing but an old wife's fable, and yet the minds of the ancients were so bewitched that they believed that Nero would be Antichrist. Paul, however, is not speaking of one individual, but of a kingdom that was to be seized by Satan for the purpose of setting up a seat of abomination in the midst of God's temple. This we see accomplished in popery. The defection has indeed spread more widely, for since Mohammed was an apostate, he turned his followers, the Turks, from Christ. All heretics have destroyed the unity of the Church by their sects, and thus there have been as many secessions from Christ.

Having warned that there would be such a dispersion that the majority would forsake Christ, Paul makes a more serious statement—there would be such confusion that the vicar of Satan would hold power in the Church and preside there in the place of God. He describes this reign of abomination under the name of a single individual, because it is a single reign, though there is a succession of individuals. My readers now understand that all the sects which have weakened the Church from the beginning have been so many channels of revolt which began to take the water away from the true course, but that the sect of Mohammed was like a raging overflow which in its violence tore away about half of the Church. It remained for Antichrist to infect the part which was left with his poison. Thus we see with our own eyes that this remarkable prediction of Paul had been confirmed by the event.

There is nothing forced in the interpretation which I offer. In that age believers fondly supposed that after their momentary distresses they were to be transported to heaven. Paul, however, forewarns them that having faced the hostility of external enemies for a certain length of time they will be oppressed by more misfortunes at home, because on all sides those who have trusted in Christ will be forced into foul treachery, and because the very temple of God will be defiled by a sacrilegious tyranny, so that Christ's greatest enemy will bear rule there. The revealing of the man of sin refers here to his open possession of tyranny, as if Paul had said that the day of Christ would not come until this tyrant showed himself openly and deliberately disorganized the whole order of the Church.

4. *He that opposeth and exalteth himself.* The two epithets, *man of sin* and *son of perdition*, express in the first place how fearful the confusion is to be, so that the revolting nature of that event may not daunt weak minds. In the second place they move the godly to a feeling of abhorrence, lest they should degenerate along with others. Paul now gives us a striking picture of Antichrist, for we may quickly deduce from these words what is the nature of his kingdom and of what it consists. By calling him an adversary, and by saying that he will appropriate to himself those things which belong properly to God, so that he is worshipped in the temple as a divine being, Paul directly contrasts his kingdom with the kingdom of Christ. As therefore the kingdom of Christ is spiritual, so this tyranny must burden men's souls if it is to rival Christ's kingdom. Paul will afterwards attribute to Antichrist the power of deception by means of godless doctrines and false miracles. To recognize Antichrist we must set him in diametrical opposition to Christ.

Where I have given the rendering *all that is called God* (*omne quod dicitur Deus*), the reading more generally found in the Greek manuscripts is *everyone that is called God* (*omnem qui dicitur Deus*). We may, however, conjecture both from the Vulgate and from some Greek commentaries that Paul's words have been corrupted. It was easy to mistake a single letter, especially where there was a very close resemblance in their shape. Where there was the reading πᾶν τὸ some copyist or exceedingly injudicious reader turned this into πάντα. This difference, however, does not very greatly affect the sense, for quite certainly Paul meant that Antichrist would seize the things which belong to God alone, his purpose being to exalt himself above every divine power, so that all religion and all worship of God should lie beneath his feet. The phrase, therefore, *all that is reckoned God*, is equivalent to *all that is reckoned as divinity (divinitas)* or σέβασμα, i.e. in which the reverence due to God consists.

We are dealing here not with the name of God Himself, but with His majesty and worship, and generally with everything to which He lays claim. 'True religion,' Paul is saying, 'is that by which the true God alone is worshipped.' It is this that the son of perdition will transfer to himself.

Now anyone who has learned from Scripture what are the things that belong particularly to God, and who on the other hand considers well what the Pope usurps for himself, will not have much difficulty in recognizing Antichrist, even though he were a ten-year-old boy. Scripture declares that God is the only Lawgiver *who is able to save and to destroy* (Jas. 4.12), and the only King whose office it is to govern men's souls by His Word. It represents Him also as the Author of all holy observances; it teaches that righteousness and salvation are to be sought from Christ alone; and it assigns the means and the method. There is not one of these things which the Pope does not claim to be his own prerogative. He boasts that it is his right to bind men's consciences with such laws as he pleases, and to consign them to eternal punishment. With regard to the sacraments, he either institutes new ones at his own whim, or corrupts and debases those which had been instituted by Christ. But more—he does completely away with them in order to put in their place the blasphemies which he has devised. He contrives means of attaining salvation which are wholly at variance with the teaching of the Gospel, and in a word does not hesitate to alter the whole of religion according to his inclination. What, I ask, does it mean to be lifted above all that is reckoned to be divine, if this is not what the Pope is doing? When in this way he deprives God of His honour, he leaves Him nothing but the empty title of God, while he transfers to himself the whole of His power. And this is what Paul adds shortly afterwards, viz. that the son of perdition would declare himself to be God. As we have said, Paul does not use the term *God* by itself, but indicates that the pride of Antichrist would be such that he would set himself apart from his position and rank as servant, mount the judgment-seat of God, and would reign with a divine and not human power. Anything that is put in the place of God, even though it does not bear the name of God, is, as we know, an idol.

In the temple of God. This one word fully refutes the error or rather stupidity of those who hold the Pope to be the vicar of Christ on the ground that he has a settled residence in the Church, however he may conduct himself. Paul sets Antichrist in the very sanctuary of God. He is not an enemy from the outside but from the household of faith, and opposes Christ under the very name of Christ. The question, however, is asked how the Church may be referred to as the den of so many superstitions, when it was to be *the pillar of the truth* (I Tim. 3.15). My answer is that it is so referred to not because it retains all the qualities of the Church, but because it has still some of them left. I admit, therefore, that it is the temple of God in which the Pope holds sway, but the temple has been profaned by sacrileges beyond number.

Remember ye not, that, when I was yet with you, I told you these things? And now ye know that which restraineth, to the end that he may be revealed in his own season. For the mystery of lawlessness doth already work: only there is one that restraineth now, until he be taken out of the way. And then shall be revealed the lawless one, whom the Lord Jesus shall slay with the breath of his mouth, and bring to nought by the manifestation of his coming. (5-8)

5. *Remember ye not?* It added considerable authority to his doctrine that they had previously heard it from Paul's lips, so that they should not imagine that it had been thought up on the spur of the moment. Since he had given them early warning about the reign of Antichrist and the devastation that was coming upon the Church when as yet no question had been raised about such matters, he quite clearly saw that the doctrine was particularly useful for them to know. This unquestionably is the case. Those whom he addressed were soon to see much that would disturb them, and when future generations saw a considerable number of those who had professed the faith of Christ abandon true religion as though stung by a gadfly or rather some raging madness, what could they do but waver? This however, was the *brazen wall,*[1] that God had arranged things in such a way because men's ingratitude deserved such punishment. Here we may see how oblivious men are when it comes to their eternal salvation. We should also note Paul's gentleness, for when he might have burst out in an angrier vein, he simply administers a modest reproof, for it is the kind of reproof a

---

[1] Calvin's reference apparently is to Horace, *Hic murus aeneus esto, / nil conscire sibi, nulla pallescere culpa* (*Epistularum*, I.i.60, 61), 'Let this be the brazen wall—to be conscious of no guilt, to blanch at no fault.'

father would administer to say that they have allowed themselves to forget a matter of such importance and profit.

6. *And now ye know that which restraineth.* Τὸ κατέχον here means properly an impediment or occasion of delay. Chrysostom, holding that it can be understood only as referring to the Spirit or to the Roman Empire, prefers to incline towards the latter view. He has good reason to do this, because Paul would not have spoken of the Spirit in an obscure way, whereas in speaking of the Roman Empire he wanted to avoid an offensive expression. He explains why the state of the Roman Empire delays the revelation of Antichrist. It is because, just as the monarchy of Babylon was overthrown by the Persians and the Medes, and the Macedonians in their turn after the defeat of the Persians took possession of the monarchy, and they were finally conquered by the Romans, so Antichrist is about to seize for himself the vacant rule of the Roman Empire. There is not one of these things that was not later confirmed in actual experience. Chrysostom, therefore, is speaking the truth as far as history is concerned. In my own view, however, Paul's meaning was different. The doctrine of the Gospel was to be spread far and wide until almost the whole world had been convicted of obstinacy and wilful malice. It is clear that the Thessalonians had heard from Paul's lips about this impediment, whatever it may have been like, for he reminds them of what he had previously told them in their presence.

The reader should now consider which of the two courses is more likely—that Paul declared that the light of the Gospel must first be spread through every part of the world before God would give Satan his rein in this way, or that the power of the Roman Empire prevented the rise of Antichrist, because he could only take forcible possession of something that was vacant. I think that at least I hear Paul speaking of the universal call of the Gentiles. The grace of God was to be offered to all, and Christ was about to enlighten the whole world by His Gospel, in order that men's impiety might be more fully attested and condemned. This, therefore, was the delay until the course of the Gospel was completed, because a gracious invitation to salvation was first in order of precedence. For this reason he adds *in his own season,* because when grace had been rejected punishment was due.

7. *The mystery of lawlessness.* This is contrasted with revelation. Since Satan had not yet amassed such strength that Antichrist could openly oppress the Church, he says that Satan is plotting secretly and by stealth what he was intending to do openly in his own good time. At that time, therefore, he was surreptitiously laying the foundations on which he would afterwards build, as in fact occurred. This gives fuller confirmation to what I have already said. The name Antichrist

does not designate a single individual, but a single kingdom which extends throughout many generations. With the same meaning John says that Antichrist will indeed come, but that many were already to be found in his own time (I John 2.18). He warns those who were alive at that time to be on their guard against this deadly contagion which was shooting up in various forms. Sects were arising which were the seeds of that ill-omened weed which has nearly choked and blighted the whole of God's field. Although Paul conveys the idea of a concealed activity, yet he has made use of the term *mystery* rather than any other. His allusion is to the mystery of salvation, about which he speaks elsewhere (Col. 1.26), for he is deliberately stressing the conflict between the Son of God and the son of perdition.

Only there is one that restraineth now. Although both his statements refer to a single individual—he says that he is supreme for a time, but that he will shortly be taken out of the way—I have no doubt that his reference is to Antichrist. The participle *one that restraineth* must be explained in the future tense. In my own view he has added for the consolation of believers that the reign of Antichrist will be temporary, since its limits have been predetermined by God. For believers could make the objection, 'What is the use of preaching the Gospel, if Satan is now plotting a tyranny which he is to hold for ever?' He therefore exhorts them to patience, because God afflicts His Church only for a time, so that He may one day set it free. On the other hand believers are to ponder upon Christ's unending reign, so that they may be sustained by it.

8. *And then shall be revealed the lawless one.* I.e. when that restraint (τὸ κατέχον) shall disappear. He does not indicate the time of the revelation when the one who at present holds the supremacy will be taken out of the way, but he has in view his previous remarks. He had said that there was something that prevented Antichrist from taking free possession of the kingdom. He then added that he was already plotting a furtive act of ungodliness. In the third place he brought them comfort on the grounds that his absolute rule would come to an end. He now repeats that the one who was still hidden would be revealed in due time. The object of his repetition is that believers should still fight hard under Christ, equipped with spiritual armour, and not allow themselves to be overwhelmed, though the deluge of ungodliness should thus flow over them.

Whom the Lord Jesus shall slay. He had predicted the destruction of the reign of Antichrist, and now describes the manner of his destruction —he will be annihilated by the word of the Lord. It is uncertain, however, whether he is speaking of the final appearing of Christ, when He will be revealed from heaven as Judge. The word, it is true, appears to have this meaning, but Paul does not think that Christ will accomplish this in a single moment. We must therefore understand the passage in this sense, that Antichrist would be completely and utterly destroyed when that last day of the restoration of all things will come. Paul indicates, however, that in the meantime Christ will scatter the darkness in which Antichrist will reign by the rays which He will emit before His coming, just as the sun, before becoming visible to us, chases away the darkness of the night with its bright light.

This victory of the Word will therefore be seen in the world, for *the breath of his mouth* means simply His word as in Isa. 11.4, the passage to which Paul appears to be alluding. In that passage the prophet takes *the rod of his mouth* and *the breath of his lips* to mean the same thing, and he also furnishes Christ with these very weapons, so that He may scatter His enemies. It is a notable commendation of true and sound doctrine that it is represented as being sufficient to put an end to all ungodliness, and as destined at all times to be victorious over all the devices of Satan. It is also a commendation when a little further on the preaching of this doctrine is referred to as Christ's coming to us.

When Paul adds *the manifestation of his coming* He intimates that the light of Christ's appearance will be such that it will swallow up the darkness of Antichrist. In the meantime he implies that Antichrist will be allowed to reign when Christ has withdrawn Himself. This is what usually happens whenever we turn our back on Him when He appears before us. It was indeed a sad departure when Christ deprived men of His light which they had wickedly and unworthily received. In the meantime Paul teaches us that His presence alone will keep all the elect of God safe against all the wiles of Satan.

Even he, whose coming is according to the working of Satan with all power and signs and lying wonders, and with all deceit of unrighteousness for them that are perishing; because they received not the love of the truth, that they might be saved. And for this cause God sendeth them a working of error, that they should believe a lie: that they all might be judged who believed not the truth, but had pleasure in unrighteousness. (9-12)

9. *Whose coming.* He confirms what he has said by an argument from the opposite side. Since Antichrist can stand firm only through the deceptions of Satan, he must of necessity disappear as soon as Christ appears. In short, because it is only in the dark that he reigns, the dawn as it arises on his kingdom scatters the darkness and puts an end to it. We now see what Paul's purpose was. He desired to inform them that Christ would find no difficulty in destroying the tyranny of Antichrist which was upheld by Satan's support alone. In the meantime, however, he points out the marks by which that man of perdition may be

recognized. He speaks of the *working* or efficacy of Satan, and alludes particularly to this when he adds *with signs and lying wonders, and with all deceit*. And certainly, if this is to be contrasted with the kingdom of Christ, it must consist partly of false doctrine and deceptions and partly of false miracles. The kingdom of Christ consists of the doctrine of truth and the power of the Spirit. Satan therefore puts on the mask of Christ for the purpose of opposing Him in the person of His vicar, but at the same time, however, he chooses the weapons with which to attack Christ directly. Christ by the doctrine of His Gospel enlightens our minds to eternal life; Antichrist, trained under the direction of Satan, deals destruction to the ungodly by his godless doctrine. Christ puts forth the power of His Spirit for our salvation and seals His Gospel by miracles; the adversary, by the efficacy of Satan, alienates us from the Holy Spirit and confirms poor worthless creatures in their error by his delusions.

By lying signs he means not simply those that clever individuals contrive with lies and deceit for the purpose of leading the simple-minded astray—the kind of fraud with which the whole of the Papacy abounds, for they are part of the supremacy which Satan has previously made his own—but he holds that falsehood consists in the fact that Satan reverses what are otherwise truly the works of God, and uses miracles in a wrong way to obscure the glory of God. In the meantime, however, it is quite clear that he deceives by means of his trickery, as we find in the case of Pharaoh's magicians (Exod. 7.11).

10. *For them that are perishing*. He limits the power of Satan so that it may not harm the elect of God, just as Christ also frees them from this danger. This shows that Antichrist enjoys such power only by His permission. Now this was a necessary consolation. But for this the godly would have been stricken with fear if they saw a gaping abyss taking up the whole of the way along which they had to pass. Although, therefore, Paul wants them to be on their guard to see that they do not fail through too great carelessness, and indeed bring their own downfall, he nevertheless bids them hope for the best, because Satan's power is restricted so that he may be able to bring destruction only upon the wicked.

Because they received not the love of the truth. To prevent the wicked from complaining that they are perishing innocently, and that they have been appointed to die by God's cruelty rather than by any fault of their own, Paul shows that there are good reasons why the punishment of God is going to come upon them with such severity. It is because they have not embraced the truth which was offered to them with the proper frame of mind. Indeed, they have rejected salvation of their own accord. This shows us more clearly, as I have already stated, that the Gospel had to be preached to the world before God accorded such liberty to Satan, for He would never have allowed His temple to be defiled in so shocking a way had He not been provoked by the extreme ingratitude of men. In short, Paul declares that Antichrist will be the minister of God's righteous punishment of those who, though called to salvation, have rejected the Gospel, and have preferred to give their mind to ungodliness and error. There is no reason, therefore, for the Papists now to object that it called in question the mercy of Christ that He should cast aside His Church in this manner. Though the rule of Antichrist has been harsh, none have perished but those who have deserved to, or who rather have died of their own choosing. And certainly, though the voice of the Son of God has been heard throughout the world, it has found men's ears deaf or rather obstinate, and though the profession of Christianity was widespread, there were still few who truly and wholeheartedly gave themselves to Christ. We need not, therefore, be surprised if like punishment has quickly followed such blasphemous contempt.

The question is asked whether the punishment for blindness falls only on those who have deliberately rebelled against the Gospel. My answer is that this particular judgment of God by which He has punished open defiance does not prevent Him from striking with wonder those who have never heard a single word about Christ as often as He wills. Paul is not taking up a general discussion of the reasons why from the beginning God has allowed Satan to proceed with his lies, but is discussing how fearful is the punishment which awaits those who treat new and unprecedented grace with callous disdain. He has used the expression *to receive the love of the truth* in the sense of to give one's heart to the love of it. From this we learn that faith is always connected with a seemly and spontaneous reverence for God, because we do not have a true belief in the Word of God, except when it is attractive to us and worthy of our devotion.

11. *A working of error.* He means that not only will errors be found, but the wicked will be blinded, so that they will fall headlong into destruction without a thought for what they are doing. God enlightens us inwardly by His Spirit so that His doctrine may take effect in us, and opens our eyes and hearts that it may reach there. So by His righteous judgment He gives up to a *reprobate mind* (Rom. 1.28) those whom He has appointed to destruction, so that they may as though hypnotized hand themselves over to be deceived by Satan and his ministers with their eyes tight shut and their mind devoid of reason. Without any doubt we have a notable demonstration of this in the Papacy. No words can express how foul is the abomination of the Papists, how massive and shameful are their nonsensical superstitions, and how far

removed their ravings are from common sense. None who have even a moderate acquaintance with sound doctrine can think of such depravity without the utmost horror. How, then, does the whole world gape in astonishment at them, unless it is because men have been blinded by the Lord and turned into dunderheads?

12. *That they all might be judged.* That is, that they may receive the punishment appropriate to their godlessness. Thus those who are put to death have no good reason for complaining to God, because they have got what they were looking for. We are to remember the passage in Deut. 13.3, where it is stated that men's hearts are weighed in the balance when false doctrines appear, for these have no effect, except among those who do not love God with a pure heart. Let those, therefore, who take pleasure in unrighteousness gather the fruit of it. When he says *all* he means that the enormous crowd and vast number who refuse to obey the Gospel are not excused for their contempt of God, for God is the Judge of the whole world, so that He will inflict punishment as much on a hundred thousand as on a single individual.

The participle εὐδοκήσαντες *(taking pleasure)* implies a voluntary propensity to evil. The ungrateful are thus deprived of any excuse when they take so much pleasure in unrighteousness that they prefer it to the righteousness of God. They will strongly insist that they have been driven to let some mad rebellion estrange them from God, though the guiding of nature led them to Him. It is clear beyond doubt that they gave their ear to falsehood knowingly and willingly.

But we are bound to give thanks to God alway for you, brethren beloved of the Lord, for that God chose you from the beginning unto salvation in sanctification of the Spirit and belief of the truth: whereunto he called you through our gospel, to the obtaining of the glory of our Lord Jesus Christ. (13-14)

13. *But we are bound to give thanks.* He now makes a clearer division between the Thessalonians and the wicked, so that their faith should not waver through fear of the coming apostasy. At the same time, however, his purpose was to consider the interests not simply of these but also of future generations. He not only establishes them so that they may not experience the same downward plunge as the world, but uses this comparison to commend further the grace of God towards them—though they see that almost the whole of the world is carried to destruction as in a wild storm, their condition in life continues peaceful and steadfast by the hand of God. It is thus fitting that we should consider the judgment of God upon the wicked, so that they

mand to do so. The Papists act with even greater stupidity in wanting to peddle the stinking conglomeration of their own superstitions as though these were the traditions of Paul. There is an end to this stuff and nonsense when we see Paul's true meaning. We may judge in part from this epistle the traditions which he commends to us, for he says *whether by word*, i.e. speech, or by *epistle*. But what do his epistles contain if not pure doctrine, which completely destroys the whole of the Papacy and every fabrication that is at variance with the simplicity of the Gospel?

16. *Now our Lord Jesus Christ.* Just as we have a clear proof of the divinity of Christ when Paul ascribes to Him a work that is wholly divine, and represents Him together with the Father as the Author of the highest blessings, so we are reminded that we cannot obtain anything from God unless we seek it in Christ Himself. And when he asks God to give them what he had prescribed for them, he is giving sufficient indication of how little effect exhortation has unless God works upon our hearts and influences them from within. We shall hear nothing but an empty sound if doctrine is not endued with power by the Spirit.

The statement which he afterwards adds, *which loved us and gave us comfort*, refers to the confidence which we have in getting what we ask for. His desire is to convince the Thessalonians that God will do what he prays for. How does he prove this? Because He once showed that they were dear to Him, while He has already treated them with remarkable kindness, and in this way has bound Himself to them for the future. This is what he means by *eternal comfort*. The term *hope* also refers to the same thing—they are to have a sure expectation that their gifts will continue without interruption. What is he asking for? He is asking that God may lift up their hearts by His comfort. This is his office, to keep them from being disheartened by anxiety or lack of trust, and also to urge them to persevere both in a godly and holy life and in sound doctrine. It is my opinion that he is speaking of this rather than of ordinary speech, so that this agrees with his earlier remarks.

may be mirrors for us in which to contemplate His mercy towards us. Our conclusion must be that it is by the singular grace of God alone that we do not share their miserable end.

His motive for calling them *beloved of the Lord* is that they may consider more carefully that the only reason why they are delivered from the all but universal destruction of the world was because God loved them with His gracious love. Thus Moses would admonish the Jews, 'God did not exalt you in such splendour because you were more powerful or more in number than others, but because He loved your fathers' (cf. Deut. 7.7f). When we hear the word *love*, we should at once remember the expression of John, *We love, because he first loved us* (I John 4.19). In brief, Paul is doing two things here. He is strengthening their faith, lest the godly should be overcome by fear and lose heart, and he is exhorting them to gratitude, so that they may value the mercy of God towards them more highly.

For that God chose you. He states why all are not submerged and crushed in the same calamity. It is because Satan has no power to keep any whom God has chosen from being saved, even though heaven and earth were thrown into disorder. There are various interpretations of this passage. The Vulgate has translated it *firstfruits*, as if in Greek it were ἀπαρχήν, but since almost all the Greek manuscripts have ἀπ' ἀρχῆς, I have preferred to follow this reading. If the former reading is preferred, the meaning will be that believers have been set apart for a sacred offering. The metaphor is derived from an ancient ceremony of the law. Let us, however, retain the more generally accepted reading, viz. that the Thessalonians have been chosen from the beginning.

Some interpret this to mean that they had been among the first to be called. But this is foreign to Paul's meaning, and is inappropriate to the context. He is not simply delivering from fear a few individuals who were brought to Christ at the very beginning of the Gospel; this consolation has reference to all whom God has chosen without exception. In saying *from the beginning*, therefore, he means that there is no danger that Satan should reverse their salvation, which is based on the eternal election of God, however chaotic an upheaval there should be. 'However universal the disorder which Satan may cause in the world, your salvation was assured before the creation of the world.' This, then, is the true haven of our security, that God, who has chosen us of old, will rescue us from all the distresses that threaten us. We are elected to salvation; we shall therefore be safe from destruction. But since it is not our business to penetrate into the secret counsel of God, there to seek the assurance of our salvation, he designates the signs or tokens of our election, which should give us sufficient confidence in it.

He says *in sanctification of the Spirit and belief of the truth.* This may be explained in two ways, either *with* sanctification or *by* sanctification. It does not make much difference which we choose, since it is certain that Paul's only intention was to describe in connexion with election the signs nearer to hand which reveal that which in itself is incomprehensible, and which are inseparably connected with election. We have no reason to ask what God decreed before the creation of the world in order to know that we have been elected by Him, but we find in ourselves a satisfactory proof of whether He has sanctified us by His Spirit and enlightened us to faith in His Gospel. The Gospel is not only a testimony to us of our adoption, but the Spirit also seals it, and those who are led by the Spirit are the *sons of God* (Rom. 8.14), and he that possesses Christ has eternal life (I John 5.12). We must note this carefully, so that we may not disregard the revelation of God, with which He bids us be satisfied, and plunge into an endless labyrinth with the desire of seeking revelation from His secret counsel, the investigation of which He compels us to abandon. We are, therefore to be satisfied with the faith of the Gospel and the grace of the Spirit by which we have been regenerated. By this means we refute the depravity of those who make the election of God a pretext for every kind of wrongdoing, for Paul connects it with faith and regeneration in such a way that he would not have us measure it by any other standard.

14. *Whereunto he called you.* He repeats the same point, though in slightly different words. The sons of God are called to a belief in the truth and to this alone. Paul, however, intended to show us here how qualified a witness he is to confirm the ministry of which he was a servant. In consequence he gives the Thessalonians his personal assurance so that they may have no doubt that the Gospel, in which they had been instructed by him, was the saving Voice of God by which they are raised from death and set free from the tyranny of Satan. He calls it *his* Gospel, not as though it had originated with him, but since he had been entrusted with the proclamation of it. The phrase which he adds, *to the obtaining or possession of the glory of Christ*, may be understood actively or passively. It may mean either that they are called so that they may one day possess a glory in common with Christ, or that Christ took them to Himself for His own glory. It will thus be another means of confirming his point to say that he will defend them as he would his own inheritance, and that in affirming their salvation he will vindicate his own glory. In my opinion this latter meaning is more appropriate.

So then, brethren, stand fast, and hold the traditions which ye were taught, whether by word, or epistle of ours. Now our Lord Jesus Christ himself, and God our Father which loved us and gave us eternal comfort

and good hope through grace, comfort your hearts and stablish the[ ] every good work and word. (15-17)

He correctly draws this word of encouragement from his pr[ ] statement, because our determination and power to persevere r[ ] our assurance of divine grace alone. But when God calls us to salv[ ] and stretches out His hand to us, when Christ offers Himself to [ ] our enjoyment by the teaching of the Gospel, and when the Sp[ ] given to us as a seal and pledge of eternal life, we are not to [ ] despondent, even though the heavens should fall. Paul, therefore,[ ] the Thessalonians stand firm not simply while others are doing so[ ] with more dogged resolution, so that even when they see that apo[ ] from the faith is well-nigh universal, they may nonetheless hold t[ ] ground. And certainly the calling of God should nonetheless defend us agains[ ] occasions for stumbling in such a way that not even the total destr[ ] tion of the world should shake, much less destroy, our constancy.

15. *Hold the traditions which ye were taught.* Some interpreters conf[ ] this to regulations concerning outward form of government, but I[ ] not like this interpretation, for he is telling them how to stand fir[ ] But to be equipped in such a way that one's strength is invincible i[ ] much higher thing than outward discipline. In my opinion, therefor[ ] Paul is using this term to include all doctrine, as if to say that they hav[ ] solid grounds on which to stand firm, if they continue in soun[ ] doctrine as he had taught them. I do not deny that the word παραδόσει[ ] is used appropriately of the ordinances which are appointed by th[ ] churches with a view to the promotion of peace and maintenance o[ ] order, and I grant that it is used in this sense when the subject o[ ] discussion is the traditions of men (Matt. 15.6). But in the next chapter[ ] Paul will use the term *tradition* to mean the rule that he had delivered[ ] to them, and the meaning of the word is general. The context, however, as I have stated, requires us to understand the word here of the[ ] doctrine in which they had been instructed as a whole. Paul is discussing the most important of all matters—that their faith may remain constant even in the terrifying disturbance of the Church.

The Papists foolishly deduce from this that their traditions are to be observed. Their argument is as follows: If Paul could enjoin traditions, other teachers could also do so, and if it was a mark of devotion to observe the former, the latter too should not be observed any the less. Granting that Paul is speaking of regulations that pertain to the outward government of the Church, I maintain nevertheless that they were not devised by him but delivered to him by God. He testifies elsewhere (I Cor. 7.35) that it was not his intention to cast a snare upon men's consciences. Neither he nor any of the apostles had any com-

CHAPTER THREE

Finally, brethren, pray for us, that the word of the Lord may run and be glorified, even as also it is with you; and that we may be delivered from unreasonable and evil men; for all have not faith. But the Lord is faithful, who shall stablish you, and guard you from the evil one. And we have confidence in the Lord touching you, that ye both do and will do the things which we command. And the Lord direct your hearts into the love of God, and into the patience of Christ. (1-5)

1. *Brethren, pray for us.* Though the Lord gave him powerful support, and though he was unsurpassed in his passion for prayer, he still has regard for the prayers of believers, by which the Lord wills to assist us. It is fitting that we too, following his example, should seek this aid and urge our brethren to pray for us.

When he adds, however, *that the word of the Lord may run,* he shows that he is concerned not so much for his own personal advantage or interest as for the entire Church. Why does he want to be commended to the prayers of the Thessalonians? So that the doctrine of the Gospel may *run* its course. He does not therefore want his personal interests alone to be considered so much as the glory of Christ and the common welfare of the Church. The course to which he refers means dissemination; while *glory* means something more, viz. that his preaching may have power and efficacy to refashion men in the image of God. Hence holiness of life and rectitude on the part of Christians is the glory of the Gospel, just as those who make profession of it with their mouths while leading wicked and rotten lives in the meantime bring the Gospel into disrepute. He says, *even as also it is with you,* for it should be an incentive to the godly to see that all others are like them. Hence those who have already entered into the kingdom of God are bidden to pray daily that it may come (Matt. 6.10).

2. *That we may be delivered.* The Vulgate has rendered ἀτόπους by *unreasonable.* This, I consider, is quite a good translation. By this word, as also by the following, *evil* (τῶν πονηρῶν), Paul is referring to unprincipled and treacherous individuals who were lurking in the Church under the name of Christians, or at least he is referring to Jews, who were attacking the Gospel violently with a frenzied zeal for the law. He knew, however, how great was the peril which threatened them from both these sources. Chrysostom is of the opinion that Paul is referring solely to those who in their malice were opposing the Gospel

with false teachings, though not, like Alexander, Hymenaeus, and others like them, by physical force. For myself, however, I apply it in general to a crisis or enemy of any kind. At that time he was travelling to Jerusalem, and was writing in the midst of his journey. Now he had already been divinely warned that bonds and afflictions awaited him there (Acts 20.23). He means, then, deliverance, so that he should emerge victorious whether by death or by life.

For all have not faith. This could be translated, 'Faith is not found in all.' But this expression would be ambiguous and less intelligible. Let us, therefore, retain the words of Paul, by which he indicates that faith is a gift of God that is too uncommon to be found in all. God, therefore, calls many who do not come to Him by faith. Many pretend to come to Him, but their hearts are very far from Him. Moreover he is not speaking of just any persons, but is referring only to those who are of the household of faith. The Thessalonians saw that very many shrank back from faith, indeed they saw how small the number of believers was. It would thus have been unnecessary to say this of outsiders. But Paul is denying that all who make a profession of faith are in fact believers. If we include all the Jews, they gave the appearance of being close to Christ, because they should have recognized Him from the Law and the Prophets. It is certain that Paul is referring particularly to those with whom he would be dealing. It is probable that these were the ones who, while they had the appearance and designation of godliness, were nevertheless far from being such. Hence the clash.

For the purpose, therefore, of showing that his fear of encounters with infamous and evil men is not groundless or unrealistic, he states that faith is not common to all, because the wicked and the depraved are always mixed together with the good, just as the tares are with the good wheat (Matt. 13.25). Whenever we are troubled by evil men who want in spite of this to be regarded as belonging to the company of Christians, we should recall that *all have not faith.* Indeed, when in some instances disturbance is being caused to the churches by disreputable partisan groups; let this be our shield against such occasions of offence. We shall not merely cause hurt frequently to godly teachers if we have doubts concerning their faith whenever enemies within the Church do them harm, but our faith will continually fluctuate unless we bear in mind that among those who boast in the name of Christian there are many who are faithless.

But the Lord is faithful. It was possible that they might be influenced by unfavourable reports and come to entertain doubts about Paul's ministry. Having, therefore, warned them that we do not always find faith in men, he now calls them back to God, and declares that He is *faithful*, for He confirms them against all the devices of men by which they will endeavour to cause them disturbance. 'They are, it is true, faithless,' he is saying, 'but in God there is a support of sufficient strength to keep you from falling.' He calls the Lord faithful, since He is consistent to the very end in safeguarding the welfare of His people, He affords them help at the proper time, and never forsakes them in danger. So in I Cor. 10.13, *God is faithful who will not suffer you to be tempted above that ye are able.*

These words, however, show that Paul was more concerned about others than about himself. Ill-intentioned individuals hurled against him the stings of their wicked conduct, and it fell upon him in all its violence. In the meantime he turns his attention to the Thessalonians, lest this temptation should cause them any harm.

The term *evil* may refer both to the fact, i.e. wickedness, as well as to the persons of the wicked. I prefer, however, to interpret it of Satan, the head of all the wicked. It would be of little account to be delivered from men's trickery or oppression, if the Lord did not protect us from all spiritual harm.

4. *And we have confidence.* He uses this preface to pass to the instruction which he will presently add. For the confidence which he states he has in them made them much more ready to obey than if he had required an obedience from them that was hesitant or untrusting. He states, however, that this hope which he had of them was founded upon the Lord, since it is His to turn their hearts to obedience and keep them obedient. Alternatively, Paul wanted to declare by this expression that it was not his intention to lay down any regulation except by the command of the Lord. This seems to me the more likely interpretation. By this phrase, therefore, he defines the limits to his demands as well as to their obedience—it should be only in the Lord. Any, therefore, who do not observe this restriction offer Paul's example for the purpose of fettering the Church and subjecting it to their laws to no purpose. He may also have intended that the respect which was due to his apostleship should not be destroyed among the Thessalonians, however evil men should attempt to depose him from his honoured position. This is the intention of the prayer which he immediately adds. Provided men's hearts remain moulded according to *the love of God* and *the patience of Christ*, all else will be well, and Paul affirms that he has no other wish. It is clear from this how far he is from seeking arbitrary power for himself alone. He is content if only they persevere in love for God and in the hope of Christ's coming. The prayer which he adds to his expression of confidence reminds us that we must not give up our dedication to prayer because we have good hope.

Paul here summarizes what he knew to be the most needful duties for Christians. Let all, therefore, strive to make progress in these two pursuits in so far as they desire to advance towards perfection. Certainly the love of God cannot reign in us unless brotherly love also prevails. *The patience of Christ (exspectatio Christi)*, on the other hand, teaches us to despise the world, put to death the flesh, and endure the Cross. The expression might nevertheless be interpreted to mean *the endurance of Christ (patientia Christi)* which is begotten in us by the doctrine of Christ, but I prefer to understand it as referring to the hope of final redemption. The only thing that bears us up in the warfare of our present life is that we await our Redeemer, and this waiting calls for endurance in the continued exercise of the Cross.

> *Now we command you, brethren, in the name of our Lord Jesus Christ, that ye withdraw yourselves from every brother that walketh disorderly, and not after the tradition which they received of us. For yourselves know how ye ought to imitate us: for we behaved not ourselves disorderly among you; neither did we eat bread for nought at any man's hand, but in labour and travail, working night and day, that we might not burden any of you: not because we have not the right, but to make ourselves an ensample unto you, that ye should imitate us. For even when we were with you, this we commanded you, If any will not work, neither let him eat.* (6-10)

He now proceeds to correct a particular misunderstanding. There were some idle creatures and at the same time inquisitive and loquacious individuals who used to wander about from house to house in order to scrape together a living at the expense of others. Because of this, Paul forbids the Thessalonians to encourage their laziness by indulging it, and teaches that it is those who provide themselves with the necessities of life by honourable and useful work that lead a life of holiness. In the first place, he uses the word *disorderly* to apply not to those who lead a dissolute life or whose reputation is stained by flagrant misdeeds, but to idlers and nonentities who do not have any honourable or useful occupation. This is truly ἀταξία (disorder), not to consider the purpose for which we were formed and not to order our lives with this end in view, for it is only when we live in accordance with the rule of God that our life is set in order. Apart from this ordering there is nothing in human life but confusion. It is worth noting this point, lest anyone should do as he pleases apart from a legitimate call from God. For God has marked out human life in such a way that each man is to give himself to the service of his neighbours. Anyone, therefore, who lives for himself alone without being of any service to the human race, and indeed who is a trouble to other people and of help to no one, is rightly to be regarded as ἄτακτος (disorderly). For this reason

Paul declares that such persons must be kept away from the fellowship of believers, so that they may not bring dishonour upon the Church.

6. *Now we command you, brethren, in the name.* Erasmus has translated this as *by the name,* as if Paul were solemnly calling God to witness. Though I do not completely reject this translation, my opinion is rather that the particle *in* is redundant, as in very many other passages. This is in accordance with the Hebrew language. The meaning will thus be that this command should be received with respect as having come not from a human being but from Christ Himself. Chrysostom interprets it in this way. This *withdrawal* of which he is speaking does not refer to public excommunication but to private fellowship. He simply forbids believers to have any friendly dealings with drones of this kind who have no decent manner of life in which to be occupied. He says explicitly *from every brother,* because if they profess themselves to be Christians, they are least of all to be tolerated, because they are the taints and blots of religion.

And not after the tradition. He will presently add the *tradition (institutionem)* to which he refers—food is not to be given to the man who refuses to work. Before coming to this, however, he refers to the example which he has given them in his own case. Doctrine has much more credibility and authority when we lay no other burden on others than we take upon ourselves. He reminds them that he worked with his hands day and night so that he might not cause expense to anyone. He had also made a reference to this point in the previous epistle, in which my readers will find a fuller explanation of this matter.

He says, *neither did we eat bread for nought at any man's hand,* and even if he had not done manual labour, he would certainly not have done such a thing. What is our rightful due is not an undeserved gift, and the value of the work which teachers do for the Church is far greater than the food which they receive from it. But Paul had thoughtless individuals in mind at this point, for not all men have such fairness and discernment as to recognize what payment is due to the ministers of the Word. Indeed, some are so tight-fisted that, even though they contribute nothing of their own, they begrudge them their upkeep as if they were men of leisure. He presently shows quite clearly that he waived his right when he refrained from taking any payment, and by this he indicates how much less they are to allow any who do not do any work to live off other people. When he says that they know how they should imitate him, he is not making the simple assertion that they should regard his example as a law. The meaning is that they knew what they had seen in him that was worthy of their imitation; or rather, the very matter with which he is dealing has been set before them for their imitation.

9. *Not because we have not the right.* Just as Paul wanted to set an example by the work that he did, so that lazy individuals should not eat other people's food like drones, so he was unwilling that this same principle should hurt the ministers of the Word, with the result that the churches would defraud them of their lawful support. In this we see his pre-eminent restraint and courtesy, and how far he was from the ambition of those who abused their powers so as to curtail the rights of their brethren. There was a danger that because the Thessalonians had received the preaching of the Gospel from the mouth of Paul without payment, they should—since men are naturally acquisitive —make this a rule for other ministers in the future. Paul therefore anticipates this danger, and teaches that he had a right to more than he had used, so that the others might still have their full freedom. As I have noted above, his intention was to fling further dishonour by this means upon those who were inactive. This is an argument from the greater to the less.

10. *If any will not work.* In the Psalm we read, *thou shalt eat the labour of thine hands: happy shalt thou be* (Ps. 128.2), and in the Proverb, *the hand of the diligent maketh rich* (Prov. 10.4). It is certain, therefore, that indolence and idle conduct are cursed by God. We know further that man was created for activity, for not only does Scripture testify to this, but nature has also taught it to the Gentiles. It is right, therefore, that those who want to excuse themselves from the common rule should also forfeit their sustenance as the reward of their work. When the apostle commanded that such persons should not eat, he does not mean that he gave the order to them, but that he forbade the Thessalonians to encourage their indolence by supplying them with food.

We should also note that there are different kinds of work. Anyone who benefits human society by his industry, either by ruling his family, administering public or private business, giving counsel, teaching, or in any other way, is not to be regarded as having no occupation. It is the inactive drones whom Paul is berating—those who live by the sweat of others while they themselves do nothing for the common good to help the human race, such as our monks and priests who acquire ample dimensions by their inactivity, except that they chant in the temples to beguile their weariness. This is truly, as Plautus says, to 'live musically'!

For we hear of some that walk among you disorderly, that work not at all, but are busybodies. Now them that are such we command and exhort in the Lord Jesus Christ, that with quietness they work, and eat their own bread. But ye, brethren, be not weary in well-doing. (11-13)

11. *For we hear of some.* It is probable that drones of this kind were

the origin of our idle monasticism. From the very beginning there were some who, under the pretext of religion, either feasted on the tables of others, or cleverly appropriated the substance of simple people. Even in the time of Augustine they had become so strong that he was forced to write a special book against idle monks in which he complains with good reason of their high-handedness, because, sneering at the warning of the apostle, they not only excuse themselves on the grounds of their infirmity, but wish to appear holier than anyone else, since they are free from manual labour. Augustine rightly attacks this unseemly situation, that while the senators are busy at work, the worker or the individual of lower rank does not simply live an idle life, but passes off his indolence for sanctity. These at least are his views. In the meantime, however, the evil has increased to such an extent that nearly a tenth of the world is occupied by idle bellies whose only religion is to be well stuffed, and to be free of any inconvenience that work may bring. They dignify this way of life which they lead sometimes with the name of some Order or other and sometimes with the name of some Rule or other.

But what, on the other hand, is the Spirit saying by the mouth of Paul? He affirms that they are all irregular and *disorderly*, by whatever title they may be known. It is unnecessary to relate here how much discontent the idle life of monks has invariably caused to persons of a sounder judgment. There is a memorable observation of an old monk recorded by Socrates in the eighth book of the Tripartite History, that he who does not labour with his hands is like a robber. I do not mention other cases, nor is there any need. Let us be content with this statement of the apostle in which he declares that they are dissolute and lawless.

That work not at all. There is a notable play on words which I have tried somehow to imitate by rendering *they work not at all, but are busybodies.* He is pointing out a fault which for the most part besets those who lead an idle life, viz. that they cause trouble to themselves and to others by their inopportune bustling. We see that those who have nothing to do are much more tired by doing nothing than if they were occupied with some very important task. They go running here and there, and wherever they go, they give the appearance of being very tired. They gather together every rumour, and spread them abroad in a meaningless jumble. One might say that they bore the burden of a kingdom upon their shoulders. Can we have a more remarkable illustration of this than we find among the monks? What group of men is less relaxed? Where does greater curiosity hold sway? Now since this disease is fatal to the general body of mankind, Paul warns that it should not be encouraged by idleness.

12. *Now them that are such we command.* He corrects both of the faults which he has mentioned—an agitated restlessness and the withdrawal from useful work. He first therefore, bids them to cultivate *quietness*, i.e. to keep themselves peacefully within the bounds of their calling, or, as we say in our own language, *sans faire bruit* (without making a noise). The matter stands thus: those who are employed in honest work are the most peaceful of all, while those who have nothing to do cause trouble to themselves and to others. He then adds another rule. They are to *work*, i.e. they are to be intent on their calling and devote themselves to lawful and honourable occupations, without which human life is lacking in direction. From this there also follows his third command, that they should *eat their own bread.* He means by this that they should be content with what belongs to them, so that they may not burden or inconvenience others. *Drink waters out of thine own cistern,* says Solomon, *and let the streams flow down to thy neighbours* (Prov. 5.15). The first law of fair-dealing is that no one is to lay claim to another's property, but use only what he can rightfully call his own. The second is that no one is to swallow what belongs to him like a whirlpool, but he is to be kindly towards his neighbours and lighten their want by his abundance. Thus the apostle bids those who had previously been idle to *work*, not simply that they may gain a livelihood, but that they may also help their brethren in their necessity, as he also teaches elsewhere (Eph. 4.28).

13. *But ye, brethren.* Ambrose is of the opinion that this remark has been added so that the rich should not withdraw from motives of envy the assistance which they are giving to the poor, because Paul had instructed them to *eat their own bread.* We certainly see how many are more ingenious than is right in seizing at a pretext for their inhumanity. Chrysostom explains it is this way—however justifiably idolent persons may be condemned, they must nevertheless be assisted if they are in want of food. In my own simple view Paul intended to provide against an occasion of offence which might arise from the inactivity of a few. It often happens that those who are otherwise particularly ready and eager to do good grow cool on seeing that they have spent their favours to no purpose by misdirecting them. Paul therefore admonishes us that although there are many who are undeserving, and others who abuse our generosity, we are not on this account to give up helping those who need our aid. His statement is worth noting—however the ingratitude, annoyance, pride, impertinence, and other unworthy behaviour on the part of the poor may trouble us, or discourage and disgust us, we must still strive never to abandon our desire to do good.

And if any man obeyeth not our word by this epistle, note that man,
that ye have no company with him, to the end that he may be ashamed.
And yet count him not as an enemy, but admonish him as a brother. Now
the Lord of peace himself give you peace at all times in all ways. The
Lord be with you all. The salutation of me Paul with mine own hand,
which is the token in every epistle: so I write. The grace of our Lord
Jesus Christ be with you all. (14-18)

14. *And if any man obeyeth not our word.* He has already stated
previously that he has no command but *from the Lord.* Refusal to obey,
therefore, would not be an insult to man, but rebellion against God
Himself. Accordingly he teaches that such persons are to be severely
punished. In the first place, he wants them to be reported to himself,
so that he may keep them in order by his influence. In the second
place, he orders them to be excommunicated, so that, having been put
to shame, they may repent. We deduce from this that we must not
spare the reputation of those who are incapable of being corrected
except by the exposure of their errors. We must, however, see to it
that we point out their diseases to the physician whose task it is to heal
them.

Have no company with him. Paul is referring, I am quite sure, to
excommunication, for apart from the fact that the disorder (ἀταξία)
to which he referred deserved to be severely punished, obstinacy is not
a fault that can be tolerated. He had previously said, 'Withdraw
yourselves from them, because they live in a disorderly fashion.' He
now says, 'Have no company with them, because they reject my
warning.' In this second expression he is stating something more than
in the former. It is one thing to withdraw from a close acquaintance
with someone, but another thing to avoid his company altogether.
In brief, he is excluding from the company of believers those who do
not obey when they have been admonished to do so. By this we are
taught that we must employ the discipline of excommunication against
all unyielding individuals who will not otherwise allow themselves to
be brought to order. They are to be exposed to ignominy until, having
been treated with compulsion and brought to submission, they learn
to obey.

That he may be ashamed. There are, of course, other purposes to be
served by excommunication, e.g. that the contamination may not
spread any further, that the personal misconduct of one individual may
not result in the public disgrace of the Church, and that the example
of severity may teach others to fear. Paul, however, mentions only
one purpose here, viz. that those who have sinned may be forced to
repentance through shame. Those who do as they want in their sins

become more and more obstinate. Thus sin is nourished by indulgence and pretence. The best remedy, therefore, is when the sinner is struck with a feeling of shame, so that he begins to feel dissatisfied with himself. The gain in getting men to have a sense of shame would, of course, in itself be small, but Paul had further progress in view, when the sinner, troubled by the recognition of his own scandalous conduct, is fully corrected by this means. Shame, like sorrow, is a useful preparation for a hatred of sin. As I have said, therefore, any who play fast and loose must be held in check by this bridle, so that they may not grow more impudent as a consequence of their remaining unpunished.

15. *Count him not as an enemy.* He thereupon modifies his harsh statement, for, as he tells us elsewhere, we must see that the sinner is not *swallowed up with his sorrow* (II Cor. 2.7), as would happen if the severity of our treatment were excessive. Hence we see that our use of this discipline ought to be such that we consider the welfare of those on whom the Church inflicts punishment. When severe treatment is excessive, it will inevitably aggravate the situation. So if we want to be of service, gentleness and restraint are necessary so that those who are reproved may still realize that they are loved. In brief, the intention of excommunication is not to drive men from the Lord's flock, but rather to bring them back again when they have wandered and gone astray.

We should note, however, that the sign by which he says that brotherly love is to be proved is not flattery or fawning respect, but *admonition.* By this means all who will not be beyond cure will feel that concern is being shown for their well-being. In the meantime excommunication is to be distinguished from anathema. With regard to those whom the Church blacklists by the severity of its censure, Paul advises that they should not wholly be abandoned, as if they were cut off from hope of salvation, but the effort is to be made to bring them back to a sound mind.

16. *Now the Lord of peace.* This prayer seems to be connected with the previous sentence for the purpose of commending the pursuit of harmony and gentle treatment. He had forbidden them to treat even the obstinate as *enemies,* but to bear with them until they were brought back to a sound mind by friendly admonition. He could appropriately have added an injunction about keeping peace, but since this truly is a work of God, he turns to prayer, though this too has the effect of a command. He may also, however, have another purpose, that God may keep unruly persons in check and prevent them from disturbing the peace of the Church.

17. *The salutation with mine own hand.* Here again he guards against

the danger which he had previously mentioned, that epistles falsely ascribed to him might find their way into the churches. It was a time-honoured wile of Satan to introduce spurious writings for the purpose of discrediting those that were genuine, and also by forging the names of the apostles to disseminate blasphemous errors for the purpose of perverting sound doctrine. By the singular kindness of God Satan's frauds had been overthrown, and the doctrine of Christ has come down to us safe and undamaged through the ministry of Paul and others. The final prayer explains how God assists those who believe in Him by the presence of Christ's grace.

INDEX OF SCRIPTURE REFERENCES

GENESIS

6.3	128, 154
6.5	161
15.6	83
17	97
17.4	195
17.7	89, 257
17.20	198
18	97
18.23	188
18.25	63
48.16	194

EXODUS

4.22	194
7.11	406
9.16	206
14.31	337
32.32	193
33.19	204

LEVITICUS

18.5	47, 87, 223

DEUTERONOMY

4.1	47
4.7f	235
4.32	195
7.7f	409
10.16	89
13.3	408
27.26	47
29.4	48
30.6	89
30.12	224
32.21	247
32.35	278

I SAMUEL

4.22	194

II SAMUEL

22.50	307

I KINGS

19.10, 18	240f

JOB

34.17	63
40.4	68

PSALMS

1.2	87
2.7	16
3.6	183
5.9	66
10.7	66
14.1	66
14.3	67
18.49	307
19.4	233
23.4	183
32.1	71
36.1	67
37.5	374
50.16	52
55.22	374
56.11	183
67.5	308
69.9	304
69.22	245
72.7	192
73.1-12	389
106.30	86
116.11	60
117.1	308
128.1	87
128.2	418

PROVERBS

2.14	38
5.15	420
10.4	418
10.7	101
16.4	208

ECCLESIASTES

9.3	389

ISAIAH

1.9	216
1.11	195
10.22f	215
11.4	405
19.18	169
26.9	380
28.16	218
28.22	215
37.4	21
42.8	296
45.9	210
52.5	54
52.15	313
53.1	232
53.5	102
59.7f	66
59.20	255f
60.1	195
60.2	368
61.1	120
65.1	236
67.5	308

JEREMIAH

7.4	195
7.13	237
9.24	32, 51
9.24	32, 51
11.7	237
18.6	210
30.22	21, 80
31.9	194
31.20	194
31.33	57, 256

EZEKIEL

11.13	212
16.25	38
36.20	54

DANIEL

6.20	21

HOSEA

1.10	214
2.23	170, 258
13.9	35

JOEL

2.2	43
2.32	229

AMOS

5.18	43

HABAKKUK

2.4	28

ZEPHANIAH

1.15	43

ZECHARIAH

13.9	231

MALACHI

1.2f	202
4.2	328

MATTHEW

3.17	189
5.10	188
5.17	81

INDEX OF SCRIPTURE REFERENCES

MATTHEW (cont.)

6.10	413
12.42	56
13.13	392
13.25	414
15.6	411
18.19	317
18.20	317
23.32	349
24.37	368

MARK

16.15	313
16.20	312
24.6	398
25.13	398

LUKE

7.37	109
11.32	56
13.24	390
24.19	312
24.25	48

JOHN

1.14	16
1.17	223
2.19	17
3.6	128
3.12	133
3.16	75, 109
5.36	312
8.36	133
9.31	109
10.18	17, 166
12.43	74
14.17	17
15.16	25
17.3	32, 392

ACTS

1.8	393
2.22	319

ACTS (cont.)

3.19	390
3.25	195, 197
6.7	18
9.15	17
13.7, 9	13
14.3	312
14.17	32
16.6ff	18
16.7	341
18.2	321
20.3	350
20.23	317, 414
20.26	345
28.26	244

ROMANS

1.13	351
1.26	67
1.28	407
3.3	194, 197
3.23	339
4.15	349
6.11	294
6.20	339
8.10	371
8.14	410
8.24	335
10.5	47
10.6	363
11.5	349
12.3	24
12.19	349
13.14	359

I CORINTHIANS

1.30	387
3.11	313
4.5	49
6.13	298
7.35	411
8.8	298
9.11	316
9.14	244
10.13	415
10.23f	300

I CORINTHIANS (cont.)

12.11	24
12.22	109
13.9	269
14.3	376
14.5	269
14.16	355
14.32	269
15.13	363
15.31	396
15.36	365

II CORINTHIANS

1.23	22
2.7	422
3.6	57
3.7	146
3.14	144
4	126
4.8	187
4.8f	106
4.16	153
5.4	365
5.20	17
5.21	160
6.8	276
9.2	315
10.10	109
11.8	345
11.14	397
13.4	16

GALATIANS

1.8	189
1.10	342
1.15	14
2.16	71
3.10	74
3.11	85
3.12	47
3.27	123, 288
4.5	130
4.9	180, 239
5.17	149
5.25	166
6.16	255

EPHESIANS

1	180
1.13	212
1.20	185
2.12	214
2.14	58
2.20	313
3.9	328
3.12	231
4.13	24
4.28	420
4.30	166
5.16	272
6	140
6.12	350
6.14	369

PHILIPPIANS

1.6	291
2.7	124
2.9f	296
2.20	352
3.3	22
3.4	239
3.13	358
4.4	374

COLOSSIANS

1.26	328, 404
1.27	328

I THESSALONIANS

4.7	19, 134
4.16	295
5.3	29
5.23	264

II THESSALONIANS

1.6, 9	188

I TIMOTHY

1.5	356
1.17	196

INDEX OF SCRIPTURE REFERENCES

I TIMOTHY (cont.)

3.2	378
3.15	402
5.1of	321

II TIMOTHY

1	180

TITUS

1.11	378
1.15	297

HEBREWS

1.2	91
1.14	189
9.15	76
10.14	127
11.1	340
11.3	31f
12.18ff	168
13.7	353

JAMES

1.3	107
2.20	79
4.11	295
4.12	401
4.13	25

I PETER

1.12	328
2.10	219
5.7	374

II PETER

1.4	105
3.8	398

I JOHN

2.18	404
2.27	361
3.2	105, 172
3.23	17
4.1	397
4.19	409
5.12	410
5.19f	171

INDEX OF NAMES

Abraham, 70f, 72, 82ff, 88f, 95, 97ff, 197
Ambrose, 17, 379, 420
Ammonius, 37
Augustine, 13, 34, 38, 71, 97, 108, 119, 142, 149, 153, 169, 179, 205, 221, 365, 419

Bucer, 19, 24
Budaeus, 193

Chrysostom, 69, 124, 159, 323, 335, 359, 375, 379, 403, 413, 417, 420
Cicero, 45, 65

Diogenes, 339
Dionysius, 389

Elijah, 240f
Epicurus, 339
Erasmus, 25, 45, 98, 100, 114, 128, 133, 149, 157f, 161, 172, 271, 274, 276, 310, 322, 334f, 347, 417
Eusebius, 34

Horace, 402
Hosea, 213

James, 79
Jerome, 69
Joel, 229
Josephus, 50

Lactantius, 34, 221, 397
Lycurgus, 53

Mohammed, 399

Nero, 399
Novatus, 77

Origen, 13, 69, 114, 366
Ovid, 53, 389

Pelagius, 112, 205
Plato, 34
Plautus, 418
Pliny, 67

Socrates (*Tripartite History*), 419
Stoics, 363

Timothy, 352f

GENERAL INDEX

Access to God, 104f
Adam, 74, 113
 and Christ, 111-18, 113f, 116f
Adoption, 167-70, 175, 194, 239, 381
Adversity, 106f, 171f, 180ff, 187, 389f
Angels, 391
Apostles, 14f, 17f, 61, 225f, 313, 371f, 393
Assurance, 170, 184, 225
Authority of Scripture, 66, 233
 civil, 280f

Baptism, 55, 89f, 116, 122f
Benefits, 42f, 91f
Blasphemy, 162, 166, 233
Blindness, spiritual, 244ff, 255
Body, 166, 263f
 of sin, 125, 154, 165
Bondage, 167ff, 173f

Calling, 181f, 201, 214, 232, 360, 381
Christ, Jesus
 and Adam, 111-18
 and Antichrist, 400, 405
 and His benefits, 183f
 death for sin, 102, 108, 126
 death and resurrection, 294
 divinity of, 295, 412
 ingrafting into, 123f
 intercession of, 186
 Jewish ancestry, 195
 kingdom of, 406
 as Mediator, 186
 and Moses, 223
 two natures of, 196
 propitiation of, 75f
 recapitulation of, 91
 reconciliation of, 104f, 110f
 Redeemer of Jews and Gentiles
  alike, 306f

resurrection of, 102, 165, 225f, 340, 363
 revelation of in OT and NT, 72
 second coming of, 339, 367
 as servant, 304
 union with believers, 165
 vengeance of, 391
Christians, regeneration of, 122, 127
Church, 233, 240, 264, 324, 333, 351, 372, 398f
Circumcision, 54ff, 69, 88-91
Commandment, see Law
Confession and faith, 227
Confidence, 186f
Conflict of believers, 98, 148f, 153
Conjecture, moral, 94, 105, 170
Conscience, 48f, 71, 91f, 104, 356
Consolation, 305
Conversion, 338
Corruption of mankind, 36f, 66ff, 111-14
Covenants, 194f, 307
Covetousness, 142, 343
Creation, 31, 172ff

Days, observance of, 291f
Dead, 362f, 365
Death, 113f, 120, 144, 154f, 157, 363, 365, 390, 392
 penalty, 283
Discipline, 421f
Dispensation, see Law and Gospel
 Mosaic, 222f
Diversity of gifts, 267f
Doctrine, 378

Edification, 299, 303, 371
Elect, 184, 232, 241, 406, 409
Election, 196-202, 205, 210f, 212ff, 241ff, 257, 335, 409

431

Enemies, loving one's, 274, 278
Eternal life, 44, 136
Excommunication, 422

Faith, 17f, 20, 28, 78f, 83ff, 91, 94, 96,
    98ff, 105, 186, 217f, 228, 230, 232f,
    250, 252, 289-96, 302, 334, 338,
    348, 370, 387, 393f, 407, 414
Fall, 111, 113
Fear, 169, 250, 283
    of God, 156
Flesh, 70, 131, 140f, 143, 151, 161f
Foreknowledge, 180, 239, 242
Freedom from the law, 139f
    from sin, 140f, 163
Free will, 148, 163

Gentiles, 32-5, 48, 53, 56, 65, 70-3, 80,
    217, 233-6, 247ff, 249ff, 307f, 312,
    327f, 403
Gifts, spiritual, 24, 192, 257, 267-70
God, absolute authority of, 204, 260f
    faithfulness of, 381
    gave up His Son, 183f
    glory of, 30
    goodness of, 42, 183, 192-5, 207,
        251f, 257, 263, 375
    hardens men's hearts, 207
    holiness of, 162f
    our hope, 309
    judgment of, 40f, 62f, 389
    love, mercy of, 107, 109f, 183, 186-9
        love for, 334
    majesty and power of, 31, 99f
    overrules evil, 64, 179
    our peace, 318f
    preserves the Church, 240
    revelation of, 30, 209
    as Saviour, 337, 356f
    searches the heart, 178
    secret counsels of, 162, 260
    sovereignty of, 280f, 294
    wisdom and knowledge of, 259, 326
    works of, 31f, 234
    wrath of, 30, 34-7, 207, 251, 349, 370

Godly, 25, 92, 148f, 154f
Gospel, 15, 25ff, 53, 194, 226, 230, 232,
    310f, 326f, 337f, 346f, 372, 413
Grace, 19, 80, 115f, 120, 121f, 132, 242

Hardening of heart, 207
Hope, 96, 106f, 173, 176f, 272, 309, 381
Hypocrites, 22, 40ff, 52f, 55, 69, 144,
    221, 230
Hypocrites, 22, 40ff, 52f, 55, 69, 144,
    221, 230

Idolatry, 36, 53
Ignorance, 31f, 66, 93, 301, 377
Implicit faith, 233
Infants, 89, 113

Jews, 16, 27, 50ff, 58f, 65, 68, 190-6,
    216f, 221f, 235, 245ff, 255, 280,
    291f, 348f
Judgment, Day of, 43f, 287f, 367
Justification, 47, 68f, 70ff, 74, 76, 84f,
    121f, 157, 182

Kingdom of God, 298
Knowledge of Christ, 15
    of God, 51f, 66, 231, 259
    of sin, 70

Law, abrogation of, 131, 136, 140
    ceremonies of, 85, 158f, 195, 218
    condemns, puts to death, 78, 93,157
    curse of, 94
    demands of, 47, 138f, 147, 223f, 356,
        379
    freedom from, 139
    and Gospel, 168f, 226
    holy and good, 145, 150
    cannot justify, 157f
    knowledge of, 48
    leads to Christ, 81, 221
    love the fulfilment of, 284f

Law (*cont.*)
revelation of God's will, 287
arouses, uncovers sin, 70, 81, 119, 141, 144
subjection to, 94, 130f
works of, 68f
Life, *see* Eternal life
Love, 220, 271, 284f, 334, 354, 356, 370, 387

Magistrate, civil, *see* Authority, civil
Man, 31, 60, 96, 124f, 128, 153f, 355f, 379f
Meats, 291f, 297f
Merit, 44, 78f, 171f, 180, 203, 217f
Ministers, Ministry of the Word, 17f, 26f, 231ff, 247f, 325, 342, 344f, 351, 354, 358, 371
Monks, 419

Nature, human, 146f

Oaths, 21, 191, 381
Obedience, 17f, 20, 131, 283, 312, 325, 339

Papists, 143, 164, 224, 263, 381, 411
Patience, 44, 106, 176, 305, 363, 373f, 388
Perseverance, 105, 412
Pope, 401f
Prayer, 170, 178, 230, 273, 317f, 355
Preaching, *see* Ministry of the Word
Predesitnation, 180f, 202f, 216, 260

Priesthood, Christian, 310f
Promises, 15, 92f, 306f

Reason, 62, 204, 265
Regeneration, 121f, 125f, 148, 157, 165
Reprobation, 201, 208, 244
Resurrection, 363-6, 396f
Righteousness, 27f, 70f, 72f, 74, 77, 83ff, 86f, 118, 133, 216f, 221, 222-8, 298

Sacraments, 89f, 122f, 401
Salvation, 16, 26f, 83, 110, 180, 197, 204f,.225, 287, 337, 370, 394, 402
Sanctification, 358, 379f
Satan, 207, 324f, 348, 350f, 353, 369f, 373, 394, 396f, 405f, 409
Schoolmen, 69, 86, 94, 115, 170, 189, 230
Scripture, 61, 269, 305, 381
Sin, 34f, 65f, 111ff, 121, 124f, 129, 136, 141, 145f, 157, 159f, 301
Spirit, Holy, 16f, 106ff, 156f, 164, 167-70, 177f, 312, 317, 337, 375f, 411f
Sword, power of, 282f

Unbelief, 59f, 251, 392, 408
Unity of Church, 306, 400
Unrighteousness, 37, 62-5

Word of God, *see* Ministry of Word
Works, 44, 69ff, 73, 86f, 92f, 201, 217f, 287
Worship, 22, 99

CALVIN'S
NEW TESTAMENT
COMMENTARIES

A NEW TRANSLATION

This volume is number 8 in a completely new translation into modern English of Calvin's commentaries on the New Testament. Those familiar with previous translations have frequently discovered that these sometimes fail to reveal the close coherence of Calvin's ideas, miss many of his characteristic images, and often translate whole passages poorly or omit them altogether. T. H. L. Parker now provides the reader with a translation that does full justice to the Reformer's qualities as an expositor of the Word of God. All who are interested in understanding the Scriptures will be enriched by it.

"This new enterprise may well be hailed as an event of high significance, whether our interest lies preeminently in Calvin studies or in biblical exegesis." —F. F. BRUCE, Professor of Biblical Criticism and Exegesis, University of Manchester.

"As Luther was the prince of translators, so Calvin was the prince of commentators. In fact, as an exegete — though by no means infallible — Calvin must be called a genius. He created the first notable Protestant commentaries, and time, the final judge of greatness, has confirmed their true worth." —PAUL K. JEWETT, Associate Professor of Systematic Theology, Fuller Theological Seminary.